COLLINS *Advanced Modular Sci*

Chemistry

AS

Series Editor: Colin Chambers

Lyn Nicholls

Mary Ratcliffe

This book has been designed to support the AQA Chemistry specification.
It contains some material which has been added in order to clarify the specification.
The examination will be limited to material set out in the specification document.

Published by HarperCollins*Publishers* Limited
77–85 Fulham Palace Road
Hammersmith
London
W6 8JB

www.CollinsEducation.com
Online support for schools and colleges

© HarperCollins*Publishers* Limited 2000
First published 2000

ISBN 0 00 327753 4

Lyn Nicholls and Mary Ratcliffe assert the moral right to be identified as the authors
of this work
All new material in this book is written by Lyn Nicholls,
with new Chapters 4, 6, 7 and 8 written by Chris Conoley.
Key Skills Assignments are written by Alan Yate.
This book draws on material from *Chemistry Core* by Lyn Nicholls and Mary
Ratcliffe, and from *Further Chemistry* by Peter Harwood, Mike Hughes and Lyn
Nicholls.

British Library Cataloguing in Publication Data
A catalogue record for this publication is available from the British Library

Edited by Pat Winter and Kathryn Senior
Cover design by Chi Leung
Book design by Ken Vail Graphic Design
Illustrations by Illustrated Arts, Tom Cross, Jerry Fowler, Hardlines, Mark Jordan,
Mainline Design and Fraser Williams
Picture research by Caroline Thompson
Index by Julie Rimington
Production by Kathryn Botterill

Printed and bound by Scotprint, Haddington

The publisher wishes to thank AQA for permission to reproduce examination
questions.

You might also like to visit
www.**fire**and**water**.com
The book lover's website

Acknowledgements

Every effort has been made to contact the holders of copyright material, but if any have been inadvertently overlooked, the publishers will be pleased to make the necessary arrangements at the first opportunity.

The publishers would like to thank the following for permission to reproduce photographs (T = Top, B = Bottom, C = Centre, L= Left, R = Right):

ACE Photo Agency/P Freytag, 19, A Hughes, 43; Barry, 200T;
Allsport/M Hewitt, 44L, S Botterill, 74TL, P Roundeau, 197;
BASF, 105;
Photos from www.JohnBirdsall.co.uk, 35R, 47T, 156L;
BT Corporate Picture Library: a BT photograph, 24;
Anthony Blake Photo Library/Maximilian Stock Ltd, 210TL, 226BL, 231, M
Brigdale, 218;
J Allan Cash Ltd, 201;
Cephas/S Boreham, 224;
Chubb Fire Ltd, 207;
Colourific! 77;
© De Beers, 27;
Dan Technology, 65R;
J Creed/Ecoscene, 74TR;
Mary Evans Picture Library, 54;
Geophotos/Tony Waltham, 2, 101, 137, 142B, 205;
GeoScience Features Photo Library, 37L;
GRAPHIS, Michel Proulx (Professor Harry Kroto, University of Sussex), 39T;
Sonia Halliday Photographs, 112R;
Robert Harding Picture Library, 142T, 150;
Robert Harding Picture Library/Westlight/Morgan, 188;
Health & Safety Executive, 182;
Michael Holford, 112TR;
Holt Studios International/N Cattlin, 100;
Hulton Getty Picture Library, 228R;
ICI Chemicals & Polymers, 177;
Image Select/Ann Ronan, 60T;

Andrew Lambert, 29, 32, 35L, 38CL, 47B, 59, 68, 70, 75, 114, 117, 118, 119, 121, 126B, 132, 134, 135, 138, 156R, 162B, 168, 181L, 191, 216C, 226TR, 225;
Niall McInerney Photography, 199, 200C;
Magnum Photos/S McCurry, 172, 173R;
Jerry Mason, 44R;
NASA, 74C, 115;
Natural History Museum, 38BR;
PA News Photo Library, 91L, 162T;
Gareth Price, 84;
Suzi Gibbons/Redferns, 133;
Rex Features Ltd, 13, 210B;
Science Photo Library, 26, 37R, 39C, 60C, 65L, 108, 113, 148L, 152, 158, 183, 184, 193, 204, 208;
Science VU/Visuals Unlimited 96;
Scott Polar Research Institute/C Swithinbank, 91R;
Emilio Segré Visual Archives, 4;
SHOUT, 169;
South American Pictures, 86, 219;
Still Pictures/D Drain, 181BR;
Tony Stone Images, 180, 181CR, 210TR, 211, 216T;
Telegraph Colour Library/Sacha Hartgers/Focus/Colorific,.173L;
Thames Water, 126T;
Janine Wiedel, 112L, 136.

Front cover:
Science Photo Library, (Top Left)
Tony Stone Images, (Centre)
Science Photo Library, (Top Right)

To the student

This book aims to make your study of advanced science successful and interesting. Science is constantly evolving and, wherever possible, modern issues and problems have been used to make your study stimulating and to encourage you to continue studying science after you complete your current course.

Using the book

Don't try to achieve too much in one reading session. Science is complex and some demanding ideas need to be supported with a lot of facts. Trying to take in too much at one time can make you lose sight of the most important ideas – all you see is a mass of information.

Each chapter starts by showing how the science you will learn is applied in an everyday setting. At other points in the chapter you may find more examples of the way the science you are covering is used. These detailed contexts are not needed for your examination but should help to strengthen your understanding of the subject.

The numbered questions in the main text allow you to check that you have understood what is being explained. These are all short and straightforward in style – there are no trick questions. Don't be tempted to pass over these questions, they will give you new insights into the work. Answers are given in the back of the book.

This book covers the content needed for the AQA Specification in Chemistry at AS-level. The Key Facts for each section summarise the information you will need in your examination. However, the examination will test your ability to apply these facts rather than simply to remember them. The main text in the book explains these facts. The application boxes encourage you to apply them in new situations. Extension boxes provide extra detail not required for your examination. These are interesting to read and will support your studies beyond AS-level.

Words written in bold type appear in the glossary at the end of the book. If you don't know the meaning of one of these words check it out immediately – don't persevere, hoping all will become clear.

Past paper questions are included at the end of each chapter. These will help you to test yourself against the sorts of questions that will come up in your examination.

The Key Skills Assignments allow you to practise for any Key Skills assessments you may have. The assignments are often starting points for work and you will need to access other books and sources of information to complete the activity.

1 Atomic structure

Crops are fed with different fertilisers containing nitrogen-15. This can be detected in the plant material to show how efficiently the crop takes up the fertiliser

A mass spectrum for a plant sample

Percentage abundance (y-axis)

10 11 12 13 14 15 16 17
m/z

Researchers in Japan are seeking the most economical nitrogen-containing fertilisers for use on upland rice, trying amino acids as well as traditional inorganic nitrogen compounds. In order to track nitrogen uptake, they 'label' the nitrogen compounds by substituting the usual nitrogen-14 atoms with nitrogen-15 atoms. Nitrogen-15 has an extra neutron in the nucleus, so that its mass is slightly heavier than normal nitrogen, and so it can be detected with a mass spectrometer.

In a **mass spectrometer**, some of the molecules in a sample lose electrons or are fragmented. The particles are sorted according to their mass and the number of each is counted. Then the data is printed out as a chart called a **mass spectrum** which shows a peak for each type of particle.

Such spectra show that upland rice absorbs substantial amounts of nitrogen-15 from some amino acids. Amino acids are the building blocks of proteins, so the results indicate that the plants have evolved a short cut to making proteins. The Japanese scientists therefore suggest that, for upland rice, amino acids would be a good alternative to traditional fertiliser.

1.1　Early ideas about the composition of matter

The nature of matter has interested people from the time of the Ancient Greeks. In their attempt to understand the material world, the Greeks observed it and made deductions about the composition of matter in it. The philosopher Democritus (460–370 BC) suggested that if you repeatedly divide up solid matter, you eventually get particles that cannot be divided further. These became known as atoms, after the Greek word *atomos* meaning 'cannot be subdivided'.

Later, Aristotle proposed that matter on Earth was composed of four 'elements' – earth, air, fire and water – with the heavens made of 'aether'. Unfortunately, Aristotle's picture of matter influenced scientific thinkers (known as natural philosophers) for the following 2000 years, and held up the progress of chemistry.

The idea of the atom was revived when scientists began to actually test their ideas

and provide evidence for them by doing practical investigations. In this chapter you will read about the evidence scientists gathered to support the picture we have today of the particles that make up matter and the way they are arranged.

In 1660, experimental scientists in Britain (by then a major centre of scientific activity in Europe) set up the Royal Society to promote knowledge of the natural world. One of its members, Robert Boyle, studied the nature and behaviour of gases and water. His ideas were to accelerate the progress of chemistry from then on. They included:

- Matter is made up of identical tiny particles that cannot be subdivided. Boyle was not aware that these indivisible particles varied. He thought that the way that they were put together made the differences in matter.

- The tiny particles are the ingredients of 'mixt bodies' which we now call compounds.

- In **solids**, the basic particles were in fixed positions, while in **liquids** and **gases** they were free to move.

- Solid material has solidity because of the connections between its particles.

After another 150 years, the English experimental chemist John Dalton continued the work on gases and compounds and refined Boyle's ideas. He named the basic particles **atoms**. By 1808, he had developed ideas that included the following:

- Atoms are indivisible and indestructible.

- All atoms of an **element** are identical and have the same **mass** and **chemical**

properties. Consequently, atoms of different elements have different masses and different chemical properties.

- Atoms react together to form what Dalton called 'compound atoms', later to be known as **molecules** and **compounds**. In forming a compound, the atoms join together in fixed proportions. Therefore, a particular compound always has the same composition.

A strength of Dalton's work was his emphasis on making measurements - quantifying results. His results match and explain the observations we make in practical chemistry today. For instance, he worked out the relative atomic masses of different elements, giving hydrogen the value of 1 and relating the masses of other elements to it.

1.2 Evidence for atomic structure

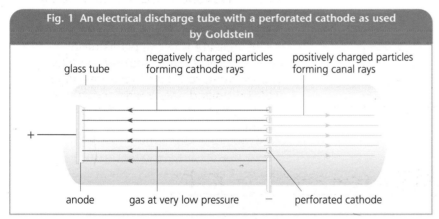

Fig. 1 An electrical discharge tube with a perforated cathode as used by Goldstein

negatively charged particles forming cathode rays

positively charged particles forming canal rays

glass tube

+

anode   gas at very low pressure   perforated cathode

In 1876 the German physicist Eugen Goldstein was investigating what happens when an electrical discharge is passed across gas at very low pressure in a discharge tube, with the anode and cathode at opposite ends of the tube (Fig.1). He found that:

- a beam which he called 'cathode rays' was attracted towards the anode (positive electrode);

- an object in their path cast a 'shadow': the object halted the rays;

- a magnetic field deflected the rays by an amount that depended on the strength of the magnetic field: a magnetic field deflects particles only if they have mass and are negatively or positively charged.

Goldstein concluded that the original gas particles were being split by the discharge into

smaller particles, that these new smaller particles made up the rays, and that those he was detecting were negatively charged and had mass.

Then in 1886, he placed a perforated cathode near the half-way point of the tube. When a discharge was passed, he observed straight yellow beams that he called 'canal rays' streaming through the holes in the cathode in the direction away from the anode. Compared with cathode rays, these beams were less deflected by a magnetic field of the same strength. These observations suggested to Goldstein that the discharge also produced gas particle fragments but that they were positively charged and more massive than the cathode ray particles.

1 Give Goldstein's evidence for the following:

a cathode rays contain negatively charged particles;

b canal rays contain positively charged particles;

c the positively charged particles were heavier than cathode-ray particles.

Values for the charges and masses of the fragments were found in later work with gas discharge tubes. The masses of positive fragments varied from one gas to another. The smallest value was for hydrogen.

Electrons, protons and neutrons

In 1897, at the Cavendish Laboratory in Cambridge, Joseph John Thomson was repeating studies on gases using more sophisticated electrical discharge tubes. Thomson's equipment was the forerunner of the present-day cathode ray tube (Fig. 2). He measured the deflections of the negative particles in cathode rays very accurately, and worked out that they had very little mass – about two-thousandth of the mass of a hydrogen atom. These particles were to be named **electrons**, the first of the sub-atomic particles to be clearly identified.

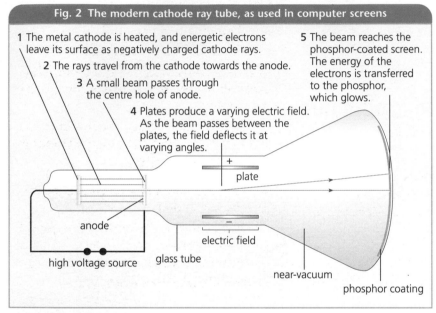

Fig. 2 The modern cathode ray tube, as used in computer screens

1 The metal cathode is heated, and energetic electrons leave its surface as negatively charged cathode rays.

2 The rays travel from the cathode towards the anode.

3 A small beam passes through the centre hole of anode.

4 Plates produce a varying electric field. As the beam passes between the plates, the field deflects it at varying angles.

5 The beam reaches the phosphor-coated screen. The energy of the electrons is transferred to the phosphor, which glows.

+ plate

anode

electric field

−

high voltage source

glass tube

near-vacuum

phosphor coating

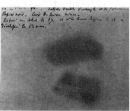

The image made by X-rays on Becquerel's photographic plate shows the shapes of the uranium salt crystals he left near it

Both Thomson's and Goldstein's results suggested that atoms could be divided into smaller particles. Thomson built up a picture of the atom containing negative electrons balanced by a positively charged part. Thomson assumed that thousands of electrons were embedded in a sphere of dispersed, positively charged material that made up most of the atom's mass (Fig. 3). He pictured the electrons

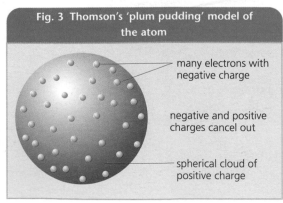

Fig. 3 Thomson's 'plum pudding' model of the atom

many electrons with negative charge

negative and positive charges cancel out

spherical cloud of positive charge

rather like fruit in a sponge pudding. For this reason, Thomson's model became known as the 'plum pudding' model of the atom.

Evidence from radioactive materials

By the late nineteenth century, scientists were looking at the mysterious radiation given out by ores of uranium, radium and other rare elements.

In 1896, Frenchman Antoine Henri Becquerel left an unexposed photographic plate wrapped in opaque (light-proof) paper in a drawer under some uranium salt crystals. Next day, to his surprise, the plate was blackened in areas that matched the shapes of the crystals (see photo). He concluded that some kind of radiation from the uranium salt could penetrate the paper and had activated the photographic emulsion. Because he was not able to identify it, Becquerel called the radiation **X-rays**. Unlike light rays, the radiation was not reflected by objects. But he did demonstrate that the radiation had energy because it could remove the charge on charged material some distance away.

The Polish physicist Marie Curie followed up Becquerel's work by investigating ores that produced X-rays, not knowing that they were dangerous and likely to cause the leukaemia she was to die from. She checked all known elements for X-rays, and discovered two new ones, radium and polonium, which emitted X-rays. It was Curie who first named the emissions **radioactivity**. She also identified negatively charged particles in the radiation as highly energetic electrons. In 1903, she and Becquerel were awarded the Nobel prize for physics in recognition of their work.

By this time, the existence of electrons was well established, and evidence was building up from other sub-atomic particles.

Ernest Rutherford was assisting Thompson's work on X-rays at Cambridge. He found two types of rays in the radiation and named them alpha (α) and beta (β) rays. He showed that they had mass and so were particles. The **alpha particle** was exactly four times heavier than hydrogen and was positively charged. This suggested to him that it contained positive particles that could be fundamental particles in atoms. The alpha particle turned out to be the same as a helium atom which had lost both its electrons. Rutherford also gave the name **beta (β) particles** to Curie's very high energy electrons. A third type of radiation, **gamma (γ) rays**, was later discovered. Gamma rays had even more penetrating power than alpha or beta rays (Fig 4).

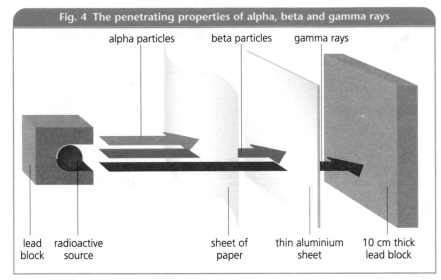

Fig. 4 The penetrating properties of alpha, beta and gamma rays

alpha particles   beta particles   gamma rays

lead block   radioactive source   sheet of paper   thin aluminium sheet   10 cm thick lead block

 2 Which of the three types of radiation in Fig. 4 could not have caused Becquerel's photographic plate to darken?

Rutherford's experiment
Rutherford moved on to Manchester University, and gathered evidence that Thomson's model of the atom as electrons in a sea of positive charge was not correct.

He fired alpha particles at very thin sheets of gold foil, only a few atoms thick (Fig. 5). He was expecting his high-energy, very fast, massive alpha particles to pass through the dispersed positive and negative charge of Thomson's atomic model, with perhaps slight deflections as the alpha particles collided with individual charged particles in the foil atoms.

Although the vast majority of alpha particles did go straight through, to his complete amazement, a few were deflected at large angles, and about one in every 10 000 was reflected back from the foil. He later recalled, 'It was almost as incredible as if you fired a fifteen inch shell at a piece of tissue paper, and it came back and hit you.' Rutherford revised Thomson's model of the atom as follows.

- Mass is not evenly spread in the atom. Nearly all the mass is densely concentrated in a minute central region, which Rutherford named the **nucleus**.

- Instead of being dispersed throughout the atom, all the positive charge is contained in the nucleus.

- The electrons circulate in the rest of the atom's volume, kept apart by the repulsion of their negative charge.

3 Give Rutherford's experimental evidence for the following.

a Most of the mass of an atom exists in the central nucleus.

b The nucleus is positively charged.

c Most of the atom is empty space.

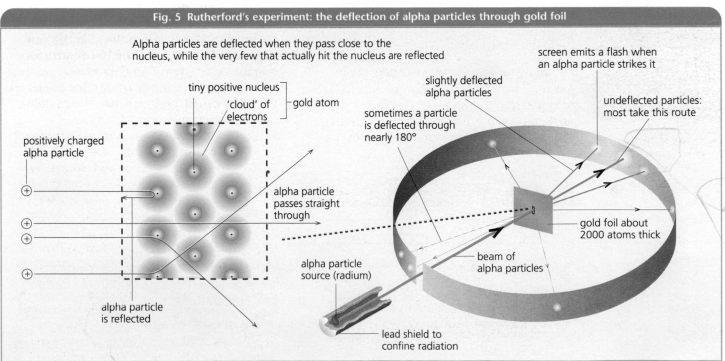

Fig. 5 Rutherford's experiment: the deflection of alpha particles through gold foil

Alpha particles are deflected when they pass close to the nucleus, while the very few that actually hit the nucleus are reflected

screen emits a flash when an alpha particle strikes it

tiny positive nucleus
'cloud' of electrons
gold atom

slightly deflected alpha particles

undeflected particles: most take this route

positively charged alpha particle

sometimes a particle is deflected through nearly 180°

alpha particle passes straight through

gold foil about 2000 atoms thick

alpha particle source (radium)

beam of alpha particles

alpha particle is reflected

lead shield to confine radiation

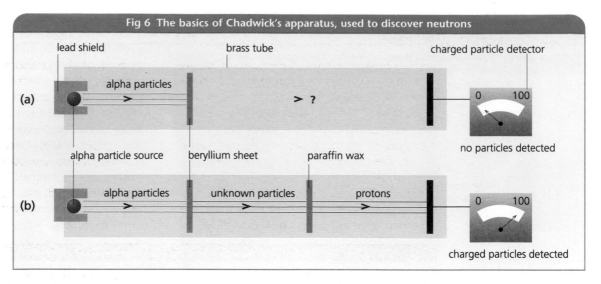

Fig 6 The basics of Chadwick's apparatus, used to discover neutrons

Particles of the nucleus

Rutherford then fired alpha particles through hydrogen gas and found that emerging particles had the mass of a hydrogen atom, yet were positively charged. By 1919 he had discovered identical particles emerging from other gases. This was evidence of a common positive particle which Rutherford was to name the **proton**.

A year later, he made a suggestion that few scientists accepted at the time - that protons did not account for the whole mass of the nucleus. He suggested that instead it also contained other particles of equal mass that were neutral in charge. It wasn't until 1932 that James Chadwick, then working for Rutherford, came up with evidence for these particles.

Chadwick was bombarding beryllium atoms with alpha particles. The beryllium gave off radiation that was undetectable because it had no charge. But the radiation dislodged protons - that were detectable - from paraffin wax (Fig. 6). The mystery particles, found to have the same mass as protons, were named **neutrons**.

In this gradual way and over many years, Rutherford built up his model of the atom that still remains today, composed of the fundamental particles electrons, protons and neutrons (Fig. 7).

We know now that the diameter of an atom is roughly 10^{-10} metres, with a nucleus that is roughly 10^{-15} metres. Scaled up, the nucleus compares to a pin-head in a sphere the diameter of the dome of St Paul's Cathedral. This model shows that the vast majority of the volume occupied by an atom is empty space. It is therefore no surprise that very few alpha particles rebounded from Rutherford's gold foil.

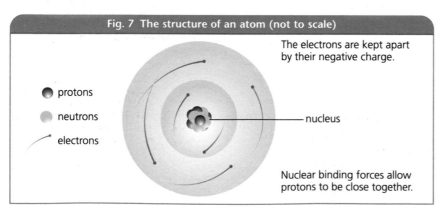

Fig. 7 The structure of an atom (not to scale)

The electrons are kept apart by their negative charge.

● protons
○ neutrons
／ electrons

nucleus

Nuclear binding forces allow protons to be close together.

1.3 Relative mass and relative charge of atomic particles

Further measurements established the masses and charges of electrons, protons and neutrons. These are summarised in Table 1. It shows that in kilograms and coulombs the values are minute numbers. For convenience in calculations, scientists use the ideas of **relative mass**. The relative mass of a proton and a neutron is 1. Also, a proton has a **relative charge** of +1, and for an electron it is –1.

The protons and neutrons of the nucleus are together called nucleons. The reason why protons in the nucleus do not repel each other (as electrons do outside the nucleus), is that a strong nuclear force acting over the short distance of the nucleus binds all the nucleons together.

Since atoms of the elements are neutral, the number of protons (positive charges) must equal the number of electrons (negative charges). The atoms of all elements (except hydrogen which has no neutrons) contain these three fundamental particles.

Table 1 The fundamental atomic particles, their mass and charge.				
Particle	Mass/kg	Charge/C	Relative mass	Relative charge
electron	9.109×10^{-31}	1.602×10^{-19}	5.45×10^{-4}	−1
proton	1.672×10^{-27}	1.602×10^{-19}	1	+1
neutron	1.674×10^{-27}	0	1	0

The mass of the electron is so small compared to the mass of the proton and neutron that chemists often take it to be zero

1.4 Atomic number, mass number and isotopes

Different elements have different numbers of electrons, protons and neutrons in their atoms. It is the *number of protons* in the nucleus of an atom that identifies which element it is. Remember that it is still the same element if an atom loses or gains electrons. It can also lose or gain one or two neutrons and still remain the same element. Using this information we can define an element according to its mass by using two numbers.

Atomic number
The **atomic number** of an element is the number of protons in the nucleus of the atom. It has the symbol Z and we place its value below the line in front of the element's symbol. Since atoms are neutral, the number of protons equals the number of electrons orbiting the nucleus.

Mass number
The **mass number** of an element is the total number of protons and neutrons in the nucleus of an atom. The symbol for the mass number is A, and its value goes above the atomic number. Note that it is not the mass of the atom and it has no units.

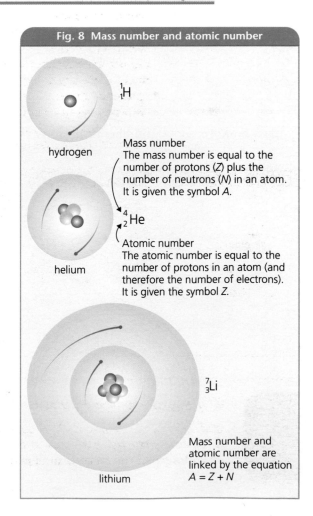

Fig. 8 Mass number and atomic number

hydrogen $^{1}_{1}H$

Mass number
The mass number is equal to the number of protons (Z) plus the number of neutrons (N) in an atom. It is given the symbol A.

helium $^{4}_{2}He$

Atomic number
The atomic number is equal to the number of protons in an atom (and therefore the number of electrons). It is given the symbol Z.

lithium $^{7}_{3}Li$

Mass number and atomic number are linked by the equation $A = Z + N$

Isotopes

We have seen that atoms of the same element have the same number of protons and hence the same atomic number Z. But they may have a different number of neutrons and so a different mass number A. For example, two isotopes of carbon are carbon-12 and carbon-14. Atoms of the same element with different mass numbers are called **isotopes**. As in Fig. 8, the notation for an isotope shows the mass number and the atomic number, like this:

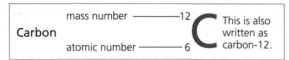

The isotopes of carbon and their sub-atomic particles are summarised in Table 2.

Table 2 Isotopes of carbon					
Name		No. of protons	No. of neutrons	No. of electrons	Relative abundance
carbon-12		6	6	6	98.9
carbon-13		6	7	6	1.1
carbon-14		.6	8	6	10^{-10}

mass number	=	number of protons	+	number of neutrons
A	=	Z	+	N

Therefore:

number of neutrons	=	mass number	–	number of protons
N	=	A	–	Z

Relative abundance is the amount of each isotope as the percentage for that element occurring naturally on Earth.

Except for hydrogen, all the isotopes of an element have the same name. The isotopes of hydrogen have these names: $^{1}_{1}\text{H}$ is hydrogen, $^{2}_{1}\text{H}$ is deuterium and $^{3}_{1}\text{H}$ is tritium.

We can calculate the number of neutrons in the isotope of an element as follows:

4 Two isotopes of chlorine are $^{35}_{17}\text{Cl}$ and $^{37}_{17}\text{Cl}$. Draw up a table to show the number of protons, neutrons and electrons in each isotope.

Properties of isotopes

The chemical properties of an element depend on the number and arrangement of the electrons. Since all the isotopes of an element have the same number and arrangement of electrons, they also all have the same chemical properties. However, because of the difference in mass, isotopes differ slightly in their physical properties, such as in the rate of diffusion which depends on mass, and their nuclear properties, such as radioactivity.

Isotopes which are not radioactive, such as chlorine-35 and chlorine-37, are called **stable isotopes**. Data books give you the relative abundance of each isotope present in such stable, naturally occurring elements.

APPLICATION A   Size, scale and simplicity

A single carbon atom measures about one ten billionth of a metre across, a dimension so small that we cannot possibly imagine it. The nucleus is a thousand times smaller again, and the electrons a hundred thousand times smaller than that!

Since the numbers involved are meaningless, and in order to make dimensions manageable in calculations, at the atomic level scientists use a different set of units to describe masses and distances. You have already come across this idea when we talked about the relative mass of a proton and a neutron as being 1 relative mass unit (see Table 1, page 7). The electron is a mere 0.000 545 units. Clearly, even with relative masses we end up with some awkard numbers.

Standard form

Numbers with many zeros are difficult to follow, so we tend to express these in standard form. Standard form is a number between 1 and 10. So how do we express the number 769 000 in standard form?

1 Locate the decimal point: 769 000.0
2 Move the decimal point to give a number between 1 and 10: 7.69 000
3 Multiply the number by ten raised to the power x where x is the number of jumps you made: 7.69×10^5

Sometimes the decimal point may move the other way. Take the mass of the electron as an example:

The mass of an electron is 0.000 545 units.
1 Find the decimal point and move it – this time it goes to the right: 00 005.45
2 Multiply the number by ten raised to the power x where x is the number of jumps you made. But this time the index will be negative: 5.45×10^{-4}

Calculations using standard form

Standard form makes multiplication and division of even the most complex numbers much easier to handle. When you multiply two numbers in standard form, you multiply the numbers and add the indices. For example:

$(3 \times 10^2) \times (2 \times 10^3) = 6 \times 10^5$

If you **divide** numbers in standard form you **divide the standard number and subtract the indices**.
For example:

$$\frac{8 \times 10^6}{4 \times 10^2} = 2 \times 10^4$$

Now use the data in Table 1 on page 7 to do the following calculations.

1 **a** An atom of hydrogen contains only a proton and an electron. Calculate the mass of the hydrogen atom in kilograms.
   b A molecule of hydrogen contains two atoms. Calculate the mass of a hydrogen molecule in grams.
   c How many electrons have the same mass as a single neutron?

2 Convert the following quantities into measurements in grams expressed in standard form:
   a the mass of a neutron
   b 200 million electrons
   c ten gold coins weighing a total of 0.311 kg

Standard prefixes

A system of prefixes is used to modify units. Prefixes that are commonly used are listed in the table.

Prefix	Symbol	Multiplier	Meaning
mega	M	10^6	1 000 000
kilo	K	10^3	1 000
deci	d	10^{-1}	0.1
centi	c	10^{-2}	0.01
milli	m	10^{-3}	0.001
micro	μ	10^{-6}	0.000 001
nano	n	10^{-9}	0.000 000 001
pico	p	10^{-12}	0.000 000 000 001

The prefixes that scientists prefer have intervals of a thousand. For example, attaching preferred prefixes to the unit metre, we have kilometre, metre, millimetre and nanometre. But others are used when they are convenient for the task in hand.

3 The smallpox virus which causes a lethal illness in humans measures 300 nm across and has a mass of 1.6×10^8 relative mass units.
   a Express the diameter of the virus in centimetres.
   b How much would a culture of 10^{17} virus particles weigh in grams?

4 The haemoglobin molecule is roughly spherical and carries oxygen in our blood. It is about 64 450 relative mass units. It is roughly 7 nm across and contains four iron atoms as ions. The atomic radius of iron is about 0.07 nm.
   a How many times larger is the diameter of haemoglobin compared with one ion of iron?
   b Express the mass of haemoglobin in kilograms in standard form.

1.5 Detecting isotopes using a mass spectrometer

The **mass spectrometer** is an instrument that sorts positively charged ions according to their mass. It was famously used to first separate the isotopes of uranium. Today, as well as being the routine tool for identifying unknown compounds in forensic science, the mass spectrometer is used in industry to record the relative abundance of isotopes in a sample.

Fig. 9 shows the basic features of the mass spectrometer. On the drawing, carefully follow the processes that the particles undergo.

1 Ionisation. A beam made up of the vaporised sample of atoms or molecules reaches the energetic electrons from the electron gun. When an electron is knocked from an atom or molecule, a positively charged ion is formed. Examples are:

$$He(g) \rightarrow He^+(g) + e^-$$
$$H_2(g) \rightarrow H_2^+(g) + e^-$$

Ions with a charge of +2 are formed when two electrons are knocked out, for example:

$$He(g) \rightarrow He^{2+}(g) + 2e^-$$

There are fewer doubly charged ions because only the more energetic electrons from the electron gun can knock out two electrons.

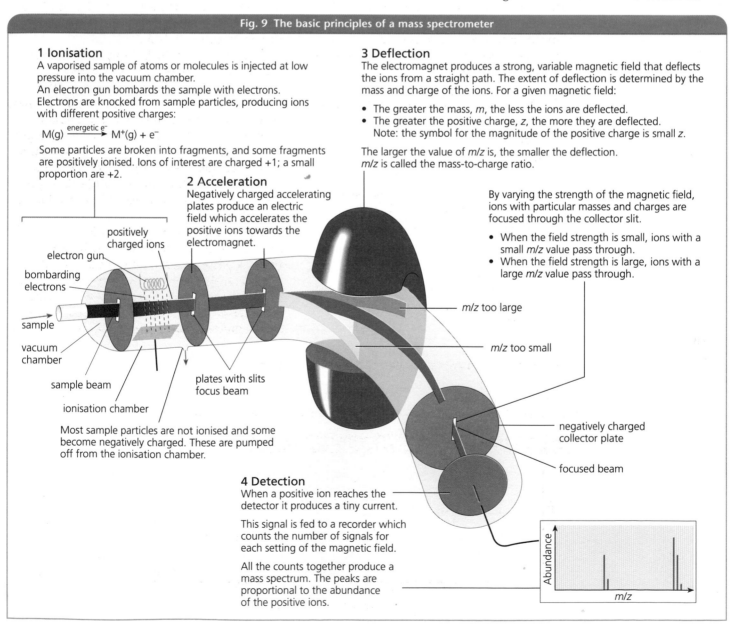

Fig. 9 The basic principles of a mass spectrometer

1 Ionisation
A vaporised sample of atoms or molecules is injected at low pressure into the vacuum chamber.
An electron gun bombards the sample with electrons. Electrons are knocked from sample particles, producing ions with different positive charges:

$$M(g) \xrightarrow{\text{energetic } e^-} M^+(g) + e^-$$

Some particles are broken into fragments, and some fragments are positively ionised. Ions of interest are charged +1; a small proportion are +2.

2 Acceleration
Negatively charged accelerating plates produce an electric field which accelerates the positive ions towards the electromagnet.

positively charged ions
electron gun
bombarding electrons
sample
vacuum chamber
sample beam
ionisation chamber
plates with slits focus beam

Most sample particles are not ionised and some become negatively charged. These are pumped off from the ionisation chamber.

3 Deflection
The electromagnet produces a strong, variable magnetic field that deflects the ions from a straight path. The extent of deflection is determined by the mass and charge of the ions. For a given magnetic field:

- The greater the mass, m, the less the ions are deflected.
- The greater the positive charge, z, the more they are deflected.
  Note: the symbol for the magnitude of the positive charge is small z.

The larger the value of m/z is, the smaller the deflection. m/z is called the mass-to-charge ratio.

By varying the strength of the magnetic field, ions with particular masses and charges are focused through the collector slit.

- When the field strength is small, ions with a small m/z value pass through.
- When the field strength is large, ions with a large m/z value pass through.

m/z too large
m/z too small
negatively charged collector plate
focused beam

4 Detection
When a positive ion reaches the detector it produces a tiny current.

This signal is fed to a recorder which counts the number of signals for each setting of the magnetic field.

All the counts together produce a mass spectrum. The peaks are proportional to the abundance of the positive ions.

Abundance
m/z

2 Acceleration. A negative electric field accelerates the beam of positive ions, and slits narrow it.

3 Deflection. The fast-moving beam of positive ions is deflected by a strong magnetic field. For each ion, the degree of deflection depends on its **mass-to-charge ratio**, **m/z**. The smaller this ratio is, the larger is the deflection. By varying the magnetic field, ions of different mass-to-charge ratios travel along the centre of the spectrometer.

4 Detection. As an ion reaches the detector, it produces a tiny current that is entered as one ion with its particular mass-to-charge value. The same applies for all the ions reaching the detector, so that the proportion of each ion in the total sample is recorded. From this record a spectrum is printed out. From a database, the identity and amounts of each ion can be found.

> **5** Write an equation for the ionisation in a mass spectrometer of:
>
> **a** hydrogen gas;
>
> **b** helium gas.
>
> **6** Ions A^+ and A^{2+} have the same mass. For the same magnetic field strength, which has the larger deflection?

The mass spectrum of chlorine gas

Two ways in which chlorine can be ionised when bombarded by energetic electrons in a mass spectrometer are:

$$Cl_2(g) \rightarrow 2Cl^+ + 2e^-$$
one molecule loses two electrons and becomes two atomic ions

$$Cl_2(g) \rightarrow Cl_2^+ + e^-$$
one molecule loses one electron and becomes one molecular ion

Each of the atomic ions has only one nucleus and so is called a **mononuclear ion**. (The molecular chlorine ion has two nuclei.) Both the mononuclear ion and the molecular ion have a charge of +1, so for each ion, $z = 1$, and therefore the m/z ratio also gives the mass of each ion.

Naturally occurring chlorine has two isotopes, ^{35}Cl and ^{37}Cl. Chlorine-35 has a lower mass than chlorine-37, and so in the mass spectrometer the same magnetic field deflects the atomic ion of chlorine-35 more than the atomic ion of chlorine-37. The spectrum in Fig. 10 shows a peak at 35 for chlorine-35. With its greater mass, the atomic ion of chlorine-37 needs a stronger magnetic field to focus it at the detector. It produces the peak at 37. The peaks at 70, 72 and 74 are for the molecular ions, which are $^{35}Cl-^{35}Cl^+$, $^{35}Cl-^{37}Cl^+$ and $^{37}Cl-^{37}Cl^+$.

The heights of the lines in the chlorine spectrum are proportional to the relative abundance of each isotope present in the sample. Fig. 10 shows that the isotope of mass number 35 is three times more abundant than mass number 37. Therefore the isotopes $^{35}Cl : ^{37}Cl$ are present in a 3:1 ratio. Similarly, for any element with several isotopes, you can use the position and size of peaks on the mass spectrum to calculate the proportion of each isotope.

Notice that the mass values for mononuclear ions have all been whole numbers. They correspond to the sum of protons and neutrons, i.e. the mass number. We will now look at a way that all chemists have agreed on to measure the mass of any atom compared with a standard mass.

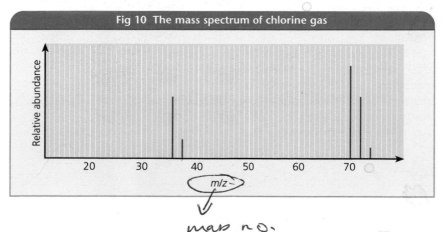

Fig 10 The mass spectrum of chlorine gas

m/z

mass no.

1.6 Relative atomic mass

The standard mass against which the mass of any atom is compared is one twelfth of the mass of an atom of the isotope carbon-12. Carbon's mass is taken as exactly 12. For any element, therefore:

The relative atomic mass, A_r, is the mass of one atom compared with one twelfth of the mass of an atom of carbon-12.

$$A_r = \frac{\text{mass of 1 atom of an element}}{\frac{1}{12} \text{ mass of one atom of carbon-12}}$$

Relative atomic masses have no units; they represent the number of times heavier one atom is compared to another, in this case, carbon-12.

Look up the value for the relative atomic mass of an element in a data book, and you will find it given as a decimal, for example, 35.453 for chlorine. This is because the value is the average of all the element's naturally occurring isotopes, taking their relative abundance into account. Using this average value is essential for accuracy in experimental calculations.

Example: Calculating relative atomic mass
In a sample of 100 atoms of copper:
69% are copper-63
31% are copper-65
So the total mass for 100 atoms
= $(0.69 \times 63) + (0.31 \times 65)$
= $43.47 + 20.15$
= 63.62
Therefore the relative atomic mass of copper is 63.62.

1.7 Relative molecular mass

To find relative molecular mass, we again use the relative atomic mass scale.

The relative molecular mass, M_r, of a molecule of an element or compound is the sum of the relative atomic masses of all the atoms in the molecule, divided by one twelfth of the mass of one atom of carbon-12.

$$A_r = \frac{\text{mass of 1 molecule}}{\frac{1}{12} \text{ mass of one atom of carbon-12}}$$

Relative molecular mass is dealt with more fully in Chapter 3.

Finding M_r values
As we have seen, the mass spectrometer is the instrument routinely used to find the relative molecular masses of compounds. In a sample of a compound injected into the mass spectrometer, some molecules do not fragment but just lose one electron to make a singly charged positive ion. The ion produced is known as the **molecular ion, M$^+$**:

$$M(g) \xrightarrow{\text{energetic e}^-} M^+(g) + e^-$$

Most other molecules in the sample split into fragments, some of them positively charged, and all the positive ions of each mass number are recorded as lines on the mass spectrum. The molecular ion has the greatest mass, and therefore its peak is furthest to the right on the mass spectrum. Its value is therefore the relative molecular mass of the compound.

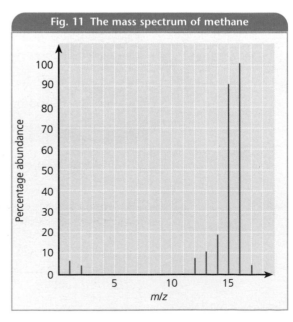

Fig. 11 The mass spectrum of methane

APPLICATION B Was there uranium at Greenham Common?

During the 1970s and 80s, women set up camp outside the US air base to protest against the storage of nuclear weapons which contained uranium

The US Air Force used to operate a base at Greenham Common in Berkshire. In the 1990s, there was an unusually high cluster of childhood leukaemia in the surrounding Berkshire region. There was a rumour of a loaded B-47 bomber leaking uranium in February 1958, and of a cover-up of the incident. This led some local residents to suspect that the uranium had caused the increased number of leukaemia cases.

Uranium occurs naturally as three isotopes, all radioactive, ^{238}U, ^{235}U and ^{234}U, with isotopic abundances as shown in the chart. This pattern of isotopic abundance is constant for all naturally occurring uranium.

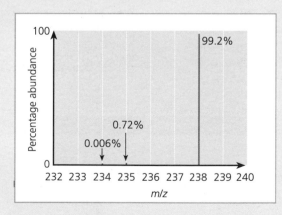

Uranium used as nuclear fuel is enriched uranium. It contains 6% ^{235}U and 94% ^{238}U. Uranium in the core of some nuclear weapons contains 93% ^{235}U and 7% ^{238}U. Depleted uranium, used in nuclear warheads, contains 0.35% ^{235}U and 99.65% ^{238}U. Any uranium released into the environment in an accident would have percentages of isotopes different from naturally occurring uranium percentages.

1 Uranium has an atomic number of 92. How many protons, neutrons and electrons are there in each naturally occurring isotope?

2 a Give the formula for the isotope responsible for the peaks at 234, 235 and 238 on the mass spectrum.
  b At a fixed magnetic field, which isotopic ion would be deflected most in a mass spectrometer? Explain your answer.
  c Calculate the relative molecular mass for a sample of uranium containing 1% ^{234}U, 1.5% ^{235}U and 97.5% ^{238}U.

A team at Southampton University measured the amounts of uranium in the Greenham Common area. Measurements showed that the uranium in the area was within the range of naturally occurring levels and percentages. The area was therefore not contaminated by activity at the air base.

Though studies did reveal contamination by uranium in the environment around the Atomic Weapons Research Establishment at Aldermaston, 5 miles away, these were well within the safety limits. Studies of childhood leukaemia show that clusters of children affected can occur for different reasons. One theory is that the disease can be caused by a virus. If a population immune to the virus but carrying it moves to an area where local people are not immune, then an outbreak can occur.

Example: Interpreting the mass spectrum of methane

In Fig. 11, the peak for the highest molecular mass is at $m/z = 16$.
It represents the molecular ion, CH_4^+
So M_r of methane = 16, and its formula is CH_4 (12 + 1 + 1 + 1 + 1).

The other lines represent fragments of methane molecules.
The line $m/z = 15$ is the CH_3^+ ion (12+1+1+1).

 7 Explain the lines at $m/z = 1$, 2, 12, 13 and 14.

1.8 First ionisation energies

Electrons move around the nucleus in particular **energy levels** (also called shells). In GCSE textbooks, diagrams often show the electrons arranged round the nucleus on rings that represent the main energy levels. The innermost ring is level 1 and contains two electrons. The next level contains eight electrons, and so on outwards. These diagrams, though useful for some purposes, are simplified versions of a fuller picture, because not all the electrons in level 2 are exactly the same. Level 2 actually has a number of sub-levels within it.

Elements other than hydrogen have more than one electron. For these, the energy required to remove the outermost electron from an atom is the first ionisation energy, and the energy to remove the next electron is the second ionisation energy:

First ionisation energy: $E(g) \rightarrow E(g)^+ + e^-$
Second ionisation energy:

$$E^+(g) \rightarrow E(g)^{2+} + e^- \text{ ...and so on.}$$

The energy for one atom is so small that, for convenience, energies are given for 1 mole of atoms, in kilojoules per mole, $kJ \, mol^{-1}$, measured at 298 K. So:

The first ionisation energy is the enthalpy change (energy transferred) when one mole of gaseous atoms forms one mole of gaseous ions with a single positive charge.

First ionisation energies have been worked out for all but a few heavy elements in the Periodic Table. Fig. 12 shows first ionisation energies for elements to caesium, atomic number 55. Note that first ionisation energies

do not give an indication of how reactive an element is, since reactivity depends on several different factors, including whether one or more electrons are lost when an element reacts. However, ionisation energies have helped us to deduce the arrangement of electrons in atoms.

Interpreting the graph of first ionisation energies

Suppose that all the electrons at energy level 2 in the elements of Period 2 were exactly the same. Then we might imagine that removing the first electron from all the elements lithium to neon would be equally easy. Or perhaps there would be a gradual uniform trend as the nuclear charge increases and the atoms increase in size. In fact, the real values do show a gradual increase, but they also include dips. In Fig. 13, Period 2 has three gentle up-slopes, with dips at the third and sixth elements. Before we can explain this pattern, we must first look at energy levels and see how electrons are added in successive elements.

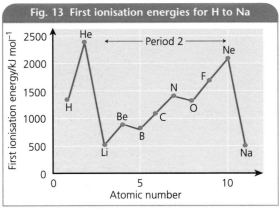
Fig. 13 First ionisation energies for H to Na

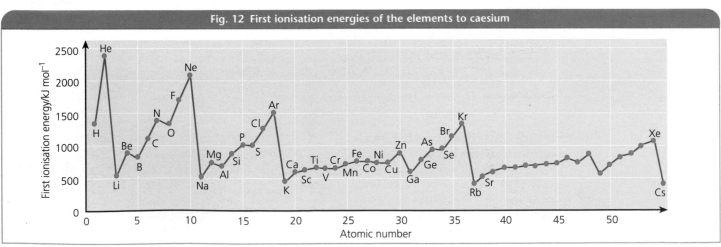
Fig. 12 First ionisation energies of the elements to caesium

1.9 Describing electrons

Energy levels and sub-levels

Within each energy level there are **energy sub-levels** (also called sub-shells). The number of sub-levels permitted for each energy level is shown in Table 3. The sub-levels are given letters, **s**, **p**, **d** and **f**. This sequence of sub-levels corresponds to an increase in energy (Fig. 14). The letters come from words used to describe emission spectral lines for the sub-levels: s = spread, d = diffuse, etc.

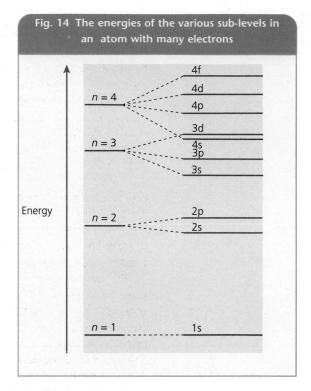

Fig. 14 The energies of the various sub-levels in an atom with many electrons

Main energy level	Sub-level	Max no. electron pairs in sub-level	Max. no. electrons in sub-level	Max. no. electrons in main energy level
1	s	1	2	2
2	s	1	2	8
	p	3	6	
3	s	1	2	18
	p	3	6	
	d	5	10	
4	s	1	2	32
	p	3	6	
	d	5	10	
	f	7	14	

Table 3 Levels, sub-levels and numbers of electrons

Each additional electron goes into the sub-level with the next lowest energy. Table 3 shows, for example, that level 1 has a maximum of 2 electrons and that they are both in sub-level s. Level 2 has a maximum of 8 electrons of which 2 are in sub-level s and 6 in sub-level p. The order of filling is the same as the order of the elements in the Periodic Table.

Electron orbitals

Electrons are constantly moving, and it is impossible to know the exact position of an electron at any given time. However, measurements of the density of electrons as they move round the nucleus show that there are regions where it is highly probable to find an electron. These regions of high probability are called **orbitals**. Each of the s, p, d and f energy sub-levels corresponds to a different shaped orbital.

The shapes of s and p orbitals are shown in Fig. 15. Each orbital can hold two electrons which spin in opposite directions. Table 4 shows the numbers of electrons and orbitals in the sub-levels.

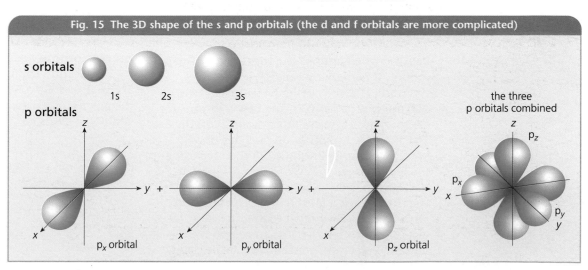

Fig. 15 The 3D shape of the s and p orbitals (the d and f orbitals are more complicated)

Table 4 Number of orbitals and maximum number of electrons per sub-level.				
Sub-level:	**s**	**p**	**d**	**f**
Number of orbitals in sub-level	1	3	5	7
Maximum number of electrons	2	6	10	14

We can now explain the pattern in Fig. 16 for the first ionisation energies of the **Period 2 elements**. Electrons with their negative charge are attracted to the positively charged nucleus. As the positive charge increases across Period 2, so the electrons experience an increasing force of attraction. This explains the overall rise in the values of first ionisation energies.

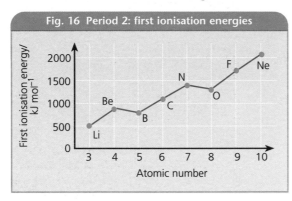

Fig. 16 Period 2: first ionisation energies

As an electron is added to each successive atom, it occupies the first available empty orbital, just as passengers on a bus prefer a double seat all to themselves before they share! In Period 2, the electron for lithium enters the empty 2s orbital. The level 1 electrons shield it from the nuclear charge, so it is relatively easy to remove and its ionisation energy is low. The electron for beryllium has opposite spin and completes the 2s orbital. Its slight increase in energy over the first 2s electron is more than offset by the increased nuclear attraction, so beryllium's first ionisation energy is higher.

Boron shows a dip in ionisation energy because its electron is the first to enter the p orbital. It is higher in energy than the 2s electrons and so is easier to remove. Then, like our bus passengers, the new electrons for carbon and nitrogen enter vacant p orbitals. The increase in ionisation energies from boron to nitrogen result from the increasing nuclear charge.

Then oxygen shows a dip. The new electron enters a p orbital with an electron already in it. They repel each other, so it takes less energy to remove it than to remove the unpaired electron from nitrogen. The rising

values for fluorine and neon match the increase in nuclear charge as electrons continue to fill the same p energy sub-level.

So the graph for first ionisation energies across Period 2 does not show electrons filling into one giant level with no sub-structure. Instead, the pattern shows electrons entering the s orbital (2 electrons), then singly into the p orbitals (3 electrons), then completing the p orbitals (3 electrons).

You can read more on page 18 about the order in which electrons fill p orbitals.

Electron configurations of atoms

The arrangement of electrons for an atom can be written down as symbols in an **electron configuration**. It includes sub-levels as well as levels, and shows the number of electrons in each:

Hydrogen has one electron in level 1, sub-level s. Its electron configuration is 1s.
Helium has two electrons with opposite spin. Its electron configuration is $1s^2$.
Lithium has two electrons in 1s and one in 2s. Its electron configuration is $1s^2 2s^1$.

We can also draw a **spin diagram** for each sub-level which shows the direction of spin of all the electrons. So we can represent the 12 electrons in magnesium in two ways:

Level/sub-level: 1s   2s   2p   3s
Electron
  configuration: $1s^2$ $2s^2$ $2p^6$ $3s^2$
Spin diagram: [↑↓] [↑↓] [↑↓][↑↓][↑↓] [↑↓]

7   Explain the meaning of 2, p and 6 in $2p^6$.

In Table 5, notice that level 1 in helium is filled. The next element with a filled level is neon with electron configuration $1s^2 2s^2 2p^6$. Since the outermost level is complete, these elements are very stable and are known as the **inert** or **noble gases**.

The electron configuration for chlorine is $1s^2 2s^2 2p^6 3s^2 3p^5$. We can abbreviate this to the previous inert gas, neon, and add chlorine's additional electrons: Cl = [Ne] $3s^2 3p^5$.

8   Using Table 5, write an abbreviated electron configurations for:

a   sulphur

b   aluminium

c   scandium

d   copper.

Table 5 Electron configurations and spin diagrams for the first 30 elements

Z	Element	Electron configuration	1s	2s	2p			3s	3p			3d					4s
1	H	$1s^1$	↑														
2	**He**	**$1s^2$**	↑↓														
3	Li	$1s^2 2s^1$	↑↓	↑													
4	Be	$1s^2 2s^2$	↑↓	↑↓													
5	B	$1s^2 2s^2 2p^1$	↑↓	↑↓	↑												
6	C	$1s^2 2s^2 2p^2$	↑↓	↑↓	↑	↑											
7	N	$1s^2 2s^2 2p^3$	↑↓	↑↓	↑	↑	↑										
8	O	$1s^2 2s^2 2p^4$	↑↓	↑↓	↑↓	↑	↑										
9	F	$1s^2 2s^2 2p^5$	↑↓	↑↓	↑↓	↑↓	↑										
10	**Ne**	**$1s^2 2s^2 2p^6$**	↑↓	↑↓	↑↓	↑↓	↑↓										
11	Na	$1s^2 2s^2 2p^6 3s^1$	↑↓	↑↓	↑↓	↑↓	↑↓	↑									
12	Mg	$1s^2 2s^2 2p^6 3s^2$	↑↓	↑↓	↑↓	↑↓	↑↓	↑↓									
13	Al	$1s^2 2s^2 2p^6 3s^2 3p^1$	↑↓	↑↓	↑↓	↑↓	↑↓	↑↓	↑								
14	Si	$1s^2 2s^2 2p^6 3s^2 3p^2$	↑↓	↑↓	↑↓	↑↓	↑↓	↑↓	↑	↑							
15	P	$1s^2 2s^2 2p^6 3s^2 3p^3$	↑↓	↑↓	↑↓	↑↓	↑↓	↑↓	↑	↑	↑						
16	S	$1s^2 2s^2 2p^6 3s^2 3p^4$	↑↓	↑↓	↑↓	↑↓	↑↓	↑↓	↑↓	↑	↑						
17	**Cl**	**$1s^2 2s^2 2p^6 3s^2 3p^5$**	↑↓	↑↓	↑↓	↑↓	↑↓	↑↓	↑↓	↑↓	↑						
18	Ar	$1s^2 2s^2 2p^6 3s^2 3p^6$	↑↓	↑↓	↑↓	↑↓	↑↓	↑↓	↑↓	↑↓	↑↓						
19	**K**	**$1s^2 2s^2 2p^6 3s^2 3p^6 4s^1$**	↑↓	↑↓	↑↓	↑↓	↑↓	↑↓	↑↓	↑↓	↑↓						↑
20	Ca	$1s^2 2s^2 2p^6 3s^2 3p^6 4s^2$	↑↓	↑↓	↑↓	↑↓	↑↓	↑↓	↑↓	↑↓	↑↓						↑↓
21	Sc	$1s^2 2s^2 2p^6 3s^2 3p^6 3d^1 4s^2$	↑↓	↑↓	↑↓	↑↓	↑↓	↑↓	↑↓	↑↓	↑↓	↑					↑↓
22	Ti	$1s^2 2s^2 2p^6 3s^2 3p^2 3d^2 4s^2$	↑↓	↑↓	↑↓	↑↓	↑↓	↑↓	↑↓	↑↓	↑↓	↑	↑				↑↓
23	V	$1s^2 2s^2 2p^6 3s^2 3p^2 3d^3 4s^2$	↑↓	↑↓	↑↓	↑↓	↑↓	↑↓	↑↓	↑↓	↑↓	↑	↑	↑			↑↓
24	Cr	$1s^2 2s^2 2p^6 3s^2 3p^6 3d^5 4s^1$	↑↓	↑↓	↑↓	↑↓	↑↓	↑↓	↑↓	↑↓	↑↓	↑	↑	↑	↑	↑	↑
25	Mn	$1s^2 2s^2 2p^6 3s^2 3p^6 3d^5 4s^2$	↑↓	↑↓	↑↓	↑↓	↑↓	↑↓	↑↓	↑↓	↑↓	↑	↑	↑	↑	↑	↑↓
26	**Fe**	**$1s^2 2s^2 2p^6 3s^2 3p^6 3d^6 4s^2$**	↑↓	↑↓	↑↓	↑↓	↑↓	↑↓	↑↓	↑↓	↑↓	↑↓	↑	↑	↑	↑	↑↓
27	Co	$1s^2 2s^2 2p^6 3s^2 3p^6 3d^7 4s^2$	↑↓	↑↓	↑↓	↑↓	↑↓	↑↓	↑↓	↑↓	↑↓	↑↓	↑↓	↑	↑	↑	↑↓
28	Ni	$1s^2 2s^2 2p^6 3s^2 3p^6 3d^8 4s^2$	↑↓	↑↓	↑↓	↑↓	↑↓	↑↓	↑↓	↑↓	↑↓	↑↓	↑↓	↑↓	↑	↑	↑↓
29	Cu	$1s^2 2s^2 2p^6 3s^2 3p^6 3d^{10} 4s^1$	↑↓	↑↓	↑↓	↑↓	↑↓	↑↓	↑↓	↑↓	↑↓	↑↓	↑↓	↑↓	↑↓	↑↓	↑
30	Zn	$1s^2 2s^2 2p^6 3s^2 3p^6 3d^{10} 4s^2$	↑↓	↑↓	↑↓	↑↓	↑↓	↑↓	↑↓	↑↓	↑↓	↑↓	↑↓	↑↓	↑↓	↑↓	↑↓

Highlighted elements are described in some detail in this chapter.

Between hydrogen and argon, electrons of increasing energy are added, one per element, in sub-level order: 1s, 2s, 2p, 3s, 3p. Then, for potassium, the next electron skips sub-level 3d and goes into 4s for the following reason. Though level 3 energies are lower overall than level 4 energies, the 3d sub-level has a higher energy than the 4s sub-level as shown in Fig. 17. So, the order of filling is the order of elements in the Periodic Table, and 4s is filled before 3d. We will see later that the chemical properties of elements reflect the energy levels of electrons.

Fig. 17 Generalised diagram of the energies of the sub-levels

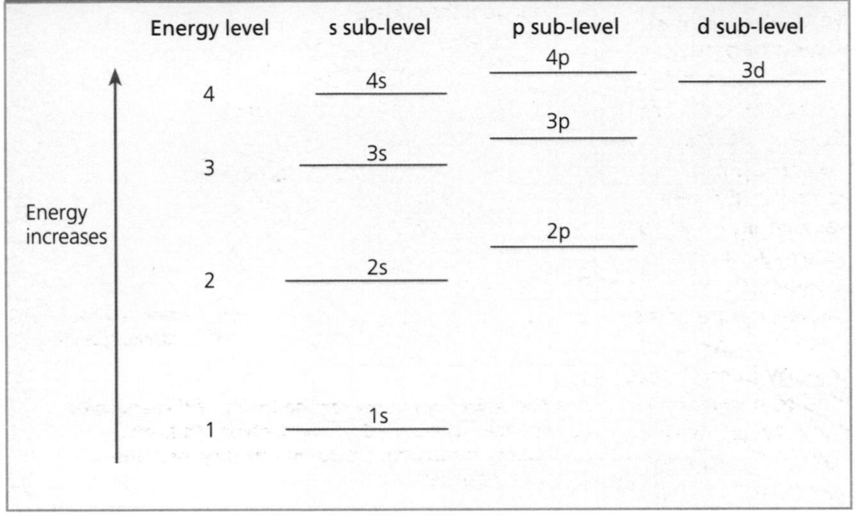

Inner electron shells have the effect of shielding outermost electrons from the positive charge of the nucleus. A full level has a strong shielding effect on a single outermost electron, which is then easy to remove, as in the case of Na^+.

9 Write the electron configuration for:
a Fe^{2+}
b Cl^-
c Al^{3+}
d S^{2-}

Hund's rule of maximum multiplicity and p electrons

We have seen that the arrows in electron spin diagrams indicate their direction of spin and whether there are one or two electrons per orbital. **Hund's rule of maximum multiplicity** states the order in which they enter orbitals:

Electrons organise themselves so that as far as possible they remain unpaired, occupying the maximum number of sub-level orbitals possible.

As we have seen, for the p sub-levels, this means that electrons first occupy empty orbitals before adding to orbitals with one electron. The incoming electrons also have the same spin. Therefore:

electron $2p^1$ in boron is:
= orbital $2p_{x1}$ (as Fig. 15)

electrons $2p^2$ in carbon are:
= orbitals $2p_{x1}$ and $2p_{y1}$

electrons $2p^3$ in nitrogen are:
= orbitals $2p_{x1}$, $2p_{y1}$ and $2p_{z1}$

After there is one electron in each orbital, the next electron goes into the first orbital, spinning in the opposite direction, so that:

electrons $2p^4$ in oxygen are:
= orbitals $2p_{x2}$, $2p_{y1}$ and $2p_{z1}$

Electron configurations of ions

An ion of an element is an atom in which either:
- one or more electrons are added, when it becomes negatively charged, or
- one or more electrons are removed, when it becomes positively charged.

Example: The electron configuration of the sodium ion, Na^+

The electron configuration of the sodium atom is $1s^2\ 2p^6\ 2s^1$.
In Na^+, the outermost electron, $2s^1$, has been removed.
This is the highest-energy electron in sodium, and so takes the least energy to remove. The electron configuration of Na^+ is $1s^2\ 2s^2\ 2p^6$.

KEY FACTS

- Electrons in an atom are arranged in energy levels, with level 1 closest to the nucleus and with least energy.
- Sub-levels s, p, d and f exist within the main levels.
- Electrons around the nucleus are located in orbitals.
- An orbital contains a maximum of two electrons spinning in opposite directions.
- The electron configuration of an atom specifies the number of electrons in each main level and sub-level of energy.

Emission spectra and electrons

Advertising signs are simply discharge tubes filled with gas, often neon which gives a strong yellow light. Pigments in the glass give other colours

When a high electrical voltage passes through a gas at low pressure in a discharge tube, radiation including light is emitted. The light can be split into its component colours using the spectroscope, an instrument designed by Robert Bunsen who also invented the burner.

We think of light as consisting of particles called photons moving in a wave-like path. Each photon has its own energy that depends on the wavelength of the photon. The shorter the wavelength, the more energetic the photon, so ultraviolet light with a shorter wavelength is more energetic than infrared light with a longer wavelength.

The light from gas in a discharge tube arises when electrons which have gained energy from the electricity then lose it as energy in the visible spectrum. An electron is excited to a higher energy level, becomes unstable and falls back after a very short time. As it falls back, it gives out the energy as a burst of radiation which a spectroscope will show up as a line of light of a particular colour. The size of the energy fall determines the energy of the radiation emitted. All the lines for an element make up an **emission spectrum** for that element.

If, as Rutherford's model suggested, the energies of electrons were not fixed, then their emission spectra would be continuous and would depend only on the energy supplied by the electricity. Instead, spectra show sharp emission lines which suggest electrons can only jump between particular levels. These levels correspond to the energy levels we now use to describe the arrangement of electrons in atoms.

Niels Bohr developed Rutherford's original ideas by suggesting that electrons exist at fixed energies. He gave each energy level the symbol n and numbered the levels 1, 2, 3 and so on; $n = 1$ represents the ground state energy level, as in the diagram of the staircase model.

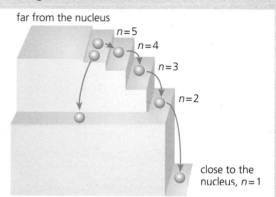

The staircase model for the levels of the energies emitted by the hydrogen electron. As shown, energy jumps can be down one step or more than one step.

Each line in the emission spectrum represents the energy difference between one of the higher energy levels to which hydrogen's electron could jump when excited, and the ground state energy level in which the unexcited electron normally stays. This is the basis of the quantum theory. Whereas Rutherford thought the world of the electron worked smoothly, Bohr showed that, in fact, it moved in small jumps or quanta.

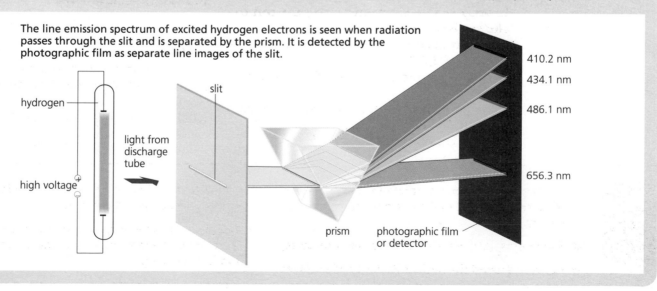

The line emission spectrum of excited hydrogen electrons is seen when radiation passes through the slit and is separated by the prism. It is detected by the photographic film as separate line images of the slit.

1.10 First ionisation energies of Group 2 elements

The Group 2 elements beryllium to barium are all reactive metals known as the alkali metals since they react in water to form alkaline or basic solutions.

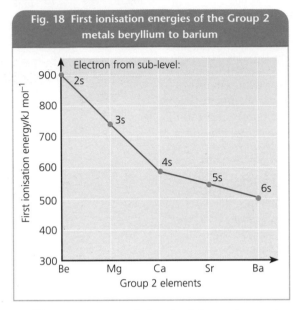

Fig. 18 First ionisation energies of the Group 2 metals beryllium to barium

The outermost sub-level of these elements contains a pair of s electrons. The graph of Fig. 18 shows that, going down Group 2, the values for the first ionisation energy decrease, and the first electron becomes easier to remove. This is because, as the number of electron shells increases between the outermost electron and the nucleus:

- the electron shells shield the outermost electron from the attraction of the positive nucleus,
- the radius of the atom increases down the group, hence the greater the distance between the nucleus and the outermost electron,
- outer electrons become easier to remove.

These effects more than offset the increase of positive charge as the number of protons increases in the nucleus. The fact that each ion has a fixed, measurable first ionisation energy is further evidence that electrons of atoms have particular energy levels.

11 The first ionisation energies in kJ mol⁻¹ for Group 1 metals are as follows: Li 519, Na 494, K 418, Ru 400, Cs 380.

a Plot a graph.
b Explain why the values decrease down Group 1.
c How does the pattern compare with the graph for Group 2 elements?

1.11 First ionisation energies of Period 3 elements

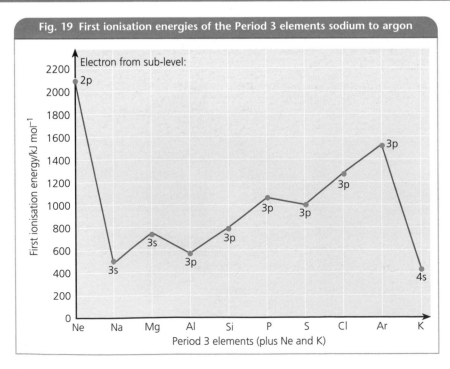

Fig. 19 First ionisation energies of the Period 3 elements sodium to argon

Period 3 includes the elements sodium to argon. Fig. 19 shows the first ionisation energies for these elements, and, in addition, neon from the end of Period 2 and potassium at the start of Period 4. Notice the following characteristics and trends in the graph:

- There is a sharp fall in first ionisation energy between neon and sodium, and between argon and potassium. This is evidence that the outer electron of the first element in a period is on its own in a new outer shell, shielded from the nuclear charge by electrons in inner shells.

- There is a general increase in first ionisation energy across Period 3. This is because of the increasing nuclear charge, from sodium with 11 protons to argon with 18 protons, exerting an attraction on the electrons as they enter the shell.

- There is a drop in ionisation energy from magnesium to aluminium because the outermost electron in aluminium is the first to enter the p sub-level in Period 3. This electron is higher in energy than the outer ($3s^2$) electron of magnesium and so is easier to remove.

- The increase in ionisation energies from aluminium to phosphorus results from the increasing nuclear charge.

- The slight fall in ionisation energy from phosphorus to sulphur is because sulphur has two electrons of opposite spin in the 3p sub-level. These electrons repel each other, so it takes less energy to remove one of them than it does to remove the unpaired electron from phosphorus. Such ionisation energy differences are evidence for the existence of sub-levels in the main levels.

- Again, the first ionisation energy increases from sulphur to argon because of the increasing nuclear charge.

Subsequent ionisation energies

These equations to show the removal of electrons from an atom of an element.

first ionisation: $Y(g) \rightarrow Y^+(g) + e^-$
second ionisation: $Y^+(g) \rightarrow Y^{2+}(g) + e^-$
third ionisation: $Y^{2+}(g) \rightarrow Y^{3+}(g) + e^-$
...and so on.

Table 6 shows the successive ionisation energies for aluminium and potassium.

After the third electron is removed from aluminium, there is a large jump in ionisation energy because the fourth electron is removed from an energy level which is closer to the nucleus. When you plot the ionisation energies for an element, as shown in Fig. 20, the electron before the largest jump will indicate the group of the Periodic Table that the element belongs to. So aluminium is in Group 3.

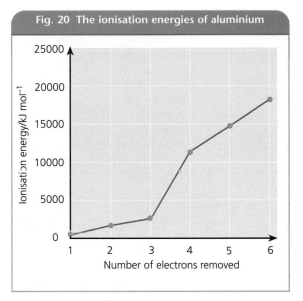
Fig. 20 The ionisation energies of aluminium

12 Plot a graph for the ionisation energies of potassium. Explain what the graph tells you about the energy levels of electrons in potassium.

Table 6 The ionisation energies for aluminium and potassium						
Ionisation energy in kJ mol⁻¹						
Element	first	second	third	fourth	fifth	sixth
aluminium	578	1817	2745	11578	14831	18378
potassium	419	3051	4412	5877	7975	9649

KEY FACTS

■ The first ionisation energies decrease down Groups 1 and 2 because the outermost electrons are increasingly shielded from the attraction of the nucleus.

■ The first ionisation energies give evidence for the existence of energy sub-levels.

1

a Fill in the **three** blank spaces below. (3)

Name of sub-atomic particle	Relative charge	Relative mass
Neutron		1
	−1	

b Give the electronic configuration of the $^{16}_{18}O^+$ ion in terms of electronic levels and sub-levels. (1)

c Give **two** reasons why a sample must first be ionised in a mass spectrometer before its mass spectrum can be determined. (2)

d Describe briefly the process by which a gaseous sample in a mass spectrometer is ionised. (2)

e Why is it **not** possible to distinguish between the ions $^{16}_{8}O^+$ and $^{32}_{16}S^{2+}$ in a low resolution mass spectrometer? (1)

f Which peak in the mass spectrometer of a compound usually gives the value of its relative molecular mass? (1)

CH01 June 1996 Q1

2

a Give the symbol, including mass number and atomic number, for the isotope which has a mass number of 34 and which has 18 neutrons in each nucleus. (2)

b Give the electronic configuration of the F^- ion in terms of levels and sub-levels. (1)

c Give the reason why it is unlikely that an F^- ion would reach the detector in a mass spectrometer. (1)

d Some data obtained from the mass spectrum of a sample of carbon are given below.

Ion	$^{12}C^+$	$^{13}C^+$
Absolute mass of one ion/g	1.993×10^{-23}	2.158×10^{-23}
Relative abundance/%	98.9	1.1

Use these data to calculate a value for the mass of one neutron, the relative atomic mass of ^{13}C and the relative atomic mass of carbon in the sample. You may neglect the mass of an electron. (6)

CH01 March 1999 Q1

3

a State the meaning of the term *atomic number*. (1)

b What is the function of the electronic gun and the magnet in the mass spectrometer? (2)

c The mass spectrum of a pure sample of a noble gas has peaks at the following *m/z* values.

m/z	10	11	20	22
Relative intensity	2.0	0.2	17.8	1.7

i) Give the complete symbol, including mass number and atomic number for one isotope of this noble gas.

ii) Give the species which is responsible for the peak at *m/z* = 11.

iii) Use appropriate values from the data above to calculate the relative atomic mass of this sample of noble gas. (6)

CH01 March 1998 Q1

4

a State the meaning of the term *mass number* of an isotope. (1)

b Define the term *relative atomic mass* of an element. (2)

c A mass spectrometer measures the relative abundance of ions with different values of *m/z*. Explain the meaning of the symbols *m* and *z*. (2)

d A sample of nickel was analysed in a mass spectrometer. Three peaks were observed with the properties shown in the following table.

Relative abundance/%	69	27	4
m/z	58	60	62

i) Give the symbol, including the mass number and the atomic number, for the ion which was responsible for the peak with *m/z* = 58.

ii) Calculate the relative atomic mass of this sample of nickel. (4)

e Complete the electronic configurations for Ni and Ni^{2+}. (2)

CH01 February 1997 Q1

5

a In terms of the numbers of sub-atomic particles, state **one** difference and **two** similarities between two isotopes of the same element. (3)

b Give the chemical symbol, including its mass number, for an atom which has 3 electrons and 4 neutrons. (1)

c i) An element has an atomic number of 23. Its ion has a charge of 3+. Complete the electronic configuration of this ion.

ii) To which block in the Periodic Table does this belong? (2)

d i) Write an equation for the process involved in the first ionisation energy of boron.

ii) Explain why the second ionisation energy of boron is greater than the first.

iii) Explain why the fourth ionisation energy of boron is much greater than the third. (6)

NEAB CH01 February 1996 Q1

6 The diagram alongside shows the electronic structure of boron.

Energy

2p ↑ — —
2s ↑↓
1s ↑↓

a The electrons are represented by arrows. What property of the electrons do these 'up' and 'down' arrows represent? (1)

b Suggest why electrons which occupy the 2p sub-levels have a higher energy than electrons in the 2s sub-level. (1)

c Complete the following energy level diagram to show the electronic structure of carbon. (2)

Energy

2p — — —
2s —

1s ↑↓

d Explain the meaning of the term *first ionisation energy*. (2)

e Explain why sulphur has a lower first ionisation energy than phosphorus. (2)

NEAB CH01 June 1998 Q1

7

a The table below gives some data for an element in the Periodic Table. Complete the table for the other elements shown. (6)

Element	Electronic configuration	Block
sodium	$1s^2\ 2s^2\ 2p^6\ 3s^1$	s
copper		
gallium		
phosphorus		

b Using the axes below, sketch the graph obtained when all the electrons are successively removed from an aluminium atom. (3)

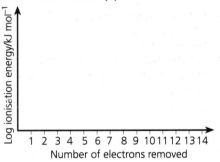

AEB Module Paper 7 June 1996 Q1

Understanding the atom

The atom is one of the most important models in modern chemistry. A model is a simple representation of a more complex system. So, thinking of atoms as simple, microscopic billiard balls allows us to explain the behaviour of solids, liquids and gases.

To explain chemical reactions we need a more complex model with electrons and shells. Radioactivity needs an even more complex model with electrons and a nucleus made up of particles even more fundamental than protons and neutrons. The atomic model has taken, off and on, over 2000 years to develop. Perhaps now we are beginning to understand how the world of materials works – and it is that understanding that allows us to look forward to a range of new materials, new chemicals and new possibilities.

1 Research the development of the atomic model. You can use textbooks (look in history books as well as science ones), CD ROM databases and the internet. Remember to keep a record of the source of all of your information.

2 Use your information to create a timeline to show the development of the atomic model. Some parts of the timeline will be fairly empty, while others will be crowded with new developments and insights.

3 Design a poster or display to allow you to show these differences. The people below all made contributions to the atomic model. They should all appear on your timeline – but they are just the starting points, you will need to add more as you discover the important milestones.

Aristotle	Albert Einstein
Becquerel	Geiger
Neils Bohr	Anton Lavoisier
Chadwick	Robert Millikan
Coulomb	Murray Gell-Mann
Marie Curie	George Zweig
John Dalton	Max Planck
Democritus	Ernest Rutherford
J.J. Thomson	

2 Bonding

Mobile phones. You see them everywhere – on trains and in cars, in shops and pubs, on the street and in the office. You either love them or hate them, but you can't avoid them. Go back to 1990 and they were rare. Go back to 1980 and they didn't exist. Go back to 1950 and even the materials they are made from didn't exist! Of course, this is also true about personal computers, video recorders, fax machines, radios and televisions. Anything with a computer chip buried in its workings depends on some of the latest science.

Everyone knows that metals conduct electricity and non-metals don't. But all our modern computers depend on a strange set of materials called semiconductors. Their limited electrical conductivity has been carefully designed into tiny slivers of silicon by chemical engineers and electronic physicists to allow us to work magic with electronic equipment. All this depends on understanding how the simplest substances in the world - the elements - link together to make some of the most complicated mechanisms - computer chips.

This chapter looks at the way atoms depend on electrons to form links with other atoms. We will look at electrovalent, covalent and metallic bonds and at the strange behaviour of semiconductors.

Mobile phones - blessing or curse? Either way, you've got chemists' understanding of the way atoms bond to thank for them!

In Chapter 1 we saw how atoms are built up from simpler particles: protons, neutrons and electrons. This chapter looks at the way atoms join together, or bond, to make the materials of the world around us. The chapter divides into three areas: different kinds of bonding between atoms, the attraction between molecules, and finally, the way the shape of molecules affects the properties of everyday materials.

There are three types of bonding at the atomic level:

- ionic bonding
- covalent bonding
- metallic bonding

2.1 Ionic bonding

Sodium chloride

The bonding in sodium chloride is **ionic** (see Fig. 1). The sodium atom loses the electron from its outer level to leave the **positively charged ion Na⁺** with an electron configuration that is the same as the inert gas neon. The chlorine atom gains an electron to become a **negatively charged ion Cl⁻** with an electron configuration that matches the inert gas argon. Both Na⁺ and Cl⁻ now have the complete outer levels of electrons of stable inert gases (see Chapter 1). No more electrons are lost or gained.

Whenever atoms bond by forming ions, they gain or lose electrons. But what holds the sodium and chloride ions together? What is the

Fig. 1 Ionic bonding in sodium chloride

sodium atom (2, 8, 1)   chlorine atom (2, 8, 7)

The 3s electron of sodium transfers to the chlorine atom

sodium ion (2, 8)   chloride ion (2, 8, 8)

As ions, sodium and chloride acquire the stable configuration of an inert gas. Opposite charges attract in ionic bonding.

'bond' between them? Let us use the notation from Chapter 1 to describe the sodium atom and the singly charged sodium ion:

Na $\rightarrow$ $Na^+ + e^-$
$1s^2\ 2s^2\ 2p^6\ 3s^1$ $\rightarrow$ $1s^2\ 2s^2\ 2p^6$
sodium atom   sodium ion

The electron from sodium is transferred to a chlorine atom. In gaining an electron, it becomes a chloride ion, Cl^-, with a single negative charge:

$Cl + e^-$ $\rightarrow$ Cl^-
$1s^2\ 2s^2\ 2p^6\ 3s^2\ 3p^5$ $\rightarrow$ $1s^2\ 2s^2\ 2p^6\ 3s^2\ 3p^6$
chlorine atom   chloride ion

The oppositely charged ions attract each other and form a giant ionic **lattice**. A lattice is not simply a random arrangement of ions stuck together - its structure has a regular repeating pattern of ions, as Fig. 2 shows.

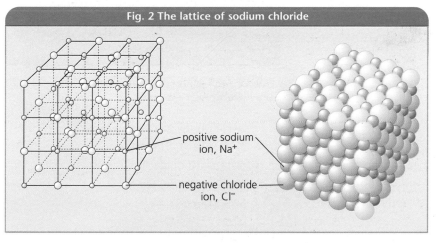

Fig. 2 The lattice of sodium chloride

positive sodium ion, Na^+

negative chloride ion, Cl^-

X-ray diffraction is the technique that allows us to investigate patterns like the lattice in the sodium chloride crystal. A machine bombards carefully prepared crystals of sodium chloride with a stream of X-rays with a particular frequency. The regular arrangement of ions acts rather like a diffraction grid and makes the X-rays scatter to form a diffraction pattern. A computer can analyse this pattern to produce an **electron density map** that represents the arrangement of the ions, the distances between them and even the positions of electrons in the crystal.

Electron density maps, such as the one in Fig. 3 for sodium chloride, cannot show individual electrons but they do indicate the likelihood of finding electrons in a particular region, and display this information as contours rather like the height contours on a

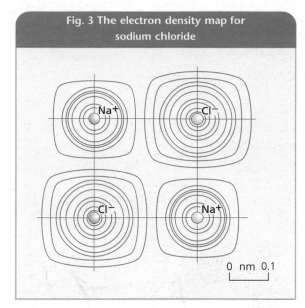

Fig. 3 The electron density map for sodium chloride

0   nm   0.1

map. The contours are lines of equal electron density. In sodium and chloride ions, the innermost ring nearest the nucleus represents the same electron density and is also the greatest density. The outermost ring in both ions is the same density and the least density. The map has two other important features:

- The ions are arranged in a regular pattern – the lattice.
- The electrons are not distributed evenly.
- The negative chloride ions occupy a greater volume than the positive sodium ions.

Sodium chloride therefore exists as a giant ionic lattice and not as molecules. Yet, to represent the 1-to-1 ratio of sodium ions to chloride ions, we use the 'molecular' formula NaCl.

Compounds made up of ions are called **ionic compounds**. The **electrostatic forces of attraction** between the ions are strong enough to make the compounds relatively stable. They are crystalline, always solid at room temperature and have high melting points. Table 1 shows two examples of ionic compounds with the electrons represented in dot and cross diagrams and including the electron configurations of the ions.

When a crystalline ionic compound is heated, there is an increase in the vibrations of the ions in their lattice positions. We can detect this increase as a rise in temperature. As more energy is added, the ions vibrate more and more strongly, until the lattice begins to break down. The ions are shaken loose from their positions. We see this as the crystal **melting**.

Table 1 Two ionic compounds, their dot and cross diagrams and ionic electron configurations			
Name	Molecular formula	Dot and cross diagram	Electron configuration of ion
calcium fluoride	CaF_2		$Ca^{2+} = 1s^2\ 2s^2\ 2p^6\ 3s^2\ 3p^6$ $F^- = 1s^2\ 2s^2\ 2p^6$
sodium oxide	Na_2O		$Na^+ = 1s^2\ 2s^2\ 2p^6$ $O^{2-} = 1s^2\ 2s^2\ 2p^6$

The lattice can also be disrupted by water. Water molecules are attracted to the charge of the ions. The water molecules surround the ions and break up the lattice. We see this as the crystal **dissolving**.

When ionic compounds are heated to melting point, or dissolved in water, the ions become free to move about. They can then **conduct electricity**, because positive and negative ions can move to the oppositely charged electrodes where they are discharged:

the ions gain or lose electrons and become neutral. Some are deposited on the electrode as the element, others are given off as gases. Deposition of the element at an electrode is used in industrial processes including electroplating, extracting metals such as aluminium, magnesium and calcium, purifying copper, and manufacturing chlorine and hydrogen. These processes are the reverse of the chemical reactions that form the ionic compounds from their elements.

Machinery parts ready to be electroplated: the electroplating tank contains a solution of a metal salt

1 Write out electron configurations for the following compounds.
a potassium oxide, K_2O
b sodium nitride, Na_3N
c iron(III) oxide, Fe_2O_3

2.2 Covalent bonding

When the atoms of two non-metals react together, they form chemical bonds called **covalent bonds**. A covalent bond forms between two atoms in a molecule when the electron in the highest energy level of each atom is shared. A hydrogen molecule contains a covalent bond (Fig. 4). Each hydrogen atom has two electrons in its only energy level, the 1s level. The electron configuration of $1s^2$ is that of helium, the first inert gas. The pair of shared electrons forms a **single covalent bond.**

Hydrogen molecules do not conduct electricity. A substance can conduct electric current only if it has electrons or other charged particles that can move independently to carry charge through the material. In hydrogen, the electrons are fixed

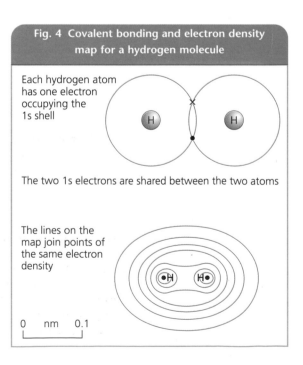

Fig. 4 Covalent bonding and electron density map for a hydrogen molecule

Each hydrogen atom has one electron occupying the 1s shell

The two 1s electrons are shared between the two atoms

The lines on the map join points of the same electron density

0   nm   0.1

in the covalent bond, in a molecule that is neutral, so hydrogen cannot be a charge carrier. The electron density map of Fig. 4 confirms that both the hydrogen atoms are identical, with an equal share of the electrons available: neither is more negative or more positive than the other.

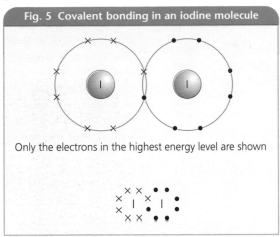

Fig. 5 Covalent bonding in an iodine molecule

Only the electrons in the highest energy level are shown

The atoms in iodine molecules are covalently bonded, as shown in Fig. 5. Each iodine atom in the iodine molecule has eight electrons in its outermost energy level, seven of its own, and one shared from the other iodine atom. This configuration totals the number of electrons in the outermost level of the inert gas neon. It is a stable electron configuration.

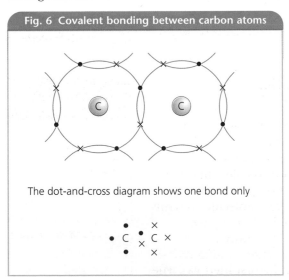

Fig. 6 Covalent bonding between carbon atoms

The dot-and-cross diagram shows one bond only

Carbon is also covalently bonded (Fig. 6). In diamond, a form of carbon, each atom is covalently bonded to four other carbon atoms. The covalent bonds link every carbon atom to four other carbon atoms in a very strong lattice. This is unusual for non-metals and is very different from the lattice produced

by ionic bonding. Carbon held in this formation has some pretty unusual properties. It is the hardest substance we know and is used to cut glass and bore through hard rock. It is also very rare.

All the carbon atoms in diamond are joined together by covalent bonds

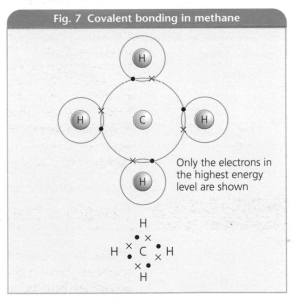

Fig. 7 Covalent bonding in methane

Only the electrons in the highest energy level are shown

Covalent bonding also occurs between different atoms, such as carbon and hydrogen atoms in methane (Fig. 7). In this molecule, the carbon atom has eight electrons in the highest energy level, the same as neon, while the hydrogen atoms each have two electrons, like helium. So both atoms have the same electronic configuration as an inert gas.

2 Explain why carbon cannot form a simple molecule, while iodine forms simple I_2 molecules.

3 Explain why iodine cannot conduct electricity.

Co-ordinate bonding: dative covalency

When ammonia vapour is mixed with aluminium fluoride vapour, $AlF_3(g)$, a white solid with the formula NH_3AlF_3 is formed:

Both of the electrons between the nitrogen atom and the aluminium atom come from the nitrogen atom: aluminium and nitrogen share these two electrons. This is slightly different from the simple covalent bond in a hydrogen molecule. Since both electrons are supplied by one of the atoms forming the covalent bond, the formula of the compound is often written like this:

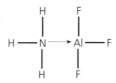

The arrow shows the origin of the shared electrons. This type of bond is called either a **dative covalent bond** or a **coordinate bond**. After a coordinate bond has been formed, it behaves in an identical way to a covalent bond.

Remember that in ionic compounds, all the ions are held in a rigid lattice. In a covalent compound, each molecule is free to move around because the forces *between* the molecules are relatively small. This means that while ionic compounds tend to be solids at room temperature with a crystalline structure, covalent compounds tend to be gases or liquids. The properties of ionic and covalent compounds are compared in Table 2.

Table 2 Comparing ionic and covalent substances		
Ionic bonding	**Covalent bonding**	
Formation	Metal elements combine with non-metallic elements to form ionic compounds; the metal atom forms the positive ion and the non-metallic atom forms the negative ion, e.g. Na^+Cl^-	Non-metallic elements combine, forming covalent bonds; the number of electrons in the highest energy level equals the maximum number of bonds that can be formed
Bond strength	Ionic bonds are strong bonds	Covalent bonds are strong bonds
Structure	Ionic compounds have giant ionic structures, containing millions of ions	Covalent substances may be individual molecules, molecular structures or giant atomic structures
Melting point and boiling point	Because of the strong bonding in ionic compounds, they have high melting points and high boiling points	Individual molecules such as CH_4, Fig. 7, have negligible forces of attraction between the molecules. They have low melting and boiling points. Molecular structures, such as that of iodine, Fig. 25, also have weak inter-molecular forces and low melting and boiling points. Giant atomic structures, eg diamond, Fig. 26, and silicon, contain strong covalent bonds between millions of atoms. They have high melting and boiling points because it is necessary to break covalent bonds in order to melt the giant molecule. Forces between individual giant molecules are weak, which explains why diamonds do not attract each other strongly and why grains of sand can be easily separated.
Conduction of electricity	Ionic compounds are insulators in the solid state, and conductors in solution or when molten	Covalent substances do not usually conduct electricity
Solubility	Many ionic compounds are soluble in water and insoluble in organic solvents such as hexane	Most covalent substances are insoluble in water and soluble in organic solvents

2.3 Metallic bonding

The bonding in metals enables them to conduct electricity. The electrons in the highest energy level of a metal atom can leave their nucleus quite easily. The orbits of these outer electrons overlap, with the overlapping extending through the metal. So the electrons are all free to move through the metal and they form a sea of negative charge surrounding the positive metal ions. They no longer belong to one particular atomic nucleus. They are said to be **delocalised**, see Fig. 8, a simplified diagram: the positive metal ions are so close as to be practically touching.

Fig. 8 A simple representation of metallic bonding

delocalised electrons

metal cation (nucleus + electrons that are not delocalised)

If a potential difference is applied across a metal, the delocalised electrons move towards the positive terminal. The flow of charge is an electric current which can be detected. The nuclei and non-delocalised electrons of the metal atoms, the metal cations, are not free to move.

On the other hand, ions in ionic compounds which are molten or in aqueous solution, are free to move. Positive ions are called **cations** (Fig. 8) because they are attracted to the negative electrode, the cathode. Negative ions are called **anions** because they are attracted to the positive electrode, the anode.

4 Give two differences between the electron arrangements in an ionic compound like sodium chloride and a metal like iron.

The metal structure is a regular lattice which is held together by the attraction between the positive ions and the delocalised electrons. Many metals have high melting points because it takes a lot of energy to remove an atom away from the attraction of these delocalised electrons and positive ions.

APPLICATION A

Predicting bonding types

It is possible to predict the types of bonding that are likely in substances by looking at their physical properties. Once you have made a prediction you can then test it with simple experiments.

1 Predict the type of bonding you would expect to find in each of the substances shown in in the photograph.

2 Describe a simple experiment you could do to test your predictions. Explain what result you would expect and how this would support your original prediction.

KEY FACTS

- In ionic bonding, electron transfer causes pairs of ions to form, one positive and one negative.

- Covalent bonds involve sharing pair(s) of electrons.

- A coordinate bond is a covalent bond in which both shared electrons come from the same atom.

- Metallic bonds involve a lattice of positively charged ions surrounded by a sea of electrons.

2.4 Electronegativity

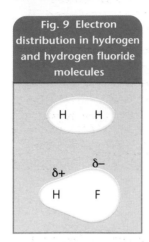

Fig. 9 Electron distribution in hydrogen and hydrogen fluoride molecules

In a covalent bond between two hydrogen atoms, the density of the electrons is distributed evenly between the hydrogen atoms (Fig. 9). In a covalent bond between hydrogen and fluorine, the electrons are drawn towards the fluorine atom.

Fluorine in hydrogen fluoride attracts electrons more strongly than hydrogen, so it distorts the electron cloud, making one end more electronegative than the other. The ability of an atom to attract the bonding electron pair in a covalent bond is called its **electronegativity**.

An atom of high electronegativity will attract electrons away from one of lower electronegativity, so fluorine is more electronegative than hydrogen.

Usually, when two atoms with different electronegativity values are joined by a covalent bond, a polar bond is produced. Bond polarity is shown by the symbols δ+, indicating a small positive charge, and δ–, indicating a small negative charge (δ is the Greek letter delta). Hydrogen fluoride is written as:

$$\overset{\delta+}{X}\!\!-\!\!\overset{\delta-}{Y}$$

Diatomic molecules like this are described as **polar** molecules.

Electronegativities cannot be measured directly. The Nobel prize-winning chemist Linus Pauling devised a scale which gives a numerical value to the power of an atom to attract electrons (Table 3). Fluorine is the most electronegative element. With a value of 0.8, the metals caesium and francium at the foot of Group I are the least electronegative elements. Electronegativity increases across the Periodic Table as atomic number increases and atomic radius decreases (see Chapter 4): the larger the nuclear charge and the smaller the atomic radius, the greater the attraction for the electron pair in the covalent bond.

Table 3 Electronegativities for the elements of Periods 1, 2 and 3							
H 2.1							He —
Li 1.0	Be 1.5	B 2.0	C 2.5	N 3.0	O 3.5	F 4.0	Ne —
Na 0.9	Mg 1.2	Al 1.5	Si 1.8	P 2.1	S 2.5	Cl 3.0	Ar —

  Why are there no values for the inert gases in Table 3?

2.5 Predicting the nature of bonds

We can use electronegativities to predict the type of bonding present in a compound. Compounds with wholly ionic or wholly covalent bonds are extreme types. Most compounds are somewhere between the two, with some degree of polarisation.

Covalent bonds

In hydrogen molecules the electrons are shared symmetrically between the two hydrogen atoms. This is not surprising since the hydrogen atoms are identical to start with. However, in hydrogen fluoride the electrons tend to be nearer the fluorine atom. Why?

Fluorine is very strongly electronegative. This means it pulls electrons towards itself and gets an 'unfair share' of the negative charge. This makes the fluorine more negative than the hydrogen atom. We describe this covalent molecule as being polar..

Linus Pauling's electronegativity scores allow us to predict how ionic a bond between two covalently bonded atoms will be. The greater the difference in electronegativity the more ionic is the bond.

The difference in electronegativities between two atoms in a covalently bonded molecule is measured in debye. So, the debye is the unit for the polarity of a bond. The higher the figure, the more polar or ionic is the bond.

Ionic bonds

Ionic bonds can also show polarity. In this case, the ionic nature of the bond can be reduced as the electron cloud is distorted by strong charges on the ions. If a cation has a high positive charge or a small size, it will tend to attract electrons towards itself. If an anion has a high negative charge or a large size, it will have an

Fig. 10 The gradual changes between ionic and covalent bonding

Pure ionic	Pure covalent
X^+ $[:Y]^-$	$X \overset{.}{\underset{.}{-}} X$

no sharing of electrons ————————→ equal sharing of electrons

complete electron transfer ←———————— no transfer of electrons

large electronegativity difference ←———————— no difference in electronegativity

polarity of the bond and gives the bond some of the characteristics of a covalent bond.

Fig. 10 shows the trends between the extremes of purely ionic compounds and purely covalent molecules.

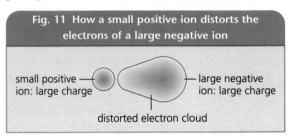

Fig. 11 How a small positive ion distorts the electrons of a large negative ion

small positive ion: large charge — large negative ion: large charge

distorted electron cloud

electron cloud which is easily distorted (Fig. 11). So large, highly charged anions can share some of their negative charge with their positively charged partners. This increases the

2.6 Period 3 halides

Study Table 4 as you follow the descriptions of bonding in Period 3 chlorides.

Sodium chloride. Sodium ions have an ionic radius of 0.102 nm. Chlorine ions have an ionic radius of 0.180 nm. Both have a single charge. Sodium chloride is ionic.

Magnesium chloride. Magnesium ions have an ionic radius of 0.072 nm. The magnesium ion has two charges. Magnesium chloride will have some covalent nature.

Aluminium chloride. Aluminium ions have a high charge, Al^{3+}. This means that the electrons in the Al^{3+} ion are drawn closely to the nucleus, making Al^{3+} a small highly charged ion. We say it has a high charge density (charge/volume). The high charge density attracts the electron cloud of the anion and results in a sharing of the electron cloud and covalent bonding. Aluminium chloride, $AlCl_3$, is a covalent molecule which

exists in two molecular structures: Fig. 12. In the second, two molecules are linked by coordinate bonds (see page 28) in which lone pairs of electrons are donated from the two bridging chlorine atoms to the two aluminium atoms.

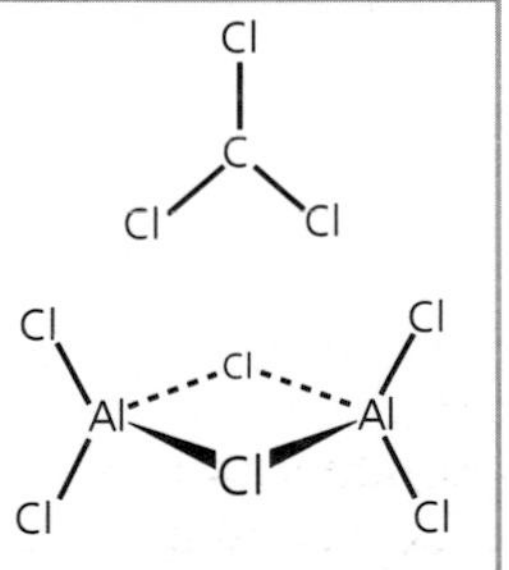

6 Explain why aluminium fluoride is highly ionic and aluminium bromide is largely covalent.

Example: Explaining bonding in lithium iodide

Lithium iodide forms a lattice with a small positive lithium ion, the cation, and a large negative iodide ion, the anion.
The small lithium cation tends to distort the electron cloud around the neighbouring anions in the crystal lattice.
Lithium iodide is described as ionic with some covalent character.

Fig. 12 Forms of aluminium chloride

	Table 4 Ions, chlorides and bonding							
Element	Na	Mg	Al	Si	P	S	Cl	Ar
Size of ion	●	●	●	–	–	◯	◯	–
	Na^+	Mg^{2+}	Al^{3+}			S^{2-}	Cl^-	
Formula of chloride	NaCl	$MgCl_2$	$AlCl_3$	$SiCl_4$	PCl_3	SCl_2	Cl_2	–
Type of bonding	ionic	ionic/covalent	covalent	covalent	covalent	covalent	covalent	–

Fig. 13 The ions of lithium iodide

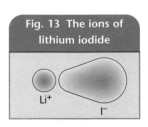

Li^+ I^-

KEY FACTS

■ Electronegativity is the power of an atom to withdraw electron density from a covalent bond.

■ Covalent bonds and ionic bonds are extreme cases. Most bonds are intermediate.

■ Differences in electronegativity between bonding atoms will result in polar bonds.

■ The charge and size of the ions affect the degree of bond polarity.

2.7 Intermolecular forces

In ionic bonds, electrons transfer between atoms to form ions. In covalent bonds, electrons are shared between atoms to form molecules. Ionic and covalent bonds hold individual atoms in place. Different types of bonds act *between* molecules. Their forces of attraction are generally weaker than for covalent bonds, and include:

- Van der Waals forces (temporary dipole–induced dipole)
- permanent dipole–permanent dipole
- hydrogen bonds

Van der Waals attractive forces (temporary dipole–induced dipole)

Van der Waals attractive forces exist between non-polar covalent molecules such as alkanes. They are very weak forces, typically less than 1% of the force of a covalent bond. If for even a moment the electron distribution in a molecule is not symmetrical, then uneven charges are set up in the molecule. The momentarily polar molecule is called a **temporary dipole** (see Fig. 14). It can disturb the electron distribution in an adjacent molecule, producing an opposite **induced dipole**, rather as the north pole of a magnet induces a weak south pole in unmagnetised iron brought near it. The two temporary dipoles attract each other and pull the molecules together. These forces operate for a short time only, because the electron density is constantly changing. The forces are continually switched on and off.

Van der Waals forces account for the differences in boiling points between ethane (185 K) and pentane (309 K). Pentane molecules are longer than ethane molecules. So more van der Waals forces can operate between pentane molecules than between ethane molecules which makes pentane molecules more strongly attracted to each other. This is why pentane's boiling point is higher than ethane's: ethane is a gas at room temperature, while pentane is a liquid.

Fig. 14 Temporary and induced dipoles in van der Waals forces

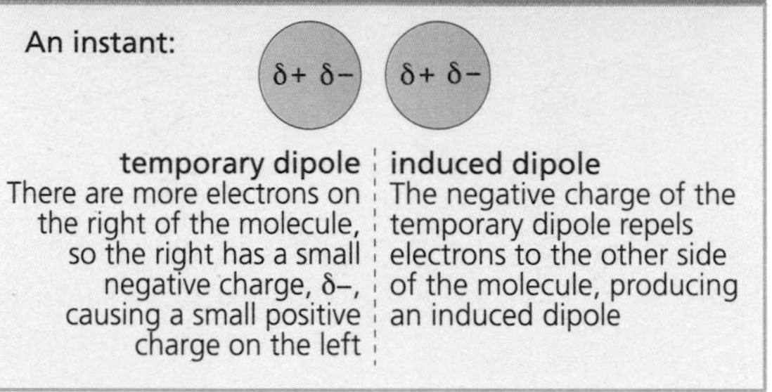

An instant:

temporary dipole | induced dipole
There are more electrons on the right of the molecule, so the right has a small negative charge, δ–, causing a small positive charge on the left | The negative charge of the temporary dipole repels electrons to the other side of the molecule, producing an induced dipole

---

Fig. 15   Van der Waals forces affecting boiling points of ethane and pentane

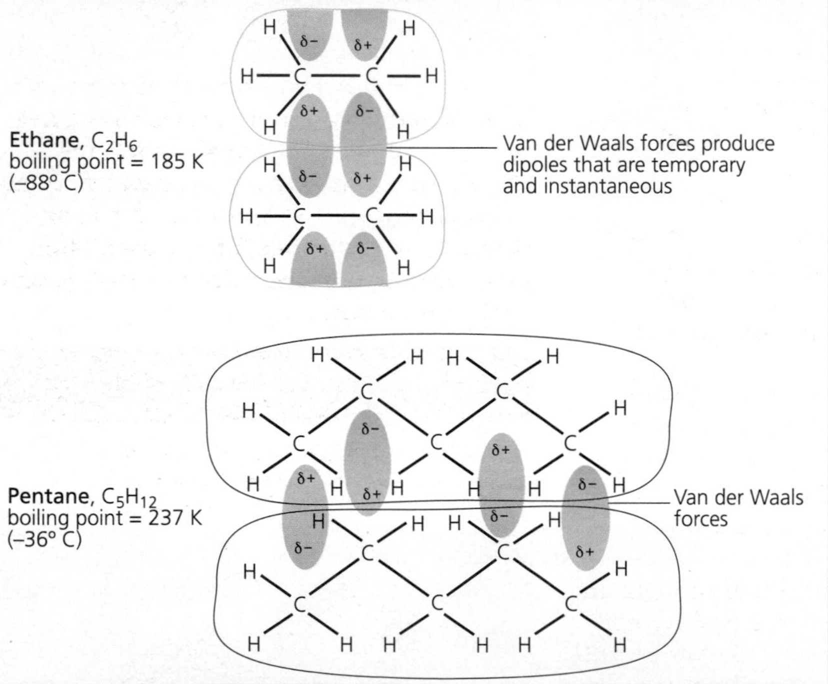

Ethane, C_2H_6
boiling point = 185 K
(–88° C)

Van der Waals forces produce dipoles that are temporary and instantaneous

Pentane, C_5H_{12}
boiling point = 237 K
(–36° C)

Van der Waals forces

EXTENSION   Chain length in cooking fats and oils

We use animal fats such as butter for cooking. Butter is a solid at room temperature. This is because it has long zig-zag chains of carbon atoms that lie parallel with van der Waals forces attracting the chains to each other.

Cooking oils are liquid at room temperature. Their structure also has long chains of carbon atoms, but the chains are not simple zig-zags. There are angles along their length where the zig-zag changes direction, and some are branched, so they cannot lie parallel. Hence, there are fewer van der Waals forces between molecules, which is why cooking oil is a liquid at room temperature.

Permanent dipole–permanent dipole forces

Polar molecules have permanent dipoles, for example $H^{\delta+}$—$Cl^{\delta-}$ (Fig. 16). Polar molecules are attracted to each other by permanent dipole–permanent dipole forces where the permanently negative end of one molecule is attracted to the permanently positive end of the other.

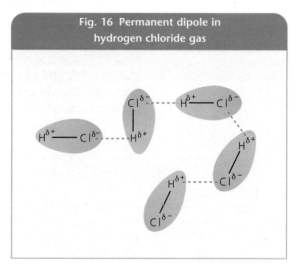

Fig. 16 Permanent dipole in hydrogen chloride gas

A permanent dipole–permanent dipole attractive force is about one hundredth the force of a covalent bond.

Hydrogen bonds

Hydrogen bonds are special cases of attractive dipole–dipole forces and are the strongest type of intermolecular force. A hydrogen bond is about one tenth the strength of a covalent bond.

The large difference in electronegativity (ability to attract electrons) between a hydrogen atom and either a nitrogen, oxygen or fluorine atom means that very polar bonds are formed, giving the molecules a strong, permanent dipole.

When two molecules are close enough, an attraction is set up between the positive end of one and the negative end of the other. This attraction is called **hydrogen bonding**.

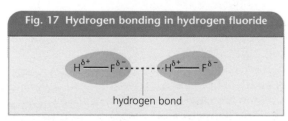

Fig. 17 Hydrogen bonding in hydrogen fluoride

hydrogen bond

A hydrogen bond is different from other dipole–dipole forces because hydrogen has no inner non-bonding electrons. An atom of nitrogen, oxygen or fluorine draws hydrogen's single electron towards itself, to expose the proton of the hydrogen nucleus. Without non-bonding electrons to repel the lone pairs of electrons in nitrogen, oxygen or fluorine, the proton is attracted strongly to their lone pair of electrons, as shown for ammonia in Fig. 18.

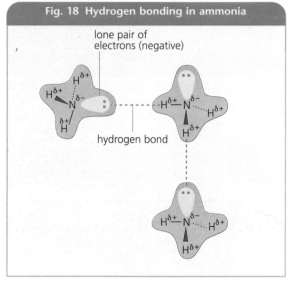

Fig. 18 Hydrogen bonding in ammonia

lone pair of electrons (negative)

hydrogen bond

In water, oxygen is more electronegative than hydrogen and strongly attracts the shared pair of electrons in the covalent bond. This makes the O—H bond very polar, and strong hydrogen bonds form between the molecules. They account for many of water's distinct properties.

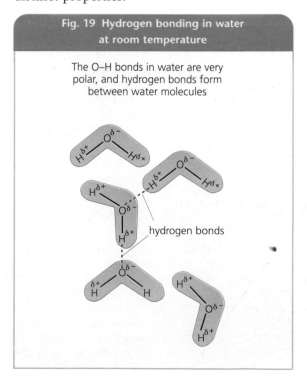

Fig. 19 Hydrogen bonding in water at room temperature

The O–H bonds in water are very polar, and hydrogen bonds form between water molecules

hydrogen bonds

Boiling points and hydrogen bonding

Fig. 20 shows the trends for boiling points of hydrides in Groups VI and VII. From Period 3 down each group to Period 5 there is a steady increase because the molecules get more massive as you go down the group. Water and hydrogen fluoride do not follow the same pattern because the hydrogen bonds present attract molecules to each other. This means that it takes more energy to form a vapour, making the boiling points unexpectedly high.

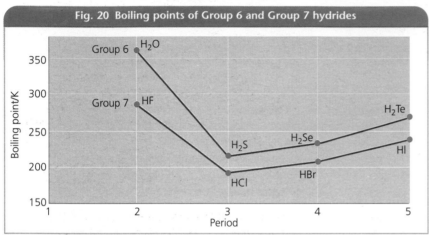

Fig. 20 Boiling points of Group 6 and Group 7 hydrides

6 Imagine that hydrogen bonds did not exist. Use the graph of Fig. 20 to suggest a value for the boiling points of water and hydrogen fluoride.

Water expands as it freezes

The water molecule is V-shaped, so we can think of it as having the oxygen atom at its negative apex. Either of oxygen's lone pairs attracts a positive hydrogen of an adjacent molecule, forming a hydrogen bond (Fig. 19). The attractive force of hydrogen bonds builds a constantly changing 3D structure in water, which explains its relatively high melting and boiling points.

As in Fig. 19, not all molecules of liquid water are hydrogen bonded at any one time. Some non-bonded molecules move more or less close than the hydrogen bonding position allows. As you heat water, the molecules gain energy, moving more rapidly and slightly further apart as their motion offsets the attraction of the hydrogen bonds. The water becomes less dense as its volume increases.

As you cool water, the reverse happens and the water becomes denser. That is, until it reaches 277 K (4 °C) when it is at its densest. But from 277 K (4 °C) to 273 K (0 °C), the

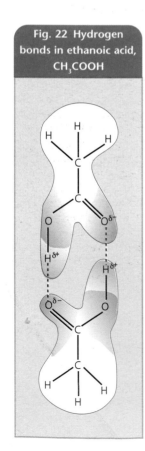

Fig. 22 Hydrogen bonds in ethanoic acid, CH_3COOH

proportion of hydrogen bonded molecules increases, and the molecules start to form a lattice structure very similar to carbon in diamond (see Fig. 26). The effect is that molecules are set slightly further apart and the water become less dense. At 273 K (0 °C), all the molecules are fixed in hydrogen-bonded positions (Fig. 21), making a rigid 3D lattice: the water has now frozen and become ice.

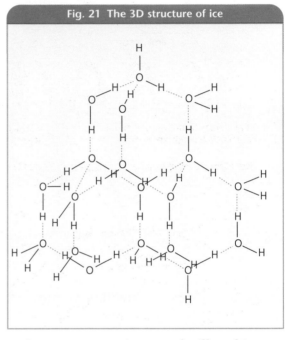

Fig. 21 The 3D structure of ice

In nature, water in a pond will cool in winter. At 277 K, it is at its densest. But if the water cools further, it becomes less dense and moves up to the surface before freezing. This still leaves liquid water below in which pond creatures can survive.

Hydrogen bonds form in ethanoic acid

Ethanoic acid has the molecular formula CH_3COOH. Hydrogen bonds form in pure ethanoic acid in the way shown in Fig. 22. These hydrogen bonds give higher than expected melting and boiling points.

7 An experiment to find the M_r of ethanoic acid gave the value as 120. Explain why.

8 Hydrogen bonds also exist in dilute ethanoic acid between the ethanoic acid molecules and the water molecules. Draw a structural diagram to show these hydrogen bonds.

EXTENSION   Hydrogen bonding in proteins

Bonding in keratin molecules

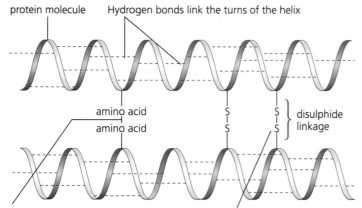

protein molecule   Hydrogen bonds link the turns of the helix

amino acid

amino acid

S-S S-S disulphide linkage

Salt linkages form between the acidic and basic parts on adjacent helices.

Disulphide linkages form between cysteine groups

The effect of breaking hydrogen bonds in the keratin helix

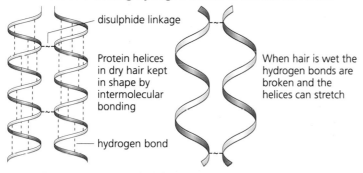

disulphide linkage

Protein helices in dry hair kept in shape by intermolecular bonding

hydrogen bond

When hair is wet the hydrogen bonds are broken and the helices can stretch

The effect of perming on disulphide bridges

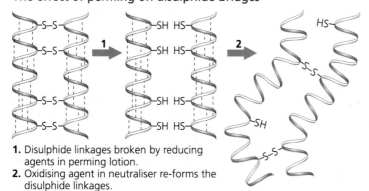

1. Disulphide linkages broken by reducing agents in perming lotion.
2. Oxidising agent in neutraliser re-forms the disulphide linkages.

People can express their personality by curling straight hair or by straightening curly hair

Hair consists mainly of a protein called alpha-keratin, α-keratin. Many thousands of keratin molecules lie side by side to make up a single hair. The top diagram shows two protein molecules.

Like all proteins, keratin consists of a long chain of amino acids. Amino acids are organic acids which have both acidic COOH and basic NH_2 groups in their molecules. The structure of hair is kept in shape by three types of **intermolecular bonding**:

- Hydrogen bonds attract the long keratin molecules to each other (not shown) and pull the keratin molecules into a spiral shape.

- **Salt linkages**: an acid group from an amino acid on one keratin molecule interacts with a base group on the next.

- **Disulphide bonds**: these are covalent linkages between two molecules of the sulphur-containing amino acid cysteine in adjacent keratin helices.

When the hair is wet, water gets between the microfibrils and breaks the hydrogen bonds. This is why wet hair can be stretched much more easily than dry hair, as shown in the diagram. Wetting the hair breaks the salt linkages too. These also break when the hair is heated with a hair-dryer.

Both the hydrogen bonds and salt linkages re-form when the hair is cool and dry. Perming or blow-dry styling will make these bonds re-form so that the hair takes up a new shape. As you would expect, permed bonds are permanent, while a blow-dry lasts until the hair gets wet again.

KEY FACTS

- Covalent and ionic bonds are strong bonds.

- Van der Waals forces are momentary and result from uneven electron distribution in molecules that creates dipoles which induce other temporary dipoles.

- Dipole–dipole interactions occur when two polar molecules attract each other.

- Hydrogen bonds are a special case of dipole–dipole interaction.

2.8 Solids, liquids and gases

The properties of a particular substance depend on the elements present and the way they are bonded. This chapter has concentrated on ideas about bonding to explain properties. For example, hydrogen bonding explains why water has a much higher boiling point than could be predicted from its small relative molecular mass. Ionic bonding explains why sodium chloride is a crystalline solid with a high melting point.

Kinetic theory

How do we explain what happens to water when it boils? The atoms and molecules remain the same but the properties of steam are very different from those of liquid water or solid ice.

Scientists use a set of ideas called **kinetic theory** to explain how the same substance can be so different at different temperatures. Simple kinetic theory assumes that all particles in a sample of material are simple spheres, and that the detailed chemical nature of the spheres is not important because they all obey the same rules.

- In the solid they move a little but their relative positions are fixed by forces acting between the particles.

- In the liquid they move more freely but forces still operate.

- In the gas there are no forces binding the particles together, and they move independently.

Fig. 23 illustrates the way that kinetic theory explains how a substance changes from a solid to a liquid to a gas. It shows the forces acting on particles as they change state. Compared to a solid, in a liquid there is only a 10% increase in the separation of particles. Then, as a gas, the volume expands enormously: 1 g of water is 1 cm^3, while 1 g of water vapour is about 1.25 dm^3.

Table 5 explains the changes further.

The solid state

The physical properties of a solid depend on the arrangement of particles in the solid. In a crystalline element or compound, the particles are arranged in a definite repeating pattern called a crystal lattice which gives the material characteristically shaped crystals.

Fig. 23 Forces on solids, liquids and gases		
Solid	**Liquid**	**Gas**
Particles vibrate around a fixed point. They are held together by ionic bonds, convalent bonds or intermolecular forces	The particles move throughout the liquid in a disordered arrangement	Gas particles move rapidly and randomly. Intermolecular forces and particle size can be ignored

Table 5 Events in phase changes, and enthalpy of fusion and vaporisation		
Solid	**Liquid**	**Gas**
Particles are in a set position. They vibrate only but do not move out of their position	Particles move randomly, with increasing energy as temperature rises. There is a 10% increase in the spaces between particles in a liquid compared to a solid: solids do not expand a great deal when melted	Particles move randomly in all directions. As the temperature increases the particles move with more energy
Increase in energy →		
We say there is an increase in heat content or the enthalpy increases		
Melting →	Boiling →	
Enthalpy of fusion is the energy required to change 1 mol of solid at X °C to 1 mol of liquid at X °C	Enthalpy of vaporisation is the energy required to change 1 mol of liquid at Y °C to 1 mol of gas at Y °C	

Lattices have a repeating pattern of more than one type of particle. We can classify crystals according to the bonding between their particles.

Ionic crystals

Ionic crystals consist of a lattice of positive and negative ions. Sodium chloride (see page **25**) has a lattice of Na^+ and Cl^- ions. Each Na^+ is surrounded by six Cl^- ions, and each Cl^- ion is surrounded by six Na^+ ions. This is called 6–6 coordination, which you can check in Fig. 2 on page 25.

The photo below shows that the lattice at atomic level is reflected in the shape of the crystals.

Crystals of sodium chloride

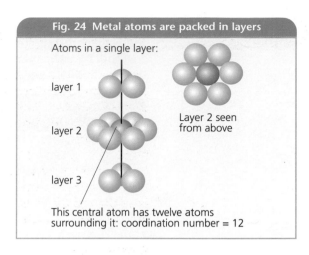

Fig. 24 Metal atoms are packed in layers

Atoms in a single layer:

layer 1

layer 2

layer 3

Layer 2 seen from above

This central atom has twelve atoms surrounding it: coordination number = 12

These are some properties of ionic crystals:

- Ionic crystals have high melting points because the ions are held firmly by strong electrostatic forces.
- Ionic crystals are hard and brittle.
- Ionic crystals do not conduct electricity when solid, but when melted or dissolved in water the ions are free to move and can then carry charge.

Metallic crystals

Crystal lattices are found only in ionic compounds. In metals, which are elements, metal cations are held in place by a sea of delocalised electrons (look back to page **29**). The cations are packed as closely as possible. Each ion has twelve adjacent ions, six in the same plane, three above and three below (Fig. 24).

This basic pattern of atoms is repeated in the metal's structure, making up small crystals or grains. These grains are often visible on the surface of the metal, as the photo in the next column shows.

The grain boundaries mark the edges of adjacent crystals

Metals can be hammered without breaking – they are **malleable**. They can also be drawn out into wires – **ductile**. This is because the layers of atoms can slide across each other and still retain their interatomic attraction.

 9 Explain why ionic crystals are not malleable.

Properties of metallic crystals

- Many metallic crystals have high melting points and high boiling points.
- Metals are malleable (can be hammered out) and ductile (can be drawn into a wire) because the layers of atoms can slide over each other.
- The free electrons can move throughout the structure and metals can conduct electricity.
- Due to their delocalised electrons, metals can also reflect light and are therefore shiny.

Molecular crystals

Molecular crystals contain molecules held together by either van der Waals forces, dipole–dipole forces or hydrogen bonding.

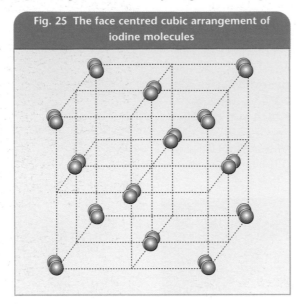

Fig. 25 The face centred cubic arrangement of iodine molecules

Iodine crystals

The iodine molecule I_2 is covalent, yet it forms crystals which contain a regular arrangement of the molecules held together by van der Waals forces. Because these attractive forces are weak, iodine crystals have a low melting point and are soft. They do not conduct electricity because there are no charged particles free to move.

Iodine crystals

Macromolecular crystals

Macromolecular crystals are giant molecular structures. The elements carbon and silicon form covalent bonds. They also form macromolecular crystals.

Diamond is one of the different forms or allotropes of carbon. **Allotropes** of an element have different structures, but are in the same state. In diamond, the carbon atoms are arranged tetrahedrally (Fig. 26) with strong covalent bonding between atoms.

Graphite is another form of carbon with covalent bonding, but it consists of two-dimensional sheets of atoms arranged hexagonally. Weak van der Waals forces hold the layers together (Fig. 27).

You can see from the structure of graphite that each carbon atom is covalently bonded to three other carbon atoms. Only three of the four valence electrons are used to form the covalent bonds.

Fig. 26 The structure of diamond

Every carbon atom bonds to four other carbon atoms

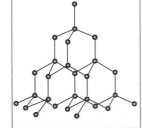

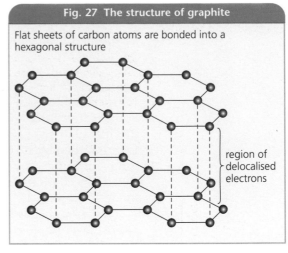

Fig. 27 The structure of graphite

Flat sheets of carbon atoms are bonded into a hexagonal structure

region of delocalised electrons

The unpaired fourth electron on each carbon atom forms a delocalised cloud above and below the plane of carbon atoms. These electrons are free to move, so graphite can conduct electricity, but only in the plane of the layers. Table 6 summarises the physical properties of diamond and graphite.

Table 6 The properties of diamond and graphite	
Diamond	**Graphite**
Very hard	Layers slide over each other because of the delocalised electrons between planes
High melting point due to strong covalent bonds	High melting point due to strong covalent bonds
Does not conduct electricity	Conducts electricity because the delocalised electrons are free to move

Diamond on graphite

The buckminsterfullerenes - buckyballs

In 1983, Harry Kroto and his team of students at the University of Sussex obtained the mass spectrum for vaporised graphite shown in the diagram.

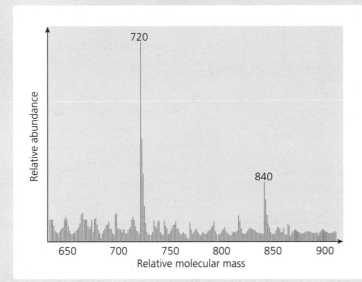

The geodesic dome that inspired the search for carbon allotropes like it

Carbon has a relative atomic mass of 12, so the peak at 720 has the molecular formula C_{60} and the peak at 840 has the molecular formula C_{70}. Until then, it was accepted that carbon had two allotropes, diamond and graphite. The mass spectrum suggested a new allotrope.

The team looked for a structure of carbon molecules with the formula C_{60} and recalled a dome made of hexagons and pentagons designed by the American architect, Robert Buckminster Fuller. They made a model based on the dome and similar to a soccer ball - a sphere with sixty points. It turned out to be a perfect model for a C_{60} molecule. This molecule, and others found with different numbers of carbon atoms, were all named buckminsterfellerenes, shortened to fullerness or buckyballs.

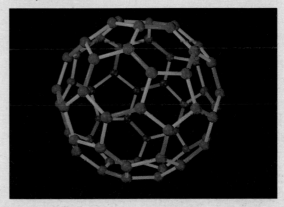

Soccer-ball structure of C_{60}

Spectroscopy confirmed the C_{60} structure. At first, chemists thought that the hexagons and pentagons that make up the fullerenes had a structure like graphite, Fig. 27, with delocalised electrons above and below the planes of hexagons and pentagons. This would have made the fullerenes quite unreactive. But fullerenes proved to be reactive because the bonding was in fact single and double bonds.

- Matter may exist as a solid, a liquid or a gas.

- To change state from solid to liquid to gas, a substance must gain increasing amounts of energy.

- Ionic crystals such as sodium chloride consist of a lattice of positive and negative ions.

- Metallic crystals such as copper consist of a lattice of positive ions and a sea of negative electrons.

- Molecular crystals such as iodine are held together by intermolecular forces.

- Giant covalent or macromolecular crystals such as diamond and graphite are held together by covalent bonds.

2.9 Shapes of molecules and ions

The shape of simple molecules and ions

The shape of simple molecules and ions is determined by the number of electron pairs surrounding the central atom or ion. The pairs of electrons can be considered as negatively charged clouds. Electron pairs repel each other and arrange themselves to minimise **repulsion** by being as far apart as possible. This determines the shape of covalently bonded molecules. In a molecule, the atoms have two types of electron pairs:

- a bonding pair of electrons involved in a chemical bond

- a non-bonding pair or **lone pair** of electrons not involved in bonding

Table 7 The shapes for different bonding			
Number of pairs of electrons	Arrangement	Angles	Name of shape
2 pairs		180°	linear
3 pairs		120°	trigonal planar
4 pairs		109° 28'	tetrahedral
5 pairs		90° 120°	trigonal bipyramidal
6 pairs		90°	octahedral

Look at Table 7 for some of the geometric shapes we can expect for different numbers of electron pairs in the highest energy level of the central atom. Note that these bonds are all single covalent bonds. The shapes will be modified by the number of lone pairs and bonding pairs, as in Table 8. Chemists use all this information to predict the shapes of molecules.

10 Calculate the number of electron pairs for each of these molecules.

a ammonia

b water

11 Sketch the structures of the molecules in question 10 and calculate the bond angles.

Lone pairs of electrons have a greater repulsion than bonding pairs. We can see this in Table 8 if we compare the bond angles of methane, ammonia and water. The repulsion between electron pairs around an atom increases in this order:

bonding pair-bonding pair
        < lone pair-bonding pair
                < lone pair-lone pair

This means that lone pair-lone pair repulsion is the greatest, and will produce the widest bond angles. In order to predict the shape of molecules you need to:

1 determine the number of electron pairs (the bond structure will give you this),
2 identify the basic shape (you can get this from Table 7),
3 look for lone pairs (these are the electron pairs not involved in bonding),
4 apply the rule above for the order of increase in repulsion between electron pairs,
5 draw out the shape of the molecule, adding bond angles.

KEY FACTS

■ The shapes of simple molecules and ions and their bond angles can be predicted from the arrangement of their outer, bonding electron pairs and the number of lone electron pairs.

■ The presence and number of lone pairs of electrons on the central atom will affect the resulting bond angles.

Table 8 The shapes of some named molecules				
Name of molecule	Dot and cross diagram	Shape	Type	Notes
Molecules with bonding electrons and no lone pairs				
Beryllium chloride	Cl Be Cl	Cl—Be—Cl 180°	Linear	The Be atom has two pairs of electrons round it. The charge clouds of electrons repel each other, so the Cl atoms are as far apart as possible
Boron trichloride	Cl B Cl Cl	Cl, Be, Cl, Cl 120° 120° 120°	trigonal	Planar means a flat shape, and trigonal implies that the Cl atoms are at the point of an equilateral triangle
Methane	H C H H H	H—C—H H 109.5° 109.5°	tetrahedral	A 3D structure, with all bond angles at 109.5°
Ethane	H H H C C H H H	H—C—C—H H H H H 109.5° 109.5°	tetrahedral	The H atoms are arranged tetrahedrally around the C atoms
Ethene	H C C H H H	H C=C H H H 120° 120° 120° 120°	trigonal planar	The double bonds hold the molecule in a flat shape. The H atoms form a trigonal planar shape around each C atom
Molecules with lone pairs and bonding pairs of electrons				
Ammonia	H N H H	lone pair H—N—H H 107° 107°		The shape is based on a tetrahedron, but the bond angles are 107°, not 109.5°. The lone pair of electrons has a greater repulsion than a bonding pair and squeezes the bonding pairs together
Water	O H H	O—H H 104.5°		The water molecule has two lone pairs. These exert a greater repulsion than one lone pair, and the hydrogen atoms are squeezed together to give an angle of 104.5°
Phosphorus(V) chloride	F F P F F F	F P F F F F 90° 120°	trigonal planar	This shape pushes the bonding pairs further apart
Sulphur hexafluoride	F F S F F	F S F F F F 90° 90°	octrahedral	All bonding angles are 90°

1 The table below shows some boiling temperatures (T_b) at a pressure of 100 kPa.

Substance	H_2	CH_4	HCl
T_b/K	21	112	188

a In liquid hydrogen, the atoms are held together by covalent bonds.
  i) What is a covalent bond?
  ii) How are the hydrogen molecules held together in liquid hydrogen? (2)
b Explain why methane has a higher boiling temperature than hydrogen. (2)
c i) Give the meaning of the term *electronegativity*.
  ii) The electronegativity of hydrogen, carbon and chlorine are 2.1, 2.5 and 3,0, respectively. Use these values to explain why the boiling temperature of hydrogen chloride is greater than that of methane. (6)
NEAB CH01 February 1997 Q4

2
a i) By using the symbols δ+ and δ–, indicate the polarity of the covalent bonds shown below. (3)

$$H_3C \longrightarrow Cl \qquad Cl \longrightarrow F \qquad CH_3CH_2N \overset{\displaystyle H}{\underset{\displaystyle H}{\diagdown}}$$

  ii) Explain the term *electronegativity*. (2)
b The structure of ethanoic acid when dissolved in benzene is shown below.

$$H_3C \longrightarrow C \overset{O\cdots\cdots H\longrightarrow O}{\underset{O\longrightarrow H\cdots\cdots O}{\diagup\diagdown}} C \longrightarrow CH_3$$

  i) Calculate the apparent relative molecular mass of ethanoic acid when dissolved in benzene. (2)
AEB Module Paper 8 June 1997 Q1

3 The boiling temperatures, T_b, of some Group IV and Group V hydrides are given below.

Compound	CH_4	SiH_4	NH_3	PH_3
T_b/K	112	161	240	185

a The polarity of a carbon-hydrogen bond can be shown as C–H [Insert δ– and δ+ above C and H]
  i) What does the symbol δ+, above the hydrogen atom, signify?
  ii) Explain briefly, in terms of its shape, why a CH_4 molecule has no overall polarity. (3)
b Name the type of intermolecular forces which exist between CH_4 molecules in liquid methane. (1)
c Explain why the boiling temperature of PH_3 is greater than that of CH_4. (3)

d Explain why the boiling temperature of NH_3 is greater than that of PH_3. (2)
e Sketch a diagram to show the shape of a molecule of NH_3 and indicate on your diagram how this molecule is attracted to another NH_3 molecule in liquid ammonia. (3)
f Suggest why the strength of the C–H bond in CH_4 is greater than that of the Si–H bond in SiH_4. State the relationship, if any, between the strength of the covalent bond in CH_4 and the boiling temperature of CH_4. (2)
NEAB CH01 March 1999 Q3

4
a Co-ordinate bonding can be described as dative covalency. In this context, what is the meaning of each of the terms *covalency* and *dative*? (2)
b Write an equation for a reaction in which a co-ordinate bond is formed. (2)
c Why is sodium chloride ionic rather than covalent? (2)
d Why is aluminium chloride covalent rather than ionic? (2)
e Why is molten sodium chloride a good conductor of electricity? (1)
f Explain, in terms of covalent bonding, why the element iodine exists as simple molecules whereas the element carbon does not. (3)
NEAB CH01 June 1999 Q2

5
a What is a polar covalent bond? (1)
b In what circumstances will a covalent bond be polar? (1)
c In what circumstances will an anion be polarised? (1)
d How does a polarised anion differ from an unpolarised anion? (1)
e i) Draw diagrams to show the shapes of the following molecules and in each case show the value of the bond angle on the diagram. $BeCl_2$, NCl_3 and SF_6.
  ii) State which if the above molecules is most likely to form a co-ordinate bond with a hydrogen ion. Give a reason for your answer. (8)
NEAB CH01 June 1997 Q3

6
a Complete the following table giving, in each case, the formula of a molecule or ion which has the bond angle shown. Use a different molecule or ion for each angle. (4)

Bond angle	90°	109° 28'	120°	180°
Formula of molecule of ion with this bond angle				

b Draw a diagram of a water molecule and on your diagram indicate the value of the bond angle. (2)
NEAB CH01 February 1997 Q5

What is the link between ironing a cotton shirt and strengthening fingernails?

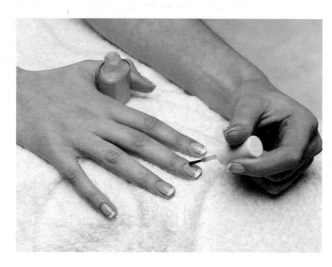

The answer to this question is **bonding**.

It is a common experience when ironing a cotton shirt that if it is too dry or the iron is not hot enough, you cannot iron the wrinkles out of the shirt fabric.

Cotton is a fibrous material made from a very large molecule called cellulose. Sticking out from the sides of the cellulose molecules are hydroxyl groups which cross-link to other cellulose molecules by hydrogen bonds. The hydrogen bonds between the cellulose molecules can be broken by increasing the temperature or by adding water.

A steam iron supplies both heat and moisture. These break the hydrogen bonds. The pressure of the iron forces the fabric flat and when it is removed the hydrogen bonds reform. The fabric is now smooth and the bonds tend to hold the fabric flat – although wearing the shirt for even a short time can undo the iron's work.

Fingernails are made from a protein called keratin. Keratin is a large fibrous protein molecule similar in some ways to cellulose. However, whereas cellulose contains only the elements carbon, hydrogen and oxygen, keratin also contains nitrogen, sulphur and phosphorus. The sulphur atoms can react together to form links between protein chains called disulphide linkages. These sulphur links can be up to one hundred times stronger than the hydrogen bonds linking cellulose molecules together. This is what helps to make keratin so strong – and explains why it is found in tough structures like fingernails, hair and animal horns and hooves.

1 Why does increasing the temperature tend to break the hydrogen bonds between the cellulose molecules?

2 The protein molecules in fingernails are held together by disulphide linkages, hydrogen bonds and van der Waals forces. Rank these three forces by their strength, starting with the strongest.

3 Research and draw a diagram to show how cross-linking occurs in the polysaccharide molecules of a cotton garment.

■ You will need to label a polysaccharide molecule, a hydroxyl group and a hydrogen bond for at least three linked molecules on your diagram.

■ It can be hand drawn or computer generated.

■ If you use other reference books, please quote the title, author, publisher and date of publication, along with the page reference.

■ Similarly, note down sources for any information you collect from the internet.

4 Research and draw diagrams to show how cross-linking between protein molecules can be broken and reformed in three different ways. You will need to write a short explanation, with suitable sub-headings for each method. Keep records of your information sources, as with the cellulose diagram.

5 Summarise the significant similarities and differences in the ways large fibrous molecules like cellulose and keratin are held together.

3 Amount of substance

Most of the titanium(IV) oxide manufactured in the UK goes into white paint and plastics. A small but increasing amount is used as the opaque white material in sun-block creams

The ideal compound to make white paint should have these properties: it should be an opaque brilliant white to reflect maximum light, it should be stable so as not to discolour, insoluble in rain and non-toxic. Titanium(IV) oxide meets all these requirements. As well as in paint, it is also the white pigment in paper, plastics and textiles, cosmetics, toothpaste and sun-block creams.

Titanium ore is mostly iron(II) titanate, $FeTiO_3$, with some iron(III) titanate, $Fe_2(TiO_3)_3$. For the manufacture of titanium(IV) oxide, industrial chemists calculate precise quantities of the reactants, which include sulphuric acid, to give best yield of the oxide at lowest cost. For their calculations, they use atomic masses, the formulas of the reactants and products, and balanced equations for the reactions. Such basic chemical knowledge is used to make calculations for any industrial process that involves chemical reactions.

Titanium(IV) oxide (left) is one of the whitest substances known. The ore (right) is first ground to a sand and reacted with sulphuric acid

3.1 Relative atomic mass

The masses of atoms vary from 10^{-24} g for hydrogen to 10^{-22} g for the heavier elements. These are masses that we cannot possibly imagine. Small numbers like these also complicate calculations.

As we saw in Chapter 1, to deal with the mass of atoms we use the idea of relative atomic mass, A_r, with mass of a carbon-12 atom as the standard.

Relative atomic mass is the average mass of an atom of an element compared to one twelfth of the mass of an atom of carbon-12.

For an element:

$$A_r = \frac{\text{average mass of an atom of an element}}{\frac{1}{12} \text{ mass of one atom of carbon-12}}$$

We use the *average* mass of an element because, if a sample has more than one isotope, not all the element's atoms have the same mass. For example, chlorine has two naturally occurring isotopes: 75.53% is $^{35}_{17}Cl$, and 24.47% is $^{37}_{17}Cl$. This gives a relative atomic mass for chlorine of 35.453, rounded up to 35.5.)

3.2 Relative molecular mass

For molecules we use the relative molecular mass, symbol M_r. In the same way as for A_r, the value for M_r has no units.

Relative molecular mass, symbol M_r, is the sum of the relative atomic masses of all the atoms in a molecule.

M_r = sum of A_r values for atoms in a molecule

We could also work out relative molecular mass as:

$$M_r = \frac{\text{average mass of one molecule}}{\frac{1}{12} \text{ mass of one atom of carbon-12}}$$

Calculating relative molecular mass
Find the relative molecular mass of sulphuric acid, H_2SO_4.

1   Look up A_r values:
    hydrogen = 1, sulphur = 32, oxygen =16.
2   Add up masses for one molecule of H_2SO_4:
    two atoms of hydrogen = 2 × 1   = 2
    one atom of sulphur   = 1 × 32 = 32
    four atoms of oxygen   = 4 × 16 = 64
    M_r of sulphuric acid = 98
The values in this calculation are accurate enough for our purposes.

1 Reread the Introduction and find the M_r of iron(II) titanate and iron(III) titanate. Use A_r values from your data book.

2 Most sulphur atoms have a mass number of 32, yet the relative atomic mass of sulphur is 32.06. Explain why.

In equations and calculations, we use the **molecular formula** of compounds:

The molecular formula of a compound gives the number of atoms of each different element in the molecule. This is the same as the number of moles of each different element in 1 mole of the compound.

For example, the molecular formula of glucose is $C_6H_{12}O_6$. This means that there are six carbon atoms in a glucose molecule - or that there are six moles of carbon atoms in a mole of glucose molecules. Similarly the molecular formula of sodium chloride is NaCl, even though sodium chloride is an ionic compounds and so does not have individual NaCl molecules.

When chemists find the composition of unknown compounds, their initial results are often a simple ratio of the number of atoms of each element in the compound. This is the **empirical formula**:

The empirical formula of a compound is the formula which gives the simplest ratio of atoms of each element in the compound.

For example, analysing glucose will give a ratio of $1 \times C : 2 \times H : 1 \times O$.
This gives an empirical formula of CH_2O.

3 Give the empirical formulae of:
a ethanoic acid, CH_3COOH
b hexane, C_6H_{12}

We can find the empirical formula of a compound if we know the *percentage by mass* of each element in the compound.

Calculating the empirical formula from percentage masses
Find the empirical formula of a compound: by mass, C = 85.7%, H = 14.3%

1 Use percentage composition in terms of 100 g: C = 85.7 g, H = 14.3 g
2 Look up A_r values in your data book: $A_r(C) = 12$ $A_r(H) = 1$
3 Divide the masses by A_r values:
carbon: $\frac{85.7}{12} = 7.1$ hydrogen: $\frac{14.3}{1} = 14.3$
4 Divide each number by the lower number to give the ratio of atoms: C:H = 1:2
5 Write the empirical formula: CH_2

Where we know the M_r of a compound and its empirical formula, we can work out its molecular formula.

Calculating the molecular formula from the empirical formula
A compound's empirical formula is CH_2, $M_r = 42$. Work out its molecular formula.

1 Calculate the empirical formula mass:
1 carbon atom = $1 \times 12 = 12$
2 hydrogen atoms = $2 \times 1 = 2$
total = 14 = empirical formula mass
2 Find the ratio of M_r to A_r:
$M_r : A_r = 42:14 = 3:1$

So M_r is three times the empirical formula. The molecular formula = $3 \times CH_2 = C_3H_6$.

4 By mass, a compound of iron, titanium and oxygen contains 28% iron, 36% titanium and has an M_r of 399
a What percentage is oxygen?
b Using data book A_r values, find its empirical and its molecular formulae

3.3 The mole and the Avogadro constant

When chemists manufacture a substance, they need to calculate the amounts of reactants and the amount of product they expect. In a chemical reaction, particles always react together in the same ratios to give a particular product. For example, when carbon is burnt in oxygen, one carbon atom always reacts with two oxygen atoms to give carbon dioxide, CO_2. This means that, if you know how many particles you start with, you can predict how many you will end up with.

Chemists dealing with quantities of particles are likely to measure the amount of a substance in **moles**, symbol **mol**. A mole always contains 6.023×10^{23} particles and is defined with reference to carbon-12 as the standard:

A mole is the amount of a substance in grams which has the same number of particles as there are atoms in 12 g of carbon-12.

But where does 6.023×10^{23} come from, and why 12 grams of carbon-12? The number 6.023×10^{23} is called the **Avogadro constant** and is named after the nineteenth century Italian physicist Amedeo Avogadro. He was investigating the number of molecules in different volumes of gases and found that, under the same conditions, one mole of gas always contained 6.023×10^{23} particles. So, a mole of carbon dioxide has the same number of particles as a mole of hydrogen, or oxygen or any other gas. This number is the number of atoms in 12 g of carbon.

The mass of a carbon-12 atom has been determined experimentally. It is 1.992×10^{-23} g.

If a mole contains 6.023×10^{23} of these atoms, then a mole has a mass of:

$6.023 \times 10^{23} \times 1.992 \times 10^{-23} = 11.998$ g

Since a mole always contains the same number of particles, we can say that a gram mole of an element is its A_r value in grams, and a gram mole of a molecule is its M_r value in grams. So a gram mole of chlorine-35 weighs 35 grams and a gram mole of sulphuric acid, H_2SO_4, weighs 98 grams.

You can have moles of an element, moles of a compound, moles of ions and moles of electrons. Anything that can be counted can be expressed in moles. For any type of particle, the number of grams in a mole is the same as its relative mass number.

Describing masses of moles for carbon and magnesium

Carbon-12 has relative atomic mass 12
Magnesium-24 has relative atomic mass 24

One magnesium-24 atom has twice the mass of one carbon-12 atom.

So 6.023×10^{23} magnesium atoms have twice the mass of 6.023×10^{23} carbon-12 atoms.

Therefore 1 mole of magnesium-24 atoms has twice the mass of 1 mole of carbon-12 atoms.

Since 1 mole of carbon-12 atoms weighs 12 grams, 1 mole of magnesium-24 atoms weighs 24 grams.

Masses and moles

It can be useful in practical work to convert masses to moles and moles to masses.

To convert the mass of a substance to moles of the substance, use:

$$\text{number of moles of an element} = \frac{\text{mass}}{A_r}$$

$$\text{number of moles of a molecule} = \frac{\text{mass}}{M_r}$$

The same procedure works for compounds, no matter how complicated.

Example: Converting masses of elements to moles

What is the number of moles in 414 g of lead?

For lead, $A_r = 207$

So number of moles $= \dfrac{414}{207}$

$= 2.00$ moles

Example: Converting masses of compounds to moles

What is the number of moles in 1 kg of glucose?
For glucose, $C_6H_{12}O_6$:
$M_r = (6 \times 12) + (12 \times 1) + (6 \times 16) = 180$
So number of moles $= \dfrac{1000}{180}$

$= 5.56$ moles

Notice that you have to convert masses to grams before dividing by M_r.

To convert the number of moles of a substance to its mass, use:

mass of an element
= number of moles × A_r in grams
mass of a molecule
= number of moles × M_r in grams

Example: Converting moles to masses

What is the mass in grams of 2.5 moles of ethanol?

For ethanol, $M_r = 46$
So mass = 2.5 × 46 g
= 115 g

5 Calculate the number of moles in the following.

a 6 g magnesium

b 60 g calcium carbonate

c 106.5 g hydrogen chloride

6 Calculate the mass in grams of the following.

a 0.72 mol oxygen

b 1.3 mol sodium chloride

c 0.1 mol aluminium oxide (Al_2O_3)

7 Find the average mass of the following.

a 1 hydrogen atom; A_r hydrogen = 1.0079

b 1 mercury atom; A_r mercury = 200.59

A 1p coin has a mass of 3.56 g, so £1's worth of pennies has a mass of 356 g. A bank clerk does not count individual coins when checking pennies. Instead, he or she often weighs them in bags each containing a total of £1. Suggest the chemical equivalent of (a) a bag, (b) the number of coins in it

3.4 Concentration and molarity

These are some examples of solutions in water: in an energy drink, the solid solute is glucose, in vinegar, the liquid solute is ethanoic acid, and in a bottle of soda water, the gas carbon dioxide is the solute.

A **solution** contains a **solute** dissolved in a **solvent**. Where the solution is a liquid, the solvent is a liquid. Water and ethanol are common solvents. The solute dissolved in the solvent can be solid, liquid or gas, as shown in the photos of some everyday solutions. You can get solutions of solids in solids such as metal alloys, but we need not deal with them here.

The **concentration** of a solution is written as the mass of solute in a given volume of solvent, such as grams per cubic decimetre, $g\ dm^{-3}$, or as the number of moles of solute in a given volume of solvent. Note that this means a mass of the solute with enough solvent to bring the volume of the solution up to a cubic decimetre; it does not mean a mass of the solute plus a cubic decimetre of solvent.

When 1 mole of solute is dissolved in 1 cubic decimetre of solution, its concentration is 1 mol dm⁻³.

We write this concentration as 1 M for short. The concentration given in $mol\ dm^{-3}$ is called the **molarity** of the solution. So, for example, the molarity of the solution in Fig. 1 is $1\ mol\ dm^{-3}$ or 1 M.

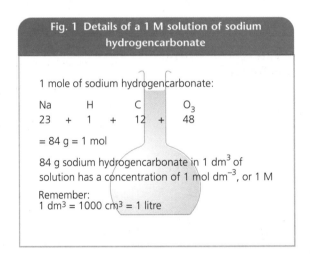

Fig. 1 Details of a 1 M solution of sodium hydrogencarbonate

1 mole of sodium hydrogencarbonate:

Na		H		C		O₃
23	+	1	+	12	+	48

= 84 g = 1 mol

84 g sodium hydrogencarbonate in 1 dm^3 of solution has a concentration of $1\ mol\ dm^{-3}$, or 1 M

Remember:
$1\ dm^3 = 1000\ cm^3 = 1\ litre$

You can calculate the number of moles of solute in a solution if you know its volume in cubic decimetres and its molarity.

Example: Calculating moles of solute in a solution

A How many moles of sodium hydrogencarbonate are there in 200 cm^3 of 1 M sodium $NaHCO_3$ solution?

Number of moles
= volume of solution in dm^3 × molarity
$$= \frac{200}{1000} \times 1$$
= 0.2 mol

The same formula works for more complex examples:

B How many moles of sodium hydroxide are there in 247 cm^3 of 0.14 M solution?

Number of moles
= volume of solution in dm^3 × molarity
$$= \frac{247}{1000} \times 0.14$$
= 0.3458 mol

8 Calculate the number of moles of solute in the following solutions.

a 1.5 dm^3 of 0.85 M sodium chloride solution

b 376.3 cm^3 of 0.2 M sodium hydroxide solution

c 16.4 cm^3 of 2 M sodium thiosulphate(VI) solution, $Na_2S_2O_3(aq)$

9 Calculate the mass of solute in the following solutions.

a 10 dm^3 of 0.85 M potassium iodide solution

b 350 cm^3 of 2 M sodium hydroxide solution

c 9.4 cm^3 of 0.01 M sodium thiosulphate(VI) solution, $Na_2S_2O_3(aq)$

KEY FACTS

■ Chemists measure amounts of particles in moles.

■ A mole contains 6.023×10^{23} particles.

■ Moles of a substance = mass in g/A_r

■ Mass of a substance in g = moles × A_r

■ The concentration of a solution can be measured in terms of its molarity where a 1 M solution contains one mole of solute in 1 dm^3 of solution.

■ Mass of a solute in a solution with molarity M = M × vol in dm^3

3.5 Chemical equations

Balancing chemical equations

A **chemical equation** is a shorthand way of writing a chemical reaction. The equation uses **chemical formulae** for the reactants and the products. Formulae use letter symbols to represent the elements, and numbers to show how many atoms of each element are involved. Chapters 1 and 2 describe how the electron arrangement of each atom in a molecule determines the number of other atoms it bonds to.

A chemical equation can also include the **state** of reactants and products:
(s)   means the solid state
(l)   means the liquid state
(g)   means the gaseous state
(aq) means aqueous, i.e. in aqueous solution

As an example, sulphur burns in oxygen to produce sulphur dioxide. This is how we write the reaction using chemical formulae:

$$\text{reactants} \qquad \text{product}$$
$$S(s) + O_2(g) \rightarrow SO_2(g)$$

A chemical equation must *balance*. This means that there must the same number of each type of atom on both sides of the arrow. In this example, there is one sulphur atom on the left and one sulphur atom on the right. There are two oxygen atoms on the left and two oxygen atoms on the right. This is therefore a **balanced equation**.

Sulphur dioxide reacts with oxygen to produce sulphur trioxide. We could use chemical formulae to write the reaction like this:

$$SO_2(g) + O_2(g) \rightarrow SO_3(g)$$

Is this equation balanced? There is one sulphur atom on the left and one on the right. But there are four oxygen atoms on the left and only three on the right. So the equation needs to be altered to balance.

One oxygen molecule contains enough oxygen atoms to react with two molecules of sulphur dioxide and produce two molecules of sulphur trioxide. So we can now write a balanced equation:

$$2SO_2(g) + O_2(g) \rightarrow 2SO_3(g)$$

This is a very simple equation. Others are more complicated, but the basic procedure is the same. Take it step by step and you should have no problems. In the Example, we look at ammonia burning in oxygen.

Example: Balancing an equation
$$NH_3 + O_2 \rightarrow NO_2 + H_2O$$

1 Look at nitrogen: there is 1 atom on either side, so the nitrogen balances.

2 Look at hydrogen: 3 on the left and 2 on the right – so use 2 ammonia molecules and 3 water molecules to give 6 hydrogens on each side:

$$2NH_3 + O_2 \rightarrow NO_2 + 3H_2O$$

3 Now the nitrogen is unbalanced - so double the nitrogen oxide on the right:

$$2NH_3 + O_2 \rightarrow 2NO_2 + 3H_2O$$

4 Now check on the oxygen, 2 on the left and 7 on the right. First of all, double both sides to get even numbers:

$$4NH_3 + 2O_2 \rightarrow 4NO_2 + 6H_2O$$

5 The nitrogen and hydrogen are still balanced. You have 14 oxygens on the right, so you need 7 molecules on the left:

$$4NH_3 + 7O_2 \rightarrow 4NO_2 + 6H_2O$$

This shows you that with each step you take you have to check whether you need more steps to rebalance the equation, until you have the same number of each kind of atom on both sides. You can often take steps in different orders.

10 Balance the following equations.

a $C_2H_5OH + O_2 \rightarrow CO_2 + H_2O$

b $Al + NaOH \rightarrow Na_3AlO_3 + H_2$

c $CO_2 + H_2O \rightarrow C_6H_{12}O_6 + O_2$

d $C_3H_8(g) + O_2(g) \rightarrow CO_2(g) + H_2O(l)$

e $Al(s) + H_2SO_4(l) \rightarrow$
$$Al_2(SO_4)_3(aq) + SO_2(g) + H_2O(l)$$

Using chemical equations and moles

Chemical equations enable us to calculate the masses of reactants we need and the masses of products formed in a chemical reaction, as the next section shows.

From balanced equations to moles

Let's look at this reaction.

$$CaCO_3(s) + 2HCl(aq) \rightarrow CaCl_2(s) + CO_2(g) + H_2O(l)$$

If we want carry out the reaction without leaving a surplus of either reactant, we need one mole of $CaCO_3$ for every two moles of HCl. So we can write the moles in the reaction as:

1 mol reacts with 2 mol to produce 1 mol + 1 mol + 1 moll

For any compound or element, we can calculate the mass of a mole. So, in this case, we can take a given amount of calcium carbonate and work out how much hydrochloric acid reacts with it exactly. We can also work out how much of each product is made.

Calcium carbonate decomposes when it is heated to make calcium oxide, sometimes called quicklime. Quicklime is added to acid soils by gardeners and farmers - you can buy bags of quicklime at most garden centres. The simple equation is:

$$CaCO_3 \rightarrow CaO + CO_2$$

So, 1 mol of calcium carbonate breaks down to give 1 mol of calcium oxide and 1 mol of carbon dioxide.

The carbon dioxide escapes into the air.

Example: Calculating the mass of product formed

How much calcium oxide would be formed from 800 kg of calcium carbonate?

1   Write a balanced equation:
$$CaCO_3(s) \rightarrow CaO(s) + CO_2(g)$$

2   Calculate the M_r for the calcium compounds:
$M_r \, CaCO_3 = 40 + 12 + 48 = 100$
$M_r \, CaO = 40 + 16 = 56$

3   Calculate the number of moles of $CaCO_3$ used:

$$\text{number of moles } CaCO_3 = \frac{\text{mass used}}{M_r}$$

$$= 800 \times \frac{1000}{100}$$

$$= 8000 \text{ mol}$$

4   From the equation, find the number of moles of calcium oxide produced:

1 mol calcium carbonate →
1 mol calcium oxide
So 8000 mol calcium carbonate →
8000 mol calcium sulphate

5   Convert moles to masses:
8000 mol calcium oxide
$= \text{mol} \times M_r$
$= 8000 \times 56$
$= 448000 \text{ g}$
So mass of calcium oxide made = 448 kg.

Example: Calculating reacting masses

Copper carbonate reacts with sulphuric acid to produce copper sulphate. What mass of copper sulphate is made when 225 g of calcium carbonate is reacted with excess sulphuric acid?

1   Write a balanced equation:

$$CuCO_3(s) + H_2SO_4(l) \rightarrow$$
$$CuSO_4(s) + H_2O(l) + CO_2(g)$$

2   Calculate the M_r for the calcium compounds:

$M_r \, CuCO_3 = 63.5 + 12 + 48$
$= 123.5$
$M_r \, CuSO_4 = 63.5 + 32 + 64$
$= 159.5$

3   Calculate the number of moles of $CuCO_3$ used:

$$\text{number of moles } CuCO_3 = \frac{\text{mass used}}{M_r}$$

$$= \frac{225}{123.5}$$

$$= 1.822 \text{ mol}$$

4   From the equation, find the number of moles of copper sulphate produced:

1 mol copper carbonate →
1 mol copper sulphate

So 1.822 mol calcium carbonate →
1.822 mol calcium sulphate

5   Convert moles to masses:

1.822 mol of copper sulphate = mol × M_r
$= 1.822 \times 159.5$
$= 290.609$

So mass of calcium sulphate made
$= 290.609 \text{ g}$.

Moles and plasterboard

As shown in the graph, a factory at Grimsby making titanium oxide pigment used to discharge 160 000 tonnes of waste sulphuric acid directly into the Humber Estuary each year.

Then in 1992 they opened a new treatment plant to react all but 20 000 tonnes of the acid with local chalk, $CaCO_3$, to form calcium sulphate:

$$H_2SO_4 + CaCO_3 \rightarrow CaSO_4 + CO_2 + H_2O$$

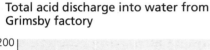

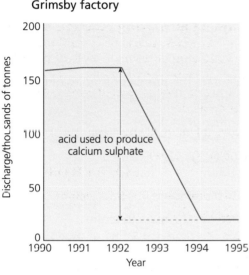

Total acid discharge into water from Grimsby factory

Calcium sulphate is made into plasterboard, the material used for the internal walls of buildings.

1 The reaction needs to be carefully managed to ensure that all of the calcium carbonate is used to make calcium sulphate. One problem is that insoluble calcium sulphate deposits onto the surface of the calcium carbonate. How will this affect the yield of calcium sulphate?

2 Calculate the theoretical yield of calcium sulphate produced annually.

The chart shows the quantities of all waste products from the plant.

3 What could account for the changes shown in the chart? For each type of discharge, explain why the quantity has changed over time.

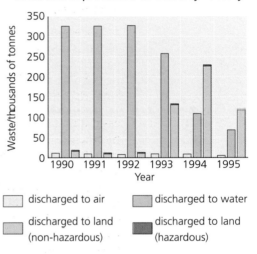

Total waste produced at Grimsby factory

- ☐ discharged to air
- ☐ discharged to water
- ☐ discharged to land (non-hazardous)
- ■ discharged to land (hazardous)

3.7 Ionic equations

An **ionic equation** shows the essential chemistry of a reaction. Ionic equations enable us to make generalisations about a reaction and to pick out the species which have lost or gained electrons.

Example: Working from a full equation to an ionic equation

A Write the ionic equation for hydrochloric acid reacting with sodium hydroxide to give sodium chloride and water.

1 First write out the full equation:

$$HCl + NaOH \rightarrow NaCl + H_2O$$

Water is covalently bonded: since it is not an ionic compound, we do not write it as ions.

2 Now write the equation as ions, and cancel.

$$H^+ + \cancel{Cl^-} + \cancel{Na^+} + OH^- \rightarrow \cancel{Na^+} + \cancel{Cl^-} + H_2O$$

The ionic equation is:

$$H^+ + OH^- \rightarrow H_2O$$

B Write the ionic equation for the reaction between zinc and hydrochloric acid.

1 Write out the full equation:

$$Zn(s) + 2HCl(aq) \rightarrow ZnCl_2(s) + H_2(g)$$

2 Write the equation as ions:

$$Zn + 2H^+ + 2Cl^- \rightarrow Zn^{2+} + 2Cl^- + H_2$$

3 Cancel to give the ionic equation:

$$Zn + 2H^+ \rightarrow Zn^{2+} + H_2(g)$$

The zinc has been **oxidised** (it has lost electrons) and the hydrochloric acid has been **reduced** (the hydrogen has gained electrons).

11 Write an ionic equation for the following reaction.

$AgNO_3 + HBr \rightarrow AgBr + HNO_3$

Calculations from ionic equations

We can also calculate amounts from ionic equations.

A mole of sodium chloride has a mass of 58.5 g. This is calculated as the mass of a mole of sodium atoms plus the mass of a mole of chlorine atoms:

23 g + 35.5 g

But sodium chloride is really a sodium ion, Na^+, and a chlorine ion, Cl^-.

Since the mass of the electrons lost or gained is very small, we can consider the mass of a mole of sodium ions the same as the mass of a mole of sodium atoms. Similarly, the mass of a mole of chlorine ions can be considered the same as the mass of a mole of chlorine atoms.

Example: Using an ionic equation to work out an amount

A Zinc metal reacts with copper sulphate solution to deposit copper metal. Calculate the amount of copper obtained using 130 g of zinc and excess copper sulphate. The chemical equation is:

$Zn(s) + CuSO_4(aq) \rightarrow ZnSO_4(aq) + Cu(s)$

1 Write out the ionic equation:

$Zn + Cu^{2+} + SO_4^- \rightarrow Zn^{2+} + SO_4^{2-} + Cu$

2 Write the equation after cancelling:

$Zn + Cu^{2+} \rightarrow Zn^{2+} + Cu$

From the ionic equation,
1 mol zinc atoms → 1 mol copper atoms.

Number of moles of zinc atoms

$= \dfrac{130}{65} = 2 \text{ mol}$

So 2 moles of copper atoms are produced.
2 mol Cu atoms
= 2 × 64 g
= 128 g

B In aqueous solution, barium chloride reacts with sodium sulphate to form a precipitate of barium chloride. Calculate the mass of barium sulphate formed when 2.5 cm³ of 0.10 M barium chloride is added to an excess of sodium sulphate. The chemical equation is:

$BaCl_2 + Na_2SO_4 \rightarrow BaSO_4 + 2NaCl$

1 Write out the ionic equation:

$Ba^{2+}(aq) + 2Cl^-(aq) + 2Na^+(aq) + SO_4^{2+}(aq)$
$\rightarrow BaSO_4(s) + 2Na^+(aq) + 2Cl^-(aq)$

2 Cancel to find the species needed in the calculation:

$Ba^{2+}(aq) + SO_4^{2+}(aq) \rightarrow BaSO_4(s)$

So 1 mole of Ba^{2+} gives 1 mole of $BaSO_4$.

3 Calculate the number of moles of barium in 2.5 cm³ of 0.10 M barium chloride:

number of moles =
 volume in dm³ × molar concentration

$= \dfrac{2.5}{1000} \times 0.10$

= 0.000 25 moles

4 Calculate the mass in grams:
mass in grams = number of moles × M_r
mass of 0.000 25 mol $BaSO_4$ = 0.00025 × 233
So mass of barium sulphate formed = 0.06 g

KEY FACTS

■ A balanced equation tells us the number of moles of reactants and products involved in a reaction.

■ An ionic equation is a simpler equation showing the species reacting. It can be derived from the full equation for the reaction.

3.8 The behaviour of gases

Calculations involving gases

For numerical work on gases and their reactions in the laboratory, we often measure gases by volume. However, the volume of a gas depends upon its temperature and pressure. So, if we want to find the mass of the gas after measuring its volume, we need to understand the way gases change in volume when temperature and pressure change. Each gas behaves very slightly differently from other gases, but for most practical purposes, the differences are small enough for us to assume that gases all behave like an imaginary 'ideal gas'.

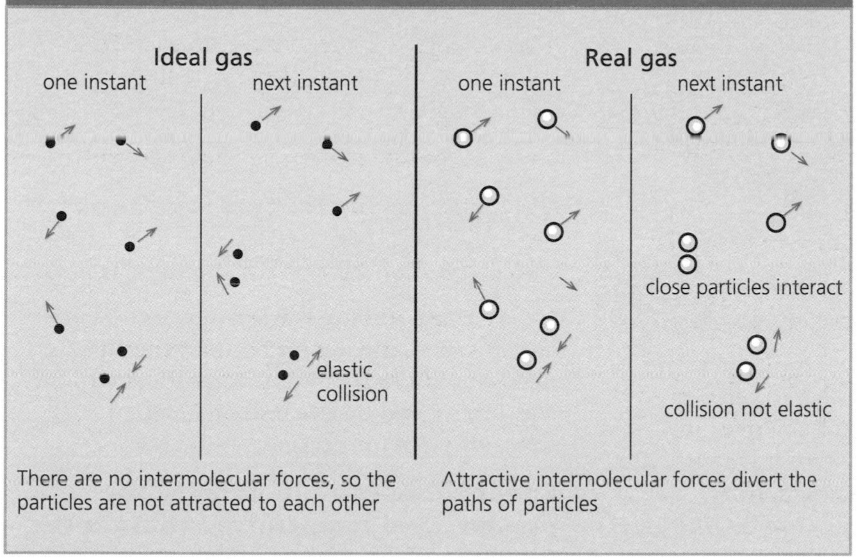

The ideal gas

These are the properties of an **ideal gas**.

- It is made up of identical particles in continuous random motion.

- The particles can be thought of as point-like, with position but zero volume.

- The particles do not react when they collide.

- Collisions between particles are perfectly elastic: the total kinetic energy, energy of motion, of the particles after a collision is the same as before the collision.

- The particles have no intermolecular forces, meaning they do not attract or repel each other.

No real gas fits this model exactly (Fig. 2). In an ideal gas there are no intermolecular forces, so the particles are not attracted to each other. In a real gas, attractive intermolecular forces divert the paths of particles. These forces explain why, under the right conditions, gases can be liquefied.

But some gases do behave like an ideal gas over a limited range of temperatures and pressures. Hydrogen, nitrogen, oxygen and the inert (noble) gases behave most like ideal gases.

Fig. 2 Movement of particles in an ideal gas and a real gas

Ideal gas — one instant — next instant

There are no intermolecular forces, so the particles are not attracted to each other

elastic collision

Real gas — one instant — next instant

close particles interact

collision not elastic

Attractive intermolecular forces divert the paths of particles

3.9 The ideal gas equation

The effect of pressure

Robert Boyle was one of the first chemists to study the behaviour of gases under different conditions. He noticed that, while keeping the number of moles of gas and the temperature constant, when he increased the pressure on a gas, its volume became smaller. He put forward this idea in 1662 in the following statement:

At constant temperature T, the volume V of a fixed mass of gas is inversely proportional to the pressure p applied to it.

When this theory proved generally to be true, it became known as **Boyle's law**. We can write it mathematically as:

$$V \propto 1/p \quad \text{when } T \text{ and the mass of gas are constant}$$

which is the same as:

$$p \times V = \text{constant} \quad \text{when } T \text{ and the mass of gas are constant}$$

The effect of temperature

About a hundred years later, the Frenchman Jacques Charles was studying gases at a time when ballooning was all the rage in France. At first, balloons were filled with hydrogen. Since its density was less than air, balloons filled with enough of it floated off from the ground. But disastrous fires put paid to using hydrogen. Instead, balloons were filled with air heated to reduce its density. As soon as the total mass of the balloon, passengers and air in the balloon was less than the air displaced, the balloon could rise into the air.

The fact that heated gases expand and become less dense led to hot-air balloons being the first safe way to become airborne

At the time, Charles was looking at the effect of changing the temperature of gases and measuring the resulting changes in volume. As temperatures were increased, the gases expanded because their density decreased. As temperatures lowered, the gases contracted as they became denser. The effect was the same for a wide range of gases, and in 1787, Charles published his law:

At constant pressure, the volume of a fixed mass of gas is proportional to its temperature.

$$V = \text{constant} \times T \quad \text{when } p \text{ and the mass of gas are constant}$$

The equation for Charles's law implies that at constant pressure, as the temperature goes down, the volume of any sample of gas decreases until, at a certain very low temperature, the volume becomes zero. Plotting the volumes of most gases against temperature and extrapolating (Fig. 3) produces a surprising result – they would all reach zero volume at the same temperature, –273.15 °C, known as **absolute zero** temperature.

At this temperature the atoms or molecules are assumed to have no kinetic energy, to have ceased moving and colliding,

and to be so close together as to occupy a negligible volume. Of course, at normal pressures, the gases would be solids at –273.15 °C, which is why we say we have to 'extrapolate' to get the value (Fig. 3). On the **Kelvin temperature scale**, this temperature is 0 K, at which an ideal gas is assumed to occupy zero volume. In your calculations using gas laws, always remember to use temperatures in kelvins, converting celsius to kelvin by adding 273.

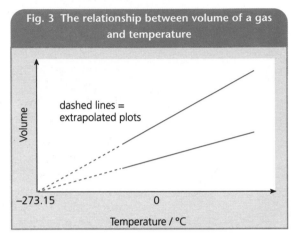

Fig. 3 The relationship between volume of a gas and temperature

dashed lines = extrapolated plots

Volume

Temperature / °C

−273.15   0

We can combine Boyle's law and Charles's law into a single ideal gas equation, but we need one more piece of information which was discovered by the Italian Amedeo Avogadro. He found that:

Equal volumes of all gases at the same pressure and temperature contain the same number of particles.

This means that the **molar volume**, the volume occupied by one mole of a gas, is the same for all gases at the same temperature and pressure. For example, Fig. 4 shows that the volume of a mole of different gases at 298 K (25 °C) is 24 dm³.

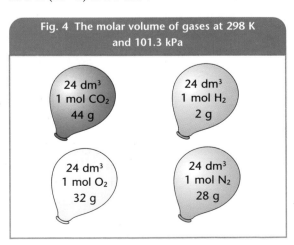

Fig. 4 The molar volume of gases at 298 K and 101.3 kPa

24 dm³
1 mol CO_2
44 g

24 dm³
1 mol H_2
2 g

24 dm³
1 mol O_2
32 g

24 dm³
1 mol N_2
28 g

As a consequence, the volume of a gas is proportional to the number of moles of the gas present when the pressure and temperature are constant. We can say that:

V = constant × n when p and T are constant

n = number of moles of the gas

The **ideal gas equation** combines all the equations for gases above into one equation:

$pV = nRT$

where:

p = pressure of the gas in Pa
V = volume of the gas in m³
n = number of moles of the gaseous particles
R = the gas constant (8.31 J K⁻¹ mol⁻¹)
T = temperature in kelvin

A simple laboratory experiment can be done to calculate the value of the gas constant R. The equipment is shown in Fig. 5. It includes a gas syringe with a friction-free plunger which which allows gas in the syringe to reach atmospheric pressure. The experimant gives values for all the quantities in the ideal gas equation necessary to calculate R.

The syringe is filled several times from the cylinder. The sum of volumes = V
The total mass of gas lost from the cylinder is recorded and the number of moles calculated = n
The temperature is recorded = T
The atmospheric pressure is recorded = p
Then the gas constant is calculated from:

$$R = \frac{pV}{nT}$$

Using the ideal gas equation

The ideal gas equation can be used to confirm the relative molecular mass of a volatile organic liquid such as propanol. The apparatus used is shown in Fig. 6.

The liquid is drawn up into the hypodermic syringe which is weighed.
A small volume of the liquid is injected through the rubber seal of the gas syringe in the oven.
The hypodermic syringe is reweighed. Subtraction gives the mass m of liquid in the gas syringe.
The oven is heated and the liquid changes completely to gas, pushing out the plunger. The apparatus is allowed to reach equilibrium. The temperature T inside the oven is recorded. The plunger is assumed to be friction free, and when it ceases to move, the pressure p inside equals the atmospheric pressure which is recorded. Volume V is also recorded.
The number of moles is calculated using the recorded values in the gas equation:

$$n = \frac{pV}{RT}$$

Then, the value of M_r is calculated from:
$$M_r = \text{mass /moles}$$

We can also use the ideal gas equation for a wide range of calculations such as those given in the Examples that follow.

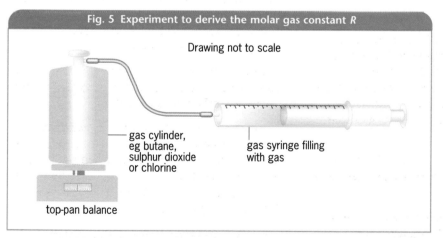

Fig. 5 Experiment to derive the molar gas constant R

Drawing not to scale

gas cylinder, eg butane, sulphur dioxide or chlorine

gas syringe filling with gas

top-pan balance

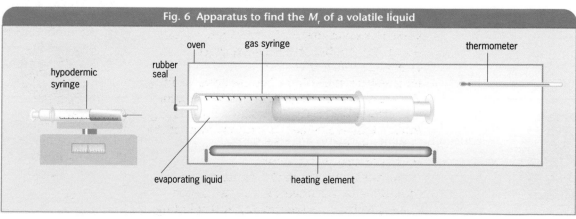

Fig. 6 Apparatus to find the M_r of a volatile liquid

oven   gas syringe   thermometer

hypodermic syringe

rubber seal

evaporating liquid   heating element

Example: Calculating moles from gas volume

How many moles of oxygen are there in $500 \, cm^3$ of gas at $25 \, °C$ and $100 \, kPa$?

1   Convert the units to the units of the ideal gas equation:
    $100 \, kPa = 100\,000 \, Pa = p$
    $500 \, cm^3 = 500 \times 10^{-6} \, m^3 = V$
    $25 \, °C = 298 \, K = T$

2   Rewrite the ideal gas equation to make n the subject:
    $$n = \frac{pV}{RT}$$

3   Insert the values:
    $$n = \frac{100\,000 \times 500 \times 10^{-6}}{8.31 \times 298}$$
    Moles of oxygen = $0.200 \, mol$

Example: Calculating the volume of a reactant gas and the mass of a gas product

In the reaction between methane and oxygen at $120 \, kPa$ and $30 \, °C$, calculate the volume of oxygen needed to react with $20 \, dm^3$ methane, and the mass of carbon dioxide produced. The equation for the reaction is:

$$CH_4(g) + 2O_2(g) \rightarrow CO_2(g) + 2H_2O(l)$$

1   The equation shows that 1 mole of methane reacts with 2 moles of oxygen to give 1 mole of carbon dioxide.
    From Avogadro's rule, at constant temperature and pressure, $20 \, dm^3$ methane therefore requires $40 \, dm^3$ oxygen for the reaction.
    Similarly, the volume of carbon dioxide produced is $20 \, dm^3$.

2   To find the mass of $20 \, dm^3$ CO_2, first use the ideal gas equation to find the number of moles:
    Using $n = pV/RT$, insert the values converted to the correct units:
    $$n = \frac{120 \times 10^3 \times 20 \times 10^{-3}}{8.31 \times 303} = 0.953$$

The reaction produces 0.953 moles of carbon dioxide.

3   Work out mass from moles:
    $$mass = moles \times M_r = 0.953 \times 44 = 41.9$$
    The mass of carbon dioxide produced in the reaction = $41.9 \, g$

Example: Calculating the volume of gas produced in a reaction of a non-gas reactant

When potassium nitrate is heated, it gives off oxygen and becomes the nitrite. Work out the volume in dm^3 of oxygen produced from $345 \, g$ potassium nitrate at $38 \, °C$ and $100 \, kPa$. The reaction is:

$$2KNO_3 \rightarrow 2KNO_2 + O_2$$

1   Work out the number of moles in $345 \, g$ of potassium nitrate:
    $M_r \, KNO_3 = 101$
    moles KNO_3
    $= mass/M_r$
    $= 345/101 = 3.42$

2   From the reaction equation, work out the number of moles of O_2:
    3.42 moles $KNO_3 \rightarrow 0.5 \times 3.42$ moles CO_2
    $= 1.71$ moles

3   Work out the temperature in kelvin:
    $T = 38 + 273 = 301$

4   Write the ideal gas equation, making V the subject, and insert the values:
    $V = nRT/p$
    $$V = 1.71 \times 8.31 \times \frac{311}{100} \times 10^3$$
    $V = 0.0442 \, m^3$

The volume of oxygen produced is $44.2 \, dm^3$.

12   Calculate how many dm^3 of hydrogen gas are produced when $19.5 \, g$ zinc metal dissolves in excess hydrochloric acid at $30 \, °C$ and $100 \, kPa$.

KEY FACTS

■ Theories about the behaviour of gases, and their equations, assume that gases are ideal gases.

■ An ideal gas has point-like particles in continuous random motion. They do not react on collision, they are elastic and have no intermolecular forces.

3.10 Reactions in solution

Calculating molarities and volumes of aqueous reagents from equations

Compounds are often reacted in aqueous solution. The chemist takes a fixed volume of solution A containing a known concentration of a solute and adds solution B of unknown concentration until the **equivalence point** is reached, which is when the solute in A has just completely reacted with the solute in B. For each reaction, an indicator is chosen which changes colour at the equivalence point, also called the **end point**.

When a solution of an acid reacts with a solution of a base, the equivalence point is known as the **neutralisation point**. This procedure is known as a **titration**. Titrations are repeated using the same volume of solution A to check the accuracy of the volume of B. An average value for volume B is calculated. Volumes of A and B are then used to calculate the concentration of solution B.

In titrations we often put an accurately measured volume of a base solution in a conical flask and add acid from a burette to neutralise the base. As an example of such an **acid–base titration**, to find the concentration of a sample of hydrochloric acid, you titrate it against a known volume of sodium hydroxide of known concentration.

Example: Calculating the concentration of an acid solution

In a titration, 25.0 cm³ of 0.100 mol dm⁻³ sodium hydroxide solution is neutralised by 19.8 cm³ hydrochloric acid. Calculate the concentration of the acid.

1 Find the number of moles of sodium hydroxide in 25.0 cm³:
Amount in moles of NaOH
= volume (dm³) × concentration (mol dm⁻³)
= 25.0 × 10⁻³ × 0.100 = 2.50 × 10⁻³ mol

2 Find the number of moles of hydrochloric acid that react with this amount of sodium hydroxide:
The equation is:

$$HCl(aq) + NaOH(aq) \rightarrow NaCl(aq) + H_2O(l)$$

1 mol HCl reacts with 1 mol NaOH
So 2.50 × 10⁻³ mol HCl reacts with a 2.50 × 10⁻³ mol NaOH

3 Find the concentration of hydrochloric acid:
concentration = mol dm⁻³ = mol/dm³

$$= \frac{2.50 \times 10^{-3}}{19.8 \times 10^{-3}}$$

So concentration of hydrochloric acid = 0.127 mol dm⁻³

Example: Calculating the volume of acid used in a titration

Sodium carbonate is a readily soluble compound used as washing soda. Calculate the volume of 0.1 M hydrochloric acid needed to react exactly with 25 cm³ 0.22 M sodium carbonate. The reaction equation is:

$$2HCl + Na_2CO_3 \rightarrow 2NaCl + CO_2 + H_2O$$

From the reaction:

2 moles of hydrochloric acid reacts with 1 mole of sodium carbonate

Volume of 0.1 M HCl that would react with 25 cm³ 0.1 M Na₂CO₃ = 50 cm³

Volume of 0.1 M HCl that reacts with 25 cm³ 0.22 M Na₂CO₃

$$= \frac{50 \times 0.1}{0.22} \ \text{cm}^3$$

$$= 22.7 \ \text{cm}^3$$

KEY FACTS

■ In a titration, a solution of one reagent is added from a burette to a fixed, accurately measured volume of another solution of a second reagent in a flask, until all the substance in the flask has reacted.

■ Unknown molarities can be calculated from acid–base titration data.

1

a The table below gives the accurate masses of two atoms.

	^1H	^{12}C
Mass/g	1.6734×10^{-24}	1.9925×10^{-23}

   i) Calculate accurate values for the mass of one mole of each atom. (The Avogadro constant (L) = 6.0225×10^{23})

   ii) Why is ^{12}C referred to when defining the relative atomic mass of an element? (3)

b i) The carbon in a sample of pure graphite has a relative atomic mass of 12.011. Suggest why this value is different from the mass of one mole of ^{12}C which you have calculated in part (a) (i).

   ii) This sample of graphite was burned completely in oxygen. The carbon dioxide occupied a volume of 1.85 dm^3 at 293 K and 98.0 kPa. Calculate the mass of carbon in the sample. (5)

c In a separate experiment, 1.54 g of carbon dioxide were produced and then absorbed in 50.0 cm^3 of a sodium hydroxide solution forming sodium carbonate (Na_2CO_3) in the solution. Calculate the molar concentration of the sodium carbonate in the solution. (3)

NEAB CH01 June 1996 Q2

2

a Define the term *relative molecular mass*. (2)

b The mass of one atom of ^{12}C is 1.993×10^{-23} g. Use this mass to calculate a value for the Avogadro constant (L) showing your working. (1)

c The following equation is not balanced.

   $MgI_2(s) + Fe^{3+}(aq) \rightarrow Mg^{2+}(aq) + I_2(s) + Fe^{2+}(aq)$

   i) In what way is the equation unbalanced?

   ii) Write the balanced equation. (2)

d A 153 kg sample of ammonia gas, NH_3, was compressed at 800 K into a cylinder of volume 3.00 m^3.

   i) Calculate the pressure in the cylinder assuming that the ammonia remained as a gas.

   ii) Calculate the pressure in the cylinder when the temperature is raised to 1000 K.

   iii) Calculate the molarity of the solution formed by dissolving the mass of ammonia in water to make 1.0 m^3 of solution. (7)

NEAB CH01 June 1999 Q1

3

a Give the meaning of the terms *empirical formula* and *molecular formula*. (2)

b The organic compound X contains the elements carbon, hydrogen and oxygen only. After analysis of a sample of X it was found to contain 38.7% by mass of carbon and 9.7% by mass of hydrogen. Calculate the empirical formula of compound X. (3)

c In a separate experiment it was found that 0.315 g of X occupied a volume of 2.0×10^{-4} m^3 at a pressure of 1.0×10^5 Pa and a temperature of 473 K.

i) Give the ideal gas equation.

ii) Use the ideal gas equation to calculate the number of moles of **X** in the experiment.

iii) From your answer to (c) (ii) calculate the relative molecular mass of **X**.

iv) From your answers to parts (b) and (c) (iii) deduce the molecular formula of **X**. (9)

NEAB CH01 June 1995 Q6

4 A tank contained 4 m^3 of waste hydrochloric acid. It was decided to neutralise the acid by adding slaked lime, $Ca(OH)_2$.

a The concentration of the acid was first determined by titration of a 25.0 cm^3 sample against 0.121 M sodium hydroxide of which 32.4 cm^3 were required.

   i) Calculate the molarity of the hydrochloric acid in the sample.

   ii) Calculate the total number of moles of HCl in the tank. (4)

b Calculate the mass, in kg, of slaked lime required to neutralise the acid. Slaked lime reacts with hydrochloric acid according to the equation shown below.

$Ca(OH)_2 + 2HCl \rightarrow CaCl_2 + 2H_2O$ (3)

c The slaked lime was manufactured by roasting limestone and then adding water.

$CaCO_3 \rightarrow CaO + CO_2$

$CaO + H_2O \rightarrow Ca(OH)_2$

Calculate the mass of limestone which is required to produce 1 kg of slaked lime. (2)

NEAB CH01 February 1996 Q3

5

a When 0.25 g of sodium metal was added to 200 cm^3 (an excess) of water, the following reaction occurred.

$Na(s) + H_2O(l) \rightarrow NaOH(aq) + \_H_2(g)$

   i) Calculate the number of moles of sodium taking part in the reaction.

   ii) Calculate the molarity of the sodium hydroxide solution which was formed.

   iii) Calculate the volume of hydrogen gas produced at 300 K. Assume that hydrogen is insoluble in water under these conditions. (6)

b In another experiment 25.0 cm^3 of 0.183 M sodium hydroxide were neutralised by 13.7 cm^3 of sulphuric acid according to the following equation.

$2NaOH(aq) + H_2SO_4(aq) \rightarrow Na_2SO_4(aq) + 2H_2O(l)$

Calculate the molartiy of the sulphuric acid. (3)

NEAB CH01 Feb 1999 Q3

Presenting titanium chemistry

Titanium(IV) oxide is used in a wide variety of products including sunblockers and cosmetics. In this assignment, you will prepare a presentation to your teaching group on the use of titanium in cosmetic products. Your presentation should last no more than 10 minutes and must contain at least one image to illustrate a complicated point in your presentation.

Your company proposes to extend the size of their plant, which produces titanium(IV) oxide. Your presentation is to argue for the importance of this plant at a Public Enquiry where the local population has a chance to question your company.

You will need to find information from the internet to prepare your presentation, and you will need to bear the following requirements in mind:

Include some basic chemistry

You can choose which aspect of the topic you wish to address, but you must ensure that your presentation includes some of the basic chemistry of titanium. The list below gives you some possible avenues to explore – but be careful you do not try to cram too much into your 10 minute presentation.

- Why are sunblockers used in cosmetic products?

- Should cosmetics be tested on animals?

- How much do people spend on cosmetic products in the UK?

- Which are the most popular types of products, e.g. skin care, shampoos, deodorants, decorative cosmetics or sun protection cosmetics?

Thorough preparation is essential

Think about your 'audience' – in this case your teaching group. They will already be familiar with chemistry and the use of chemical conventions like symbols and equations, but they may not have the in-depth knowledge of some of the detailed chemistry you want to present. Since you know the group, you can decide what assumptions to make about their background knowledge.

Choose your images carefully

Are they simply there to add interest or do they carry important information? If they carry information, how can you make sure your audience takes time to study the images and extract the relevant material? How will you display your images – OHT slides, handouts, video or computer screen?

Cosmetics containing titanium dioxide.

Make the presentation interesting

How will you help your listeners to remember your main points? Will you use summaries on a flip chart or handouts? If you use handouts will you give them out at the beginning or at the end of your presentation?

How will you involve you audience? Asking questions is a useful technique – but do not hope to make them up on the spot. Plan your questions in advance and think about the kind of answers you might get.

Practice makes perfect

Try practising your presentation in front of someone you know to help you sort out any little problems. This is a very good way to prepare for the real thing. Keep everything you use to develop your presentation – this will help to form the evidence of your efforts.

After it's all over

Once you have completed your presentation, ask for some feedback. Note down your group's comments – they may be useful when you prepare for another presentation.

Finally, make a list of the ways you would modify your presentation so that it would be suitable for the following groups:

a Students following advanced level courses in history and economics.

b Students following a range of GCSE courses including science.

4 Periodicity

About 150 years ago, the Russian chemist Dmitry Mendeleev was teaching at St Petersburg University. There were no decent textbooks for his students, so he decided to write one himself. To set out the elements, he used a file of cards, one for each element, its properties and atomic mass. By trying different arrangements of the cards, he built up the Periodic Table much as we know it today. The word 'periodic' means repeating. By arranging the elements in order of atomic mass he found that, if he left a few gaps, chemically related elements recurred at regular intervals.

Mendeleev first published a version of his table of 1869. Other chemists had incorrectly recorded the properties of some elements, and his groupings showed the correct trends in properties which were later confirmed by experiments. The gaps prompted a search for new elements.

Mendeleev gave the name eka-silicon to an unknown element below silicon in Group IV. His predictions for its properties and those found for the element germanium when it was discovered, are listed in the table. Mendeleev's table closely predicted the properties of germanium and several other elements found in the twenty years following his first table. From then on, the Periodic Table was accepted as one of the most important stages in the progress of chemistry.

	Silicon	Predicted properties of eka-silicon	Germanium
Atomic mass	28	72	72.59
Density/g cm^{-3}	2.3	5.5	5.3
Appearance	grey non-metal	grey metal	grey metal
Formula of oxide	SiO_2	EkO_2	GeO_2
Reaction with acid	none	very slow	slow with conc. acid

			Ti=50	Zr=90	?=180.
			V=51	Nb=94	Ta=182.
			Cr=52	Mo=96	W=186.
			Mn=55	Rh=104,4	Pt=197,4
			Fe=56	Ru=104,4	Ir=198.
			Ni=Co=59	Pl=106,6	Os=199.
H=1			Cu=63,4	Ag=108	Hg=200.
	Be=9,4	Mg=24	Zn=65,2	Cd=112	
	B=11	Al=27,4	?=68	Cr=116	Au=197?
	C=12	Si=28	?=70	Sn=118	
	N=14	P=31	As=75	Sb=122	Bi=210
	O=16	S=32	Se=79,4	Te=128?	
	F=19	Cl=35,5	Br=80	I=127	
Li=7	Na=23	K=39	Rb=85,4	Cs=133	Tl=204
		Ca=40	Sr=87,6	Ba=137	Pb=207.
		?=45	Ce=92		
		?Er=56	La=94		
		?Yt=60	Di=95		
		?In=75,6	Th=118?		

Mendeleev's Periodic Table was published in his textbook *Principles of Chemistry* in 1869. The horizontal rows represent groups of elements as they appear in the modern Periodic Table. In a later publication, Mendeleev followed the familiar arrangement of the groups in vertical rows.

Dmitri Mendeleev

4.1 Classification of the elements in s, p and d blocks

The detailed structure of the atom was unknown when Mendeleev was devising his Periodic Table. Later, the relative atomic masses of the elements were accurately measured and showed that the order in the table did not always follow the order of masses.

In 1913 at Manchester University, Henry Moseley showed that the table's order of elements was related to another property, the atomic number, Z, which is also the proton number of an atom. In a few cases, the atomic number order was not the same as relative atomic mass order, so Mendeleev's table needed slight changes to produce the modern form of the Periodic Table (Fig. 1).

The horizontal rows of elements in the table are the **periods**, numbered 1 to 7. For each successive element there is an increase of one proton (and one electron) , and hence an increase of 1 in atomic number. The vertical columns given roman numbers I to VII and O are the **groups** of elements. Chemical properties are similar in each group.

1 From his experiments, Moseley identified three missing elements with atomic numbers 43, 61 and 75. All of these have now been discovered. What are their names?

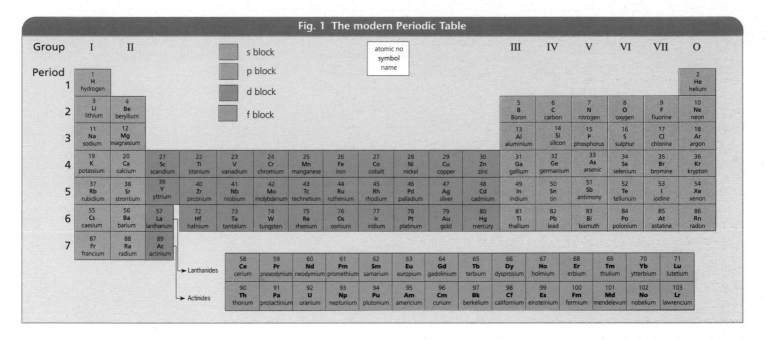

Fig. 1 The modern Periodic Table

2 Element 43 does not occur naturally and was the first element to be made in the laboratory by the Italian Emilio Segrè in 1937.He gave it a name meaning 'artificial'. One of its isotopes has 56 neutrons.

a What is its mass number?

b How many electrons does it have?

Fig. 2 shows the electronic structures for the outermost energy sub-levels of the first 36 elements. Going down each group, the elements have the same number of electrons in their outermost sub-level. So Group II always has a full s^2 sub-level and Group VII always has an $s^2 p^5$ sub-level. The total number of electrons in the outer level (shell) is the same as the element's group number. For example, nitrogen's highest energy level

is level 2 and contains $2s^2\ 2p^3$ electrons, totalling 5, which is its group number.

The Periodic Table is divided into blocks, as in Fig. 3, according to the sub-level being filled. Groups I and II are called **s block** elements because electrons are being added to s sub-levels. Groups III to VII, and Group O (the inert gases), are the **p block** elements because their p sub-levels are being filled. In the **transition elements**, also called the **d block** elements, it is the d sub-levels which are being filled. Finally, in the **lanthanide** and **actinide** elements, electrons are filling inner f sub-levels, so they make up the **f block**.

Since it is electronic structure that determines properties, when you get to know the position of elements in the Periodic Table, you can predict their properties.

The Periodic Table is given in full on page 232.

Fig. 2 The first 36 elements of the Periodic Table and their outer electronic structures

Group	I	II										III	IV	V	VI	VII	O
Period 1						H $1s^1$											He $1s^2$
2	Li $2s^1$	Be $2s^2$										B $2p^1$	C $2p^2$	N $2p^3$	O $2p^4$	F $2p^5$	Ne $2p^6$
3	Na $3s^1$	Mg $3s^2$										Al $3p^1$	Si $3p^2$	P $3p^3$	S $3p^4$	Cl $3p^5$	Ar $3p^6$
4	K $4s^1$	Ca $4s^2$	Sc $3d^14s^2$	Ti $3d^24s^2$	V $3d^34s^2$	Cr $3d^54s^1$	Mn $3d^54s^2$	Fe $3d^64s^2$	Co $3d^74s^2$	Ni $3d^84s^2$	Cu $3d^{10}4s^1$	Zn $3d^{10}4s^2$	Ga $4p^1$	Ge $4p^2$	As $4p^3$	Se $4p^4$	Br $4p^5$	Kr $4p^6$

3 Write the full electronic structure of elements with the following atomic numbers. State which block in the Periodic Table each element belongs to.

a 9

b 20

c 30

4 An element has the electron configuration $1s^2\ 2s^2\ 2p^6\ 3s^2\ 3p^6\ 3d^{10}\ 4s^2\ 4p^4$.

a In which period is the element?

b In which block is the element?

c In which group is the element?

d How many electrons in its outer shell?

5 For each of the following elements, use the Periodic Table to name the block it is in and to write out its electron configuration.

a strontium

b fluorine

c gold

d aluminium

e iron

f germanium

6 Explain why there are ten d block elements and only six p block elements in Period 4.

APPLICATION A **Predicting properties of an unstable element**

The element astatine, At, comes after iodine in Group VII. The Italian physicist Emilio Segrè and his team first produced it in the laboratory at the University of California in 1940. They bombarded bismuth with helium ions, He^{2+} (also called alpha particles) to produce this new element with atomic number 85. No more than 0.5 micrograms has ever been made.

Its longest lived isotope has a half-life of only 8.3 hours, meaning that half the astatine in a sample decays in 8.3 hours. It was named astatine, the Greek for 'unstable', because of this short half-life.

Use the data given in the table to answer the following questions. Where appropriate, sketch graphs.

1 In which block of the Periodic Table is astatine?

2 Give the outermost sub-level electron structure of astatine.

3 Predict the following values for astatine:
a density as a liquid
b melting point
c first ionisation energy

4 Give the formulae of these compounds:
a sodium astatide
b hydrogen astatide

	Fluorine	Chlorine	Bromine	Iodine
Relative atomic mass	19	35.5	79.9	127
Density as a liquid /g cm^{-3}	1.11	1.56	2.93	4.93
Melting point/°C	−220	−101	−7.2	113.5
Appearance at room temperature	colourless gas	green gas	orange liquid	purple solid
Formula of hydrogen halide	HF	HCl	HBr	HI
First ionisation energy/kJ mol^{-1}	1680	1260	1140	1010

KEY FACTS

■ Elements in the Periodic Table are arranged in order of atomic number.

■ The electron configuration of an element determines its properties.

■ The Periodic Table is divided into blocks.

■ Elements are classified as s, p or d block elements according to their position in the Periodic Table

■ The Periodic Table can be used to deduce the electron configuration of any element.

4.2 # Trends across Period 3

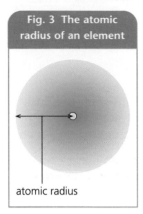

Fig. 3 The atomic radius of an element

atomic radius

Periodicity is the term we use for repeating patterns or trends in the properties of elements in the Periodic Table. The trends found in one period – a horizontal row – is repeated in other periods. In this section, we are going to examine some of the periodic trends of the elements in Period 3.

Atomic radius in Period 3

Atoms are extremely small. Rutherford first determined the size of an atom: he found the radius of a gold atom to be about 10^{-10} metre. The **atomic radius** is the distance from the centre of the nucleus of an atom to its outermost electrons, as shown by Fig. 3.

Fig. 4 shows the trend in atomic radii of the Period 3 elements. Note that the atomic radii decrease across the period from sodium to chlorine.

Fig. 4 Atomic radii of elements in Period 3 measured in nanometres (10^{-9} m)

Na	Mg	Al	Si	P	S	Cl	Ar
0.154	0.145	0.130	0.118	0.110	0.102	0.099	–

In Period 3 all of the outer electrons are in the third energy level: $n = 3$. Going across the period, as a proton is added to the nucleus of each element, so the increasing nuclear positive charge pulls with greater force on the negative electrons. This applies both to the inner level electrons ($n = 1$ and 2) and the outer level electrons. Since the inner electrons remain the same, there is no increase in the number of electrons shielding the outer electrons from the nuclear charge. However, as the inner level electrons have been drawn nearer to the nucleus, the outer level electrons can also be drawn closer to the nucleus before they are themselves repelled by the inner level electrons.

The overall effect is to pull all electrons closer to the nucleus. For example, sodium is larger than magnesium because the nuclear charge of magnesium is greater than that of sodium but the outer electrons are in the same energy level, with the same amount of shielding by the inner electrons. For the same reason, magnesium is larger than aluminium.

First ionisation energy in Period 3

The **first ionisation energy** is the energy required to remove one mole of the outermost electrons from one mole of atoms of an element in the gaseous state.

Fig. 5 plots the first ionisation energies of the Period 3 elements against their atomic numbers. A similar pattern is repeated across other periods when s and p electrons are being removed. This is why we can say that first ionisation energies show periodicity. As Fig. 5 shows, the overall trend is of first ionisation energy increasing across Period 3. We would expect it to take more energy to remove an electron as we go across the period. This is because, as the number of protons is increasing, the positive charge on the nucleus increases, pulling with increasing force on electrons which are all in the same, outermost energy level.

However, the increase in first ionisation energy across Period 3 is not a steady rise. There is a rise for two elements, then a dip and a rise for three. Then another dip followed by a rise for three more. This 2,3,3 pattern suggests that electrons removed from the third energy level are arranged in different sub-levels.

The first two values of this pattern are for electrons taken from the 3s sub-level. The value for magnesium is greater than for sodium because magnesium has one more

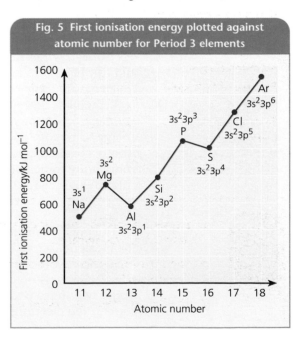

Fig. 5 First ionisation energy plotted against atomic number for Period 3 elements

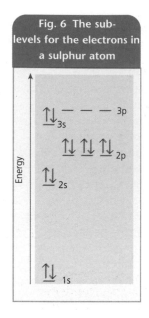

Fig. 6 The sub-levels for the electrons in a sulphur atom

proton attracting the electrons. Then, there is a decrease for aluminium, where the first electron is taken from the 3p sub-level. This electron is at a higher energy level than those in the 3s sub-level and so is easier to remove.

Aluminium, silicon and phosphorus show the expected increase in the energy required to remove each unpaired 3p electron as the increasing positive charge exerts more force on electrons in the same sub-level. Then another dip occurs at sulphur as the first paired electron is removed. There is more electrostatic repulsion between paired electrons, and so it is easier to remove the fourth electron in the 3p sub-level (Fig. 6).

After sulphur, the expected increase in the first ionisation energy appears again due to the increasing positive charge attracting the electrons more strongly.

 Explain why there is a general increase in first ionisation energies as you go across the elements in Period 2.

Electronegativity in Period 3

Electronegativity is the power of an atom to attract electron density from a covalent bond.

The more electronegative an atom is, the more strongly it attracts a pair of electrons in a covalent bond. Electronegativity can be used to predict the polarity of a covalent bond. When a compound contains one atom of very low electronegativity (low electron attraction) and one of very high electronegativity (high electron attraction), electron transfer occurs and an ionic compound is produced. Compounds containing elements of intermediate electronegativities have polar covalent bonds and can be said to have varying degrees of covalent and ionic character.

Remember that no atom has a tendency to *lose* electrons, shown by the fact that it takes energy to remove its first electron. Also, wholly covalent bonding (as in hydrogen) and wholly ionic bonding (as in sodium chloride) are two extremes. For many compounds, the covalent character of bonds varies.

The positive nuclear charge increases in the elements across Period 3, and is reflected in an increase in their electronegativity (Fig. 7). There is no change across the period in the two inner electron levels: they all contain ten electrons. These partially shield

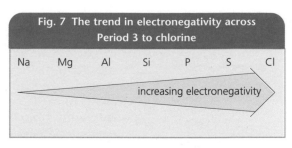

Fig. 7 The trend in electronegativity across Period 3 to chlorine

| Na | Mg | Al | Si | P | S | Cl |

increasing electronegativity

the outer, bonding electrons from the positive charge of the nucleus. But positive nuclear charge increases across the period, and with each additional proton, the positive charge pulls the inner electron levels closer to the nucleus. There are no additional inner electrons to shield the nucleus so the attraction of the nucleus for electrons in a covalent bond increases and electronegativity increases.

Sodium on the left of Period 3 (nuclear charge +11) is the least electronegative element. On the right, chlorine has a nuclear charge of +17. Since its inner-electrons shield outer electrons no more than sodium's, chlorine is the period's most electronegative element.

You might expect argon (+18) to have an even greater electronegativity. However, its outer energy sub-levels are full ($3s^2 3p^6$). There is a large energy gap before the next energy sub-level, and as argon does not form covalent bonds with other atoms, it is given an electronegative value of zero.

Electrical conductivity in Period 3
Conductivity and metallic bonding

Metals are good **electrical conductors** and non-metals are poor electrical conductors. For any substance to conduct, there must be charged particles which are free to move. In the case of elements, it is the electrons which must be free to move.

Electrons in a conductor are delocalised, meaning they are not associated with any particular atom. This means that they are free to move through the element when a potential difference is applied.

When the terminals of a battery are attached to each end of a metal wire, a potential difference is produced down the wire. This then results in the flow of electrons that we call a current.

Electrical conductivity increases from sodium to aluminium. Sodium atoms have only one outermost electron which is delocalised, while magnesium has two and

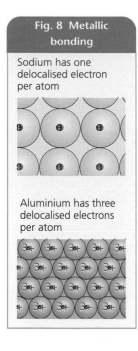
aluminium has three. So electrical conductivity is greatest in aluminium because it has the most delocalised electrons able to move and carry charge.

Conductivity and covalent bonding

Semiconductors

Silicon is a very poor conductor at room temperature. This is because the four outer electrons are held firmly in the four covalent bonds which make up the giant lattice seen in Fig. 9.

Very few electrons gain the energy to enter the higher energy levels where they can become delocalised. At higher temperatures, more of the outer electrons are promoted (excited) to higher energy levels as they gain energy. They then become delocalised. This is why silicon is referred to as a semiconductor. To make silicon a better semiconductor and the most useful material in the computer industry, other elements are added which enable electrons to become delocalised at room temperature.

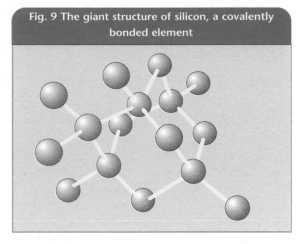

Fig. 9 The giant structure of silicon, a covalently bonded element

Non-conductors Period 3

The other elements in Period 3 from phosphorus to chlorine do not conduct electricity at all. The electrons are held in covalent bonds and are not free to move when a potential difference is applied. Argon holds its electrons very tightly in its stable third energy level, so again there is no electrical conduction.

EXTENSION   Silicon the superb semiconductor

The grooves in this magnified chip separate the tracks of the circuit which are the raised areas of silicon. These areas have been doped

The biggest use of silicon is in semiconductor components – silicon chips – used in the circuits in all our electronic equipment, from the radio alarm and personal computer to the TV and CD player.

At room temperature, very few electrons in a silicon lattice gain enough energy to become delocalised. Heating silicon to promote more electrons to higher energy levels is not practical in today's modern devices. One way to improve the electrical conductivity of silicon at room temperature is to add extra electrons to the silicon lattice. Arsenic and phosphorus atoms, which are both non-metals in Group V, have five outermost electrons. When added in trace amounts to silicon, a technique called doping, atoms of these elements take the place in the lattice of some of the silicon atoms. Just like silicon atoms, they form four covalent bonds but leave a fifth, non-bonding electron which is free to become delocalised. The extra electrons turn silicon into a useful semiconductor. Since the extra electrons are negative, the material is called n-type silicon.

Silicon chips have revolutionised information technology

Boron is also used to dope silicon, but the mechanism of conduction is different. Boron is a non-metal in Group III. In the silicon lattice, it can only form three covalent bonds, so its neighbouring silicon atom at that position has an unpaired electron, while the boron has a 'hole' that could accommodate an electron.

When a potential difference is applied across the boron-doped silicon, electrons from the silicon atoms move to fill these holes. This creates other holes in the lattice which are filled by other electrons moving, creating further holes, and so on. This process allows electrons to move through the doped silicon lattice, so the silicon conducts electricity. Since the holes represent the absence of electrons, they are considered positive, which gives rise to the name p-type for boron-doped silicon.

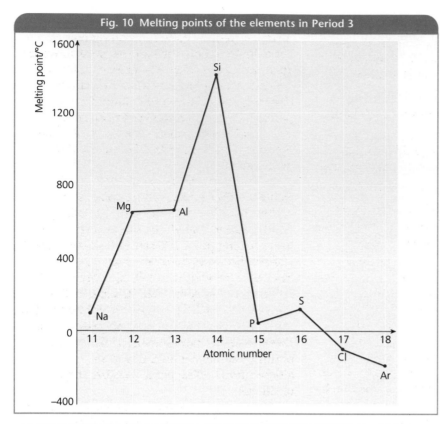

Fig. 10 Melting points of the elements in Period 3

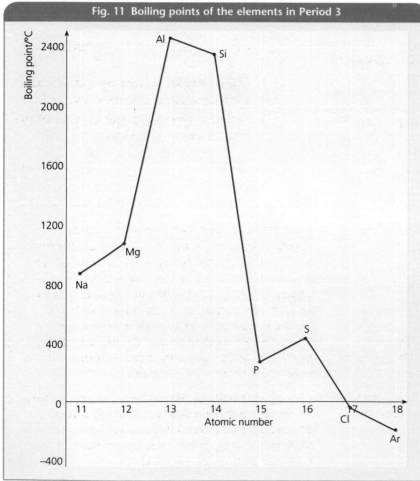

Fig. 11 Boiling points of the elements in Period 3

Melting and boiling points in Period 3

The melting points and boiling points across Period 3 show a pattern that is irregular and not repeated across other periods (see Figs. 10 and 11).

Melting points

The melting points pattern shows that they rise to a maximum at Group IV's silicon, and then decrease dramatically.

When an element melts, the particles have to break free of the forces holding them together. The greater the force between the particles, the higher the melting point. For the metals sodium, magnesium and aluminium held together by metallic bonds, this force is the electrostatic attraction between the delocalised electrons and the positive ions. For these metals, the melting point increases as the attraction between ions and delocalised electrons increases.

The charge on the positive ion increases as you pass along Period 3, so sodium has a charge of +1 while magnesium is +2 and aluminium +3. Consequently there is a similar increase in the number of delocalised electrons available from one in sodium to three in aluminium.

The increased charge and availability of delocalised electrons will increase the attraction between the atoms and so strengthen the metallic bonding holding the solid together.

A further effect concerns the decrease of the ionic radius as you pass from sodium to aluminium. The increased charge on the nucleus tends to draw the electrons closer to the nucleus as explained on page 63 with reference to atomic radii. The same trend is noticeable in ions so the ionic radius falls giving a smaller ion with a lower surface area and a denser charge. So, aluminium has a greater charge density on its surface than a magnesium ion which in turn is greater than for the sodium ion.

Table 1 Ionic radii	
Element	**Ionic radius / nm**
Sodium	0.102
Magnesium	0.072
Aluminium	0.053

7

a List four factors that explain the trend in the strength of the metallic bonding in Period 3 from sodium to aluminium.

b State the diameter of an aluminium ion.

c Calculate the surface area for each of the ions in Table 1.

d Calculate the percentage difference between the ionic and atomic radii for the elements in Table 1.

The next element, silicon, is a non-metal with the highest melting point of all the Period 3 elements. This is due to the giant covalent lattice structure of silicon (Fig. 9), which is similar to that of diamond (Fig. 26 on page 38). All the silicon atoms are held by strong covalent bonds. For silicon to melt, many of these covalent bonds must be broken. This needs a considerable input of energy, and so gives silicon a very high melting point.

The non-metals phosphorus to argon are all made up of separate molecules held together by weak intermolecular forces. The phosphorus molecule exists as P_4, sulphur as S_8, chlorine as Cl_2, and argon as Ar. In the process of melting, the element breaks up into small lumps - groups of molecules - which can move relative to each other. Though phosphorus, sulphur and chlorine molecules have strong intramolecular covalent bonds, there are only weak van der Waals forces of attraction between molecules. Their strength is in the order $S_8 > P_4 > Cl_2 > Ar$, so the energy required to break the forces decreases in the same order, as shown by their decreasing melting points in Fig. 10.

Boiling points

A similar trend is shown by boiling points. For a liquid to boil, the particles must move far apart from each other. The energy required depends on the forces holding the particles close together in the liquid phase. The boiling points increase from sodium to aluminium because of the increase in the forces of metallic bonding already described for the melting point trend.

Silicon does not follow the pattern of these elements. Though its melting point is much higher than that of aluminium, its boiling point is lower. It might be supposed that the lower boiling point is because all silicon's bonds were broken in the process of melting, but the difference between the melting point 1683 °C and the boiling point 2628 °C suggests that liquid silicon still has some covalent bonds that must be broken for it to become gaseous. But these bonds are not as strong as the metallic bonds in liquid aluminium, and so aluminium's boiling point is higher than that of silicon.

The rest of the non-metals have low boiling points, reflecting the weak intermolecular forces of non-metals in the liquid phase.

8 Look at Figs. 10 and 11. For phosphorus and sulphur:

a State the types of bonding and describe the magnitude of the forces involved.

b Explain the melting points in terms of the forces between molecules.

KEY FACTS

■ Periodicity is the term used to describe repeating pattern of properties at regular intervals in the Periodic Table.

■ Across Period 3, the atomic radius of the elements decreases as the nuclear charge increases.

■ The general trend across Period 3 is of an increase in first ionisation energy as the nuclear charge increases. The fall in value at Mg-Al and P-S is due to the arrangement of electrons in sub-levels.

■ Electronegativity increases from Na to Cl because the number of filled inner electron levels stays the same whilst nuclear charge increases.

■ From Na to Al there is an increase in electrical conductivity as the number of delocalised electrons in the metallic bond increases. The non-metal Si is a semiconductor with a very low electrical conductivity at room temperature because only a very tiny proportion of electrons are free. P to Cl do not conduct electricity as the electrons are firmly held in covalent bonds or stable sub-shells. Non-bonding Ar has a very stable electron structure with none free to conduct.

■ Melting and boiling points increase to the middle of Period 3 and then decrease. Melting points depend on the forces between particles in the solid, and boiling points depend on forces between particles in the liquid.

4.3 Group II elements

Elements in Group II

Having looked at the trends in some of the properties of elements across a period, let us consider the trends we find in a group. Remember that elements with similar properties are grouped together in eight vertical columns in the Periodic Table. We are going to consider the elements in Group II, and the trends in properties of the elements and their compounds.

9

a Write down the full electron configurations of beryllium, magnesium and calcium.

b To which block of the Periodic Table do the Group II elements belong? Explain why.

Atomic radius in Group II

For each element in Group II, there is an additional level of electrons as you pass down the group. This means that the outer electrons are increasingly shielded from the attraction of the nucleus. Electrons in each inner level are successively closer to the nucleus as its charge increases but the additional level results in an increase in atomic radius. See Table 2.

First ionisation energy in Group II

We have seen that, going down a group, atoms get larger with the outermost electrons further away from the nucleus, and shielding increases. These features make it easier to remove the outer electrons, as shown in Fig. 12 by the decrease in ionisation energy.

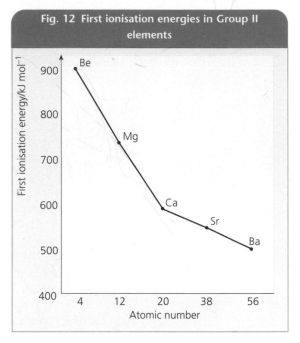

Fig. 12 First ionisation energies in Group II elements

Trend in electronegativity

Electronegativity decreases as you go down Group II (Fig. 13) because increasing atomic radius and extra shielding reduce the attraction of the positive nucleus for bonding electrons. With the exception of beryllium, going down the group, compounds formed by the elements are essentially ionic.

Table 2 Some properties of Group II elements						
Atomic number	Element	Outer electron configuration	Atomic radius/nm	Ionic radius/nm	First ionisation energy/kJ mol-1	Electronegativity (scale 0 to 4)	Melting point/°C
4	Be	$2s^2$	0.112	0.031	900	1.5	1278
12	Mg	$3s^2$	0.160	0.065	736	1.2	650
20	Ca	$4s^2$	0.197	0.099	590	1.0	850
38	Sr	$5s^2$	0.215	0.113	548	1.0	768
56	Ba	$6s^2$	0.222	0.135	502	0.9	714
88	Ra	$7s^2$	0.220	–	510	0.9	See q.10

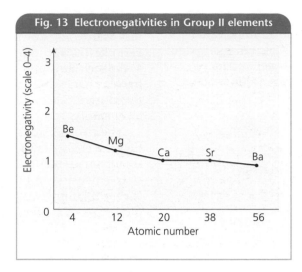

Fig. 13 Electronegativities in Group II elements

Melting points in Group II

Because the Group II elements are metals, their melting points are high. The radii of the ions increases down the group (see Table 2), and because the number of delocalised electrons in their metal lattices remains the same, the attraction between metal ion, M^{2+}, and electron cloud decreases down the group. This gives rise to the general trend seen in Fig. 14 of decreasing melting point as we go down the group.

The dip in the graph for magnesium is because it and beryllium have a different metallic structure from the elements below them in the group: beryllium and magnesium are hexagonal close-packed and calcium and strontium are face centred cubic; barium is body centred cubic.

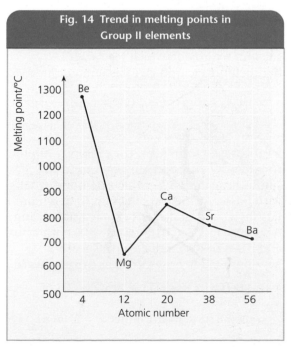

Fig. 14 Trend in melting points in Group II elements

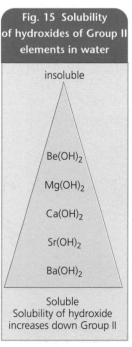

Fig. 15 Solubility of hydroxides of Group II elements in water

insoluble

Be(OH)₂

Mg(OH)₂

Ca(OH)₂

Sr(OH)₂

Ba(OH)₂

Soluble
Solubility of hydroxide increases down Group II

10

a Going down Group II, what it the general trend in melting points?

b What does this tell you about the strength of forces in Group II metallic lattices?

c Look at Table 4.2. Radium is a radioactive element at the bottom of Group II. Predict its melting point.

Reactions of Group II elements with water

Beryllium is totally unreactive in water, and does not react even in steam. Magnesium has an extremely slow reaction with cold water which takes several days to be apparent. In hot water it reacts slowly to give hydrogen gas and magnesium hydroxide.

$$Mg(s) + 2H_2O(l) \rightarrow Mg(OH)_2(aq) + H_2(g)$$

When heated in steam, magnesium burns to form magnesium oxide:

$$Mg(s) + H_2O(g) \rightarrow MgO(s) + H_2(g)$$

Calcium, strontium and barium react with increasing vigour with cold water to produce the metal hydroxide and hydrogen. In the equation below, M could stand for Ca, Sr or Ba.

$$M(s) + 2H_2O(l) \rightarrow M(OH)_2(aq) + H_2(g)$$

We can also write this as an ionic equation:

$$M(s) + 2H_2O(l) \rightarrow M^{2+}(aq) + 2OH^- + H_2(g)$$

So the general trend for the reaction of the Group II elements with water is of an increase in reactivity down the group.

Solubility of the Group II hydroxides

The solubility of a substance is the maximum amount that will dissolve in a given volume of solvent. Solubility is usually given in grams or moles per 100 g of water. The solubility of the Group II hydroxides increases down the group. Magnesium hydroxide is **sparingly soluble**, which means only a very small amount dissolves.

11 Solutions of sodium hydroxide and magnesium chloride are mixed together. Write an equation for the reaction, and explain what you would observe.

A suspension of magnesium hydroxide in water, commonly called Milk of Magnesia, is taken as a medication to neutralise acid indigestion because magnesium hydroxide is a very weak alkali and any excess does not disturb digestion. It is also an important ingredient of toothpaste. Calcium hydroxide is much more soluble in water and its solution is the familiar reagent limewater.

12

a What is the function of magnesium hydroxide in toothpaste?

b What is limewater used for in the laboratory?

Solubility of the Group II sulphates

The solubilities of the Group II sulphates decrease down the group (Fig. 16), which is opposite to the trend for the hydroxides. Magnesium sulphate, which is very soluble in water, is used as a laxative called Epsom salts. Calcium sulphate is sparingly soluble in water and is precipitated when concentrated solutions containing calcium and sulphate ions are mixed.

The soluble compounds of barium are very poisonous, yet barium sulphate is the barium meal given to patients to improve the contrast of X-ray images. Since barium sulphate is so very insoluble, it can pass through the body without dissolving in any of the body fluids. Barium sulphate's insolubility is used to test solutions for sulphate ions. When barium chloride (or nitrate) solution and dilute hydrochloric acid are added, a white precipitate of barium sulphate indicates the presence of sulphate ions in solution:

$$Ba^{2+}(aq) + SO_4^{2-}(aq) \rightarrow BaSO_4(s)$$

Fig. 16 The solubility of the sulphates of the Group II elements in water

soluble

$BeSO_4$

$MgSO_4$

$CaSO_4$

$SrSO_4$

$BaSO_4$

insoluble
Solubility of sulphate decreases down Group II

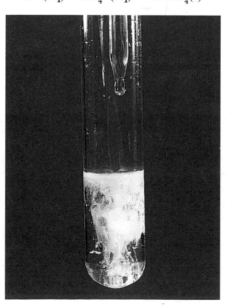

Testing for sulphate ions. The white precipitate of BaSO₄ confirms the presence of sulphate ions.

Atypical beryllium

Just as in going down any group in the Periodic Table, the Group II atoms get larger, as do their ions (see Table 3). The ions have a charge of 2+ when the atoms lose the two outermost-level electrons, leaving this level empty.

The two electrons of the Be^{2+} ion occupy the first energy level only, so the ion is very small. Small, highly charged ions have a high charge density, and the charge density of Be^{2+} is very high indeed. As a consequence, the properties of beryllium and its compounds are not typical of the other Group II elements.

Covalent character of beryllium compounds

Chapter 2 dealt with the polarisation of anions by cations of high charge density. The Be^{2+} cation polarises anions strongly, forming compounds that have a high covalent character. Beryllium chloride, $BeCl_2$, is a typical example: chloride anions are so polarised that beryllium chloride is essentially covalent. Its relatively low melting point of 405 °C, its solubility in organic solvents and its poor electrical conductivity when molten, confirm its covalent character.

13 Explain why Group II chlorides become more ionic in their bonding down the group.

The amphoteric character of beryllium hydroxide

Bases react with acids to form salts. This is true for the s block hydroxides such as calcium hydroxide which reacts with hydrochloric acid to give calcium chloride:

$$Ca(OH)_2(aq) + 2HCl(aq) \rightarrow CaCl_2(aq) + 2H_2O(l)$$

Non-metal oxides are covalent and react with bases to form salts. For example, sulphur trioxide, SO_3, dissolves in water to form sulphuric acid, H_2SO_4, which then forms salts with bases. At the top of Group II, beryllium has metal and non-metal characteristics, and its hydroxide, $Be(OH)_2$, reacts with both acids and bases to form salts. For this reason, beryllium oxide is described as **amphoteric**.

$$Be(OH)_2 + H_2SO_4 \rightarrow BeSO_4 + 2H_2O$$

$$Be(OH)_2 + 2NaCl \rightarrow BeCl_2 + 2NaOH$$

The formation of complex ions

The Be^{2+} ion is so small and highly charged with such strong polarising power that it probably does not exist as a simple ion at all. When beryllium compounds dissolve in water, the Be^{2+} ion forms co-ordinate – or dative covalent - bonds with water to give a hydrated beryllium ion (Fig. 17). Dative means 'giving': the oxygen atom in water donates an electron pair and forms a coordinate covalent bond with the beryllium ion.

The ion $[Be(H_2O)_4]^{2+}$ in Fig. 17 is called a complex ion, or just a complex. A **complex** is formed when a central metal atom or ion is surrounded by species - ions, atoms or molecules - which donate lone pairs of electrons. A species which donates a lone pair of electrons in a complex is called a ligand, meaning joined. Water is the ligand in this case. The charge on the complex ion is +2 because this is the charge of the central beryllium ion, and water is a neutral ligand.

Fig. 17 The Be^{2+} ion accepts lone pairs of electrons from water molecules to form four coordinate bonds

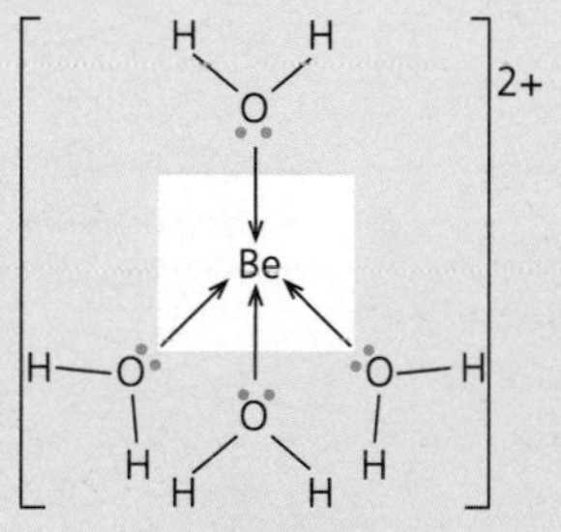

$[Be(H_2O)_4]^{2+}$

14 Predict the bond angles between the water ligands in $[Be(H_2O)_4]^{2+}$. Hint: Look at page 40 to remind yourself about electron pair repulsion.

The Be^{2+} ion is very small and there is only enough room for it to form co-ordinate bonds with four water molecules. The larger Mg^{2+} ion can form six coordinate bonds to water, to give the ion $[Mg(H_2O)_6]^{2+}$. The remaining Group II metal ions have too small a charge density for them to form coordinate bonds with water, and these larger ions hold water by the attraction of the ions for the water dipole.

Fig. 18 Two other complexes of beryllium

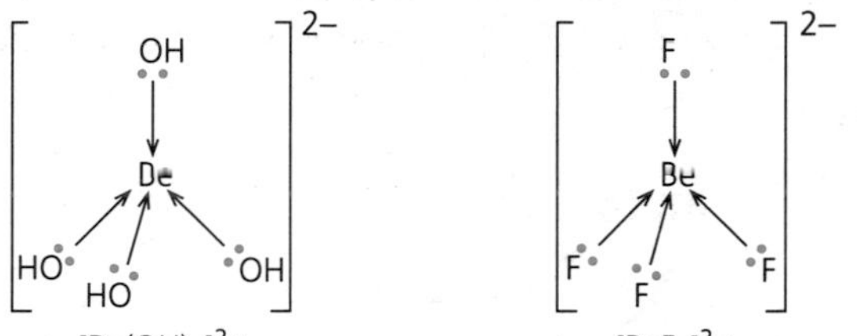

$[Be(OH)_4]^{2-}$ $[BeF_4]^{2-}$

15 Fig. 18 shows two other complexes formed when ligands attach to the central Be^{2+} ion. Explain the value of the charges on these complex ion. Hint: What charge does each ligand have before it bonds to Be^{2+}?

a $[Be(OH)_4]^{2-}$

b $[BeF_4]^{2-}$

KEY FACTS

- Going down Group II, there is an increase in atomic radius and first ionisation energy.
- Electronegativity and melting point decrease down Group II.
- The vigour of the reaction of elements with water increases going down Group II. Beryllium is unreactive and magnesium reacts only slowly in hot water. When the elements react with water, hydrogen is produced.
- The solubility of the Group II hydroxides increase down the group.
- The solubility of the Group II sulphates decreases down the group.
- $BaSO_4$ is insoluble and the formation of its precipitate is used as the test for sulphate ions.
- The Be^{2+} ion is very small and has a very high charge density, This gives beryllium compounds atypical properties:
- they are covalent (e.g. in $BeCl_2$) rather than ionic;
- $Be(OH)_2$ is amphoteric rather than basic;
- Be^{2+} forms complex ions with a maximum co-ordination number of four.

1

a Explain the meaning of the term *periodic trend* when applied to trends in the Periodic Table. (2)

b Explain why atomic radius decreases across Period 3 from sodium to chlorine. (2)

c The table below shows the melting temperatures, T_m, of the Period 3 elements.

Element	Na	Mg	Al	Si	P	S	Cl	Ar
T_m/K	371	923	933	1680	317	392	172	84

Explain the following in terms of structure and bonding.

i) Magnesium has a higher melting temperature than sodium.

ii) Silicon has a very high melting temperature.

iii) Sulphur has a higher melting temperature than phosphorus.

iv) Argon has the lowest melting temperature in Period 3. (8)

NEAB CH01 June 1998 Q6

2 The table below shows the melting points of the Period 3 elements except for silicon.

Element	Na	Mg	Al	Si	P	S	Cl	Ar
m.p./K	371	923	933		317	392	172	84

a Explain in terms of bonding why the melting point of magnesium is higher than that of sodium. (3)

b State the type of bonding between atoms in the element silicon and name the type of structure which silicon forms. (2)

c Predict the approximate melting point of silicon. (1)

d Explain why chlorine has a lower melting point than sulphur. (2)

e Predict the approximate melting point of potassium and give one reason why it is different from that of sodium. (2)

NEAB CH01 June 1997 Q5

3 The diagram below shows the trend in electronegativity of the elements in Period 3.

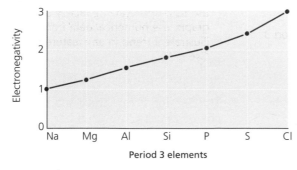

a Define the term *electronegativity*. (2)

b Explain briefly the trend in electronegativity across Period 3. (2)

c State and explain the trend in electronegativity down

Group II. (2)

d Give the type of bonding between phosphorus and oxygen in P_4O_{10}. Explain how the type of bonding in P_4O_{10} can be predicted from electronegativity values. The electronegativity of oxygen is 3.5. (2)

e Write an equation for the reaction of P_4O_{10} with water. (1)

NEAB CH01 February 1996 Q6

4 The graph below shows the trend in first ionisation energy from oxygen to magnesium.

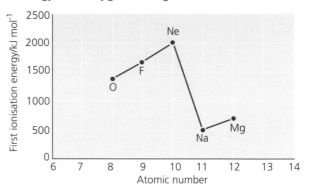

a Using crosses, mark on the graph the first ionisation energies of nitrogen and of aluminium. Label each of your crosses with the symbol for the element. (2)

b Explain why the first ionisation energy of neon is greater than that of sodium. (2)

c Of the elements neon, sodium and magnesium, predict which one has the largest second ionisation energy. Explain your answer. (3)

d Published values of electronegativity are available for oxygen, fluorine, sodium and magnesium but not for neon.

i) Explain why a value of electronegativity is not available for neon.

ii) Of the elements oxygen, fluorine, sodium and magnesium, predict which one has the smallest electronegativity value. (2)

NEAB CH01 June 1999 Q5

KEY SKILLS ASSIGNMENT

Looking for patterns in the Periodic Table

Table A1 Data on selected elements from the Periodic Table			
Element	Melting point/°K	Density/kgm^{-3}	First Ionisation Energy/kJmol^{-1}
Aluminium	933.52	2698	577.4
Barium	1002	3594	502.8
Beryllium	1551	1847.7	899.4
Boron	2573	2340	800.6
Caesium	301.6	1873	375.7
Calcium	1112	1550	589.7
Carbon	3820 (diamond)	3513	1086.2
Gallium	302.9	5907	578.8
Germanium	1210.6	5323	762.1
Indium	429.32	7310	558.3
Lead	600.65	11350	715.5
Lithium	453.7	534	513.3
Magnesium	922	1738	737.7
Potassium	336.8	862	418.8
Rubidium	312.2	1532	403.0
Silicon	1683	2329	786.5
Sodium	371.0	971	495.8
Strontium	1042	2540	549.5
Tellurium	576.7	11850	589.3
Tin	505.1	7130	708.6

1 Table 1 is organised alphabetically by element name. Using data from this page and the Periodic Table, construct the following graphs.

a Melting point against atomic number for Period 3.

b Ionisation energies against atomic number for Group II.

c Atomic number against density for Group I.

For each graph you will need to identify any trends in the graphs and explain these trends using ideas from this chapter.

2 Many computer spreadsheets have built-in graph drawing routines. Select a suitable program and use its graph drawing facility to construct another graph: use numerical data from the table above to illustrate a trend in any feature of the elements in Group V.

5 Energetics

These three photographs all show fuels in use. The space shuttle uses hydrogen, the Brazilian car runs on an ethanol and petrol mixture called gasohol and the athlete is 'burning' sugar in his muscle cells. The basic reactions are the same – a fuel reacting with oxygen to give out useful energy – but obviously the way the reaction is controlled and used is very different.

The branch of chemistry that looks at the way energy is transferred during reactions is called **energetics**. Combustion is the most obvious example of energy transfer by chemical reactions. Engine designers, oil company chemists and personal coaches for athletes all need a good understanding of the energetics of these energy-supplying reactions. This chapter looks at how we can explain the energy transfers that occur in reactions and how we can predict energy yields from new fuels – whether they are hydrogen, petrol and alcohol or a good plate of pasta!

5.1 Energy

The technology of handling energy has probably had more effect on the human race than any other branch of science. The first human beings who learnt how to manage fire started a process that led eventually to their distant descendants walking on the Moon! But what is energy?

Energy is the ability of a system to *do work*. Energy technology is so important because energy can do so many different things. Energy can be used to cook a meal, light a room, transmit a TV picture or contract a muscle or... the list is endless. However, we cannot see the energy – only the things that it *does*. So, energy (which we cannot see) creates effects (which we can see) when it transfers (which we can measure) from one system to another. This explains why energy can do so many different things – it is all down to how it transfers.

You may have heard about different 'forms' of energy, for example heat, light, sound, movement etc. This is probably unhelpful. The forms listed are the *effects* of energy transfer – so transferring energy to a beaker of water can raise its temperature. We

often call this the transfer of 'heat energy'. However, the same energy could produce light in a light bulb or sound from a loudspeaker. For this reason all energy 'forms' are measured in the same units – joules. An older unit, the calorie, is still commonly used to express the energy stored in foods, and you have probably heard of calorie-controlled diets. These are diets that contain measured amounts of energy so that people can lose weight by using more energy than their food supplies. There are 4.18 joules to a calorie.

Energy transfers in chemical reactions can produce a variety of effects. These are often changes in temperature (down as well as up) but can include the release of light and, in muscles, movement. In this chapter we will use the term heat energy for simplicity as the vast majority of reactions we will look at involve changes in temperature. To sum up:

- Energy is the ability to do work.
- We detect the *effects* of energy transfer rather than the energy itself.
- Energy is measured in joules, symbol J.

5.2 Enthalpy change

To understand enthalpy change you need to understand the difference between the system and its surroundings. In the photo above, the **system** is the methane and oxygen, and the carbon dioxide and water produced when methane and oxygen react. The **surroundings** include the metal gas burner, the wok, the food, the air around the system – in fact everything that is not the chemical system. In this reaction, there is a transfer of energy from the system to the surroundings. The methane reacts with oxygen according to the simple equation:

$$CH_4(g) + 2O_2(g) \rightarrow CO_2(g) + H_2O(l)$$

This equation tells us the products formed and the amounts, but tells us nothing about how much heat we can get out of the reaction. To calculate the energy transferred by the reaction, that is the heat produced, we need to use the idea of enthalpy change.

In the laboratory we can carry out a reaction between chemicals in a vessel open to the atmosphere, where any gases produced are allowed to escape, so we can measure the heat energy transferred when the chemicals react at constant pressure. We call this heat energy transfer the **enthalpy change**, and give it the symbol ΔH where Δ means 'change in' and H stands for heat energy. Notice that an enthalpy change is not just any change in heat energy – it must be in a reaction *at constant pressure*. So:

Enthalpy change is the amount of heat energy taken in or given out during any change in a system, provided the system is kept at constant pressure.

Cooking depends on an enthalpy change that releases heat, and it is easy to see the energy change and its effects. However, *all* chemical reactions show enthalpy changes, not just combustion reactions. Methane burning is only one familiar example of a reaction which gives out heat energy. A reaction which gives out heat energy is called an **exothermic** reaction and the enthalpy change is given a negative sign.

Endothermic reactions take in energy, so the vessel in which the reaction takes place gets colder, and the enthalpy change is given a positive sign. Table 1 shows some reactions with negative and positive enthalpy changes.

1 Define these terms.
a energy
b enthalpy change
c exothermic
d endothermic

Table 1 Exothermic and endothermic reactions		
Reaction	**Temperature change**	**Enthalpy change**
Exothermic:		
burning coal	vessel gets hotter	negative
acid + base	solution gets slightly hotter	negative
$Al + Fe_2O_3$	iron and Al_2O_3 formed get very hot	negative
Endothermic:		
NH_4NO_3 dissolving in water	vessel gets cooler	positive
$CH_4 + H_2O$ reacting	CO and H_2 formed are cooler	positive
$NaHCO_3 + HCl$ reacting	$NaCl + H_2O + CO_2$ formed are cooler	positive

5.3 Standard enthalpy changes

Values for an enthalpy change depend on the temperature and pressure at which the reaction is carried out. So that we can compare ΔH values, we must measure enthalpy changes under the same reaction conditions. These are called **standard conditions**. The standard conditions most commonly used are a reaction temperature of 298 K (25 °C) and a pressure of 100 kPa. Sometimes the temperature is included after ΔH.

All reactants must be in their **standard state**. Their standard state is their normal, stable state at 100 kPa and 298 K. For example, the standard state of oxygen is as a gas and sulphur is as a solid. If a substance has two possible standard states, they must be made clear. Water can be $H_2O(l)$ or $H_2O(g)$ under standard conditions and the appropriate state symbols must be used. At 289 K, carbon has two allotropes, diamond and graphite. We must state either C(graphite) or C(diamond). We use the symbol $^\ominus$ to show that an enthalpy change is measured under standard conditions.

The enthalpy change for a reaction under standard conditions at 298 K and 100 kPa, with all substances in their standard state, is called the standard enthalpy change of reaction.

$$2NaOH(aq) + CO_2(g) \rightarrow Na_2CO_3(aq) + H_2O(l)$$
$$\Delta H^\ominus_{298} = -109 \text{ kJ mol}^{-1}$$

This equation tells us that when 2 moles of sodium hydroxide in aqueous solution are reacted with 1 mole of carbon dioxide gas (bubbled through the solution), 1 mole of sodium carbonate in solution and 1 mole of water are formed, and that under standard conditions, 109 kJ of energy are transferred to the surroundings as heat.

Standard enthalpy change of combustion, $\Delta H^\ominus_C$

Combustion reactions are so important that a particular value for enthalpy change is defined specifically for combustion reactions. This is the **standard enthalpy change of combustion**.

The standard enthalpy change of combustion is the enthalpy change when 1 mole of a compound is burnt completely in oxygen under standard conditions (298 K and 100 kPa), all reactants and products being in their standard state.

The reaction that we looked at earlier between methane and oxygen is a combustion reaction, and the standard enthalpy change of combustion of methane is –890 kJ mol⁻¹:

$$CH_4(g) + 2O_2(g) \rightarrow CO_2(g) + H_2O(l)$$
$$\Delta H^\ominus_{C,298} (CH_4) = -890 \text{ kJ mol}^{-1}$$

Other standard enthalpy changes of combustion are given in Table 2. Note that the figures are for the combustion of the main component of the fuels. Each fuel is almost always a mixture and so cannot have a standard enthalpy change of combustion. To overcome this, fuels are often given a joulerific value. The joulerific value is the total heat energy transferred when a measured amount, usually a gram, of the fuel is burnt. This allows people to compare the energy stored in a wide variety of different fuels.

2 Explain this reaction in words, including references to any energy transfers:

$$C_3H_8(g) + 5O_2(g) \rightarrow 3CO_2(g) + 4H_2O(l)$$
$$\Delta H^\ominus_{298} = -2219 \text{ kJ mol}^{-1}$$

Table 2 Standard enthalpy changes of combustion			
Fuel	**Main constituent**	**Formula and standard state**	**$\Delta H^\ominus_C$ of main constituent/kJ mol⁻¹**
hydrogen, compressed	hydrogen	$H_2(g)$	–286
natural gas, liquid (CNG)	90% methane	$CH_4(g)$	–890
liquid petroleum gas (LPG)	95% propane	$C_3H_8(g)$	–2219
methanol	methanol	$CH_3OH(l)$	–726
ethanol	ethanol	$C_2H_5OH(l)$	–1367
petrol	octane	$C_8H_{18}(l)$	–5470

Crude oil, the source of many fuels, cannot have a standard enthalpy change of combustion because it is a mixture. It does burn well though!

3

a Convert the value for hydrogen to a joulerific value in kJ g^{-1}.

b The joulerific value for liquid petroleum gas is –47.5 kJ g^{-1} . Using the data in Table 1, work out if the 5% that is not propane has a higher or lower joulerific value than propane.

Standard enthalpy change of formation, $\Delta H_f^{\ominus}$

Another useful standard enthalpy change is the **standard enthalpy change of formation**.

The standard enthalpy change of formation is the enthalpy change when 1 mole of a compound is formed from its elements under standard conditions (100 kPa and 298 K), all reactants and products being in their standard state.

$$H_2(g) + S(s) + 2O_2(g) \rightarrow H_2SO_4(l)$$
$$\Delta H_f^{\ominus} = -814.0 \text{ kJ mol}^{-1}$$

Note that we would not make sulphuric acid by reacting hydrogen, sulphur and oxygen together in this way.

Unlike the standard enthalpy change of combustion, the value for $\Delta H_f^{\ominus}$ is not a simple, directly-measurable value. We cannot measure the enthalpy *content* of a compound. We can only measure the enthalpy *changes* that happen in reactions. The standard enthalpy change of formation of an *element* is always zero, since no energy is actually needed to produce an element from its elements! $\Delta H_f^{\ominus}$ is used in a variety of energy calculations and can be used to predict the stability of a compound. We will look at $\Delta H_f^{\ominus}$ more closely when we consider Hess's law on page 81.

KEY FACTS

■ Energy is the ability of a system to do work.

■ All chemical reactions involve a transfer of energy. This is often described as an enthalpy change and the transfer of energy is described as a change in heat energy.

■ In an exothermic reaction, heat energy is transferred from the system to the surroundings.

■ In an endothermic reaction, heat energy is transferred from the surroundings to the system.

■ The standard enthalpy change of combustion is the enthalpy change when 1 mole of a compound is burnt completely in oxygen under standard conditions (298 K and 100 kPa), all reactants and products being in their standard state.

■ The standard enthalpy change of formation is the enthalpy change when 1 mole of a compound is formed from its elements under standard conditions (298 K and 100 kPa), all reactants and products being in their standard state.

5.4 Calorimetry

The term **calorimetry** is the process of measuring the enthalpy changes of reactions. We can do experiments in the laboratory to measure enthalpy changes: we measure temperature changes and use specific heat capacities to calculate energy transfers.

The specific heat capacity of a substance is the heat required to raise the temperature of one gram of the substance by 1 kelvin. It is measured in J g⁻¹ K⁻¹.

The energy given out can be used to raise the temperature of a known volume of water. One gram of water needs 4.18 J of energy to raise its temperature by 1 kelvin or 1 degree celsius. The value of 4.18 J g⁻¹ K⁻¹ is the **specific heat capacity** of water.

So to calculate the energy q transferred to a known mass of water in a combustion reaction, we use the equation:

q = mass m of water × specific heat capacity c of water × temperature change ΔT.

$$q = m \times c \times \Delta T$$

4

a A beaker of water increased in temperature by 29.6 °C. How much energy was transferred to the water to produce this rise?

b 400 J of energy raises the temperature of a beaker of water by 25 °C. How much water is in the beaker?

Enthalpy change in neutralisation reactions

The equation in the previous section is used to measure the enthalpy changes of neutralisation reactions between compounds in aqueous solutions.

It is relatively easy to measure temperature changes for reactions in aqueous solution. An expanded polystyrene cup absorbs very little of the heat energy transferred during the reaction and also acts as a good insulator to prevent heat escaping to the surroundings.

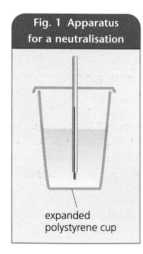

Fig. 1 Apparatus for a neutralisation

expanded polystyrene cup

Example: Measuring the enthalpy change for a neutralisation reaction

1 Measure out 50 cm³ of 1.00 M sodium hydroxide solution into an expanded polystyrene cup.

2 Measure 50 cm³ of 1.00 M hydrochloric acid into a glass beaker.

3 Measure the temperature of the sodium hydroxide solution, and then every minute until the fourth minute. Stir the solution before taking the temperature.

4 At minute 4, add the 50 cm³ of hydrochloric acid. Continue stirring and record the temperature at the fifth minute.

5 Continue taking the temperature every minute until the tenth minute.

Table 3 Sample results	
Time/min	**Temperature/°C**
0	21.0
1	20.5
2	20.0
3	20.0
4	acid added
5	25.6
6	25.1
7	25.0
8	24.8
9	24.7
10	24.6

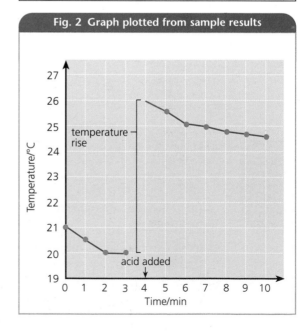

Fig. 2 Graph plotted from sample results

temperature rise

acid added

6   Graph the results and extrapolate backwards to find the temperature rise at 4 minutes when the acid was added.

7   Calculate the heat energy given out:
    heat given out
    = mass × 4.18 × temperature change
    = 100 × 4.18 × 60
    = 25 080 J = 25.08 kJ

8   Calculate moles of reactants:
    moles of acid and alkali
    = volume in litres × molarity
    = 50/1000 × 1
    = 0.05 moles

9   Calculate the molar heat of neutralisation:
    molar heat of neutralisation = joules/moles
    = 25080/0.05
    = –50.2 kJ mol^{-1}

Enthalpy change in combustion reactions

Combustion reactions are exothermic, so the value for their enthalpy change of combustion is always negative.

Polystyrene cups cannot be used for combustion reactions since the flame would destroy the cup. To overcome this problem, chemists often use a small copper container called a calorimeter to hold the reacting material. The container is placed over water whose temperature is recorded. However, not all of the heat from the reaction goes into the water: a lot is lost to the surroundings, and the copper of the calorimeter itself also rises in temperature. Both factors greatly reduce the energy available to raise the temperature of the water. Consequently, this method inevitably underestimates the energy transfer in the combustion reaction.

Example: Measuring the enthalpy change of combustion for ethanol, C_2H_5OH

The equation for the reaction is:

$$C_2H_5OH(l) + 3O_2(g) \rightarrow 2CO_2(g) + 3H_2O(l)$$

1   Weigh the spirit lamp containing ethanol.
2   Set up the equipment as in the diagram. The distance between the spirit burner and the bottom of the calorimeter should be less than 5 cm.
3   Add 100 cm^3 of water to the calorimeter. Stir and take the temperature of the water.
4   Light the wick of the spirit lamp. Keep stirring and taking the temperature.
5   When the temperature has risen by approximately 30 °C, record the temperature accurately and extinguish the spirit lamp.
6   Reweigh the spirit lamp.

Table 4 Sample results
mass of spirit lamp + ethanol at start = 55.56 g
mass of spirit lamp + ethanol at end = 55.02 g
mass of ethanol burnt = 0.54 g
temperature of water at start = 21.0 °C
temperature of water at end = 48.6 °C
temperature rise = 27.6 °C

7   Calculate heat energy given out:
    heat energy
    = mass × 4.18 × temperature change
    = 100 × 4.18 × 27.6
    = 11 536.8 J = 11.54 kJ

8   Calculate number of moles of ethanol burnt:
    M_r ethanol, C_2H_5OH, = 46
    moles of ethanol = mass in g/M_r
    = 0.54/46
    = 0.0117 moles

9   The exothermic reaction has a negative enthalpy change of combustion. Calculate this value:
    ΔH_c = heat energy given out/moles burnt
    = 11.54/0.0117
    ΔH_c = –986 kJ mol^{-1}

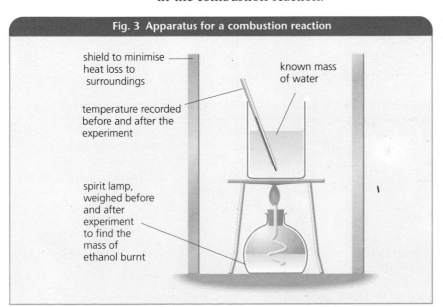

Fig. 3 Apparatus for a combustion reaction

shield to minimise heat loss to surroundings

known mass of water

temperature recorded before and after the experiment

spirit lamp, weighed before and after experiment to find the mass of ethanol burnt

Accuracy of the result

The figures above make no allowance for energy absorbed by the copper calorimeter or for heat lost to the air. We cannot measure heat lost to the air, but let us consider the energy absorbed by the copper calorimeter, given that it weighs 78 g and the specific heat capacity of copper is 0.387 J g⁻¹ K⁻¹. The temperature change is assumed to be the same as for the water, 27.6 °C.

$$\begin{matrix} \text{energy} \\ \text{absorbed} \end{matrix} = \begin{matrix} \text{mass of} \\ \text{calorimeter} \end{matrix} \times \begin{matrix} \text{specific heat} \\ \text{capacity of} \\ \text{copper} \end{matrix} \times \begin{matrix} \text{temperature} \\ \text{change} \end{matrix}$$

$$= 78.0 \times 0.387 \times 27.6$$
$$= 833.1336 \text{ J} = 0.833 \text{ kJ}$$

This amount of heat energy can be added to the result calculated in the Example. The new total is –986.833 kJ mol⁻¹, or –987 kJ mol⁻¹ to three significant figures.

5

a The standard enthalpy change of combustion for ethanol is –1367 kJ mol⁻¹. Suggest why the experimental value is lower.

b Suggest three ways the result obtained by the calorimeter experiment could be made more accurate.

EXTENSION

The bomb calorimeter

In this apparatus, a fuel is ignited by an electrically heated wire in an oxygen atmosphere. The fuel burns and the temperature change in the surrounding water bath is monitored. The air-filled insulation jacket reduces heat loss from the water bath. The bomb calorimeter gives more accurate values than the spirit burner experiment because the heat loss is minimised.

The bomb calorimeter is used by food scientists to calculate the energy value of foods. In our body cells, energy is released from the products of digestion (such as glucose) during respiration. Overall, the process of respiration is similar to combustion, but respiration is much slower because respiration is controlled by biological catalysts called enzymes.

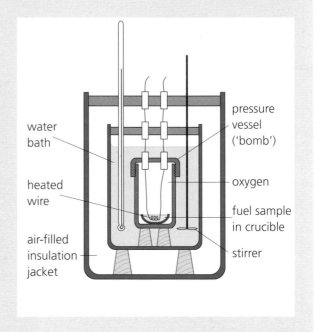

KEY FACTS

■ The specific heat capacity of a substance is the heat required to raise the temperature of one gram of the substance by 1 K. It is measured in J g⁻¹ K⁻¹.

■ The energy transferred to a body can be calculated using the equation:

$$\text{energy transferred} = \text{mass} \times \begin{matrix} \text{specific} \\ \text{heat} \\ \text{capacity} \end{matrix} \times \begin{matrix} \text{temperature} \\ \text{change} \end{matrix}$$

■ Experimental methods for determining enthalpy changes in combustion reactions typically give values lower than the actual values because heat is lost from the system.

5.5 Hess's law

Some enthalpy changes cannot be measured directly in the laboratory, but they can be calculated from known enthalpy changes from other reactions. The method is based on the idea that energy cannot be created or destroyed – only transferred from one system to another. The **law of conservation of energy** summarises this idea. It states that:

Energy cannot be created or destroyed, but only changed from one form to another.

The chemist Germain Henri Hess modified this law in terms of enthalpy changes (remembering that these must occur at constant pressure). **Hess's law** and states that:

The enthalpy change of a reaction depends only on the initial and final states of the reaction and is independent of the route by which the reaction may occur.

Hess's law means that you can never create a reaction that 'makes' energy. Look at Fig. 4 which shows a simple network of reactions, complete with some imaginary ΔH values. Note that these values are for amounts of A, B and C that are not 1 mole, so the unit mol^{-1} is omitted from the values. The network obeys Hess' law, because the enthalpy change from A to B is -500 kJ whether the route is direct or through C.

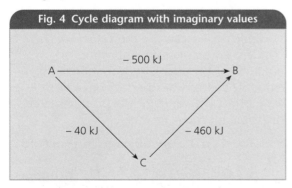

Fig. 4 Cycle diagram with imaginary values

Now let's break Hess's law and make the A → C reaction yield 80 kJ rather than 40 kJ. Why is this a problem?

The direct reaction A → B yields 500 kJ. We can drive B back to A by putting in 500 kJ. If we let A go to B through C, and if A → C were -80 kJ, then 540 kJ mol^{-1} of energy would be produced. We could then use 500 kJ to drive B back to A and come out with 40 kJ

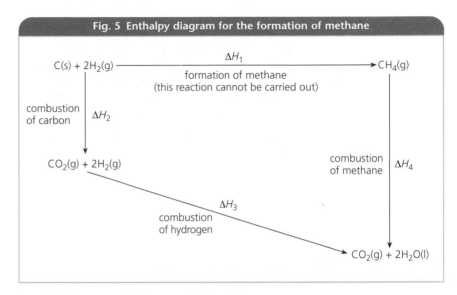

Fig. 5 Enthalpy diagram for the formation of methane

'profit'. This would allow us to 'make' energy by cycling through the reaction over and over again. But this is impossible as it breaks the law of the conservation of energy.

Hess's law also gives a way of calculating enthalpy changes that cannot be determined experimentally. Methane (CH_4) cannot be made directly from its elements, carbon and hydrogen. In Fig. 5, the top line, value ΔH_1, is the unknown step in the sequence of reactions that takes carbon and hydrogen all the way to carbon dioxide and water. Since we can determine experimentally the enthalpy changes for combustion of carbon, ΔH_2, hydrogen, ΔH_3, and methane, ΔH_4, we can work out the value of the unknown energy step for methane formation from:

$$\Delta H_1 = \Delta H_2 + \Delta H_3 - \Delta H_4$$

Example: Using Hess's law to calculate enthalpy of formation

Construct a diagram for the reactions and values given in Table 5. The diagram should show the enthalpy changes and clearly identify the unknown value. Then calculate

Table 5 Reactions for the formation of methane from its elements	
Equation	**Value of $\Delta H^{\ominus}$/kJ mol^{-1}**
$C(s) + O_2(g) \rightarrow CO_2(g)$	ΔH_1 -393
$2H_2(g) + O_2(g) \rightarrow 2H_2O(l)$	ΔH_2 -286
$CH_4(g) + 2O_2(g) \rightarrow CO_2(g) + 2H_2O(l)$	ΔH_3 -890
$C(s) + 2H_2(g) \rightarrow a\ CH_4(g)$	ΔH_4 unknown

the enthalpy change of formation of methane, balancing the number of moles used.

1 Look at Table 5 and work out an appropriate sequence for the reactions, so that there are two routes in the network.

2 Draw a stepped diagram like Fig. 6, using your routes for the reactions. Include each equation at an appropriate level. For exothermic reactions, use arrows going down (endothermic reactions use arrows going up).

3 Insert the values from the table. For each, indicate whether the standard enthalpy is of formation or of combustion. Add chemical symbols to indicate the substance involved.

4 To calculate the enthalpy change of formation of methane, ΔH_4, work out the equation for enthalpies:

From Hess's law:

$$\Delta H_1 + \Delta H_2 = \Delta H_3 + \Delta H_4$$

$$\Delta H_4 = \Delta H_1 + \Delta H_2 - \Delta H_3$$

5 Balance the equations: note that the equation for the combustion of hydrogen has 2 moles of hydrogen. Therefore, the value in the right column, for 1 mole, has to be doubled.

Inserting the values:

$$\Delta H_4 = -393 + (2 \times -286) - (-890)$$
$$\Delta H_4 = 75$$
So, by Hess's law, the enthalpy of formation of methane, ΔH_f° is -75 kJ mol^{-1}.

6 Calculate ΔH_f° of the following.

a ethyne, $C_2H_2(g)$

b ethanol, $C_2H_5OH(l)$
ΔH_C° carbon(s) = -393 kJ mol^{-1}
ΔH_C° hydrogen(g) = -286 kJ mol^{-1}
ΔH_C° ethyne(g) = -1300 kJ mol^{-1}
ΔH_C° ethanol(l) = -1367 kJ mol^{-1}

7 Methanol can be produced from methane by a two-step process:
Step 1: $CH_4(g) + H_2O(g) \rightarrow CO(g) + 3H_2(g)$
Step 2: $CO(g) + 2H_2(g) \rightarrow CH_3OH(g)$

Use the following enthalpies of combustion to calculate the enthalpy change for each of the two steps. ΔH_C°:
$CH_4(g)$ -808 kJ mol^{-1},
$CO(g)$ -283 kJ mol^{-1},
$H_2(g)$ -245 kJ mol^{-1},
$CH_3OH(g)$ -671 kJ mol^{-1}

Standard enthalpy change of reaction

In the reaction of methane with oxygen to give carbon dioxide and water, the methane and oxygen are the reactants and carbon dioxide and water are the products. We can calculate the **standard enthalpy change of the reaction**, ΔH_r°, by taking the sum of the standard enthalpies of formation of the products, $\Sigma\Delta H_f^\circ$(products), and subtracting the sum of the standard enthalpies of formation of the reactants, $\Sigma\Delta H_f^\circ$(reactants). This is much simpler as an equation, with the symbol sigma, Σ, meaning 'sum of'. So for any reaction:

Standard enthalpy change of reaction ΔH_r°

$$= \Sigma\Delta H_f^\circ \text{(products)} - \Sigma\Delta H_f^\circ \text{(reactants)}$$

Similarly, we can use the values for the standard enthalpies of combustion of products and reactants to work out standard enthalpy changes of reaction, but this time, we subtract the value for the products from the value for the reactants:

Standard enthalpy change of reaction ΔH_r°

$$= \Sigma\Delta H_C^\circ \text{(reactants)} - \Sigma\Delta H_C^\circ \text{(products)}$$

This is easier to understand when you consider that some reactions of formation are the reverse of the reactions of combustion, as is the case for carbon dioxide and water, seen in the next section on photosynthesis. Whenever you carry out calculations of this kind, always work from basic principles and consider what type of reaction a particular value applies to.

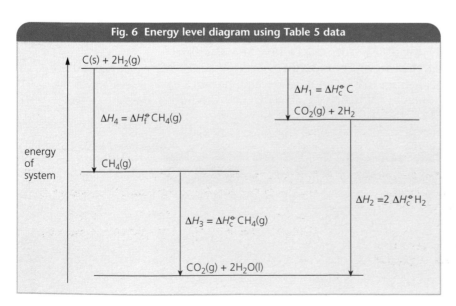

Fig. 6 Energy level diagram using Table 5 data

$C(s) + 2H_2(g)$

$\Delta H_1 = \Delta H_C^\circ$ C

$CO_2(g) + 2H_2$

$\Delta H_4 = \Delta H_f^\circ$ $CH_4(g)$

energy of system

$CH_4(g)$

$\Delta H_2 = 2 \Delta H_C^\circ$ H_2

$\Delta H_3 = \Delta H_C^\circ$ $CH_4(g)$

$CO_2(g) + 2H_2O(l)$

Standard enthalpy change for photosynthesis

We can use Hess's law to calculate the enthalpy change of a reaction by using values in data books for the enthalpies of formation of reactants and products. For example, we can calculate the overall standard enthalpy change for photosynthesis. The reaction of photosynthesis takes place in all green plants where glucose is synthesised from carbon dioxide and water using energy from sunlight. The reaction equation is:

$$6CO_2(g) + 6H_2O(l) \rightarrow C_6H_{12}O_6(aq) + 6O_2 \quad (\Delta H_1)$$

We cannot directly measure this enthalpy change of formation, but data books will tell us the enthalpies of formation from their elements of carbon dioxide, water and glucose. These are the reactions that match the equation above:

formation of carbon dioxide:
$$6C(s) + 6O_2(g) \rightarrow 6CO_2(g) \quad \Delta H_f^\circ = -393.5 \text{ kJ mol}^{-1}$$
formation of water:
$$6H_2(g) + 3O_2(g) \rightarrow 6H_2O \quad \Delta H_f^\circ = -285.8 \text{ kJ mol}^{-1}$$
formation of glucose:
$$6C(s) + 6H_2(g) + 3O_2(g) \rightarrow C_6H_{12}O_6$$
$$\Delta H_f^\circ = -1273.3 \text{ kJ mol}^{-1}$$

We know from Hess's law that the overall enthalpy change in going from the constituent elements to glucose must be the same as the enthalpy change in going from the elements to carbon dioxide and water and then to glucose. With this information we can draw the energy cycle for the reactions leading to photosynthesis shown in Fig. 7. ΔH_1 is the standard enthalpy change for photosynthesis. This is the value we are calculating.

$\Delta H_1 + \Delta H_2 + \Delta H_3 = \Delta H_4$.
Therefore:
$$\Delta H_1 = \Delta H_4 - \Delta H_2 - \Delta H_3 \quad (1)$$

$$\Delta H_2 = 6 \times -393.5$$
$$= -2361 \text{ kJ mol}^{-1}$$
$$\Delta H_3 = 6 \times -285.8$$
$$= -1714.8 \text{ kJ mol}^{-1}$$
$$\Delta H_2 + \Delta H_3 = -4075.8 \text{ kJ mol}^{-1}$$

$$\Delta H_4 = -1273.3 \text{ kJ mol}^{-1}$$

Note that the ΔH_f° of oxygen is 0 by definition. From equation (1):

$$\Delta H_1 = -1273.3 - (-4075.8) \text{ kJ mol}^{-1}$$
So ΔH_f°(photosynthesis) = 2802.5 kJ mol^{-1}

8 Calculate the enthalpy change of formation for propane using standard enthalpies of combustion and Hess's law.

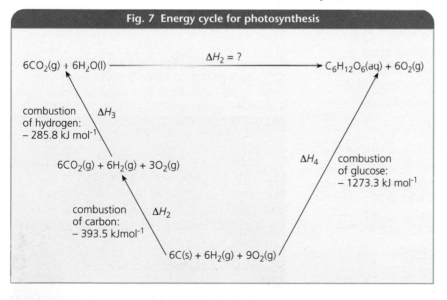

Fig. 7 Energy cycle for photosynthesis

$6CO_2(g) + 6H_2O(l)$ ———— $\Delta H_2 = ?$ ————→ $C_6H_{12}O_6(aq) + 6O_2(g)$

combustion of hydrogen: -285.8 kJ mol^{-1} $\quad \Delta H_3$

$6CO_2(g) + 6H_2(g) + 3O_2(g)$

combustion of carbon: -393.5 kJmol^{-1} $\quad \Delta H_2$

$6C(s) + 6H_2(g) + 9O_2(g)$

ΔH_4 / combustion of glucose: -1273.3 kJ mol^{-1}

KEY FACTS

- Hess's law states that the enthalpy change of a reaction depends only on the initial and final states of the reaction and is independent of the route by which the reaction may occur.

- Hess's law allows chemist to work out enthalpy changes for reactions that cannot be measured directly in the laboratory.

- Standard enthalpy change of reaction $\Delta H_r^\circ = \dfrac{\Sigma \Delta H_f^\circ}{\text{(products)}} - \dfrac{\Sigma \Delta H_f^\circ}{\text{(reactants)}}$

- Standard enthalpy change of reaction $\Delta H_r^\circ = \dfrac{\Sigma \Delta H_c^\circ}{\text{(reactants)}} - \dfrac{\Sigma \Delta H_c^\circ}{\text{(products)}}$

5.6 Bond enthalpies

When chemical reactions occur, bonds between atoms are broken and new bonds are made. The amount of energy needed to break a particular bond is called its **bond enthalpy**.

The standard molar enthalpy change of bond dissociation, $\Delta H^{\ominus}_{diss}$, is the enthalpy change when one mole of bonds of the same type are broken in gaseous molecules under standard conditions.

The simplest example is the energy needed to break apart a hydrogen molecule into its two atoms:

$$H—H(g) \rightarrow H(g) + H(g)$$

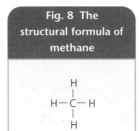

In this case, $\Delta H^{\ominus}_{diss}$ is 436 kJ mol^{-1}. All hydrogen molecules are identical and there is no difference between the atoms in the molecules. The bond that breaks is always the same and in the same environment.

Looking at methane we find four equal C—H bonds. But as soon as we start to pull apart the methane molecule, the remaining C—H bonds exist in a different environment: the first C—H bond is broken in a CH$_4$ molecule, but the second C—H bond is broken from a CH$_3$ fragment. The third bond to break is in a CH$_2$ fragment. Since the energy needed to break the bonds is affected by the environment of the bond, the eventual figure for the enthalpy change for the dissociation of C—H bonds in methane will be an average of four values. How much does this affect the value?

When methane is broken into its atoms, 1664 kJ mol^{-1} of energy is absorbed:

$$CH_4(g) \rightarrow C(g) + 4H(g) \quad \Delta H^{\ominus}_{diss} = 1664 \text{ kJ mol}^{-1}$$

This process involves breaking four C—H bonds, so the mean C—H bond enthalpy in methane is 1664/4 kJ mol^{-1}, or 416 kJ mol^{-1}. We write this as:

$$\Delta H^{\ominus}_{diss} \text{ (C—H in CH}_4) = 416 \text{ kJ mol}^{-1}$$

However, considering the first part of this reaction, to break one bond only:

$$CH_4(g) \rightarrow CH_3(g) + H(g) \quad \Delta H^{\ominus}_{diss} = 423 \text{ kJ mol}^{-1}$$

The value of 423 kJ mol^{-1} is the true bond dissociation enthalpy for the first C—H bond in a gaseous methane molecule. This is clearly different from the mean value of 416 kJ mol^{-1}, and is due to the changing environment of the C—H bond as the methane molecule is pulled apart.

Since bond enthalpies vary with the environment, it is often more useful to use mean bond energies when applying data to other compounds. Note that the values for C—H bonds in data books are not just an average of the values for methane but an average of C—H bonds in a wide variety of molecules, and is often given as 413 kJ mol^{-1}. This means the value is adequate for most situations, but remember that they are only approximations.

9 Water is H—O—H.
Breaking the first O—H bond:
$$H—O—H(g) \rightarrow H(g) + O—H(g)$$
$$\Delta H^{\ominus}_{diss} = 502 \text{ kJ mol}^{-1}$$
Breaking the second O-H bond
$$O—H(g) \rightarrow O(g) + H(g)$$
$$\Delta H^{\ominus}_{diss} = 427 \text{ kJ mol}^{-1}$$

a Calculate the mean bond enthalpy likely to be found in data books for the O—H bond.

b Explain any difference between the value you have calculated from the example above and the actual value in a data book.

Methane burns with a pale blue flame to give out 890.3 kJ mol^{-1}

Using bond enthalpies to calculate the enthalpy change of a reaction

So far in this chapter, we have calculated enthalpy changes from experiments and by using Hess's law. Another way to calculate the enthalpy change of a reaction is to consider which bonds are broken and which are made. When bonds are broken, energy is required, so breaking bonds is endothermic. When bonds are made, energy is released, so making bonds is exothermic. The enthalpy change we can measure in a combustion reaction, for example, is the result of the breaking and making of all of the bonds involved. As for all other enthalpy values, average bond enthalpies are measured in kJ mol^{-1}. They are given in data books as positive values, for the endothermic process of breaking bonds. When considering the remaking of bonds, which are exothermic processes, you need to give the values a negative sign

Example: Calculating bond enthalpies in the combustion of ethanol

These are the steps required to work out the enthalpy changes when bonds in ethanol are broken in combustion and reformed in the products.

1 Write out the equation using molecular structures:

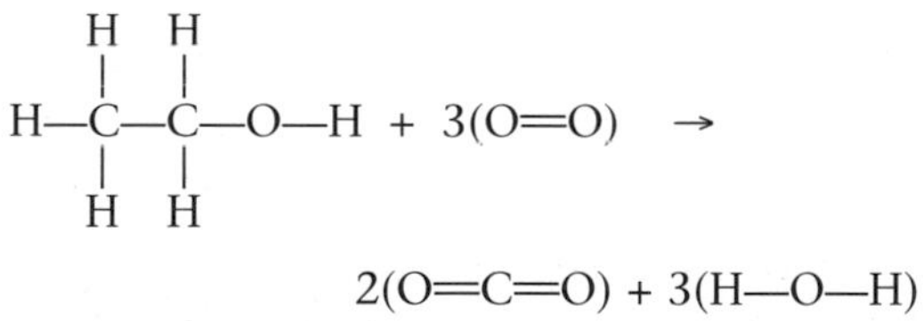

$$\begin{array}{cc} \text{H} & \text{H} \\ | & | \\ \text{H}\!-\!\text{C}\!-\!\text{C}\!-\!\text{O}\!-\!\text{H} + 3(\text{O}\!=\!\text{O}) & \rightarrow \\ | & | \\ \text{H} & \text{H} \end{array}$$

$$2(\text{O}\!=\!\text{C}\!=\!\text{O}) + 3(\text{H}\!-\!\text{O}\!-\!\text{H})$$

2 For each reactant, list the type of bonds broken to give its atoms and count the number of each type. Look up the average bond enthalpy for each bond type and calculate the enthalpy change. Do this for bonds broken and then for bonds made.

These are the enthalpy changes when bonds are broken in kJ mol^{-1}. As endothermic processes, the values are positive.
5 × (C—H) = 5 × 413 = 2065
3 × (O=O) = 3 × 498 = 1494
1 × (C—O) = 1 × 360 = 360
1 × (O—H) = 1 × 463 = 463
Total enthalpy change = 4382 kJ mol^{-1}

These are the enthalpy change when bonds are formed in kJ mol^{-1}. As exothermic processes, the values are negative.
4 × C=O = 4 × –743 = –2972
6 × (O—H) = 6 × –463 = –2778
Total enthalpy change = –5750 kJ mol^{-1}

Fig. 9 is a diagram of energy levels for the molecules and atoms at different steps in the reaction. It shows that the products are at a lower energy level than the reactants, since energy is produced as heat in the reaction, so overall the enthalpy change is negative.

3 Calculate the overall enthalpy change and convert this into a standard enthalpy change
Overall enthalpy change
= 4382 – 5750 = –1368 kJ mol^{-1}
This is the theoretical standard enthalpy change of combustion for ethanol.

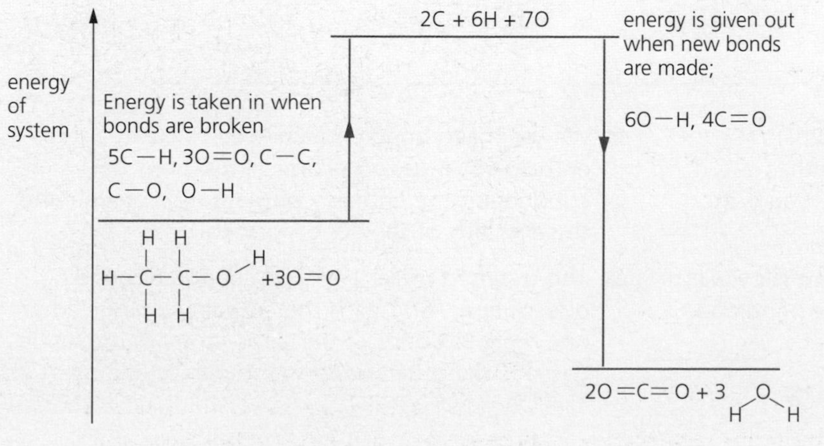

Table 6 Some mean bond enthalpies/kJ mol^{-1}			
H—H	436	H—C	413
C—C	348	H—O	463
C=O	743	C—O	360
O—O	146	O=O	498

10 Use the mean bond enthalpies in Table 6 to calculate the enthalpy change of combustion for burning propane in oxygen.

Fig. 9 Bond enthalpies for combustion of ethanol

energy of system

Energy is taken in when bonds are broken
5C—H, 3O=O, C—C, C—O, O—H

2C + 6H + 7O

energy is given out when new bonds are made;

6O—H, 4C=O

H H
| |
H—C—C—O^H +3O=O
| |
H H

2O=C=O + 3 O
H   H

APPLICATION A   Alcool

In 1975, Brazil set up the world's biggest programme to produce an alternative fuel, known as Alcool. Brazil does not have sufficient oil reserves for its needs, but it does have a climate ideal for growing sugar cane. The sugar cane is used to produce ethanol, C_2H_5OH, by fermentation, and the ethanol is either blended with petrol or used neat as car fuel.

Ethanol is a bio-fuel, a fuel made from biomass, which is vegetable matter. The source is renewable because we can easily grow more sugar cane to replace that used in fuel production. Fuels such as oil and coal are non-renewable. It would take millions of years to replace the oil and coal we are using today. So, effectively, once the fuels have been used they have gone forever.

Both petrol, whose main ingredient is octane, and ethanol produce carbon dioxide when burnt. Carbon dioxide is a greenhouse gas which increases global warming. The equations for combustion reactions for ethanol and octane are:

$$C_2H_5OH + 3O_2 \rightarrow 2CO_2 + 3H_2O$$
$$C_8H_{18} + 12\tfrac{1}{2}O_2 \rightarrow 8CO_2 + 9H_2O$$

1 Use ΔH_f values from your data book to calculate the ΔH_c for ethanol and octane.

You have worked out the enthalpy change of combustion for each fuel.

2
a Which fuel produces more energy in combustion? To the nearest whole number, how many times more energy does it produce?

To get the same energy from the less energetic fuel, you can multiply its combustion equation by this number.

3
a How many moles of carbon dioxide does it produce now?
b For the same energy output, compare the number of moles of carbon dioxide produced by ethanol and by octane.
c Explain why environmental scientists concerned about global warming prefer ethanol fuel to petrol.

4 Gasohol is a mixture of petrol and alcohol. Why is it impossible to quote a ΔH_c for gasohol?

KEY FACTS

■ In a diatomic molecule, the molar enthalpy change of bond dissociation is the enthalpy change for breaking one mole of like bonds in gaseous molecules.

■ In polyatomic molecules, the bond enthalpy will depend upon the environment of the bond and the molecule itself.

■ Mean bond enthalpy values are used for polyatomic molecules.

■ We use mean bond enthalpies to calculate enthalpy changes for chemical reactions by considering the enthalpy of the bonds broken and the enthalpy of the bonds formed.

■ The standard molar enthalpy change of bond dissociation, $\Delta H^{\ominus}_{diss}$, is the enthalpy change when one mole of bonds of the same type are broken in gaseous molecules under standard conditions.

EXAMINATION QUESTIONS

1 Below are some standard enthalpy changes including the standard enthalpy of combustion of nitroglycerine, $C_3H_5N_3O_9$

$\frac{1}{2}N_2(g) + O_2(g) \rightarrow NO_2(g)$ $\Delta H_f^\ominus = +34$ kJ mol^{-1}

$C(s) + O_2(g) \rightarrow CO_2(g)$ $\Delta H_f^\ominus = -394$ kJ mol^{-1}

$H_2(g) + \frac{1}{2}O_2(g) \rightarrow H_2O(g)$ $\Delta H_f^\ominus = -242$ kJ mol^{-1}

$C_3H_5N_3O_9(l) + \frac{11}{4}O_2(g) \rightarrow$
$3CO_2(g) + \frac{5}{2}H_2O(g) + 3NO_2(g)$
$\Delta H_c^\ominus = -1540$ kJ mol^{-1}

a Standard enthalpy of formation is defined using the term *standard state*. What does the term *standard state* mean? (2)

b Use the standard enthalpy changes given above to calculate the standard enthalpy of formation of nitroglycerine. (4)

c Calculate the enthalpy change for the following decomposition of nitroglycerine.
$C_3H_5N_3O_9(l) \rightarrow$
$3CO_2(g) + \frac{5}{2}H_2O(g) + \frac{3}{2}N_2(g) + \frac{1}{4}O_2(g)$ (3)

d Suggest one reason why the reaction in part (c) occurs rather than combustion when a bomb containing nitroglycerine explodes on impact. (1)

e An alternative reaction for the combustion of hydrogen, leading to liquid water, is given below.
$H_2(g) + \frac{1}{2}O_2(g) \rightarrow H_2O(l)$ $\Delta H^\ominus = -286$ kJ mol^{-1}
Calculate the enthalpy change for the process
$H_2O(l) \rightarrow H_2O(g)$ and explain the sign of ΔH in your answer. (2)

NEAB CH01 March 1999 Q4

2 The tables below contain data which are needed to answer the questions.

Name	hydrazine	ethane
Formula of compound	N_2H_4	C_2H_6
Boiling temperature /K	387	184

Formula and state of compound	$C_2H_6(g)$	$CO_2(g)$	$H_2O(l)$
Standard enthalpy of formation (at 298 K)/kJ mol^{-1}	−85	−394	−286

a Suggest why hydrazine has a much higher boiling temperature than ethane. (2)

b When liquid hydrazine burns in oxygen it forms nitrogen and water. The standard enthalpy change for this reaction when one mole of hydrazine forms water in the liquid state is −624 kJ mol^{-1}.

i) Write a balanced equation for the combustion of hydrazine in oxygen.

ii) Calculate the standard enthalpy of formation of liquid hydrazine. (4)

c i) Write an equation for the complete combustion of ethane.

ii) Use the appropriate standard enthalpies of formation to calculate the standard enthalpy of combustion of ethane. (4)

d Suggest one reason why hydrazine is more suitable than ethane for use as a rocket fuel. (1)

NEAB CH01 June 1998 Q5

3

a In $\Delta H^{\ominus}$, what does the symbol $^{\ominus}$ indicate? (1)

b Some mean bond enthalpies are given below.

Bond	C–C	H–H	Cl–Cl	C–H
Mean bond enthalpy/kJ mol^{-1}	348	436	242	412

i) Write down the equation for the reaction used to define the bond enthalpy of a chlorine–chlorine bond. Include state symbols.

ii) Why is the term *mean bond enthalpy* used in the table instead of just *bond enthalpy*?

iii) Use the data above to predict what happens first when a sample of propane, C_3H_8, is cracked in the absence of air and explain your prediction. (5)

c Use the following data to calculate the standard enthalpy of formation of propane.
$C_3H_8(g) + 5O_2(g) \rightarrow 3CO_2(g) + 4H_2O(l)$
$\Delta H^{\ominus} = -2220$ kJ mol^{-1}
$H_2(g) + \frac{1}{2}O_2(g) \rightarrow H_2O(l)$ $\Delta H^{\ominus} = -286$ kJ mol^{-1}
$C(s) + O_2(g) \rightarrow CO_2(g)$ $\Delta H^{\ominus} = -394$ kJ mol^{-1}
(4)

NEAB CH01 March 1998 Q4

4

a Define the term *standard enthalpy of formation* ($\Delta H_f^\ominus$). (3)

b Give the chemical equation for which the enthalpy change is the standard enthalpy of formation of methane. (2)

c Use the following data to calculate a value for the enthalpy of formation of methane.
$C(s) + O_2(g) \rightarrow CO_2(g)$ $\Delta H = -394$ kJ mol^{-1}
$H_2(g) + \frac{1}{2}O_2(g) \rightarrow H_2O(g)$ $\Delta H = -242$ kJ mol^{-1}
$CH_4(g) + 2O_2(g) \rightarrow CO_2(g) + 2H_2O(g)$
$\Delta H = -802$ kJ mol^{-1} (3)

d Use the following data to calculate mean bond enthalpy values for the C–H and the C–C bonds.
$CH_4(g) \rightarrow C(g) + 4H(g)$ $\Delta H = 1648$ kJ mol^{-1}
$C_2H_6(g) \rightarrow 2C(g) + 6H(g)$ $\Delta H = 2820$ kJ mol^{-1}
(3)

NEAB CH01 June 1995 Q4

5

a Write a chemical equation, including state symbols, for the reaction which is used to define the enthalpy of formation of one mole of aluminium chloride ($AlCl_3$). (2)

b State the additional condition necessary if the enthalpy change for this reaction is to be the standard enthalpy of formation. $\Delta H_f^\ominus$, at 298 K. (1)

c Use the standard enthalpies of formation given below to calculate a value for the standard enthalpy change for the following reaction.

$AlCl_3(s) + 6H_2O(l) \rightarrow AlCl_3.6H_2O(s)$ (3)

	$AlCl_3(s)$	$H_2O(l)$	$AlCl_3.6H_2O(s)$
$\Delta H_f^{\ominus}$/kJ mol^{-1}	−695	−286	−2680

NEAB CH01 February 1996 Q5

6

a Define the term standard molar enthalpy change of formation. (3)

b State *Hess's law*. (1)

c The equation below shows the reaction between ammonia and fluorine.

$NH_3(g) + 3F_2(g) \rightarrow 3HF(g) + NF_3(g)$

  i) Use the standard molar enthalpy change of formation ($\Delta H_f^{™}$) data below to calculate the molar enthalpy change for this reaction.

Compound	NH_3	HF	NF_3
$\Delta H_f^{\ominus}$/kJ mol^{-1}	−46	−269	−114

(4)

  ii) Use the average bond enthalpy data below to calculate a value for the molar enthalpy change for the same reaction between ammonia and fluorine.

$NH_3(g) + 3F_2(g) \rightarrow 3HF(g) + NF_3(g)$

Bond	N–H	F–F	H–F	N–F
Average bond enthalpy/kJ mol^{-1}	388	158	562	272

(3)

d The answer you have calculated in (c) (i) is regarded as being the more reliable value. Suggest why this is so. (3)

AEB Module Paper 6 Summer 1997 Q2

Identifying bias in a scientific article

When someone writes an article, they want to promote their ideas and usually have a target audience in mind. This can affect the style and content of the article - in other words, it can be biased.

Scientists often pride themselves on the fact that their writing is 'objective' - but you need to be aware that a science-based article can be biased. Think about these questions when reading an article:

■ What is the background of the author - do they work for a particular organisation which might have a vested interest in putting a particular view forward?

■ If 'evidence' for a point of view is presented - does the author quote where it comes from?

■ Do phrases like 'Everyone knows that' or 'It's a well-known fact that' keep appearing without any idea of where these 'facts' come from?

■ Are there attempts in the writing to name drop in order to impress the reader - so-called 'appeals to authority' which you may never have heard of before?

Following on from this tactic, some authors will put in words like 'obviously', 'clearly' or 'it can easily be shown that' in order to appeal to the reader's vanity (implying that you are as clever as the author is trying to be.)

■ Is there an over-reliance on technical jargon which the reader cannot question and has to accept?

■ Does the author try to belittle any opponents by resorting to sarcasm or innuendo? It is fairly easy to imply a low opinion of another person by making an amusing description of their case.

■ Does the author make assumptions in arguments? Even worse, are these assumptions then used to build a case?

■ Are the fears or prejudices of the reader being played on to win an argument? This is most typically found by looking at the type of publication the article appears in, where the readership is expected to have certain ideas. Having your own prejudices confirmed is a technique used by polititians who are trying to win your vote.

■ Does the author use rhetorical questions, such as: Do we really want to see more beautiful countryside disappear? This tactic encourages the reader to provide the answer subconsciously and so be more receptive to any arguments that follow.

■ Environmental issues like gobal warming and fuel use can often bring out the worst in journalists! The temptation to be sensationalist and to campaign rather than to report facts can be impossible to resist.

1 Your task is to locate chemistry based articles about fuel use and the environment which illustrate five of the tactics outlined above. You may use articles from magazines, newspapers, advertising literature or from the Internet.

It may be possible to find an article which illustrates all five examples in the same article or you may have to use examples from several articles.

For each tactic, provide the evidence by highlighting the parts of the article/s, and producing a written explanation of why you think this tactic is being used.

Remember to quote :
where the article is from,
who wrote it,
who published it and the date of publication.

6 Reaction kinetics

Sell-by dates on foods are the norm nowadays. They ensure that we don't have to put up with sour milk or stale bread. Yet it may be a bit over the top when even bottled water has a sell-by date!

Like milk and bread, strawberries and butter are called perishable foods because they change substantially as they age. We sense this change when the strawberries grow mould and the butter tastes rancid. The changes are caused by numerous reactions. It is no good blocking one or two reactions because there are far too many of them. What we need to preserve the food is to stop all the reactions, or at least slow them down. The simplest way is to do this is to cool the food.

Chill cabinets in supermarkets keep the temperature of the foods below 10 °C. This extends the life of perishable foods considerably. The table shows the effect of temperature on milk becoming sour. But keeping food cool costs money – and the cooler you keep it the more it costs. The cost has to be weighed up against the costs of keeping it at a higher temperature and risking some food going off before it is sold. Of course, customers are not pleased to be sold rotten food!

Storage temperature/°C	Time until milk sours/hours
0	96
5	48
10	24
15	15
20	6
25	4

6.1 The rates of chemical reactions

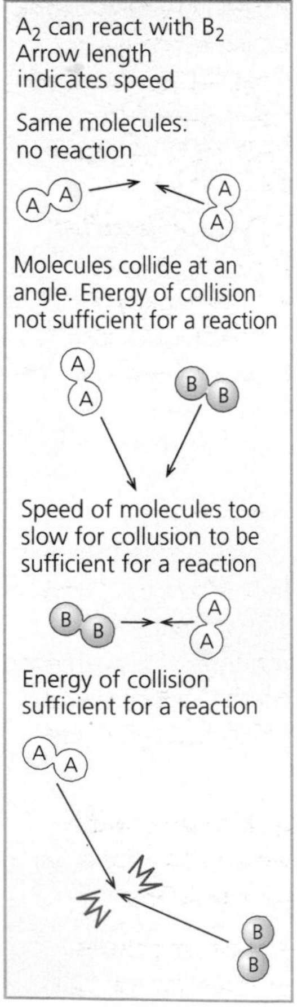

The chemical reactions that cause milk to go sour obey the same rules as all other reactions. Reaction rate is measured as amount of reactant used up or product made in a certain time, often per second. The rate at which the reactions occur is not fixed - it changes according to conditions. In this chapter we look at the factors that affect the rates of all chemical reactions. These are:

- the temperature of the reactants
- the concentration of the reactants and products
- the surface area of reactants
- the presence of any catalysts

We will look at each of these factors in turn and see how they affect the rates of reactions and how they can be used to control reaction rates. But first we look at individual molecules in gases, and what makes them likely to react.

Collisions between molecules

For a reaction to occur between molecules, they must collide. The explanation of reactions as the result of collisions between particles is called **collision theory**. In a gas, molecules are in constant motion and constantly colliding with each other and with the walls of their container. For example, in one cubic centimetre of a gas at atmospheric pressure and room temperature, there are about 10^{27} collisions every second. Because of the connection between particle movement and reactions, the study of reaction rates is called **kinetics**, from the Greek word meaning to move.

If all collisions in reacting gases caused a reaction, then reactions would be over in microseconds. But, clearly, not all collisions actually result in a reaction. For example, oxygen and nitrogen molecules can react, yet they coexist in the air around us without reacting. Whether or not a reaction occurs depends on whether the energy of the collisions is great enough.

Fig. 1 shows collisions in two types of gas molecules which are able to react together. The energy of head-on collisions is greater than the energy of collisions at an angle, so head-on collisions are more likely than angular collisions produce a reaction. The energy of their collisions depends on both the angle at which they collide and the speed at which they are moving. The speed in turn depends on how much energy a molecule possesses - all molecules have some energy. We now look at energy in more detail.

Fig. 1 Colliding molecules

A_2 can react with B_2
Arrow length indicates speed

Same molecules: no reaction

Molecules collide at an angle. Energy of collision not sufficient for a reaction

Speed of molecules too slow for collusion to be sufficient for a reaction

Energy of collision sufficient for a reaction

6.2 Maxwell–Boltzmann energy distribution

Temperature and energy

We use temperature as an indication of the amount of energy of the particles in matter. For instance, the temperature of a gas sample tells us something about the average amount of energy that each molecule of the gas possesses. Taking the gas sample as a whole, whether a reaction takes place or not depends on:

- the energy of the colliding particles,
- the number of collisions.

Let us look at this in more detail.

This fire was caused by a gas leak. The very fast reaction that began it took only a second or so

Reactions slow down when temperatures are lowered, so materials at Scott's base in Antarctica will decay very slowly

At a given temperature, the molecules do not all have the same energy, so they are moving at different speeds. At any instant in time, a tiny fraction of molecules have very high energies: these move fastest. A tiny fraction have very low energies: these move very slowly. But most molecules have energies between the two extremes. The distribution of energies amongst molecules was calculated statistically by the Scots physicist James Clerk Maxwell in 1859, and was applied by the Austrian physicist Ludwig Eduard Boltzmann in 1871. The result is the **Maxwell–Boltzmann distribution of molecular energies**. The distribution curve for molecular energies of molecules in a gas sample at a particular temperature, T_1, is shown in Fig. 2. Note that no molecules have zero energy.

Activation energy

We can use the Maxwell–Boltzmann distribution to explain why only a certain proportion of collisions results in a reaction at a particular temperature. For a reaction to take place, the minimum energy of a collision between molecules is called the **activation energy**, E_A, measured in kilojoules per mole, kJ mol^{-1}:

Activation energy is the minimum energy with which particles need to collide to cause a reaction.

For most reactions, the most important factor that determines how fast the reaction

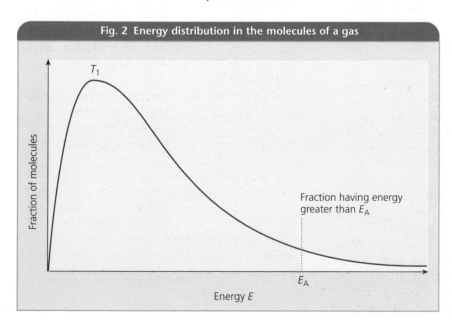

Fig. 2 Energy distribution in the molecules of a gas

Fraction of molecules (vertical axis)

T_1

Fraction having energy greater than E_A

E_A

Energy E

will occur is its activation energy. Each reaction has its own activation energy, and different reactions have different activation energies. At the same temperature, a reaction with a low activation energy goes faster than one with a high activation energy.

Only the proportion of molecules above the threshold activation energy value have sufficient energy to react when they collide. Fig. 2 shows that at T_1 the fraction of molecules with sufficient energy to react is small.

As the temperature rises, the energy distribution moves to the right as shown by the curve for T_2 in Fig. 3(a). The total area underneath the curves stays the same because we are dealing with the same total number of molecules. However, at higher temperatures, more molecules have higher energies and so

more molecules have energies equal to or above the activation energy. Therefore more collisions result in a reaction.

Now we look at the energy of molecules in a sample of gas at two widely differing temperatures. Fig. 3(b) shows typical energy distribution curves for a gas at T_1 of 25 °C (298 K) and at T_2 which is about 4.5 times higher, namely 1067 °C (1340 K).

Molecules would have no energy if they could exist at absolute zero temperature. We take the increase in energy to be roughly proportional to increase in absolute temperature. The peaks in the graph represent the energy possessed by the maximum proportion of molecules in the gas sample. The peak for the T_2 curve has an energy about 4.5 times greater than the peak for the first curve. Note also that, again, at the higher temperature, the molecules have a wider range of energies than at the lower temperature.

1. Hydrogen reacts with both chlorine and iodine. The activation energies for these reactions are:
   $H_2(g) + Cl_2(g) \rightarrow 2HCl(g)$ $E_A = 25 \text{ kJ mol}^{-1}$
   $H_2(g) + I_2(g) \rightarrow 2HI(g)$ $E_A = 157 \text{ kJ mol}^{-1}$
   Predict which reaction will be faster at a particular temperature. Explain your answer.

2. Using the concept of activation energy, explain why food spoilage reactions are slowed down using a refrigerator or freezer.

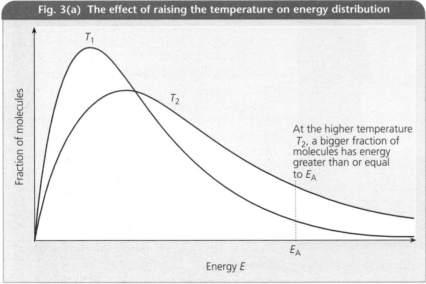

Fig. 3(a) The effect of raising the temperature on energy distribution

Fraction of molecules

T_1

T_2

At the higher temperature T_2, a bigger fraction of molecules has energy greater than or equal to E_A

E_A

Energy E

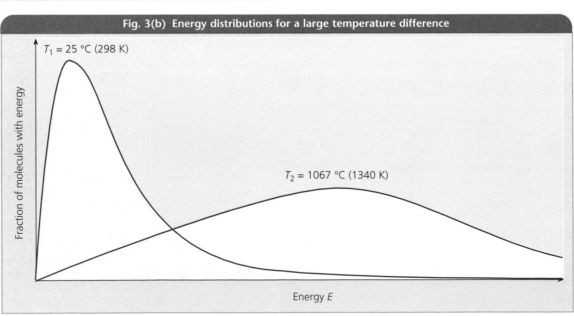

Fig. 3(b) Energy distributions for a large temperature difference

Fraction of molecules with energy

$T_1 = 25 \text{ °C (298 K)}$

$T_2 = 1067 \text{ °C (1340 K)}$

Energy E

APPLICATION A Nitrogen oxides from vehicle exhausts

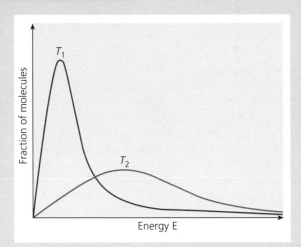

Fraction of molecules

T_1

T_2

Energy E

The two main gases in air are nitrogen and oxygen. Under normal conditions, these do not react with each other. But inside a petrol engine the temperature can reach 2500 °C. At this temperature, the activation energy for the reaction is exceeded and nitrogen reacts with oxygen to form nitrogen monoxide, NO. Nitrogen dioxide, NO_2, is also formed when nitrogen monoxide reacts with oxygen. Nitrogen oxides are the main contributors to pollution in towns and cities and they cause respiratory problems and acid rain.

1 Write balanced equations for:
a the formation of NO,
b the reaction of NO with O_2.

2 What is meant by the term activation energy?

The graph shows Maxwell-Boltzmann energy distribution curves for a mixture of nitrogen and oxygen at two temperatures. In the laboratory, when an electric arc is passed through nitrogen-oxygen mixtures at 3500 °C, the yield of nitrogen monoxide is about 2%.

3 a Predict where on the graph the activation energy would be marked.
b What percentage of nitrogen monoxide would you expect at 25 °C?

4 The reaction to produce nitrogen dioxide from nitrogen monoxide and oxygen occurs readily at room temperature. What does this tell you about the activation energy for this reaction compared to the value for the reaction between nitrogen and oxygen?

Fig. 4 An energy profile diagram for an exothermic reaction

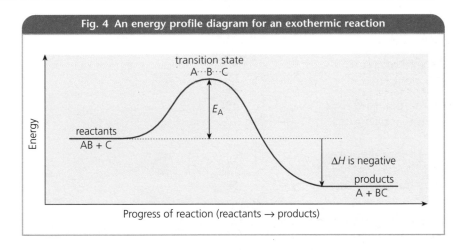

Energy

transition state
A··B··C

E_A

reactants
AB + C

ΔH is negative

products
A + BC

Progress of reaction (reactants → products)

Mechanism of activation energy
Fig. 4 is called an **energy profile**. It is for the exothermic (heat-producing) reaction between AB and C. They cannot react unless they gain more energy represented by E_A, the **energy barrier**. The reactants then reach a form called the **transition state**, when bonds are being broken and formed.

In the reaction, some bonds will re-form the reactants, while others will form products. The level of energy for product molecules is lower than for the reactants, so there is an energy output for this reaction: it is exothermic.

KEY FACTS

■ Kinetics is the study of rates of reaction.

■ The distribution of molecular energies in a gas is shown by the Maxwell–Boltzmann distribution curve.

■ An increase in temperature changes the distribution of molecular energies to give a higher proportion of molecules with higher energy levels.

■ Reactions can occur only when collisions between particles having sufficiently high energy.

■ Most collisions between reactants do not lead to a reaction.

■ For a reaction, the activation energy is the minimum energy which molecules need for collisions to cause a reaction. It is measured in kJ mol^{-1}.

6.3 Factors affecting reaction rates

The rate of a reaction is measured as the rate at which a reactant is used up, or the rate at which a product is formed. The rate of reaction is affected by the:

- temperature of the reactants
- concentration of reactants and products
- surface area of reactants
- presence of any catalysts

The effect of temperature

We have seen that increasing the temperature of gas molecules increases their energy and shifts the energy distribution curve to the right. The speeds of molecules increase, giving more collisions per second. In a reacting mixture, more of these collisions exceed the activation energy and the rate of reaction increases. But by how much?

Fig. 5 shows energy distribution curves for a mixture of reacting gases at a 10 °C interval, namely at 27 °C and at 37 °C. The fraction of molecules above the activation energy has almost doubled, leading to a doubling of the rate of reaction. The rates of many different reactions double for a 10 °C rise in temperature. With all other conditions constant:

An increase in temperature of 10 °C will double the rate of a reaction.

This explains why small temperature rises can lead to a large increase in reaction rate.

Yet remember that most collisions in the reaction mixture do not lead to a reaction. Only collisions with energies equal to or above the activation energy are likely to be effective in causing a reaction.

3 A reaction takes 20 minutes at 20 °C. Estimate the time for the same reaction to occur if the reagents were mixed at 100 °C.

The effect of concentration

Chemists define the rate of reaction as the rate at which a product is formed, or the rate at which a reactant is used up. It is measured as a change in concentration of products or reactants over time. For reactions in solution, the units of rate are mol dm^{-3} s^{-1}, meaning change of concentration per cubic decimetre of solvent per second.

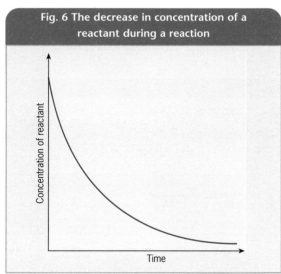

Fig. 6 shows how the concentration of a reactant decreases during the course of a typical reaction. If the rate of reaction were constant, the graph would be a straight line with a downward slope. Clearly, the rate changes with time, being fastest at the start of the reaction, when the concentration of reactants is greatest. At the end of the reaction we say that the rate is zero – at least one of the reactants must have been used up, so no more collisions between reactant particles can occur and lead to a reaction.

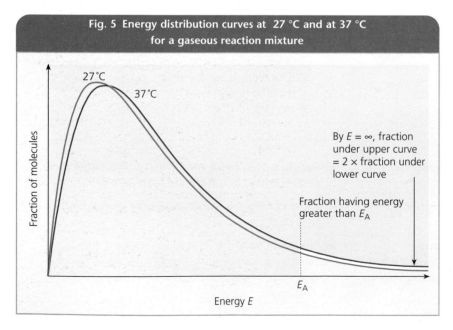

Fig. 7 is a graph for the increase in concentration of a product during a typical reaction. Again, the rate of formation of the product is fastest at the start of the reaction, slowing to zero at completion.

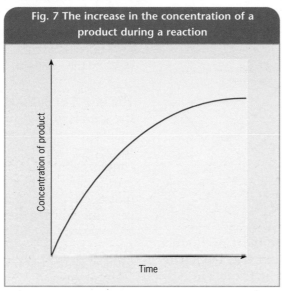

Fig. 7 The increase in the concentration of a product during a reaction

The graph is known as a **rate curve**. The rate of reaction at any instant is given by the gradient (the slope) of the curve at that instant.

4

a What do Figs. 6 and 7 tell you about how the rate of reaction changes during the course of a reaction?

b Explain the shape of the graph in Fig. 7.

Explaining the effect of concentration

In the reaction between powdered zinc and a solution of hydrochloric acid, zinc chloride and hydrogen gas are formed:

$$Zn(s) + 2HCl(aq) \rightarrow ZnCl_2(aq) + H_2(g)$$

Either dilute or concentrated acid can be used. Fig. 8 on page 96 shows energy distribution curves for reaction mixtures of zinc and hydrochloric acid where the only change in conditions is in the concentration of the acid. The temperature of both mixtures is the same. But the higher concentration of acid has the effect of increasing the number of collisions between particles that can react with each other, and so the number of collisions that reach the activation energy also increases.

EXTENSION **Finding the rate of reaction at a particular time**

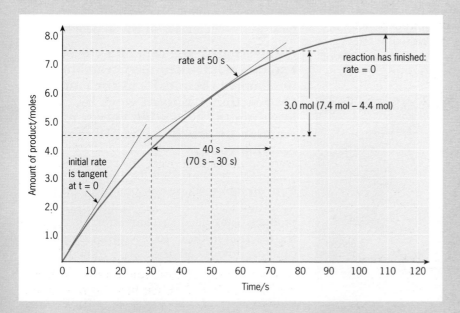

The **gradient** or slope at any point on a rate curve gives the rate of the reaction at that time, measured in moles per unit of time. We find the gradient by drawing the tangent to the curve and making it the hypotenuse in a triangle, with the horizontal line ending at convenient times. Then we read off the moles and time as shown on the graph, and calculate the gradient.

The graph is a rate curve for the products of a reaction. It includes two tangents. The tangent at time zero is called the **initial rate**, which occurs when the reactants are first mixed. The gradient of this tangent is the steepest of any taken along the rate curve, since the reaction is fastest at the start. The rate at 50 seconds is calculated as follows:

Rate at 50 s = gradient of tangent at 50 s
$$= \frac{3.0 \text{ mol}}{40 \text{ s}} = 0.75 \text{ mol s}^{-1}$$

If you calculate the gradient of the tangent at time zero you will find that it is much greater than that at 50 seconds.

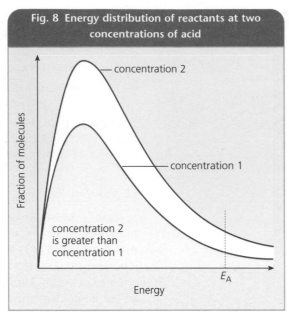

Fig. 8 Energy distribution of reactants at two concentrations of acid

Therefore an increase in the concentration of a reactant causes an increase in the rate of reaction. This is especially noticeable in laboratory work at the start of reactions: the initial rate of the reaction is much faster in many reactions where concentrated reagents are used.

Concentration in gaseous reactions

We can apply to reactions in gases the same idea about concentration as we applied to reactions in solution. At a given temperature, raising the pressure of a mixture of gases increases the concentration of molecules and in turn the rate of collisions, hence the reaction rate increases. The collision theory again explains why increasing the pressure of gases increases the rate of reaction.

In 1977 in New Orleans, an explosion in a grain silo killed 37 people. A spark ignited very fine flour dust mixed in the air in one of the silos and the terrifyingly fast rate of combustion with oxygen in the air caused the explosion

5 In the Haber process for making ammonia (NH_3), nitrogen and hydrogen are reacted together. Increasing the pressure speeds up the rate of this reaction.

a Write down a balanced equation for this reaction.

b Use the collision theory to explain why increasing the pressure speeds up the rate of this reaction.

The effect of surface area of solid reactants

If a solid is in large lumps, each lump has a small surface area compared to the total surface area of all the reactant molecules it contains. Only reactant molecules at the surface can take part in collisions with other molecules. If a solid fragment is ground to a very fine powder, then many more molecules are exposed to collisions with sufficient energy to cause a reaction. So increasing the surface area of a solid reactant increases the reaction rate.

Miners have always known of the hazards of coal dust explosions, but dust explosions are not confined to underground mines. Milling flour has the same risk of explosion.

Effect of catalysts

Catalysts play a crucial role in the lives of everybody. Protein catalysts called enzymes dramatically increase the rates of chemical reactions that take place in our bodies. Catalysts are involved in the manufacture of most of the chemicals on which people rely.

Catalysts alter the rate of a chemical reaction while themselves remaining unchanged chemically at the end of the reaction. Catalysts work by lowering the activation energy of a reaction by providing an alternative reaction route.

We saw in Fig. 4 that reactants interact to form an intermediate compound called the transition state before they can form the product. They need the activation energy for the reaction in order to reach that state. But a catalyst provides an alternative route with alternative intermediate forms, lowering the activation energy required. This can be seen in the energy profiles of Fig. 9. With the catalyst, the energy barrier is smaller, so more molecules have enough energy when they collide to pass over it. This is why catalysts speed up the rate of reactions.

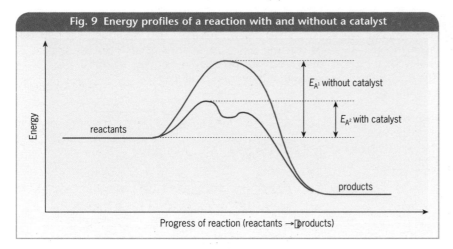

Fig. 9 Energy profiles of a reaction with and without a catalyst

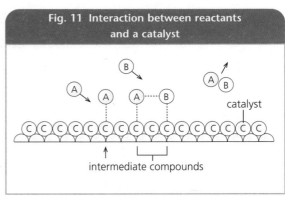

Fig. 11 Interaction between reactants and a catalyst

The Maxwell-Boltzmann energy distribution curve in Fig. 10 shows that when a catalyst is used at any particular temperature, more molecules have energies greater than the new activation energy. In terms of the collision theory this means that more molecules are going to collide with sufficient energy to react.

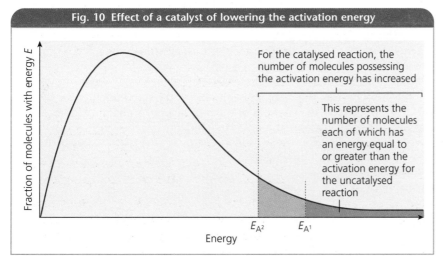

Fig. 10 Effect of a catalyst of lowering the activation energy

Catalysts are made with a large surface area, as material which is finely divided, or as a mesh or honeycomb. This increases their surface area. They interact with the reactants as shown in Fig. 11. Because the reaction leaves a catalyst unchanged chemically, a reaction with a large amount of reactant requires only a small amount of catalyst.

6 A main step in an early method for manufacturing sulphuric acid was the conversion of sulphur dioxide to sulphur trioxide, with nitrogen dioxide used as the catalyst. The reaction steps were:

$SO_2 + NO_2 \rightarrow SO_2 + NO$ (a rapid reaction)
$NO + \frac{1}{2}O_2 \rightarrow NO_2$ (also a rapid reaction)
$SO_2 + \frac{1}{2}O_2 \rightarrow SO_3$

The sulphur trioxide was then dissolved in water:
$SO_3 + H_2O \rightarrow H_2SO_4$
Explain why NO_2 is acting as a catalyst in the first two reactions.

KEY FACTS

- Rate of reaction is the rate at which a reactant is used up, or the rate at which a product is formed.

- Increasing the temperature of a reaction speeds it up because the number of collisions increases and more reactant molecules possess sufficient energy to react.

- Small temperature changes lead to a large increase in rate, as explained by looking at Maxwell-Boltzmann energy distributions at different temperatures.

- Changes in concentration (pressure for gases) affect reaction rate. The more particles there are in a given volume, the more collisions there will be with activation energy or higher.

- Changes in surface area of solid reactants affect reaction rates. The larger the surface area the faster the reaction.

- Catalysts alter the rate of a chemical reaction while themselves remaining unchanged chemically at the end of it. They provide an alternative reaction route with a lower activation energy.

1

a The diagram below shows the Maxwell-Boltzmann energy distribution curves for molecules of a gas under two sets of conditions A and B. The total area under curve B is the same as the total area under curve A.

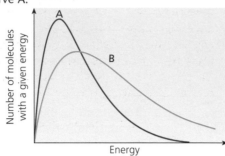

i) What change of condition is needed to produce curve **B** from curve **A**?
ii) What is represented by the total area under curve **A**?
iii) Why is the total area under curve **B** the same as that under curve **A**? (3)

b i) Explain the meaning of the term activation energy.
ii) In a reaction involving gas molecules, if all other conditions are kept constant, state the effect, if any, on the value of the activation energy when: a catalyst is added, the volume of the vessel is decreased. (3)

c Explain why the reactions between solids usually occur very slowly, if at all. (2)

NEAB CH03 June 1998 Q1

2

a The curve below shows the distribution of energies at a temperature, T_1, for the molecules in a mixture of gases which react together.

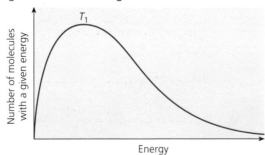

i) On the same axes, add a second curve for the distribution of energies in the same sample at a higher temperature, T_2, and label the curve T_2.
ii) At which temperature is the rate of reaction between the gases in the mixture higher? Give a reason for your choice.
iii) Why do collisions between molecules of gaseous reactants not always lead to a reaction? (5)

b The curves below, labelled 1 to 5, could be obtained by reacting an excess of zinc with different solutions of hydrochloric acid and measuring, at 25 8C, the volume of hydrogen produced.

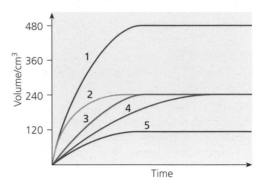

The reaction of an excess of zinc with 100 cm³ of 0.1 M hydrochloric acid at 25 8C gave curve 3. Which one of the curves, labelled 1 to 5, could have been produced by reacting excess zinc with each of the following. (Each curve may be used once, more than once or not at all.)

i) 50 cm³ of 0.2 M hydrochloric acid at 25 8C?
ii) 100 cm³ of 0.1 M hydrochloric acid at 15 8C?
iii) 100 cm³ of 0.2 M hydrochloric acid at 25 8C?
iv) 100 cm³ of 0.1 M hydrochloric acid at 25 8C in the presence of a catalyst? (4)

NEAB CH03 June 1997 Q1

3 The diagram below shows the distribution curve for the energies of the molecules in a mixture of two gases at a given temperature.
E_a is the activation energy for the reaction between the two gases.

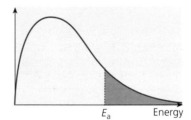

a Label the vertical axis. (1)

b i) How do the molecules in a gas exchange energy?
ii) What effect, if any, does the exchange have on the distribution shown above? (2)

c What does the shaded area on the graph represent? (2)

d Give two changes to this reaction mixture which would cause the shaded area to increase. (2)

NEAB CH03 February 1997 Q1

Are catalytic converters really 'green'?

Road vehicles produce some 90% of all emissions of the toxic gas carbon monoxide. To solve this pollution problem, catalytic converters are now fitted to car exhaust systems. This item is about how solving this carbon monoxide problem can itself cause a problem, namely the production of another polluting gas, sulphur dioxide.

The catalysts used in these converters are usually platinum and rhodium. The hot, finely powdered platinum reduces the energy barriers which impede the complete oxidation of hydrocarbons and carbon monoxide to carbon dioxide. The job of the rhodium catalyst, also a fine powder, is to convert the various nitrogen oxides back to oxygen and nitrogen.

Both of these metals are quite difficult to extract from their ores. They occur in very low concentrations in sulphide ores which also contain copper and nickel. In removing the sulphides, another pollutant, sulphur dioxide, is produced as a waste gas. Sulphur dioxide causes acid rain – a different but serious environmental problem. So if the whole 'life cycle' of the catalytic converter is analysed, on the one hand you have a product which is intended to reduce pollution, but on the other hand, producing the raw materials for the car industry puts another pollutant in its place!

Canadian metal extraction plants have developed an effective means of removing the sulphur dioxide: they fit scrubbers to their smokestacks. However, Russian extraction plants do not, and continue to pour out sulphur dioxide and also nitrogen oxides into the air. Researchers in Germany estimate that these metal extraction processes put back a quarter of the volume of the pollutants that the catalytic converters are designed to remove.

1 Why are platinum and rhodium used as a very fine powders?

2 Write down balanced chemical equations to represent:

  a carbon monoxide and oxygen conversion to carbon dioxide by the platinum.

  b the reaction nitrogen oxides, NO_x, at the rhodium surface.

3 How does the catalytic converter help to solve one problem while creating another?

4 Prepare to conduct a discussion about the issue described below. Your job will be to chair the discussion and to keep a track of the claims made. You will need to understand the science likely to be discussed so that you can spot any lies or misunderstandings.

■ Plans have been submitted to your local authority to construct a processing plant to produce platinum metal for the world-wide catalytic converter industry.

■ Its supporters argue that with more countries insisting on catalytic converters to reduce pollution from traffic, there will be an increased demand for the metal. This will make it economical to import the platinum ore as the chemical technology in this country is very efficient.

■ It will also provide jobs and improve the overall economy of the area. There may even be government grants for the area to start up the plant.

■ Local people are divided on the issue – some are very keen on the promise of new work and money. Others are very worried about the potential pollution the new plant could cause.

7 Equilibria

While an oil shortage may well be the world economic concern now, a hundred years ago the fear was of a shortage of nitrogen compounds. Bird droppings metres deep in Peru and sodium nitrate in the deserts of Chile were the main sources of nitrogen fertiliser – and these were running out.

Agriculture in Europe and North America expanded in the nineteenth century to feed rapidly growing populations. In industry, the explosives TNT and nitroglycerine, used for mining and in weapons of war, also needed nitrogen as nitrates as their raw material. The demand for nitrates threatened to outstrip supply.

At the start of the twentieth century, Germany was preparing for war. Britain controlled the seas and was likely to threaten the import of Chilean nitrate, so Germany wanted to produce nitrogen compounds from nitrogen gas. Nitrogen is plentiful in the air, but very unreactive. Many chemists tried to convert it to a form that could be used for nitrate production.

Fritz Haber made the breakthrough in 1909, taking nitrogen and hydrogen and synthesising 100 g of ammonia (NH_3), the starting material for making nitrogen compounds including nitrates. In 1913, Carl Bosch, a chemical engineer, scaled up Haber's process to the first industrial plant.

Fritz Haber is one of chemistry's great heroes and villains. As a hero he showed the way to make fertilisers that keep millions of people all over the world alive today. As a villain he also contibuted to the development of the poison gas weapons and explosives used in the first world war.

Commercially made fertilisers make intensive agriculture possible, increasing food production and so reducing food shortages

7.1 ## The dynamic nature of equilibria

This chapter is about the chemical rules behind Haber's success in finding a reaction to produce ammonia, and behind the design of all industrial reactions.

The word **equilibrium** means a state of balance. **Equilibria** exist for many chemical reactions, including the chemistry of life. For example, in the lungs, oxygen from air reacts with haemoglobin in blood to form oxyhaemoglobin. The blood flows to the body tissues where, because conditions are different, the reaction is reversed and oxygen is released for use by the tissues. Therefore, different conditions can alter the position of the equilibrium for a reaction and so control the direction in which the reaction proceeds.

Many chemical reactions are reversible

If you burn magnesium in air you will see a brilliant white flame as the white powdery solid, magnesium oxide, is produced:

$$2Mg(s) + O_2(g) \rightarrow 2MgO(s)$$

The single-headed arrow in this equation indicates that *all* the magnesium forms magnesium oxide. We say that the **reaction goes to completion**. We also say the reaction is **irreversible** and, for practical purposes, it is. Some apparently irreversible reactions are reversible to a very small extent, but so little that we can ignore it.

However, many reactions are reversible. A **reversible reaction** is one that can take place in both directions and so is incomplete. A stunning reversible reaction forms stalactites and stalagmites in caves. As water seeps through the ground above the caves, it absorbs carbon dioxide, a gas which is acidic in aqueous solution. If this solution seeps through limestone (calcium carbonate), a reaction occurs to give a solution of calcium ions Ca^{2+} and hydrogencarbonate ions HCO_3^-.

$$CO_2(g) + CaCO_3(s) + H_2O(l) \rightarrow Ca^{2+}(aq) + 2HCO_3^-(aq)$$

As the solution drips through a cave ceiling, the reverse reaction occurs:

$$Ca^{2+}(aq) + 2HCO_3^-(aq) \rightarrow CaCO_3(s) + CO_2(g) + H_2O(l)$$

The calcium carbonate forms the beautiful stalactites and stalagmites you see in the photograph.

These magnificent limestone structures are formed because a reversible reaction takes place between carbon dioxide, limestone and water

Reactions in dynamic equilibrium

Let us look at a reversible reaction between hydrogen and iodine.

$$H_2(g) + I_2(g) \rightleftharpoons 2HI(g)$$

The gases are sealed in glass bulbs and kept at a constant temperature of 445 °C. At particular time intervals, the reaction is stopped by cooling the bulbs rapidly and their contents are analysed. The results are shown in Fig. 1. The vertical axis represents the amount of HI present in the reaction mixtures from the start of the reaction.

The lower curve (blue) is for reaction mixtures of 0.5 moles of hydrogen and 0.5 moles of iodine, and plots the amount of HI formed in these mixtures at different times. If the reaction went to completion, there would

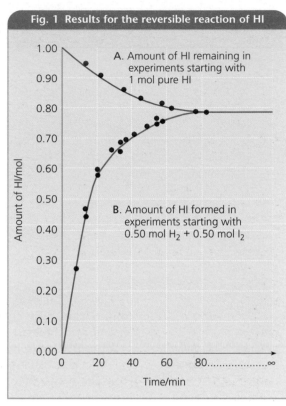

Fig. 1 Results for the reversible reaction of HI

A. Amount of HI remaining in experiments starting with 1 mol pure HI

B. Amount of HI formed in experiments starting with 0.50 mol H_2 + 0.50 mol I_2

Amount of HI/mol (vertical axis)

Time/min (horizontal axis)

be 1 mole of hydrogen iodide in the flask, and zero moles of H_2 and I_2. But this did not happen. Only 0.78 moles of HI were present.

The upper curve (red) shows that by starting with 1 mole of HI in the flask, at the same temperature, the same amount, 0.78 moles, was left after 84 minutes. However much time elapsed after 84 minutes, the amounts of all three chemicals were identical: after 84 minutes, the reaction had reached its **equilibrium position**.

1

a Explain why rapid cooling apparently stops the reaction.

b Imagine that, instead of being reversible, the reaction goes to completion. If the starting mixture contains 2 moles of H_2 and 1 mole of I_2, how many moles of HI would be formed?

c Explain the shapes of the curves in Fig. 1 in terms of reaction rates. Hint: You may need to look back at Chapter 6 to remind yourself about rates of reaction.

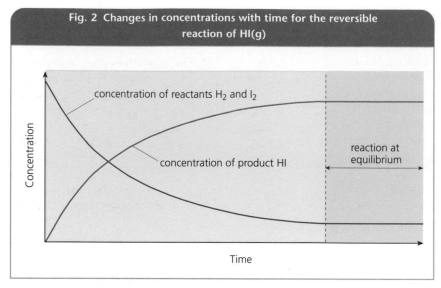

Fig. 2 Changes in concentrations with time for the reversible reaction of HI(g)

The importance of a closed system

The glass bulbs used for these experiments were sealed so that none of the gases could escape. This is an example of a **closed system**, where no material is exchanged with the surroundings. There is therefore no loss of reactant or product materials to affect their equilibrium concentrations. An equilibrium is maintained only with constant concentrations, and from Chapter 6 you learnt that rate of reaction depends on concentration. A lowered concentration of reactant slows down the forward reaction; a lowered concentration of product slows down the backward reaction. In both cases, the equilibrium shifts.

Fig. 2 is a different way of presenting the results. The graph shows the concentration of H_2 and I_2 in blue and concentration of the product HI in red, as the reaction progresses.

We can see that the concentrations of the gases do not change once equilibrium has been set up. Does this mean that reactions stop when equilibrium is reached? The answer is No, and this is where the term **dynamic** comes in. Though the concentrations of reactants and product remain constant, both the forward and reverse reactions still continue, which is why we say that the equilibrium is dynamic.

When a reaction is in dynamic equilibrium, the forward and reverse reactions are occurring at the same rate.

At first the rate of the forward reaction between H_2 and I_2 is at its fastest since the reactants are at their highest concentrations. The forward rate slows down because reactant concentrations go down as the concentration of HI builds up. The backward rate increases as there is more HI to break down, until both rates meet and become equal.

2 If you removed some HI from the equilibrium mixture, predict what would happen:

a to the rate of the reverse reaction,

b to the position of the equilibrium.

The equilibrium mixture of hydrogen, iodine and hydrogen iodide gases is an example of a **homogeneous equilibrium**. This means that the equilibrium is for materials all in the same phase, in this case the gas phase.

3 State in which of the following there is a dynamic equilibrium.

a An unopened bottle of fizzy lemonade.

b A bottle of fizzy lemonade with the top left off.

c A sealed bag containing wet washing.

d Wet washing hanging on a washing line on a windy day.

KEY FACTS

- Many chemical reactions are reversible.
- In a closed system an equilibrium can be established.
- Equilibria are called dynamic because the forward and reverse reactions continue to proceed at the same rate.
- Once an equilibrium is established, the concentrations of reactants and products remain constant.

Changes that affect a system in equilibrium

Changes in temperature, pressure and concentration all have an effect on equilibrium. We shall not be considering quantitative changes here, meaning we shall not be calculating quantities. We will consider the qualitative effect of altering a condition. Here, the word qualitative means judging whether we can get more or less product, and how the position of equilibrium is shifted.

The position of equilibrium in a reaction tells us the proportion of products to reactants. If product concentrations at equilibrium are high and hardly any reactants are left, then we say that the position of the equilibrium lies to the right. If reactant concentrations are high and product concentrations are very low, then we say the position of equilibrium lies to the left.

Le Chatelier's principle
In 1884, the French chemist Henri Le Chatelier formulated his famous principle which can be simply stated as:

The position of the equilibrium of a system changes to minimise the effect of any imposed change in conditions.

By 'imposed change' we mean any change in temperature or pressure or concentration made to the system. Le Chatelier's principle applies to any reaction that reaches equilibrium. Fritz Haber knew this principle, and applied it to the manufacture of ammonia.

Temperature and equilibria
When nitrogen gas and hydrogen gas are heated to 1000 °C with an iron catalyst at atmospheric pressure, the equilibrium position lies well towards the reactants, that is, to the left. In fact, the reaction mixture at equilibrium contains less than 1% of ammonia. The reaction equation is:

$$N_2(g) + 3H_2(g) \rightleftharpoons 2NH_3(g) \quad \Delta H^\ominus = -92 \text{ kJ mol}^{-1}$$

We can predict the effect of increasing the temperature on the position of the equilibrium for this reaction. Le Chatelier's principle tells us that, in any reaction, if you raise the temperature, and so *increase* energy, the equilibrium shifts to *absorb* energy. The negative sign in $\Delta H^\ominus$ above tells you that the reaction is exothermic in the forward direction. Therefore, raising the temperature

shifts the equilibrium in the endothermic direction, so that the system absorbs energy. This is to the left, and so raising temperature drives down the equilibrium yield of ammonia. Yet Haber needed a high temperature to increase the rate of a reaction and bring it to equilibrium faster.

4 Look at these equilibria and predict the effect of increasing the temperature. Give your reasons.

a $N_2(g) + O_2(g) \rightleftharpoons 2NO(g)$
$$\Delta H^\ominus = +90 \text{ kJ mol}^{-1}$$

b $2SO_2(g) + O_2(g) \rightleftharpoons 2SO_3(g)$
$$\Delta H^\ominus = -98 \text{ kJ mol}^{-1}$$

Pressure and equilibria
Haber used Le Chatelier's principle to predict that if he increased the pressure at a fixed temperature, the equilibrium would shift to the right and give a better yield of ammonia. He wrote:

'It was clear that a change to using maximum pressure would be an advantage. It would improve the position of equilibrium and probably the rate of reaction as well.'

Why did Haber think pressure would move the equilibrium to the right? Look at the equation. There are fewer moles of gaseous reactant on the right than moles of gaseous product on the left. In a gas, pressure depends on the number of molecules acting on a particular area. When Haber increased the pressure, the equilibrium shifted to the right, as the reaction opposed the change imposed on it. More ammonia was formed, while the pressure remained constant.

By comparison, in this reversible reaction:

$$H_2(g) + I_2(g) \rightleftharpoons 2HI(g)$$

the number of molecules is the same on both sides, so an increase in pressure has no effect on the equilibrium position. This is also true of equilibria for reactions which do not include gases.

5 Use Le Chatelier's principle to predict the effect of increasing the pressure on each of these equilibrium reactions.

a $CH_4(g) + H_2O(g) \rightleftharpoons CO(g) + 3H_2(g)$

b $CO(g) + H_2O(g) \rightleftharpoons CO_2(g) + H_2(g)$

c $2NO_2(g) \rightleftharpoons N_2O_4(g)$

Concentration and equilibria

The equilibrium positions for reactions in the liquid phase are not affected by pressure changes. But equilibrium positions are affected by changes in the concentration of products and reactants.

You may have used cobalt chloride paper, which is blue, to test for water. When cobalt chloride ions are added to water, this reaction rapidly reaches an equilibrium as the ions undergo a reaction to form the pink hexaaquacobalt(II) ion, $[Co(H_2O)_6]^{2+}$. Adding concentrated hydrochloric acid promotes the reverse reaction, accompanied by a colour change from pink back to blue. The ionic equation is:

$$[Co(H_2O)_6]^{2+} + 4Cl^- \rightleftharpoons [CoCl_4]^{2-} + 6H_2O$$
$$\text{pink} \qquad\qquad\qquad \text{blue}$$

The amount of colour change depends on the amount of acid added. Adding concentrated acid increases the concentration of chloride ions on the left of the equation. The effect is to increase the forward reaction since, as Le Chatelier's principle states, the equilibrium position shifts to minimise the imposed change.

Catalysts and equilibria

A catalyst does not alter the equilibrium *position*: the equilibrium concentrations of reactants and products remain the same. The effect of adding a catalyst is to increase the *rate* of forward and backwards reactions to the same extent, so that it takes a shorter time to reach equilibrium. Haber did more than 6000 experiments just to find the most effective catalyst to speed up the reaction between nitrogen and hydrogen and so obtain ammonia more quickly.

APPLICATION A

Le Chatelier's principle and car exhaust gases

Amongst the oxides of nitrogen that form in vehicle engines is nitrogen monoxide, NO:

$$N_2(g) + O_2(g) \rightleftharpoons 2NO(g) \qquad \Delta H^\oplus = +90 \text{ kJ mol}^{-1}$$

At room temperature, the equilibrium for this reaction is so far to the left as to be considered non-reversible. Even at the temperature of a car engine, the yield is less than 1%.

1 When the nitrogen monoxide leaves the engine, it cools very rapidly. Why does this prevent NO decomposing back to N_2 and O_2?

2 Lowering the pressure (compression ratio) in the engine is one way to reduce the high temperature in the engine so that less NO forms.

a What is the effect of reducing (i) the pressure and (ii) the temperature on the equilibrium which produces NO? Explain your answers.

b Reducing the pressure in the engine reduces the engine's efficiency. Why is this not a good idea?

KEY FACTS

- Le Chatelier's principle states that the position of the equilibrium of a system changes to minimise the effect of any imposed change in conditions.

- Increasing the temperature displaces the equilibrium position in the endothermic direction.

- Decreasing the temperature displaces the equilibrium position in the exothermic direction.

- For a gaseous system, increasing the pressure displaces the equilibrium position in the direction which has fewer numbers of gas molecules, because this reduces the pressure.

- For a gaseous system, decreasing the pressure displaces the equilibrium position in the direction which has larger numbers of gas molecules, because this increases the pressure

- Increasing the concentration of a reactant shifts the equilibrium position to the products side.

- Increasing the concentration of a product shifts the equilibrium position to the reactants side.

7.3 Importance of equilibria in industrial processes

Haber and his assistant Robert le Rossignol found the optimum conditions for producing ammonia in the laboratory, and then needed to scale up the process for industrial production by the manufacturer BASF. They had to convince BASF that a reasonable yield of ammonia could be produced at a fast enough rate.

One condition for Haber's reaction was a pressure of about 200 atmospheres. This is roughly the pressure at the base of a brick wall 1.5 kilometres high! It posed great technical problems for BASF's engineer, Carl Bosch. But by 1913, the first industrial plant was producing 30 tonnes of ammonia a day. Efforts were spurred on by the needs of the impending war. Ammonia is a starting material for the manufacture of nitric acid, HNO_3, which is used for the production of explosives (see Application C on page 108).

However, it was the use of ammonia to manufacture fertilisers that had a more beneficial social impact. Haber received the Nobel prize for chemistry in 1918 for devising the process, followed in 1931 by Carl Bosch, for inventing and developing the high pressure technology.

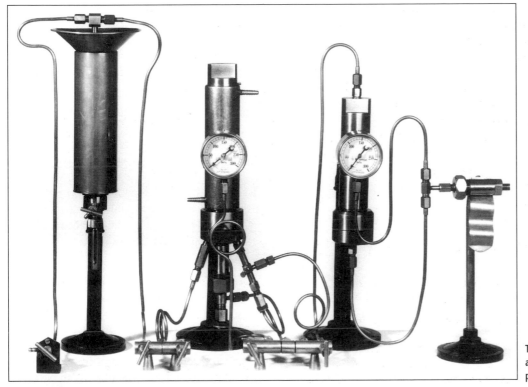

The original laboratory apparatus Haber used to produce ammonia

APPLICATION B

Equilibria in organic reactions

Esters are sweet-smelling organic compounds. Most are neutral liquids with a pleasant fruity smell. They are made industrially and used mainly as solvents. In addition, they are added to materials such as plastics to keep them flexible, and are used as food flavourings such as raspberry and pear. One reaction to form an ester, which requires a catalyst, is:

$$CH_3COOH(l) + C_2H_5OH(l) \rightleftharpoons CH_3COOC_2H_5(l) + H_2O(l)$$

| ethanoic acid | ethanol | | ethyl ethanoate | water |
| acid | + | alcohol $\rightleftharpoons$ | ester | + water |

1 Describe what happens to the equilibrium position when the following takes place at equilibrium.
 a Ethanol is added to the reaction mixture.
 b The ester is added to the reaction mixture.
 c The ester is removed from the reaction mixture.

The modern Haber process

The Haber process has to prepare a 1:3 mixture of nitrogen and hydrogen to manufacture ammonia. The source of hydrogen is a hydrocarbon, and in the UK it is methane in natural gas, CH_4. Water (as steam), and air which contains the nitrogen, are introduced, so all the reactants are relatively cheap.

Several of the reactions in the process are designed to remove the unwanted compounds in order to reach maximum purity of the nitrogen:hydrogen mixture. Fig. 3 shows a flow diagram for the industrial plant with the stages and reactions in the modern Haber process.

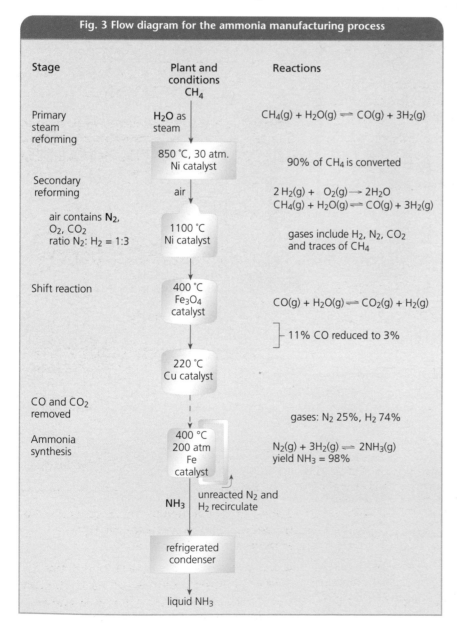

Fig. 3 Flow diagram for the ammonia manufacturing process

Stage	Plant and conditions	Reactions
	CH_4	
Primary steam reforming	H_2O as steam	$CH_4(g) + H_2O(g) \rightleftharpoons CO(g) + 3H_2(g)$
	850 °C, 30 atm. Ni catalyst	90% of CH_4 is converted
Secondary reforming	air	$2H_2(g) + O_2(g) \rightarrow 2H_2O$ $CH_4(g) + H_2O(g) \rightleftharpoons CO(g) + 3H_2(g)$
air contains N_2, O_2, CO_2 ratio N_2 : $H_2 = 1:3$	1100 °C Ni catalyst	gases include H_2, N_2, CO_2 and traces of CH_4
Shift reaction	400 °C Fe_3O_4 catalyst	$CO(g) + H_2O(g) \rightleftharpoons CO_2(g) + H_2(g)$
		11% CO reduced to 3%
	220 °C Cu catalyst	
CO and CO_2 removed		gases: N_2 25%, H_2 74%
Ammonia synthesis	400 °C 200 atm Fe catalyst	$N_2(g) + 3H_2(g) \rightleftharpoons 2NH_3(g)$ yield NH_3 = 98%
	NH_3 | unreacted N_2 and H_2 recirculate	
	refrigerated condenser	
	liquid NH_3	

Producing hydrogen

At the **primary steam reforming** stage, methane and steam react to give carbon monoxide and hydrogen:

$$CH_4(g) + H_2O(g) \rightleftharpoons CO(g) + 3H_2(g)$$
$$\Delta H^\ominus = +210 \text{ kJ mol}^{-1}$$

Let us apply Le Chatelier's principle to this equilibrium by looking at the effect of changing two conditions.

Increasing temperature. The forward reaction is endothermic because the sign of ΔH is positive: as the forward reaction proceeds, energy is absorbed. Raising the temperature increases the rate of the forward reaction, displacing the equilibrium position to the right.

Decreasing pressure. There are two moles of molecules on the left of the equation and four moles on the right. Using a low pressure displaces the equilibrium position towards the right. But, although the equilibrium mixture would contain a higher proportion of the required products, the actual yield would be low, since a low pressure would require the vessel to contain only a small amount of reactants.

Industrial conditions are not always the ones that Le Chatelier's principle says would give the highest equilibrium yield: these conditions could require high energy costs or the use of expensive equipment; or reaching equilibrium may take too long. Instead, conditions used may be a *compromise* between best equilibrium yield and fastest rate of production, to give as cheap a product as possible.

The reaction above that gives hydrogen is maintained at 850 °C. This high temperature gives a very fast reaction and also displaces the equilibrium to the right. The pressure of 30 atmospheres moves the equilibrium position to the left, but is cost-effective. In addition, higher pressures increase *rates* of reaction, so the overall productivity is increased.

A nickel catalyst is used. This does not alter the position of equilibrium, but shortens the time it takes to achieve equilibrium. Under these conditions, about 90% of the methane is converted to hydrogen.

6 The shift reaction removes most of the carbon monoxide:

$$CO(g) + H_2O(g) \rightleftharpoons CO_2(g) + H_2(g)$$
$$\Delta H^\ominus = -41 \text{ kJ mol}^{-1}$$

What conditions of temperature and pressure does Le Chatelier's principle suggest would give the best yield of hydrogen from this equilibrium reaction?

Synthesising ammonia

The synthesis reaction is:

$$N_2(g) + 3H_2(g) \rightleftharpoons 2NH_3(g)$$
$$\Delta H^\ominus = -92 \text{ kJ mol}^{-1}$$

Applying Le Chatelier's principle to this reaction, the equilibrium yield of ammonia will be high if:

- the temperature is low, because the reaction is exothermic,

- the pressure is high, because the number of moles of gaseous product is less than the number of moles of gaseous reactant.

However, to increase the reaction rate, a balance is struck between equilibrium yield and rate of reaction. Figs. 4 to 6 show the effect of temperature and pressure on the the percentage of ammonia in the equilibrium mixture.

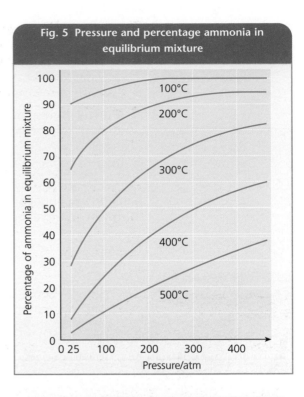

Fig. 5 Pressure and percentage ammonia in equilibrium mixture

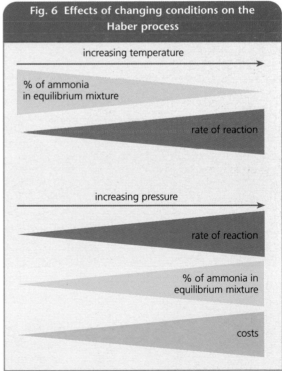

Fig. 6 Effects of changing conditions on the Haber process

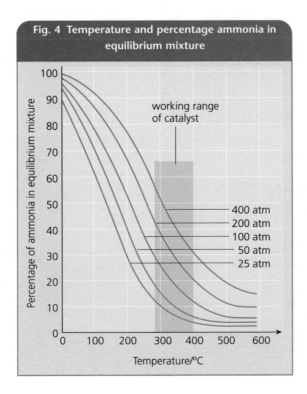

Fig. 4 Temperature and percentage ammonia in equilibrium mixture

Today, ammonia manufacturers generally use the following conditions for the final ammonia-producing reaction:

- A temperature between 400 °C and 450 °C. This is a compromise temperature. The rate of reaction is fast enough to give a good yield in a short time at the expense of a lower equilibrium yield.

- A pressure of about 200 atmospheres. A higher pressure would have high energy costs, and thicker-walled pipes would make the construction of the plant more expensive.

- A finely divided iron catalyst. This speeds up both the forward and the reverse reactions equally, so that equilibrium is reached sooner.

Under these conditions, the yield of ammonia is about 15%. The unreacted nitrogen and hydrogen are recycled until eventually the conversion of hydrogen and nitrogen is about 98%.

7 In the ammonia synthesis stage:

a The iron catalyst is finely divided on an inert support, rather than as large lumps. Explain why.

b What is the effect of reducing the concentration of ammonia in the equilibrium mixture by removing it in the ammonia condenser in Fig. 3?

APPLICATION C | **Manufacturing nitric acid**

Gauze covered in platinum and rhodium provides a huge surface area on which to catalyse the oxidation of ammonia

Nitric acid is made using ammonia and oxygen as starting materials. Almost 80% of the world production of 50 million tonnes of nitric acid is used to manufacture ammonium nitrate (NH_4NO_3), and most of this is used as fertiliser.

There are two stages in nitric acid manufacture:

- Ammonia is oxidised, with oxygen supplied in excess air.

- Nitrogen oxides are absorbed in water to form nitric acid.

Stage one involves this reaction:

$$4NH_3(g) + 5O_2(g) \rightleftharpoons 4NO(g) + 6H_2O(l)$$
$$\Delta H^\ominus = -909 \text{ kJ mol}^{-1}$$

The catalysts used are platinum and rhodium, and the conditions are 900 °C and 10 atmospheres.

In stage two, dinitrogen tetroxide (N_2O_4) is formed:

$$2NO(g) + O_2(g) \rightleftharpoons 2NO_2(g)$$
$$\Delta H^\ominus = -115 \text{ kJ mol}^{-1}$$
$$2NO_2(g) \rightleftharpoons N_2O_4(g) \qquad \Delta H^\ominus = -58 \text{ kJ mol}^{-1}$$

Low temperatures are used (about 40 °C) and the pressure is 7 to 12 atmospheres.

1 What is the effect of a low temperature on the position of these equilibria?

2 Describe the difference in yields of dinitrogen tetroxide you would expect at 40 °C and at 75 °C, with all other conditions the same.

3 Le Chatelier's principle suggests using a high pressure to convert NO to N_2O_4. What are the advantages of using a lower pressure?

Finally, the dinitrogen tetroxide is absorbed into a stream of cold water with which it reacts to produce nitric acid:

$$3N_2O_4(g) + H_2O(l) \rightleftharpoons 4HNO_3(l) + 2NO(g)$$
$$\Delta H^\ominus = -103 \text{ kJ mol}^{-1}$$

4 Why should the water be cold?

Manufacturing sulphuric acid

It was said in the mid nineteenth century that you could judge a nation's prosperity by how much sulphuric acid it used. For chemical and manufacturing industries this probably still applies today. These are just a few of the huge range of substances that use sulphuric acid in their production: paints, pigments and dyes, soaps and detergents, plastics and fibres, and fertilisers.

The contact process

The raw materials for manufacturing sulphuric acid are sulphur, air and water. The series of reactions involved is called the **contact process**. It has three stages:

1 Molten sulphur is burnt in air to give sulphur dioxide:

$$S(s) + O_2(g) \rightarrow SO_2(g) \quad \Delta H^{\ominus} = -297 \text{ kJ mol}^{-1}$$

2 Sulphur dioxide is reacted with oxygen to give sulphur trioxide:

$$SO_2(g) + \tfrac{1}{2}O_2(g) \rightleftharpoons SO_3(g)$$
$$\Delta H^{\ominus} = -98 \text{ kJ mol}^{-1}$$

3 The sulphur trioxide is dissolved in concentrated sulphuric acid:

$$SO_3(g) + H_2SO_4(l) \rightleftharpoons H_2S_2O_7(l)$$
$$\Delta H^{\ominus} = -230 \text{ kJ mol}^{-1}$$

$$H_2S_2O_7(l) + H_2O(l) \rightarrow H_2SO_4(l)$$

Let us look at the equilibrium of the stage 2 reaction in detail. The oxidation of sulphur dioxide to sulphur trioxide is a slow one, so manufacturers use the catalyst vanadium(V) oxide, V_2O_5. As you can see, ΔH is negative, so the reaction is exothermic. Applying Le Chatelier's principle, using a low temperature shifts the equilibrium position to the right. However, a low temperature also means the reaction slows down, so a moderate temperature of 450 °C is used.

The equilibrium equation 2 tells us that there are three molecules on the left for every two on the right. So a high pressure would shift the equilibrium position to the right. However, despite this Le Chatelier prediction, a high pressure is not used. This is because the equilibrium position already lies well to the right, so the extra cost of high-pressure equipment is not necessary. A pressure of just above 10 atmospheres is used to push the gases around the plant.

8

a In stage 2, the concentration of reactants is kept high. Explain why.

b The sulphur trioxide formed is continually removed. Explain why.

c The conversion of sulphur dioxide to sulphur trioxide in modern chemical plants is 99.5%. What are the benefits of this (i) economically and (ii) environmentally?

KEY FACTS

■ Le Chatelier's principle is used to determine the conditions which will give the highest equilibrium yield of products in industrial processes involving reversible reactions.

■ Higher temperatures give a higher equilibrium yield of products when the reaction is endothermic (ΔH is positive).

■ Lower temperatures give a higher equilibrium yield of products when the reaction is exothermic (ΔH is negative).

■ In gaseous reactions that have fewer moles of product than of reactant, high pressures shift the equilibrium position to the right. It would move left if there were fewer moles of reactant than product.

■ In industrial processes, compromise temperatures are often used to speed up the rate of reaction and so produce a good yield of product in a reasonable time, even though the equilibrium yield is not at a maximum.

■ Even if it lowers yield, a compromise high pressure may be used to reduce energy costs and to avoid the cost of building and maintaining a very high pressure plant.

1 Each of the equations A, B, C and D represents a dynamic equilibrium.

A $N_2(g) + O_2(g) \rightleftharpoons 2NO(g)$ $\quad \Delta H^\circ = +180 \text{ kJ mol}^{-1}$
B $N_2O_4(g) \rightleftharpoons 2NO_2(g)$ $\quad \Delta H^\circ = +58 \text{ kJ mol}^{-1}$
C $3H_2(g) + N_2(g) \rightleftharpoons 2NH_3(g)$ $\quad \Delta H^\circ = -92 \text{ kJ mol}^{-1}$
D $H_2(g) + I_2(g) \rightleftharpoons 2HI(g)$ $\quad \Delta H^\circ = -10 \text{ kJ mol}^{-1}$

a Explain what is meant by the term *dynamic equilibrium*. (1)

b Explain why a catalyst does not alter the position of any equilibrium reaction. (2)

c The graphs below show how the yield of product varies with pressure for three of the reactions A, B, C and D given above.

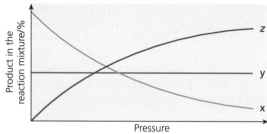

i) Identify a reaction from **A**, **B**, **C** and **D** which would have the relationship between yield and pressure shown in graphs x, y and z. (3)

ii) Explain why an industrial chemist would not use a very low pressure for the reaction represented in graph x. (2)

iii) Explain why an industrial chemist may not use a very high pressure for the reaction represented in graph z. (1)

iv) Add to the above graphs a line to show how the product yield would vary with pressure if the reaction which follows curve z was carried out at a temperature higher than that of the original graph. (1)

NEAB CH06 June 1998 Q4

2 The equilibrium yield of product in a gas-phase reaction varies with changes in temperature and pressure as shown below.

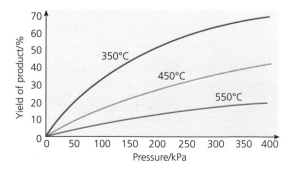

a Use the information given above to deduce whether the forward reaction involves an increase, a decrease, or no change in the number of moles present. Explain your deduction. (4)

b Use the information given above to deduce whether the forward reaction is exothermic or endothermic. Explain your answer. (3)

c i) Estimate the percentage yield of product which would be obtained at 350 8C and a pressure of 250 kPa.

ii) State what effect, if any, a catalyst has on the position of the equilibrium. Explain your answer. (4)

d A 70% equilibrium yield of product is obtained at a temperature of 350 °C and a pressure of 400 kPa. Explain why an industrialist may choose to operate the plant at

i) a temperature higher than 350 °C

ii) a pressure lower than 400 kPa (2)

NEAB CH02 February 1997 Q3

3

a Ammonia is synthesised in the Haber process.

i) Write an equation for this synthesis from nitrogen and hydrogen.

ii) State the catalyst used in this process.

iii) A typical ammonia synthesis plant operates at 450 °C. By reference to this reaction, for which $\Delta H = -92 \text{ kJ mol}^{-1}$, explain why this is a compromise temperature.

iv) A typical ammonia synthesis plant operates at a pressure of 2×10^4 kPa. By reference to this reaction, explain why this is a compromise pressure. (8)

b Six equations are given below which show the equilibria established when gaseous reactants, A(g) and B(g), form gaseous products, C(g) and D(g). In each case the enthalpy change in the reaction is stated.

1. $A(g) + B(g) \rightleftharpoons C(g) + D(g)$ Endothermic
2. $A(g) + B(g) \rightleftharpoons C(g) + D(g)$ Exothermic
3. $2A(g) + B(g) \rightleftharpoons C(g) + D(g)$ Endothermic
4. $2A(g) + B(g) \rightleftharpoons C(g) + D(g)$ Exothermic
5. $A(g) + B(g) \rightleftharpoons 2C(g) + D(g)$ Endothermic
6. $A(g) + B(g) \rightleftharpoons 2C(g) + D(g)$ Exothermic

Select from this list the number of the equation for which the equilibrium yield of products is always

i) increased when temperature is increased and pressure is increased.

ii) increased when temperature is increased and pressure is decreased.

iii) decreased when temperature is decreased and pressure is increased.

iv) decreased when temperature is increased but is unaffected by a change in pressure. (4)

NEAB CH02 June 1996 Q1

4 The following reaction is used to remove traces of carbon monoxide from synthesis gas.

$$CO(g) + 3H_2(g) \rightleftharpoons CH_4(g) + H_2O(g)$$
$$\Delta H^\circ = -206.1 \text{ kJ mol}^{-1}$$

The reaction is carried out at 325 8C in the presence of

a nickel catalyst.

a State the effect of the catalyst on
  i) the rate of the forward and backward reactions at equilibrium;
  ii) the equilibrium position. (3)

b State the effect on the equilibrium position of removing water from the reaction mixture. Explain your answer. (2)

c Give one reason why, in practice, a high temperature is used. (1)

NEAB CH02 February 1996 Q2

5 When a colourless solution containing thiocyanate ions, NCS⁻, is added to a pale yellow solution containing iron(III) ions, a dynamic equilibrium is established which can be represented by the following equation.

$$Fe^{3+}(aq) + NCS^-(aq) \rightleftharpoons Fe(NCS)^{2+}(aq)$$
                                    Deep red

a State what is meant by the term *dynamic* as applied to an equilibrium. (1)

b Give the term used to describe an equilibrium in which all reactants and products are in the same phase. (1)

c An aqueous solution containing iron(III) ions is added to the equilibrium mixture at a fixed temperature. State and explain the changes, if any, to the colour of the equilibrium mixture. (2)

d The red colour of the equilibrium mixture fades when the mixture is heated but reappears on cooling. State what can be deduced from this observation. (1)

NEAB CH02 June 1997 Q2

4 The equation for the synthesis of hydrazine by the direct combination of the elements is given below.
$$N_2(g) + 2H_2(g) \Leftrightarrow N_2H_4(g)$$

a Explain why the concentrations of reactants and products remain constant once a dynamic equilibrium has been established. (2)

b Explain why this reaction is described as *homogenous*. (1)

c Predict how the addition of a catalyst will affect the position of equilibrium. (1)

NEAB CH02 March 1998 PartQ4

Making ammonia

Ammonia is the starting material for many nitrogen-containing chemicals. Originally, the Haber process was developed to manufacture explosives but it was then used to more worthwhile ends manufacturing the raw materials for fertilisers.

The final reaction, which is exothermic, is simple:

$$N_2(g) + 3H_2(g) \rightarrow 2NH_3(g)$$

The conditions that would give the maximum yield from the reaction are not used by manufacturers. Instead, they use a set of conditions which are a compromise that is more cost-effective.

The data in the table below shows the percentage yield of ammonia under different conditions.

1 Describe the effect of temperature on the yield of ammonia.

2 Describe the effect of raising the temperature on the yield of ammonia.

3 Draw a graph to show the figures in the table. You must include all of the data on a single set of axes.

a What conditions give the best yield of ammonia?

b These conditions are not used in practice. Suggest why.

c Use the Internet to research the production of ammonia worldwide. List the top ten producers and consumers of ammonia and suggest reasons for the order of countries.

	Percentage yields of ammonia								
	Pressure/ atm								
Temperature/ °C	**0**	**50**	**100**	**150**	**200**	**250**	**300**	**350**	**400**
350	0	25	38	46	53	58	62	66	68
400	0	15	25	32	39	44	48	52	56
450	0	9	18	23	28	32	36	40	42
500	0	6	11	15	20	23	26	29	31
550	0	4	8	11	13	16	19	21	23

8 Oxidation and reduction

About 30 000 years ago, the inhabitants of southern France and northern Spain decorated their caves with lively paintings of the animals that they hunted for food. The pigments which the artists used to make paint were minerals which they ground up and mixed into a paste using mud or oil.

Their choice of pigments is fortunate, because minerals decay very slowly compared with organic pigments, and so after thousands of years we can still enjoy pictures such as the prehistoric painting shown here of a bison in the caves of Altamira in northern Spain. The red colour is iron(III) oxide, the yellow is iron(II) carbonate, and for black the artists used either manganese(IV) oxide or soot.

Until recently, paints contained mineral compounds of lead and chromium. But these elements are now known to be a health hazard, so safer, organic red and yellow pigments have replaced them.

Just like paintings, pottery has been around for thousands of years. The ancient Egyptians and later the Greeks and Romans produced beautiful ceramic pieces. Like today's potters, they included beautiful coloured pigments in the glaze. Like old paint pigments, these are usually transition metal oxides.

Makers of stained glass also use transition metal oxides. The blue comes from adding cobalt(II) oxide and blue-green from copper(II) oxide. The red results from reducing copper(II) oxide to copper(I) oxide using a strong reducing agent.

The range of colours is related to the different oxidation states of transition metals in their compounds, and different oxidation states come about through oxidation and reduction reactions.

8.1 Oxidation and reduction

Nearly every element known reacts to form compounds – even some 'inert' gases form compounds. When elements react, electrons in their atoms are redistributed. Either electrons are completely transferred from one atom to another, forming an ionic bond; or electrons are shared, forming covalent or co-ordinate bonds.

When an element in a molecule or a compound reacts, it may undergo oxidation. If this happens, then in the reaction as a whole, a different element has to undergo the opposite, reduction. If the element is reduced, then a different element must be oxidised.

The reaction as a whole is called a **redox reaction**. Redox is short for **red**uction-**ox**idation. Redox reactions are the subject of this chapter.

Oxidation

The brilliant white of the firework in the photograph is the result of magnesium powder reacting with oxygen:

$$Mg(s) + \tfrac{1}{2}O_2(g) \rightarrow MgO(s)$$

From your GCSE science course you will have learnt that oxidation was defined as the addition of oxygen to a compound. It is easy to see from the equation above that magnesium has been oxidised. Looking at what happens to magnesium alone, we can write this half-equation:

$$Mg \rightarrow Mg^{2+} + 2e^-$$

So in the reaction, magnesium undergoes both the addition of oxygen and the loss of electrons. Note that state symbols appear in the full equation, so can be left out in the half-equation.

Now we can extend the definition to take this into account:

Oxidation is the process of electron loss.

We call the last equation a **half-equation** because it covers only one half of the reaction, the part in which something has been oxidised. Note that the charges balance because we include electrons, e⁻, and that the half-equation shows that each magnesium atom loses two electrons.

Reduction

Now we look at the oxygen part of the reaction between magnesium and oxygen. The half-equation is:

$$\tfrac{1}{2}O_2 + 2e^- \rightarrow O^{2-}$$

In combining with magnesium, each atom in the oxygen molecule is reduced because it gains two electrons. We can now redefine reduction:

Reduction is the process of electron gain.

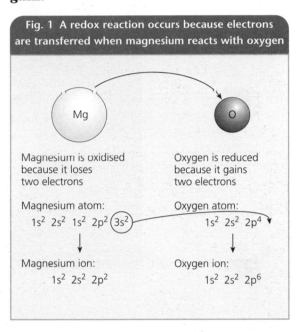

Fig. 1 A redox reaction occurs because electrons are transferred when magnesium reacts with oxygen

The half-equation represents the other half of the whole redox reaction. In any reaction which involves oxidation, something has to be reduced at the same time, and in this case, when magnesium is oxidised, oxygen is reduced.

OIL RIG – a memory aid

Use OIL RIG as an easy way to remember what happens in redox reactions:

Oxidation Is Loss of electrons

Reduction Is Gain of electrons

Oxidant and reductant

An **oxidant** is the species (atom, ion or molecule) which does the oxidising. It is often called the **oxidising agent**.

Magnesium burning in chlorine

When magnesium burns in chlorine, the following reaction occurs:

$$Mg(s) + Cl_2(g) \rightarrow MgCl_2(s)$$

The two half-equations for this reaction are:

$$Mg \rightarrow Mg^{2+} + 2e^-$$
$$Cl_2 + 2e^- \rightarrow 2Cl^-$$

Chlorine is the oxidant because it oxidises magnesium. Each atom in the chlorine molecule gains an electron. These electrons come from magnesium atoms, so we say that magnesium has been oxidised.

At the same time, chlorine has been reduced because magnesium atoms have given electrons to chlorine atoms. We say that magnesium is the **reductant**, or **reducing agent**, because it has reduced chlorine.

We can say that:

Oxidants take electrons from another species and are themselves reduced. Reductants give electrons to another species and are themselves oxidised.

Rules for writing half-equations

These are important rules to follow when writing any half-equation for an oxidation or a reduction:

- Only one element gains or loses electrons.
- The equation must balance for atoms (this applies also to full equations).
- The equation must balance for charge (this applies also to full equations).

We return to the subject of writing half-equations on page 121.

1 For the following reactions: (i) write down the full equation; (ii) write down the half-equations; (iii) state which species is being oxidised and which is being reduced; (iv) state which species is the oxidant and which is the reductant.

a Sodium reacting with bromine to form sodium bromide.

b Sodium burning in oxygen to form sodium oxide (Na_2O).

c Calcium reacting with iodine to form calcium iodide (CaI_2).

d Magnesium reacting with nitrogen to form magnesium nitride (MgN_3).

KEY FACTS

- Oxidation is the process of electron loss.
- Reduction is the process of electron gain.
- Redox reactions are reduction-oxidation reactions.

- Any reaction which involves oxidation must also involve reduction.
- An oxidant oxidises a species by taking electrons from it, while a reductant reduces a species by giving it electrons.

Oxidation states

The redox reaction of hydrogen and oxygen propels the US space shuttle beyond our atmosphere. The shuttle piggy-backs a lift on giant tanks containing 1.74 million litres of liquid hydrogen and 0.65 million litres of liquid oxygen.

In reactions which give rise to ionic compounds it is easy to see where electrons have been lost or gained. But what happens when there are covalent bonds in a reaction? For example:

$$H_2(g) + \tfrac{1}{2}O_2(g) \rightarrow H_2O(l)$$

It is not possible to write half-equations for this reaction, so, using our current definition of oxidation as a process of electron loss, how do we know hydrogen has been oxidised? This is where the concept of **oxidation states** comes in. No electrons are *transferred* in the formation of a covalent bond, we can *pretend* that they are.

In the covalent bond between hydrogen and oxygen in water, oxygen is the more **electronegative** element. This means that it has more power than hydrogen to attract electron density in the covalent bond (see page 30).

When we assign an oxidation state to oxygen we pretend that oxygen has taken two electrons, one from each hydrogen. We give oxygen an oxidation state of –2 because we think of it as having a charge of 2–.

In the same way, we assume that each hydrogen has 'lost' an electron, and has a charge of 1+. Thus the oxidation state of each hydrogen is +1.

Note that in oxidation states, the + or – comes in front of the number, while in charge, it is after the number (as for ions, eg Mg^{2+}).

In reality, electrons are not transferred when a covalent bond is formed. But, using this concept, we have a way of assigning a state of oxidation or reduction to an atom or ion.

We can now define oxidation and reduction in terms of changes in oxidation states:

Oxidation occurs when the oxidation state of an element in a reaction increases.

Reduction occurs when the oxidation state of an element in a reaction decreases.

The oxidation state of atoms in the molecules of an element is zero. So molecular hydrogen and oxygen atoms have an oxidation state of zero.

We can now see that for the reaction forming water from hydrogen and oxygen, hydrogen is oxidised because its oxidation state increases from 0 to +1, while oxygen is reduced because its oxidation state decreases from 0 to –2.

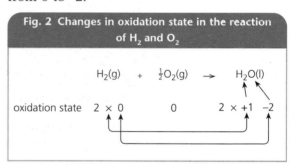

Fig. 2 Changes in oxidation state in the reaction of H_2 and O_2

Non-redox reactions

At this point, it is worth mentioning that not all reactions are redox reactions. Take for example the reaction between the base aluminium oxide and hydrochloric acid:

$$Al_2O_3 + 6HCl \rightarrow 2AlCl_3 + 3H_2O$$

In Al_2O_3, to be combined with three oxygens, total oxidation state –6, the two aluminium atoms must have a total oxidation state of +6. In $2AlCl_3$, the six chlorine atoms total –6, so again the aluminium atoms must total +6. Similarly, the oxidation states of the other elements do not change. Therefore the reaction is not a redox reaction. This applies to acid–base reactions in which a salt and water are formed.

Table 1 Simple rules for assigning oxidation states

1 The oxidation state of an atom in an element is always zero.

2 The oxidation state of a simple ion is its charge.

3 The oxidation state of fluorine in a compound is always −1 as it is the most electronegative element.

4 The oxidation state of oxygen is nearly always −2 (except in the peroxides and F_2O).

5 The oxidation state of chlorine in a compound is usually −1 (except when combined with F or O).

6 The oxidation state of hydrogen is +1 (except when it is bonded to a metal ion, in which case it is −1).

7 The sum of the oxidation states of all the atoms and ions in a compound is always zero.

8 The sum of the oxidation states in a polyatomic ion is always the charge on the ion.

Example: Assigning oxidation states

Work out the oxidation state of:

a lithium in lithium oxide;
b sulphur in sulphuric acid;
c chlorine in the chlorate(V) ion, ClO_3^-.

a Lithium is a Group I metal. It forms Li^+ ions. Since the charge on this ion is 1+, it is assigned an oxidation state of +1 (rule 2 in Table 1).

b The formula of sulphuric acid is H_2SO_4. We know that oxygen has an oxidation state of −2 (rule 4) and hydrogen +1 (rule 6). This just leaves the oxidation state of sulphur to determine. Since the oxidation states of all atoms and ions in a compound must add up to zero (rule 7), sulphur has an oxidation state of +6:

$$\begin{array}{ccc} H_2 & S & O_4 \\ (2 \times +1) + & (+6) + & (4 \times -2) = 0 \end{array}$$

c The charge on the ClO_3^- ion is 1−. According to rule 8, the oxidation states in a polyatomic ion must add up to its charge. The oxidation state of oxygen is −2 and there are three oxygen atoms, making a total of −6. This means that chlorine has to be +5 for the total of all the oxidation states to add up to 1−, the charge on the ion:

$$\begin{array}{ccc} Cl & O_3 & {}^- \\ +5 + & (3 \times -2) & = -1 \end{array}$$

Rules for assigning oxidation states

To work out the oxidation states of elements in compounds we use some simple rules. These are given in Table 8.1.

The box below the table shows how these rules can be applied.

2 Write down the oxidation states of each element in the following.

a NaCl
b HNO_3
c MnO_4^-
d K_2SO_4
e H_3PO_4
f $Cr_2O_7^{2-}$

Naming inorganic compounds and ions

Many compounds in daily use have traditional names, for example, ammonia. But the name ammonia does not tell you that it contains nitrogen and hydrogen atoms. So chemists give compounds more systematic names that are internationally agreed. Besides, systematic names are easier to work out and remember!

Iron oxide is a confusing name since it can refer to more than one oxide of iron. FeO and Fe_2O_3 are two common iron oxides. Since we know that oxygen has an oxidation state of −2, we can work out the oxidation state of iron in each oxide.

The iron ion in FeO must be Fe^{2+}, giving it an oxidation state of +2:

$$\begin{array}{cc} Fe^{2+} & O^{2-} \\ +2 + & -2 = 0 \end{array}$$

We name this compound iron(II) oxide. The roman numerals give the oxidation state of the iron. The Fe^{2+} ion is called the iron(II) ion. Note that the oxidation state is written without a space after the element to which it refers.

Fe_2O_3 is named iron(III) oxide because the iron has an oxidation state of +3. Each of its two metal ions is Fe^{3+} and is called iron(III).

Some elements exhibit several different oxidation states in their compounds, and so this type of systematic naming clarifies their oxidation state.

If a metal can have only one oxidation state in its compounds, we do not bother to put its oxidation state in its name. So NaCl is called sodium chloride, not sodium(I) chloride.

3 Name these compounds and ions systematically, using oxidation states.

a Cu_2O

b CuO

c MnO_2

d PbO

e $PbCl_4$

f Mn^{2+}

g Mn_2O_3

h SnO

4 Write the formulae of these compounds.

a iron(II) sulphate

b titanium(IV) oxide

c manganese(II) hydroxide

d copper(II) nitrate

e iron(II) bromide

Naming of oxoanions

Oxoanions are negative ions which contain oxygen. Oxoanions containing a metal require a systematic name to indicate the oxidation state of the metal. This can be calculated as shown in Table 2.

Table 2 also shows how to calculate the oxidation state of central non-metal atoms in some oxoanions that occur in aqueous acids.

Acids with oxygen in their oxoanions are named after these anions. The systematic names of HNO_3 and HNO_2 are nitric(V) acid and nitric(III) acid. Though their traditional names – nitric acid for HNO_3 and nitrous acid for HNO_2 – are still widely used, it is better to use their systematic names.

5 Name the following oxoanions of chlorine systematically.

a ClO^-

b ClO_2

c ClO_3^-

d ClO_4^-

6 The traditional names of sulphuric acid for H_2SO_4 and sulphurous acid for H_2SO_3 are still used. What are their systematic names?

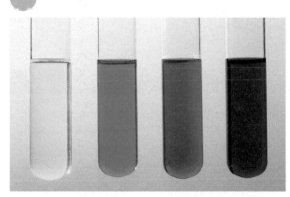

Vanadium has several oxidation states. It is at its highest at +5 in VO_2^+, the vanadyl(V) ion. This is yellow and in aqueous solution can be reduced by zinc to these oxidation states: +4 blue, +3 green, and +2 purple

Species	No. of oxygen atoms	Total oxidation no. for oxygen	Overall charge on the ion	Oxidation state of central atom	Name
MnO_4^-	4	−8	1−	+7	manganate(VII)
$Cr_2O_7^{2-}$	7	−14	2−	+6 each	dichromate(VI)
NO_3^-	3	−6	1−	+5	nitrate(V)
NO_2^-	2	−4	1−	+3	nitrate(III)

Table 2 Calculating the oxidation state of the central atoms in some oxoanions

KEY FACTS

■ Oxidation states show the states of oxidation or reduction of elements in a compound.

■ Oxidation occurs in a reaction when the oxidation state of an element increases: the new oxidation number is higher.

■ Reduction occurs in a reaction when the oxidation state of an element decreases: the new oxidation number is lower.

■ Oxidation states can be assigned to elements in compounds using a simple set of rules.

■ The oxidation state of an atom in an element is always zero. The oxidation state of a simple ion is its charge.

■ Systematic names are used to name metal ions and their compounds, particularly those with different oxidation states in different compounds.

■ Metal oxoanions and acids containing oxoanions are systematically named.

8.3 Oxidation and reduction of s and p block elements

Will an element in a covalently bonded compound be oxidised or reduced in a reaction? This is equivalent to asking: How easily does the element lose or gain electrons to form ions compared to the other elements in the compound? Ease of losing or gaining electrons is indicated by the element's electronegativity. Let us consider some of the redox reactions in which s and p block elements take part.

s block: Group I and Group II metals

Group I elements have one electron in their outermost shell (energy level). This outer electron can be transferred to non-metal atoms in reactions, which is why the Group I metals are so reactive. It also explains why they are good reductants. Because all metals lose electrons to form positive ions, they can all act as reductants.

The half-equation for lithium losing its electron and acting as a reductant is:

$$Li(s) \rightarrow Li^+(aq) + e^-$$

When lithium reacts with water, hydrogen is given off and lithium hydroxide is formed:

$$2Li(s) + 2H_2O(l) \rightarrow 2LiOH(aq) + H_2(g)$$

Let us examine these half-equations for the reaction:

$$2Li \rightarrow 2Li^+ + 2e^-$$
$$2H_2O + 2e^- \rightarrow 2OH^- + H_2$$

We can see that water has been reduced by lithium. But it may not be obvious which element in the water has been reduced. It becomes clear when we examine the water reduction half-equation more closely and assign oxidation numbers to the elements as in Table 3.

Table 3 Calculating which element in water is reduced							
$2H_2O(l)$	+	$2e^-$	$\rightarrow$	$2OH^-(aq)$		+	$H_2(g)$
+1 for each hydrogen −2 for oxygen			$\rightarrow$	−2 for each oxygen +1 for each hydrogen		+	0 for hydrogen as element
$(4 \times +1)$ + (2×-2) +		−2	$\rightarrow$	(2×-2) + $(2 \times +1)$ or 2×-1 (rule 8)		+	0
0	+	−2	$\rightarrow$	−2		+	0

Lithium reacts with water to form aqueous lithium hydroxide and hydrogen. Phenolphthalein indicator turns magenta in the presence of the OH⁻ ions formed

This calculation shows that some of the hydrogen atoms in water have been reduced because their oxidation state decreases from +1 to zero.

7 Calcium is a Group II element which reacts with cold water.

a How many electrons are present in the outer shell of calcium atoms?

b Write a balanced equation for the reaction of calcium with water.

c Write the two half-equations for this reaction.

d Why is calcium metal a good reductant?

p block: Group V elements

At the top of Group V are the non-metals nitrogen and phosphorus. These are vital for healthy plant growth and are constituent elements in all living things. The element nitrogen is in all proteins and nucleic acids, such as DNA which transmits our genetic characteristics. Phosphorus, too, is present in nucleic acids and in bones and teeth.

8 A 70 kg human being contains about 3.5 kg of the compound $Ca_5(PO_4)_3OH$ which is a major constituent of bones and teeth. What is the oxidation state of phosphorus in this compound?

Nitrogen is a very unreactive element, which is why 78 per cent of our atmosphere is still nitrogen. Even in the hot cylinders of a car engine, very little of it reacts. The spark temperature can reach 2500 °C, which provides enough energy to break the very strong triple bond of the nitrogen molecule and to form nitrogen oxides, NO_x, with oxygen.

9 Nitrogen monoxide is the main compound formed from the reaction of nitrogen and oxygen in a car engine.

a Write a balanced equation for this reaction.

b (i) What is the oxidation state of nitrogen in nitrogen monoxide in this reaction?
(ii) What is the systematic name for this compound?

c Dinitrogen oxide (N_2O) and nitrogen dioxide (NO_2) are also formed in car engines. What are the oxidation states of nitrogen in these compounds?

The Haber process uses a series of reactions to convert nitrogen to ammonia (see Chapter 7). The equation for the final reaction is:

$$N_2(g) + 3H_2(g) \rightarrow 2NH_3(g)$$
$$0 + 0 \rightarrow (2 \times -3) + (6 \times +1)$$

In this case, nitrogen is acting as an oxidant and it has been reduced from oxidation state 0 to oxidation state –3. This reaction also illustrates another rule about assigning oxidation numbers, based on the

---

APPLICATION A

The thermite reaction

Igniting a fuse of magnesium ribbon provides the energy that starts the thermite reaction. Then, aluminium powder reacts spectacularly with iron(III) oxide to produce aluminium oxide and molten iron

Aluminium is a good reductant, reducing many metal oxides to the metal. In the thermite reaction, aluminium powder reduces iron(III) oxide to iron and forms aluminium oxide. The thermite reaction is so vigorous and generates so much heat that the iron produced is molten.

1 Aluminium is a Group III element.
 a To which block of the Periodic Table does it belong?
 b How many electrons are in its outer shell?
 c What oxidation state does aluminium have in its compounds?

2 Write a balanced equation for the thermite reaction, and underneath each reactant and product write the oxidation states of the elements present (see Table 3).

3 Explain in terms of oxidation states which element has been oxidised and which reduced.

4 Identify the oxidant in this reaction.

fact that we pretend that a more electronegative element takes electrons from the less electronegative element:

The more electronegative element in a compound is always taken as the negative element.

When a non-metal reacts with a metal, the non-metal acts as an oxidant because it gains electrons to form an ion. This is what happens when magnesium nitride is formed. Some nitride is always produced when magnesium is burnt in air:

$$3Mg(s) + N_2(g) \rightarrow Mg_3N_2(s)$$

The nitride ion is N^{3-}. The oxidation state of nitrogen in this ion is therefore -3.

When Mg_3N_2 is added to water, ammonia is evolved; this is not a redox reaction:

$$Mg_3N_2(aq) + 6H_2O(l) \rightarrow 3Mg(OH)_2(aq) + 2NH_3(g)$$

p block: Group VII elements

When Group VII elements react with metals they form compounds containing halide ions. This is certainly true of their reactions with s block elements. For example:

$$Ca(s) + Cl_2(g) \rightarrow CaCl_2(s)$$
$$2K(s) + I_2(s) \rightarrow 2KI(s)$$

In all these compounds the halogen has an oxidation state of -1.

The halogens are good oxidants because their atoms readily gain an electron to acquire a noble gas electron configuration. When they react with metals that can exist in two or more oxidation states, the metal often gains the higher oxidation state. So, when chlorine is passed over hot iron wire, iron(III) chloride, $FeCl_3$, is formed, rather than iron(II) chloride, $FeCl_2$.

In reactions with non-metals (and some p block and transition metals), Group VII elements form covalent compounds. In most of these the oxidation state is -1. Examples include $SiCl_4$, PCl_3 and PCl_5.

Oxidation states of sulphur

Sulphur is in Group VI. It can exist in several different oxidation states. We can illustrate this with the reactions of solid sodium halides with concentrated sulphuric acid. For example, the reaction for sodium chloride with sulphuric acid is:

$$NaCl(s) + H_2SO_4(l) \rightarrow NaHSO_4(aq) + HCl(g)$$

The oxidation state of sulphur is +6 in H_2SO_4 and +6 in $NaHSO_4$, so no oxidation or reduction has taken place. However, if we repeat the same reaction with sodium bromide, the concentrated sulphuric acid will oxidise a little of the HBr produced to Br_2:

$$NaBr(s) + H_2SO_4(l) \rightarrow NaHSO_4(aq) + HBr(g)$$
$$2HBr(g) + H_2SO_4(l) \rightarrow 2H_2O + SO_2(g) + Br_2(g)$$

In the second reaction, the sulphur in the concentrated sulphuric acid is reduced from +6 to +4 in sulphur dioxide. Concentrated sulphuric acid is a strong oxidant, but it is not strong enough to oxidise all of the hydrogen bromide present.

When solid sodium iodide is used, most of the hydrogen iodide formed is oxidised, and this is one of the reactions:

$$8HI + H_2SO_4 \rightarrow H_2S(g) + 4H_2O(l) + 4I_2(g)$$

10 Consider the reaction between solid sodium iodide and concentrated sulphuric acid. It follows the pattern for the other sodium halides.

a Write an equation to show the formation of hydrogen iodide.

b When sulphuric acid acts as an oxidant, one of the reactions, shown in the equation above, produces hydrogen sulphide. What is the oxidation state of sulphur in this compound?

c Reread this section carefully. What is the trend in ease of oxidation of the hydrogen halides?

KEY FACTS

■ s block metals lose electrons in their reaction and are good reductants.

■ Group VII elements gain electrons in their reactions and are good oxidants.

■ Many p block elements exhibit more than one oxidation state when they form compounds.

Redox equations

In this chapter we have seen that for every reduction reaction an oxidation reaction happens at the same time and vice versa, and that half-equations can be used to represent either the oxidation or the reduction.

More on writing half-equations

Many redox reactions occur in aqueous solution and they often involve ions. Writing balanced equations for the overall reaction and then writing half-equations, helps us to work out what is being oxidised or reduced. The two half-equations must add up to the balanced equation for the whole reaction. Look back at page 114 for the rules.

Redox reaction for Cu(II) and Zn

Let's consider the redox reaction between zinc and copper(II) ions in a solution of copper(II) sulphate and zinc. The overall equation for this reaction is:

$$Zn(s) + CuSO_4(aq) \rightarrow ZnSO_4(aq) + Cu(s)$$

Since the reaction involves ions, we can write these ions into a full equation:

$$Zn(s) + Cu^{2+}(aq) + SO_4^{2-}(aq) \rightarrow$$
$$Zn^{2+}(aq) + SO_4^{2-}(aq) + Cu(s)$$

Note that the sulphate ions do not change. They remain free and unreacted in the solution. As they take no part in the reaction, they are sometimes called **spectator ions** and can be omitted from an equation, leaving:

$$Zn(s) + Cu^{2+}(aq) \rightarrow Zn^{2+}(aq) + Cu(s)$$

From the reaction equation, the two half-equations are:

oxidation of zinc: $\quad Zn(s) \rightarrow Zn^{2+}(aq) + 2e^-$
reduction of copper(II) ions:
$$Cu^{2+}(aq) + 2e^- \rightarrow Cu(s)$$

When zinc is dipped into aqueous copper(II) sulphate, a redox reaction occurs. Copper(II) ions are reduced to copper which can be seen coating the zinc. Some of the zinc has been oxidised to zinc ions and enters the solution which changes from blue to colourless

11

a For the reaction between zinc and aqueous copper(II) sulphate, explain in terms of loss and gain of electrons why zinc is oxidised and copper is reduced.

b Write two half-equations for this reaction:
$$Cu(s) + 2AgNO_3(aq) \rightarrow$$
$$Cu(NO_3)_2(aq) + 2Ag$$
Label them as either oxidation or reduction half-equations.

c Describe what you would see if you dipped a copper rod into a solution of silver nitrate.

Redox reaction for Mg and HCl

Another redox reaction occurs when magnesium reacts with hydrochloric acid. We can write the full equation for this reaction:

$$Mg(s) + 2HCl(aq) \rightarrow MgCl_2(aq) + H_2(g)$$

Written as ions, this equation is:

$$Mg(s) + 2H^+(aq) + 2Cl^-(aq) \rightarrow$$
$$Mg^{2+}(aq) + 2Cl^-(aq) + H_2(g)$$

which shows that the chloride ions do not take part in the reaction – they are the spectator ions.

Magnesium reacts with dilute hydrochloric acid to form aqueous magnesium chloride and hydrogen gas

We also know what the reactant are: Mg and H^+; and we know the products: Mg^{2+} and H_2. We can now construct the two half-equations:

oxidation of magnesium:
$$Mg(s) \rightarrow Mg^{2+}(aq) + 2e^-$$
reduction of hydrogen:
$$2H^+(aq) + 2e^- \rightarrow H_2(g)$$

We can work out the oxidation states of elements in oxygen-containing compounds and oxoanions.

Redox reaction for sulphur dioxide and chlorine

Let's look at the oxidation by chlorine of sulphur dioxide to sulphuric acid:

$$SO_2(g) + Cl_2(aq) + 2H_2O(l) \rightarrow H_2SO_4(aq) + 2HCl(aq)$$

Chlorine gas, Cl_2, with an oxidation state of 0, is being reduced to Cl^- with an oxidation state of −1. We can construct a reduction half-equation to show this:

$$Cl_2(g) + 2e^- \rightarrow 2Cl^-(aq)$$

The oxidation half-equation is a little more complicated, and we will build it up in stages. We know that sulphur dioxide changes to sulphuric acid, and in aqueous solution the sulphuric acid is present as H^+ and SO_4^{2-} ions. A review of the oxidation numbers tells us that this is an oxidation:

$$\begin{array}{cc} S & O_2 \\ +4 & 2(-2) \end{array} \rightarrow \begin{array}{cc} S & O_4^{2-} \\ +6 & 4(-2) \end{array}$$

The oxidation number of sulphur changes from +4 to +6. This means that sulphur loses two electrons:

$$SO_2(g) \rightarrow SO_4^{2-}(aq) + 2e^-$$

But this does not balance in terms of atoms or charges. This is where the water shown in the balanced reaction equation comes in:

$$SO_2(g) + 2H_2O(l) \rightarrow SO_4^{2-}(aq) + 4H^+(aq) + 2e^-$$

You will often see the involvement of water and H^+ ions in half-equations.

We can now bring the two half-equations together:

$$SO_2(g) + 2H_2O(l) \rightarrow SO_4^{2-}(aq) + 4H^+(aq) + 2e^-$$
$$Cl_2(g) + 2e^- \rightarrow 2Cl^-(aq)$$

Adding the equations, combining the acid ions and cancelling the electrons, gives the reaction equation:

$$SO_2(g) + Cl_2(aq) + 2H_2O(l) \rightarrow H_2SO_4(aq) + 2HCl(aq)$$

Redox reaction for nitric acid and copper

Copper reacts with dilute nitric acid to produce nitrogen monoxide and copper(II) nitrate. We can build up the reaction equation by first working out the half-equations. The copper must have been oxidised to produce the copper(II) nitrate which contains copper(II) ions:

oxidation: $Cu(s) \rightarrow Cu^{2+}(aq) + 2e^-$

Copper's oxidation state changes from 0 to +2.

We now work out the reduction half-equation by considering what happens to the nitrogen in nitric acid. Nitric acid in dilute solution is made up of H^+ ions and NO_3^- ions, so:

$$\begin{array}{cc} N & O_3^-(aq) \\ +5 & 3(-2) \end{array} \rightarrow \begin{array}{cc} N & O(g) \\ +2 & -2 \end{array}$$

Nitrogen is therefore reduced from +5 to +2, which means it has lost three electrons:

$$NO_3^-(aq) + 3e^- \rightarrow NO(g)$$

This is unbalanced for charges and atoms. As in the reaction with sulphur dioxide and chlorine above, water and H^+ ions must be involved to balance the half-equation:

reduction:
$$NO_3^-(aq) + 4H^+(aq) + 3e^- \rightarrow NO(g) + 2H_2O(l)$$

To obtain the reaction equation, we need the same number of electrons on both sides. To do this, we multiply the oxidation half-equation given above for copper by 3, and the reduction half-equation by 2.

$$3Cu(s) \rightarrow 3Cu^{2+}(aq) + 6e^-$$
$$2NO_3^-(aq) + 8H^+(aq) + 6e^- \rightarrow 2NO(g) + 4H_2O(l)$$

Adding the equations and cancelling the electrons gives the reaction equation:

$$3Cu(s) + 2NO_3^-(aq) + 8H^+(aq) \rightarrow$$
$$3Cu^{2+}(aq) + 2NO(g) + 4H_2O(l)$$

Redox reaction for potassium manganate(VII) and iron(II) ions

In the presence of acid, the manganate(VII) anion, MnO_4^-, is a powerful oxidising agent. The concentration of a potassium manganate(VII) solution can be standardised by titrating it against a standard solution of iron(II) ions acidified with dilute sulphuric acid.

The manganate(VII) ion is reduced to the manganate(II) ion:

$$MnO_4^-(aq) \rightarrow Mn^{2+}(aq)$$

The oxidation state of manganese changes from +7 to +2. This reduction must involve gaining five electrons:

$$MnO_4^- + 5e^- \rightarrow Mn^{2+}$$

But this equation is not balanced for oxygen. Oxygen combines with hydrogen ions in the acidic solution to form water. Therefore the balanced half-equation for the reduction is as follows:

reduction:
$$MnO_4^-(aq) + 8H^+(aq) + 5e^- \rightarrow Mn^{2+}(aq) + 4H_2O(l)$$

The half-equation is now balanced: the numbers of atoms are equal on both sides, and the total charge on the left equals the total charge on the right.

While the manganate(VII) is reduced, the iron(II) is oxidised to iron(III). The half-equation is:

oxidation: $Fe^{2+}(aq) \rightarrow Fe^{3+}(aq) + e^-$

Redox reaction for dichromate(VI) ion

As for the manganate(VII) ion, in acidic solution the dichromate(VI) ion, $Cr_2O_7^{2-}$, is a strong oxidising agent. It is commonly used in volumetric analysis to estimate concentrations of reducing agents. For example, for the reducing agent Fe^{2+}, the redox equations are:

oxidation: $\qquad 6Fe^{2+}(aq) \rightarrow 6Fe^{3+}(aq) + 6e^-$

reduction: $\ Cr_2O_7^{2-}(aq) + 14H^+(aq) + 6e^- \rightarrow 2Cr^{3+}(aq) + 7H_2O(l)$

Adding these and cancelling the electrons gives the full reaction equation:

$$6Fe^{2+}(aq) + Cr_2O_7^{2-}(aq) + 14H^+(aq) \rightarrow$$
$$6Fe^{3+}(aq) + 2Cr^{3+}(aq) + 7H_2O(l)$$

Redox reaction for the element silver and magnesium(II) ions

When we place magnesium in a solution of silver ions, there is a redox reaction which produces magnesium ions and silver. We can work out the half-equations from this information.

oxidation of magnesium:
$$Mg(s) \rightarrow Mg^{2+}(aq) + 2e^-$$
reduction of silver ions: $\quad Ag^+(aq) + e^- \rightarrow Ag(s)$

We can combine these to give an overall redox equation. All the electrons released from the magnesium atoms must combine with the silver ions. This means that the number of electrons in the oxidation half-equation must be the same as the number of electrons in the reduction half-equation. In that case we need to multiply the silver half-equation by 2:

$$2Ag^+(aq) + 2e^- \rightarrow 2Ag(s)$$

Now that the electrons in both half-equations are equal, we can combine them:

$$Mg(s) + 2Ag^+(aq) \rightarrow Mg^{2+}(aq) + 2Ag(s)$$

12 Work out the overall redox equation for the reaction between acidified aqueous manganate(VII) ions and iron(II) ions using the half-equations in the example in the left column.

KEY FACTS

- Half-equations can be written for the oxidation and reduction half-reaction which occur in a redox reaction.

- Provided the reactants and products are specified a half-equation can be worked out.

- To combine half-equations to give an overall redox equation, the electrons in both half-equations must be the same.

1 Hydrazine, N_2H_4, and dinitrogen tetroxide, N_2O_4, react together to form nitrogen and water.
a Give the oxidation states of nitrogen in N_2H_4 and in N_2O_4.
b Write an equation for the reaction between N_2H_4 and in N_2O_4. (3)
NEAB CH02 March 1998 PartQ4

2 The following is an equation for a redox reaction.
$$2H_2O + SO_2 + 2[CuCl_4]^{2-} \rightarrow 4H^+ + SO_4^{2-} + 4Cl^- + 2[CuCl_2]^-$$
a Identify the element being oxidised in this reaction and write a half-equation for the oxidation of the species containing this element. (2)
b Identify the element being reduced in this reaction and write a half-equation for the reduction of the species containing this element. (2)
NEAB CH02 June 1998 Q5

3 The concentration of sulphur dioxide in air can be measured using an acidified solution of potassium manganate(VII) which oxidises sulphur dioxide to sulphate ions, SO_4^{2-}.
a State, in terms of electrons, what happens to a species when it is oxidised. (1)
b State the oxidisation states of sulphur in SO_2 and in SO_4^{2-}. (2)
c Deduce the half-equation for the oxidisation of sulphur dioxide to sulphate ions in the presence of water. (1)
d Write the half-equation for the reduction of manganate(VII) ions in acid solution. (2)
NEAB CH02 February 1996 Q5

4
a Use the concept of oxidisation states to deduce whether either of the reactions given below involves redox processes. Explain your answers and, where appropriate, identify the element which is being oxidised.
i) $2NH_3 + 3Cl_2 \rightarrow N_2 + 6HCl$
ii) $CuO + 2HCl \rightarrow CuCl_2 + H_2O$

b i) Potassium manganate(VII), $KMnO_4$, can be used in the quantative estimation of ethanedioate ions, $C_2O_4^{2-}$, in an acidified aqueous solution. In this reaction, ethanedioate ions are converted into carbon dioxide. Deduce half-equaitons for the redox processes involved and hence derive an equation for the overall reaction. (3)
ii) A 1.93 g sample of a crystalline ethanedioate salt dissolved in water and made up to 250 cm³. 25.0 cm³ of this solution, after acidification, was found to react with 30.4 cm³ of 0.0200 M $KMnO_4$. Calculate the percentage by mass of ethanedioate ions in the original salt.
NB If you are you are unable to deduce the overall ratio $C_2O_4^{2-} : MnO_4^-$ for this reaction you may assume the ratio 5 : 3 (This is not the correct ratio). (6)
NEAB CH02 February 1997 Q7

5
a State the meaning of the term *oxidising agent*.
b When solid potassium manganate(VII) is heated, it decomposes according to the equation below.
$$2KMnO_4 \rightarrow K_2MnO_4 + MnO_2 + O_2$$
Explain, in terms of the oxidisation states, why this is a redox reaction. (3)
NEAB CH02 March 1999 Q6

6 When an acidified solution containing $Cr_2O_7^{2-}$ ions is added to an aqueous solution containing Sn^{2+} ions, a redox reaction occurs. The products of this reaction can be considered as Sn^{4+} ions, Cr^{3+} ions and water. Derive half-equations for the reduction of $Cr_3O_7^{2-}$ ions in an acidified solution and the oxidisation of Sn^{2+} ions and hence deduce the overall equation. (3)
NEAB CH02 June 1996 Q6

Colourful pottery

Metal oxides have been used to colour pottery for thousands of years. The table below shows some of the colours available from different transition metal pigments.

1 Prepare an article for the magazine The Ceramicist, in a series of articles about the science behind the development of pottery over the last 2000 years. You have been asked to write about the use of pigments and glazes in a style suitable for a non-scientific readership. Your article must be less than 200 words and include at least two diagrams.

2 The compound giving the white colour when fired in an oxidising atmosphere is titanium(IV) oxide with a formula of TiO_2. From the table, copy the metal oxide column and add their chemical formulae.

The percentage addition column in the table refers to the percentage of the glaze that is the relevant metal oxide. So, to produce a yellowish green colour the potter will need to use 2 g of chromium(III) oxide in every 100 g of glaze, and fire in an oxidising atmosphere. If the glaze has the wrong concentration, the colour will be wrong. Glaze manufacturers make random colour checks on every consignment of glaze they produce.

Testing for iron(II) oxide concentration

To test iron(II) oxide concentration in a glaze sample:

1 Weigh out 10 g of glaze and warm it with dilute sulphuric acid to dissolve the iron(II) oxide.

2 Filter off any residue (impurities in the glaze) and make up the iron(II) sulphate solution to 250 cm^3 with dilute sulphuric acid.

3 Titrate 25 cm^3 portions of this solution against 0.005 mol dm^{-3} potassium manganate(VII) solution. The solutions react as shown:

$$MnO_4^-(aq) + 8H^+(aq) + 5Fe^{2+}(aq) \rightarrow Mn^{2+}(aq) + 4H_2O(l) + 5Fe^{3+}(aq)$$

4 The purple potassium manganate(VII) solution is decolourised. But as soon as all of the iron(II) ions have reacted, the next drop of potassium manganate(VII) solution gives a pink tinge.

5 The volume of potassium manganate(VII) solution can then be used to calculate the moles of iron(II) ions in the original solution and so the mass of iron(II) oxide in the original sample.

Mass of glaze sample	9.85 g
Concentration of potassium manganate(VII) solution	0.005 mol dm^{-3}
Volume of potassium manganate(VII) solution	23.9 cm^3

3 Use the data above to calculate:

a the concentration of the iron(II) sulphate solution;

b the mass of iron(II) oxide in the original glaze sample;

c the percentage of iron oxide in the glaze.

d What colour would the glaze sample give when used in a reducing atmosphere?

Transition metal oxides used in glazes			
Metal oxide	Addition to glaze as a %	Colour when fixed in oxidising atmosphere	Colour when fixed in reducing atmosphere
Titanium(IV)		white	
Vanadium(V)	6	yellow	
Chromium(III)	2	yellowish green	emerald green
Manganese(IV)	4	purple	brown
Iron(III)	1		willow green
	2	tan	olive green
	4	brown	mottled green
	10	black-brown	red-brown
Cobalt(II)	0.5	medium blue	medium blue
	1	strong blue	strong blue
Nickel(II)		grey	grey-blue
Copper(II)	0.5		copper red
	1	turquoise	deep red
	2	turquoise	red and black
	8	blue-green	black

9 Halogens

How many lives can an element save? And which element is the biggest life-saver? Oxygen? Silver? Gold? In fact, the title of Life-saving Element should probably go to chlorine, or at least one of the halogens. Millions of people across the world are alive today because of chlorine's ability to kill bacteria.

In the UK we take chlorine's effect on our water supplies for granted. But in London less than 150 years ago, water-borne cholera killed thousands of people every year. Adding chlorine to drinking water cut the number of deaths to almost nothing, and now, cholera is almost unknown in the UK. The story is similar elsewhere: chlorine has wiped out many of the diseases carried by dirty water. It is impossible to work out exactly how many lives have been saved, but we can assume that it runs into many millions.

These cylinders contain enough chlorine to treat the water for millions of people for weeks

9.1 The halogens

Chlorine is one of a group of elements called the halogens. Halogen is another name for the Group VII elements. The word halogen comes from a Greek word meaning 'salt producing' and was used because halogens were known to occur in salts in the sea.

1 Use the Periodic Table to deduce the electronic configuration for fluorine, chlorine and bromine.

Table 1 The halogens		
Atomic number	**Symbol**	**Notes**
9	F	Fluorine is a pale yellow gas at room temperature
17	Cl	Chlorine is a yellow-green gas at room temperature
35	Br	Bromine is a dark red liquid at room temperature
53	I	Iodine is shiny grey-black crystalline solid at roomtemperature
85	At	Astatine is very radioactive and very rare

Occurrence

The halogen elements are not found in nature because they are too reactive. They are always combined with other elements. Chlorine is the commonest halogen, ranking as the eighteenth most common element. Chlorine occurs mostly in sodium chloride in sea water, see Table 2, and in salt deposits. Fluorine is the next most common halogen and is found in rock deposits such as fluorspar, CaF_2, and cryolite, Na_3AlF_6. Bromine and iodine are less common. Both occur as ions of salts in sea water: bromine is actually extracted from sea water, where it is present at between 65 and 70 parts per million.

Table 2 Average composition of sea water	
Ion	**Mass of dissolved salts/%**
Anions	
chloride (Cl^-)	55.042
sulphate (SO_4^{2-})	7.682
hydrogencarbonate (HCO_3^-)	0.406
bromide (Br^-)	0.189
borate ($H_2BO_3^-$)	0.075
fluoride (F^-)	0.029
Cations	
sodium (Na^+)	30.612
magnesium (Mg^{2+})	3.689
calcium (Ca^{2+})	1.160
potassium (K^+)	1.102
strontium (Sr^{2+})	0.038

2

a Work out the electron configurations for the chloride, bromide, fluoride and sodium ions.

b How did these ions get into sea water?

Uses of fluorine and chlorine
Fluorine
Fluoride ions, naturally present in some water supplies, strengthen tooth enamel, and compounds of fluorine are added to many toothpastes to reduce tooth decay. Some water companies add fluorides to the water supply if there is little naturally present. Fluorine compounds are used to make non-stick coatings for pots and pans and plastics such as PTFE, poly(tetrafluoroethene). Fluorine is also an ingredient of CFCs and anaesthetics.

Chlorine
Chlorine has many uses that depend on its disinfecting properties. We use it to purify water supplies and swimming pools. But it was also used with devastating effect as a chemical warfare gas during World War I. Many troops were killed and many more maimed for the rest of their lives.

Bleach solution contains chlorine which whitens paper pulp and fabrics, and is used in the home to bleach and disinfect. Chlorine compounds are used to manufacture plastics such as PVC and polyester for a whole range of consumer goods including trainers and cosmetics. Many manufactured insecticides contain chlorine. They include DDT and BHC. Chlorine is also present in the medicine used to treat leukaemia.

Chlorine is so useful that its compounds, many of them manufactured, are increasingly building up as waste around the world. This is of concern to environmentalists who point to the damage done to wildlife caused by DDT.

DDT (**d**ichloro**d**iphenyl**t**richloroethane.) is an insecticide containing chlorine. It was developed to wipe out the malaria mosquito and was spectacularly successful at first: cases of malaria fell dramatically as the numbers of mosquitoes that carried the disease fell.

The problem was that DDT not only kills insects but accumulates to toxic levels in other organisms. It is a very stable molecule, so it persists in the environment and becomes more concentrated as it passes up food chains. As an example of its toxic effect, DDT was linked to thinner shells in birds' eggs. In the UK during the 1960s, there was a sharp decline in the number of sparrow hawks which, as birds of prey, are secondary consumers and so more likely to accumulate DDT in their cells.

Because some malaria mosquitoes developed immunity to DDT, other insecticides were developed, and the use of DDT was banned in one country after another. In the UK, the number of sparrow hawks is now healthy and increasing. Yet DDT still persists in the environment, and it will be decades before it clears completely from the biosphere.

3 List the benefits and problems associated with the widespread use of chlorine compounds.

APPLICATION A | **Concentrating DDT**

Organism	Main food source	DDT level/p.p.m.
cormorant	larger fish	26.4
heron	small fish	3.57
herring gull	scavenger	6.00
osprey	larger fish	13.8
tern	small fish	3.91
needlefish	small fish	2.07
pickerel fish	small fish	1.33
sheepshead minnow	plant eater	0.94
silverside minnow	plant eater	0.23
Plankton	photosynthetic	0.04
Water	–	0.000 05

The table shows the levels of the insecticide DDT found in organisms in a coastal estuary. The levels are given in parts per million. DDT is a fat-soluble chemical, so it tends to accumulate in the fatty tissues of living organisms. A predator feeding on a DDT-containing organism will tend to extract the DDT and store it in its own fatty tissues. Generally, a predator tends to be larger than its prey and will eat lots of them over its lifetime. In this way, predators accumulate DDT.

1

a Give data from the table that supports the idea that DDT accumulates in the biosphere.

b The American eagle is a carnivorous bird which can attack and eat smaller birds like the tern or the osprey. What prediction can you make about the levels of DDT in its body?

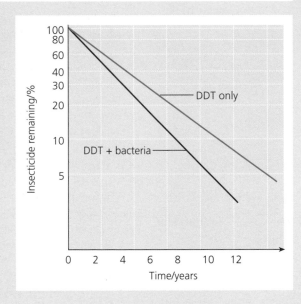

Scientists in New Zealand investigated the rate of breakdown of DDT in the type of soil used in hen-houses where DDT is used to kill insect parasites on poultry. The soil was made up of waste paper and chicken manure contaminated with DDT, and certain bacteria were added. They appeared to increase the rate of DDT breakdown, as shown in the graph.

2 If adding bacteria to the mixture doubles the rate of breakdown, how long will it take to reduce the DDT level to 20% of its original value?

3 Give the advantages and disadvantages of an insecticide which is broken down to harmless chemicals in the environment within 5 days of application.

Table 3 Physical properties of the halogens							
Halogen	Electron configuration	Atomic radius/nm	Ionic radius/nm	Melting point/°C	Boiling point/°C	Electronegativity	Electron affinity/ kJ mol^{-1}
fluorine	$1s^2\ 2s^2\ 2p^5$	0.071	0.133	−220	−188	4.0	333
chlorine	$1s^2\ 2s^2\ 2p^6\ 3s^2\ 3p^5$	0.099	0.180	−101	−35	3.0	348
bromine	$[Ar]\ 3d^{10}\ 4s^2\ 4p^5$	0.114	0.195	−7	59	2.8	340
iodine	$[Kr]\ 4d^{10}\ 5s^2\ 5p^5$	0.133	0.215	114	184	2.5	297
astatine	$[Xe]\ 5d^{10}\ 6s^2\ 6p^5$	0.140	–	?	?	–	–

9.2 Physical properties of the halogens

The halogens are non metallic elements that exist as diatomic molecules, for example, Cl_2 and I_2. Table 3 gives some physical data for the halogens.

Atomic radius

The atomic radius increases down the group because the number of electron shells increases. The positive charge of the nucleus also increases and pulls the electrons shells closer, which tends to reduce the size of the atom. However, the addition of shells more than counteracts this. Each outer shell is to some extent shielded from the pull of the nucleus by the inner shells, so that, overall, the atomic radii increase down the group.

Boiling point

Van der Waals forces are attractive forces that act between molecules because of the uneven distribution of electrons in molecules. The electron distribution changes from one instant to the next, each time causing a temporary dipole with one end of the molecule more negative and the other end less negative. This induces an adjacent molecule to become a temporary dipole also. The result is that electron distribution in halogen molecules is always changing, but that the attraction between oppositely charged ends tends to hold the molecules together.

The boiling point of fluorine is –188 °C. The dipoles formed by its few electrons do not produce sufficiently strong intermolecular van der Waals forces for it to be a liquid at room temperature. With more electrons, chlorine's dipoles produce a greater intermolecular attraction, so its boiling point is higher, at –35 °C.

Bromine, with boiling point at 59 °C, is one of the few elements liquid at room temperature, while iodine is a solid at room temperature. With larger molecules and more electrons than chlorine, bromine and iodine have successively greater van der Waals forces. For iodine to change from a liquid to a gas requires energy to overcome these intermolecular forces. This means that, at 184 °C, iodine's boiling point is the highest of the first four Group VII elements. We say that **volatility** – the tendency for a substance to become gaseous – decreases down Group VII.

4 Use data in Table 3 to estimate the melting point and boiling point of astatine.

Electronegativity

The electronegativity of an atom is a measure of the force of attraction of its nucleus for the electrons of other atoms bonded with it. Atoms which attract electrons strongly are said to be strongly electronegative, and high electronegativity tends to make an element very reactive. The electronegativity of all the halogens is high, but it decreases down the group, as seen in Table 3.

Fluorine is a small atom, so that another atom bonded to it gets close to the fluorine nucleus. Also, with few electron shells to shield the other atom from its nucleus, the attractive force is particularly strong. In fact, fluorine is the most electronegative of all the elements: it has the strongest attraction for the electrons of an atom covalently bonded to it, such as the electron of hydrogen in the gas hydrogen fluoride. In such a compound, the electron cloud is strongly distorted towards the fluorine atom.

Chlorine is a bigger atom with one more shell of electrons to shield the electrons of another, covalently bonded atom from the attractive force of its nucleus. Though not quite so electronegative as fluorine, chlorine is still a very reactive element.

As the size of the atom increases in bromine and iodine, so do the number of shells of electrons shielding the nucleus. Both size and number of shells reduce the power of the nucleus to attract other electrons. So bromine is less reactive than chlorine, and iodine is less reactive than bromine: F > Cl > Br > I.

5 In general, Group O elements are inert and do not form compounds. An exception is xenon tetrafluoride with the formula XeF_4. Would you expect xenon to react with iodine? Give a reason for your answer.

Formation of ions

In a compound with two atoms of different elements, the larger the difference in electronegativities of the atoms, the greater is the ionic character of the compound. Halogens have high electronegativities, and an element with a low electronegativity in a compound with a halogen will readily donate an electron to the halogen. For example, the Group I metals have low electronegativities, and in compounds such as sodium chloride and potassium iodide, they lose an electron to the halogen atom, forming strongly ionic compounds. The ionic nature decreases down Group VII. In gaining an electron, the halogen gains the stable electron configuration of an inert gas.

A fluorine atom accepts one electron from a weakly electronegative atom bonded to it, to become a fluoride ion in an ionic compound. The fluoride ion, F^-, has the electron configuration $1s^2\ 2s^2\ 2p^6$, which is the electron configuration of the noble gas neon. Similarly, a chlorine atom readily accepts an electron to form a chloride ion, Cl^-, with an electron configuration of $1s^2\ 2s^2\ 2p^6\ 3s^2\ 3p^6$, the electron configuration of argon. With decreasing electronegativities, bromine and iodine compounds have decreasing ionic character.

Like electronegativity, **electron affinity** is a measure of the electron-attracting power of an atom:

Electron affinity is the amount of energy required to remove an electron from a gaseous negative ion.

As energy, it is measurable, in kJ mol^{-1}. For halogens, electron affinity is the amount of energy to remove the electron from the ion Hal^-. The values are high, see Table 3, reflecting the attraction of the halogens for an additional electron, and explaining why halogens are not found free in nature.

APPLICATION B **Plasticisers**

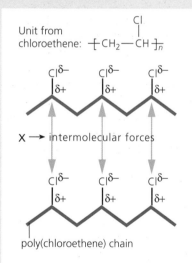

Unit from chloroethene:

$X \longrightarrow$ intermolecular forces

poly(chloroethene) chain

Plasticiser molecules inserted at **X** push chains apart and reduce intermolecular forces

The plastic called PVC is polyvinylchloride or, to give it its chemical name, poly(chloroethene). It is a long-chain molecule, a polymer of chloroethene. The diagrams show the structural formula of a unit, the intermolecular forces between molecules of poly(chloroethene), and the position of plasticiser molecules when they are added between the molecules.

The bonded C–Cl groups make permanent dipoles that attract the molecules to each other by van der Waals forces, so that PVC is a very strong, rigid plastic, ideal for drainpipes and guttering.

But cling-film and the soles of trainers, which need to be flexible, can also be made from PVC when it has been treated with a plasticiser chemical. The plasticiser molecules fit between the PVC molecules. This pushes the PVC molecules further apart and so reduces the van der Waals forces between them. However, plasticiser molecules are liable to evaporate when the material containing them is heated, even if only gently, and they can have toxic effects.

1 Explain why a dipole exists in the carbon–chlorine bond.

2 Suggest why, in time, PVC items treated with a plasticiser can lose their flexibility.

KEY FACTS

- The halogens, the Group VII elements, are fluorine, chlorine, bromine, iodine and astatine.

- Halogens are reactive elements and are always combined in nature.

- Halogens have many uses but can also cause environmental problems.

- The boiling points of the halogens increase down Group VII because of the increasing van der Waals forces.

- The electronegativity decreases down the group as the size of the atoms increases.

9.3 Chemical properties of the halogens

All the halogens react to gain one electron and reach the electron configuration of an inert gas. With metals they form ionic compounds containing the ion Hal⁻, and with non-metals they form covalent compounds containing the single covalent bond –Hal.

Halogens as oxidising agents
When halogens react, they usually either share electrons in a covalent bond in a molecular halide, as in hydrogen chloride gas, or they accept an electron and form a negative ion in an ionic compound called a **halide**, such as sodium chloride.

The ability of the halogens to accept an electron to form an ionic halide makes them very good **oxidising agents**. Remember, oxidation is electron loss, so an oxidising agent is one that is an electron acceptor. The order of oxidising power is $F_2 > Cl_2 > Br_2 > I_2$, and is reflected in the following.

- The weakness of the molecular bond, Hal–Hal. The less energy it takes to break the bond, the stronger the oxidising ability. Bonds in all the halogens are weak, with F–F the weakest.

- Electron affinity. As already seen, halogens all have high electron affinities: it takes a lot of energy to remove the electron gained in Hal⁻. Table 3 on page 128 gives the values: they are similar for all the halogens.

- The lattice energy of ionic halogen compounds. This is the energy required to break the bond in a halogen-metal lattice. The values are high, while decreasing down Group VII.

- Hydration energy of the halogen. This is the energy released when the element dissolves in water. The hydration energies are high, decreasing down the group. Many reactions with halogens are carried out in aqueous solution in which the halogen molecule is a particularly good oxidising agent.

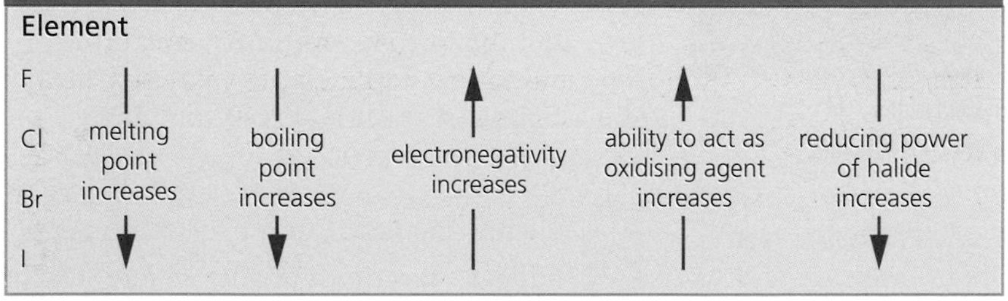

6 Which are ionic and which are molecular?

a chlorine molecules

b calcium fluoride

c potassium bromide

Reactions of halogens with metals
The oxidising ability of all the halogens is clearly seen in their reactions with metals, though it decreases down the group. Fluorine reacts readily with every metal, including gold and platinum, which are usually very unreactive. Chlorine reacts with most metals.

If chlorine gas is passed over heated iron wire, brown iron(III) chloride forms. Chlorine is the oxidising agent and is itself reduced as each atom accepts an electron from iron:

$$3Cl_2(g) + 2Fe(s) \rightarrow 2\ FeCl_3$$

7 Explain how you would expect bromine and iodine to react with the following. Give reasons for your answers.

a gold

b aluminium

c potassium

Fig. 1 Summary of physical and chemical trends in Group VII

Element					
F					
Cl	melting point increases	boiling point increases	electronegativity increases	ability to act as oxidising agent increases	reducing power of halide increases
Br					
I					

KEY FACTS

- Halogens act as oxidising agents because they readily accept electrons.

- The oxidising ability of the halogens decreases down the group.

9.4 Reactions of ionic halides

Displacement reactions with halogens

The trend in the oxidising power of the halogens is shown by their reactions with solutions of halide ions. For example, chlorine dissolves in water to give a pale yellowish-green solution. When it is added to a colourless solution of potassium bromide a reddish-brown solution of bromine forms as the bromide ion is oxidised by the chlorine to bromine. The overall reaction is:

$$Cl_2 + 2KBr \rightarrow 2KCl + Br_2$$

The ionic half-equations are:

oxidation: $2Br^- \rightarrow Br_2 + 2e^-$

reduction: $Cl_2 + 2e^- \rightarrow 2Cl^-$

When bubbled through potassium iodide solution, chlorine gas displaces iodine because chlorine is a stronger oxidising agent than iodine

Bromine is formed because chlorine is a stronger oxidising agent than bromine and so withdraws an electron from each bromide ion to leave bromine atoms and negatively charged chloride ions. The bromine atoms then combine to form molecules of bromine which give the solution its new colour. This reaction is called a **displacement reaction**: chlorine displaces bromine from a solution of its salt. Both chlorine and bromine will displace iodine from iodides.

8 Describe the reactions, if they occur, between these halogen molecules and halide ions.

a $Cl_2(aq) + KI(aq)$
b $I_2(aq) + NaBr(aq)$
c $Br_2(aq) + KCl(aq)$
d $Br_2(aq) + NaI(aq)$

Write an equation for the reactions that do occur.

Detecting ionic halides

Aqueous halides with silver nitrate and ammonia solutions

Most halides are soluble. But we can detect them in solution by adding dilute nitric acid, then silver nitrate solution. We then get silver chloride, bromide and iodide which are insoluble, meaning that they form as a precipitate. Their different colours, white, cream and yellow, make it possible to identify the halide present, as shown in the photo.

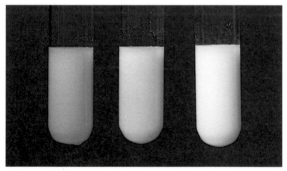

Distinguishing between white, cream and yellow is not always easy, so we use a second test, adding aqueous ammonia, to confirm our results. This tests for the solubility of the silver halide in ammonia solution. Table 4 summarises the reactions.

9 Identify the halide in the following tests.

a Adding a few drops of silver nitrate solution produced a yellow precipitate which did not dissolve in concentrated ammonia solution.

b Adding a few drops of silver nitrate solution produced a cream precipitate. The precipitate did not dissolve in dilute ammonia solution, but did dissolve when concentrated ammonia solution was added.

Halide	Reaction with silver nitrate solution	Reaction with aqueous ammonia
fluoride	$Ag^+(aq) + F^-(aq) \rightarrow AgF(aq)$ No precipitate: AgF is water soluble	No precipitate
chloride	$Ag^+(aq) + Cl^-(aq) \rightarrow AgCl(s)$ White precipitate of silver chloride	Silver chloride turns violet in light, then in dil. $NH_3(aq)$, diamminesilver(I) ion, $[Ag(NH_3)_2]^+(aq)$, is formed which is soluble and colourless
bromide	$Ag^+(aq) + Br^-(aq) \rightarrow AgBr(s)$ Cream precipitate of silver bromide	Sparingly soluble in dil. $NH_3(aq)$, silver bromide dissolves in conc. $NH_3(aq)$, when $[Ag(NH_3)_2]^+(aq)$ is formed, which is colourless
iodide	$Ag^+(aq) + I^-(aq) \rightarrow AgI(s)$ Pale yellow precipitate of silver iodide	In conc. $NH_3(aq)$, silver iodide does not dissolve but turns white

Table 4 Testing for halides

Silver halides and photography

Chemists have known for 250 years that silver halides were sensitive to light and decomposed to form finely divided silver (which looks grey or black). Film coated with a layer of a silver halide will gradually darken when it is exposed to light. The more intense the light, the darker the image. This gives a negative image from which a positive print can be made.

In taking a picture the silver halide is briefly exposed to light to differing extents. Where exposed, the silver halide is converted to silver metal which blackens. It is necessary to stop the unexposed silver halide from decomposing and producing a completely black picture.

In the early nineteenth century, silver halides (but not metallic silver) were found to dissolve in sodium thiosulphate solution. So, after a picture was taken the film was removed from the camera in a darkened room and the unreacted silver halide was removed by dissolving it in thiosulphate solution. This

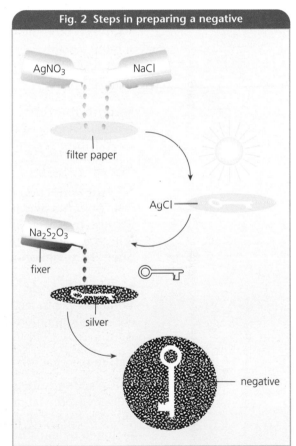

Fig. 2 Steps in preparing a negative

left just the black particles of silver in the exposed areas. The same basic chemistry is still used today when developing photographic film.

You can prepare your own negative by following the steps shown in Fig. 2.

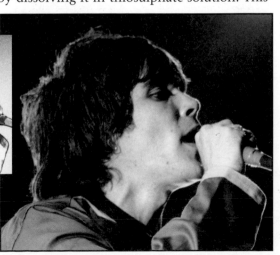

Stone Roses negative and positive

10 Explain why the silver halide on photographic film produces a negative image.

Solid ionic halides and concentrated sulphuric acid

Solid ionic halides can be detected and identified by their reactions with concentrated sulphuric acid. First, the corresponding hydrogen halide is formed. All are gases at room temperature. Differences in reaction then partly depend on the reducing nature of the hydrogen halide and the moderately strong oxidising ability of concentrated sulphuric acid. Hydrogen fluoride is not a reducing agent, but the other hydrogen halides are increasingly so.

Concentrated sulphuric acid does not react with hydrogen fluoride or hydrogen chloride, but it does oxidise hydrogen bromide and hydrogen iodide to the free halogens. Hydrogen bromide reduces sulphuric acid to sulphur dioxide, while hydrogen iodide, an even stronger reducing agent, converts the acid mainly to hydrogen sulphide.

Sodium fluoride

With concentrated sulphuric acid, sodium fluoride forms hydrogen fluoride gas:

$$NaF(aq) + H_2SO_4(l) \rightarrow HF(g) + NaHSO_4(l)$$

No further reaction occurs and there is no change in the oxidation state of the elements. Because hydrogen fluoride attacks glass and skin, this reaction must be carried out carefully in a plastic container.

Sodium chloride

When concentrated sulphuric acid is dripped on to sodium chloride, hydrogen chloride gas is formed:

$$NaCl(aq) + H_2SO_4(l) \rightarrow HCl(g) + NaHSO_4(l)$$

This reaction is used to prepare hydrogen chloride in the laboratory. Dry hydrogen chloride gas is colourless. It is very readily hydrated by moisture in the air to form fumes. No further reaction occurs.

Sodium bromide

When sulphuric acid is added to sodium bromide, hydrogen bromide is given off:

$$NaBr(aq) + H_2SO_4(l) \rightarrow HBr(g) + NaHSO_4(l)$$

As a moderately strong oxidising agent, concentrated sulphuric acid oxidises hydrogen bromide to bromine, forming brown fumes of the gas. The reaction also produces the colourless gas sulphur dioxide, and water:

When concentrated sulphuric acid is added to sodium bromide, fumes of bromine are produced

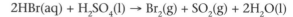

$$2HBr(aq) + H_2SO_4(l) \rightarrow Br_2(g) + SO_2(g) + 2H_2O(l)$$

The aqueous bromide ion from hydrogen bromide is oxidised to form bromine:

$$2Br^- \rightarrow Br_2 + 2e^-$$

The hydrogen bromide and the acid each provide $2H^+$ ions, and the electrons from bromine are transferred to the sulphate ion:

$$4H^+ + SO_4^{2-} + 2e^- \rightarrow SO_2 + 2H_2O$$

While the oxidation state of the two bromine atoms goes up from −1 to zero, total +2, the oxidation state of the sulphur atom is reduced from +6 in the sulphate ion to +4 in sulphur dioxide, total −2. The next equation comes from adding the last two equations.

$$2Br^- + 2e^- + 4H^+ + SO_4^{2-} \rightarrow$$
$$Br_2 + 2e^- + SO_2 + 2H_2O$$

The electrons cancel out to give the reaction equation above.

Sodium iodide

When sulphuric acid is added to sodium iodide, several reactions occur. In one, hydrogen iodide is produced:

$$NaI(aq) + H_2SO_4(l) \rightarrow HI(g) + NaHSO_4(l)$$

In another reaction, hydrogen iodide is oxidised according to the equation below, to form violet fumes of iodine. As in the reaction with bromide, the sulphur atom is reduced from oxidation state +6 to +4, giving sulphur dioxide and water:

$$2HI(aq) + H_2SO_4(l) \rightarrow I_2(g) + SO_2(g) + 2H_2O(l)$$

In the predominant reaction, hydrogen iodide is again oxidised to iodine, but this time the sulphuric acid is reduced to hydrogen sulphide and water:

$$8HI(aq) + H_2SO_4(l) \rightarrow 4I_2(s) + H_2S(g) + 4H_2O(l)$$

In this case,

$$8HI \rightarrow 8H^+ + 8I^-$$

The iodide ion is oxidised to iodine:

$$8I^- \rightarrow 4I_2 + 8e^-$$

The bromide provides eight hydrogen ions and the acid two:

$$10H^+ + 8e^- + SO_4^{2-} \rightarrow H_2S + 4H_2O$$

The oxidation state of the eight iodine atoms goes up from −1 to zero, total +8. Hydrogen sulphide is a covalently bonded compound and, as we saw in section 8.2, for covalent compounds we say that the element that gains electrons (is reduced) is the more electronegative element. The electronegativities are: H = 2.1 and S = 2.5. So the sulphur atom is reduced, from +6 in the sulphate ion to –2 in hydrogen sulphide, total –8.

The next equation is made by adding the last two equations:

$$10H^+ + 8I^- + 8e^- + SO_4^{2-} \rightarrow 4I_2 + 8e^- + H_2S + 4H_2O$$

The electrons cancel out.

When concentrated sulphuric acid is added to sodium iodide, fumes of iodine are produced

Summarising redox reactions

The halogens are strong oxidising agents because they readily accept electrons to become halides. The halides, in turn, can act as reducing agents when they donate electrons and are oxidised to the halogens:

    reduced   oxidised
    halogen → halide → halogen

As seen above, hydrogen fluoride and fluoride ions are the most difficult to oxidise and are therefore the weakest reducing agents. On the other hand, hydrogen iodide and iodide ions are the easiest to oxidise and are therefore the strongest reducing agents. The trend is that the oxidising power of the halogens decreases down the group, and the reducing power of the halides increases down the Group VII.

11 Predict the products formed in the reaction between sodium astatide, NaAt, and concentrated sulphuric acid.

9.5 Halogens and disinfection

Water has to be treated chemically to make it safe to drink

Chlorine and drinking water

Domestic water must be fit to drink. At the treatment works, chlorine is pumped into the water, which is then stored for about two hours. This is long enough for complete disinfection, meaning that any harmful bacteria and viruses are killed. Just sufficient chlorine – less than 1 p.p.m. – is added to ensure that the water is bacteria-free when it reaches people's homes, without affecting its taste.

Reaction of chlorine in water

Chlorine reacts with water to form an acidic solution, a mixture of hydrochloric acid and chloric(I) acid:

$$Cl_2(aq) + H_2O(l) \rightarrow HOCl(aq) + HCl(aq)$$
$$\text{chloric(I) acid}$$

This is an example of a **disproportionation** reaction, in which a single compound is simultaneously oxidised and reduced. Here, the oxidation state of one

chlorine atom increases from 0 in Cl_2 to +1 in HOCl as it is oxidised. The other chlorine changes from 0 in Cl_2 to –1 in HCl as it is reduced.

 What does the (I) in chloric(I) acid mean?

Chloric(I) acid dissociates to H^+ and OCl^-. The OCl^- is responsible for the disinfecting action, killing microorganisms.

Water in swimming pools is disinfected in a similar way. Chlorine used to be added directly from cylinders but it was found to corrode the metal and plastic parts of the pool. Today chlorine compounds are added that dissolve in water to produce chloric(I) acid at a concentration of about 6 p.p.m. The chloric(I) acid is responsible for the swimming pool smell.

APPLICATION C

Water treatment: the halogens compared

While chlorine is used for water treatment, bromine and iodine are not used. How do they compare as disinfectants?

A group of water analysts set out to answer this question, comparing the effects of the three halogens on microorganisms called amoebic cysts. Where they are in the sewage in tropical countries, they can reach water supplies and cause amoebic dysentery. Sufferers have diarrhoea which, if serious, can cause dehydration and death.

Amoebic cysts and can survive treatment with disinfectants at levels that would kill most other microorganisms. The graphs show the effect of chlorine, bromine and iodine on amoebic cysts in water at different pH values. The analysts found that bromine was the best killer of cysts in water, but that in sewage, iodine was best. All of the halogens performed better at low pH.

1

a Which halogen is the most effective at killing amoebic cysts in water at pH 8?

b Which halogen is the most effective at killing amoebic cysts in water across the pH range 6–8?

c Bromine reacts with water to form bromic(I) acid (HOBr) in the same way that chlorine reacts to form chloric(I) acid. Write an equation for the reaction of bromine with water.

d Suggest why chlorine is used to treat water and not bromine.

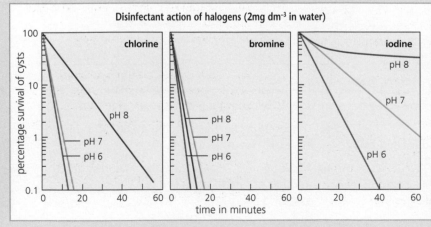

Disinfectant action of halogens (2mg dm^{-3} in water)

Campers using water from a river or lake can make it safe with water-purifying tablets. These tablets release chlorine which kills any bacteria in the water

Reactions of chlorine with sodium hydroxide solution

When chlorine is added to cold (15 °C) dilute sodium hydroxide solution, a mixture of chlorate(I) and chloride ions are formed. The reaction equation is:

$$Cl_2(aq) + 2NaOH(aq) \rightarrow NaOCl(aq) + NaCl(aq) + H_2O(l)$$
sodium chlorate(I)

When the mixture is heated, the sodium chlorate(I) then disproportionates to form chlorate(V) ions and more chloride ions. The reaction equation is:

$$3NaOCl(aq) \rightarrow NaClO_3(aq) + 2NaCl(aq)$$
sodium chlorate(V)

In NaOCl, the oxidation number of the chlorine atom is +1 because oxygen is –2 and sodium is +1. In NaCl the oxidation number of the chlorine atom is –1 because sodium is +1. In $NaClO_3$ the oxidation number of the chlorine atom is +5 because oxygen is –2 (×3 = –6) and sodium is +1.

So some chlorine atoms increase in oxidation number and are oxidised, while others decrease in oxidation number and are reduced.

Sodium chlorate(I) is domestic bleach which is sold under a wide variety of trade names. It is also used industrially to bleach paper and fabrics. Sodium chlorate(V) is a powerful weed-killer.

12 The reaction of chlorine with cold dilute sodium hydroxide is also disproportionation. Explain why.

13 With cold dilute sodium hydroxide solution, bromine reacts in a similar way to chlorine. Write equations for its reactions and name the products formed.

14 When damp blue litmus is placed in chlorine gas, it first turns red and then white. Explain why.

Determining chlorine in bleach

Commercial bleach can made by passing chlorine through cold dilute sodium hydroxide solution. As seen above, the products are a mixture of sodium chloride and sodium chlorate(I). Sodium chlorate(I) is a powerful bleach because in acid solution it releases chlorine which oxidises the chemicals in stains to colourless compounds.

One of these is much cheaper than the other, but is it really better value or just dilute bleach?

The strength of a bleach depends on the amount of chlorine it can release from a given volume of bleach solution. This can be measured either as the percentage of available chlorine by mass, or simply as the mass available per dm^3 of bleach. It can be determined in the laboratory as shown in Fig. 3 and described next.

Potassium iodide solution acidified with a few drops of hydrochloric acid liberates the chlorine from the bleach. The chlorine then reacts with the potassium iodide solution to displace the iodine. Unlike chlorine, the iodine does not escape from the mixture but remains in solution, colouring the liquid brown.

$$Cl_2(aq) + 2KI \rightarrow 2KCl(aq) + I_2(aq)$$

The ionic equation is:

$$Cl_2(aq) + 2I^-(aq) \rightarrow 2Cl^-(aq) + I_2(aq)$$

The amount of iodine can now be measured by titrating against a standard solution of sodium thiosulphate. Remember that a standard solution is one in which the concentration is exactly known. In this experiment, 0.1M is a suitable concentration. The reaction is:

$$I_2(aq) + 2Na_2S_2O_3(aq) \rightarrow 2NaI(aq)$$

Iodine, which gives a brown solution, is reduced to colourless iodide ions by sodium thiosulphate, while the sodium thiosulphate is oxidised to sodium tetrathionate, $Na_2S_4O_6$. It is a redox reaction. The ionic equation is:

$$I_2(aq) + 2S_2O_3^{2-}(aq) \rightarrow 2I^-(aq) + S_4O_6^{2-}(aq)$$

As the reaction proceeds and the iodine is converted to iodide, the brown colour fades. When the solution is just straw coloured, a few drops of starch solution are added as indicator: iodine turns the starch blue-black. It is much easier to see the colour change from blue-black to colourless at the end point than a change from pale yellow to colourless. The starch cannot be added earlier because the iodine molecules would be locked up by the large starch molecules and so would not be free to react.

15 Explain why the reaction between iodine and sodium thiosulphate is an oxidation reaction.

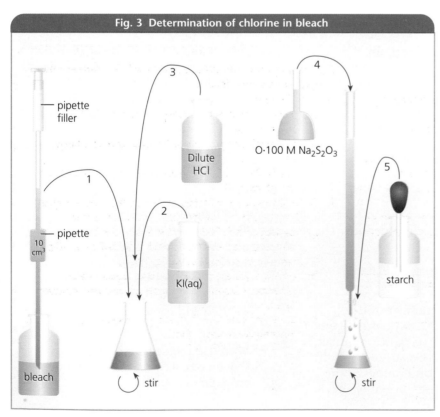

Fig. 3 Determination of chlorine in bleach

pipette filler

pipette

10 cm³

bleach

stir

3

Dilute HCl

1

2

KI(aq)

4

0·100 M Na₂S₂O₃

5

starch

stir

Example: Calculating the chlorine in bleach

From the equations, 1 mole of chlorine gas releases 1 mole of iodine and 1 mole of iodine reacts with 2 moles of sodium thiosulphate.

10.0 cm³ of bleach are added to excess acidified potassium iodide solution and a brown coloured mixture is obtained. This is titrated against 0.1M sodium thiosulphate solution and 32.0 cm³ of the 0.10 M sodium thiosulphate are needed to react exactly. What mass of chlorine is available from 1 dm³ of bleach?

16 20.0 cm³ of bleach solution were added to excess acidified potassium iodide solution. This required 44.0 cm³ of 0.10 M sodium thiosulphate to react completely. Calculate the mass of chlorine available from 1 dm³ of the bleach solution.

Number of moles of sodium thiosulphate in 32.0 cm³ of 0.10 M sodium thiosulphate solution	$= 32.0/1000 \times 0.10 = 3.20 \times 10^{-3}$ mol
Number of moles of iodine present	$= 3.20/2 \times 10^{-3} = 1.60 \times 10^{-3}$ mol
Number of moles of chlorine present	$= 3.20 \times 10^{-3}$ mol
1 mol chlorine contains 71 g chlorine.	
So mass of chlorine in 3.20×10^{-3} mol	$= 3.20 \times 10^{-3} \times 71 = 0.23$ g chlorine.
This is the amount of chlorine available in 10 cm³ of bleach. Mass in 1 dm³ of bleach	$= 0.23/10 \times 1000 = 23$ g chlorine.

KEY FACTS

- Chlorine reacts with water to form hydrochloric acid and chloric(I) acid.

- Chloric(I) acid disinfects water supplies and swimming pools.

- Disproportionation is a redox reaction in which part of the molecule is oxidised and part is reduced.

- Chlorine reacts with cold dilute sodium hydroxide to produce chloride ions and chlorate(I) ions.

- The active ingredient in bleach is sodium chlorate(I).

- The available chlorine in bleach can be estimated by reacting bleach with potassium iodide solution to displace the iodine, and then titrating the mixture against standard sodium thiosulphate solution.

- The reaction of iodine with sodium thiosulphate solution is a redox reaction.

EXAMINATION QUESTIONS

1
a i) Define the term *electronegativity*.
  ii) State and explain the trend in electronegativity of the halogens fluorine to iodine. (5)
b State and explain the trend in boiling points of the halogens fluorine to iodine. (3)
c Describe what is observed when aqueous bromine is added to separate aqueous solutions of sodium chloride and sodium iodide. Write equation(s) for any reaction(s) occurring.
d State and explain the trend in reducing properties of the halide ions shown by the experiments in part (c). (6)
NEAB CH02 June 1995 Q4

2 Select appropriate data from the table to answer the questions which follow.
a Explain why
  i) iodide ions can be oxidised more easily than bromide ions,
  ii) the electronegativity of fluorine is much larger than that of chlorine,
  iii) the boiling point of bromine is higher than that of chlorine. (9)
b The halogen below iodine in Group VII is astatine(At). Predict, giving an explanation, whether or not
  i) hydrogen sulphide will be evolved when concentrated sulphuric acid is added to a solid sample of sodium astatide, NaAt,
  ii) astatine will be precipitated as a solid when chlorine is bubbled through an aqueous solution of sodium astatide,
  iii) silver astatide will dissolve in concentrated aqueous ammonia. (10)
NEAB CH02 June 1996 Q7

Element X	Atomic number	Atomic radius nm	Radius of X⁻/ nm	Boiling point/K	Electronegativity
F	9	0.064	0.133	86	4.0
Cl	17	0.099	0.181	238	3.0
Br	35	0.111	0.196	332	2.8
I	53	0.130	0.219	456	2.5

3

a When solid sodium iodide was warmed with concentrated sulphuric acid the following products were obtained.

$NaHSO_4$, HI, S, SO_2, H_2S, I_2

i) State which of these were formed by reduction.

ii) State which of these products were formed by oxidation.

iii) State how, without carrying out any further chemical tests, you would know that iodine and hydrogen sulphide were among the products.

iv) State the role of sulphuric acid in the formation of hydrogen iodide.

v) Construct a half-equation for the conversion of H_2SO_4 into H_2S and water in the presence of excess acid.

b Identify one halide ion, in addition to iodide, which is converted into the halogen when the solid sodium halide, NaX, is warmed with concentrated sulphuric acid. (1)

c The presence either of chloride or of bromide ions in aqueous solution can be detected by the addition of aqueous silver nitrate. State what would be observed if

i) chloride ions were present

ii) bromide ions were present (2)

d Explain how aqueous ammonia would help you to distinguish between the products obtained in part (c). (2)

NEAB CH02 February 1997 Q5

4 Concentrated sulphuric acid can behave as both an acid and an oxidising agent.

a State, in terms of electron transfer, what is meant by the term oxidising agent. (1)

b Identify one halide ion which reacts with warm concentrated sulphuric acid without being oxidised. Write an equation for the reaction. (2)

c Identify one halide ion which is ionised by warm concentrated sulphuric acid forming hydrogen sulphide as one of the reduction products. Write half-equations for each reaction and use these to deduce an overall equation. (4)

NEAB CH02 June 1997 Q4

5 A pale green solution is formed when chlorine gas is bubbled into water. When sodium hydroxide is added to this solution, the green colour disappears and then reappears when an excess of hydrochloric acid is added.

a Write an equation for the equilibrium reaction which occurs when chlorine is added to water. (1)

b Identify the species responsible for the green colour. (1)

c Explain why the green colour disappears when sodium hydroxide is added and write an equation for the reaction occurring. (3)

d Write an equation to show why the green colour reappears when hydrochloric acid is then added to the reaction mixture. (1)

e One of the products formed in the reaction between chlorine and sodium hydroxide is used commercially as a bleach. Identify this compound and give the oxidation state of chlorine in it. (2)

NEAB CH02 June 1996 Q5

6

a Describe what is observed when chlorine is bubbled through a solution of potassium iodide. Identify the role of chlorine and write an ionic equation for the reaction. (3)

b i) Write an equation for the reaction which occurs when chlorine is bubbled into a cold dilute aqueous solution of sodium chloride.

ii) Chlorate(V) ions, ClO_3^-, and chloride ions are produced when chlorine bubbled into a hot concentrated aqueous solution of sodium hydroxide.

Write half equations for the conversion of chlorine into chloride ions and for the conversion of chlorine into chlorate(V) ions. Use these half-equations to deduce the overall equation for the reaction. (6)

NEAB CH02 March 1998 Q2

7 The composition of a mixture of two solid sodium halides was investigated in two separate experiments.

Experiment (1)

When a large excess of chlorine gas was bubbled through a concentrated solution of the mixture, orange-brown fumes and a black precipitate were produced.

Experiment (2)

0.545 g of the solid mixture was dissolved in water and an excess of silver nitrate solution was added. The mass of the mixture of silver halide precipitates formed was 0.902 g. After washing the mixture of precipitates with an excess of concentrated aqueous ammonia the mass of the final precipitate was 0.546 g.

Write an equation for each of the reactions occurring in these experiments and explain how these results enable you to identify the halide ions present. Use the information given above to calculate the percentage by mass of each halide ion present in the solid mixture. (15)

NEAB CH02 June 1999 Q7

KEY SKILLS ASSIGNMENT

Chlorine chemistry

In the early 1800s, many people died of cholera each year in Britain. In one bad outbreak over 50 000 people died in London alone. Today, 98% of Western Europe's drinking water is made safe by chlorination, and water-borne diseases like cholera have become a thing of the past.

Some 85% of medicinal drugs are made using chlorine and its compounds. Thousands of consumer products, such as items made from PCV, depend on chlorine chemistry at some point in their production e.g. polyvinyl chloride (PVC). Even natural chlorine compounds, notably common salt, NaCl, are economically important.

On the other hand, environmental groups are becoming increasingly concerned about the effects of some chlorine compounds on ourselves and other living things. For example, CFCs (chlorofluorocarbons) were originally chosen back in the 1930s as suitable refrigerants because they were non-toxic. They also made good propellants in aerosols and formed the gas bubbles in foam rubber and plastics.

Unfortunately, CFCs are now causing problems in the ozone layer by converting ozone into oxygen and thus depriving us of protection against harmful ultra violet rays.

Although PVC is a very useful plastic for many applications, the vinyl chloride it is made from is a known carcinogen, so workers in PVC manufacture have to be carefully monitored. It is also thought that burning PVC releases highly toxic dioxins that fine their way into the atmosphere and soil.

Another group of chlorine based chemicals which are giving concern are **chlorinated solvents**. They include trichloroethene (TCE) used in the dry cleaning industry and adhesives, and tetrachloroethene (perchloroethylene PCE) used to degrease machinery and as paint thinners and antifreeze as well as in dry cleaning. If these compounds get into surface water, they sink to the bottom and slowly dissolve in the groundwater, contaminating water supplies.

However, there may be some help on the way in the form of a bacterium tentatively named *Dehalococcoides ethenogenes* Strain 195 which strips away the chlorine atoms from PCE, eventually producing ethene.

1 Research the article in the journal *Science, June 6 1997* by the research team at Cornell University concerning the bacterium, *Dehalococcoides ethenogenes* Strain 195. Give a brief outline of the possible uses of this bacterium, particularly how the bacterium derives its energy from the decomposition of chlorinated compounds. You can access this article from the internet.

2 What can you say about the density of TCE and PCE? What evidence do you have for this?

3 Draw the structure of PCE and then four other structural diagrams which illustrate what happens to this structure when the bacterium *Dehalococcoides ethenogenes* Strain 195 strips away the chlorine atoms one at a time. You may use computer graphics for this question.

4 Name each chemical compound at each stage of the bacterium's work, eventually ending with ethene.

5 Write an account of the place of chlorine and its compounds in modern society, giving reasons for statements you make.

Some of your text will show how chlorine has been useful, other parts may list the dangers of chlorine and its compounds. You will need to support your argument with referenced articles and facts – and you may find the internet useful to research some of the laterst chlorine applications.

Your eventual article should include diagrams or charts to illustrate your points and it should be no longer than 500 words.

10 Extraction of metals

Over three thousand years ago, the Ancient Egyptians believed that iron was a magical metal because they knew of it only in meteorites. They called iron 'the metal that falls from the sky', and it was valued for the strength and sharpness of the blades they made from it.

Later in history, someone discovered how to extract iron from its ores. This could have happened by chance. One suggestion is that beads of metal were formed when charcoal was burnt on ground rich in iron ore. From then on, iron ceased to be rare, and the Iron Age began.

King Tutankhamun's dagger, made about 3400 years ago. The blade is iron from a meteorite, and the hilt is decorated with gold

10.1 Iron, aluminium and titanium

Iron is used extensively today, especially in steels which are alloys of iron. After aluminium, iron is the second most abundant metal in the Earth's crust (see Table 1) and the fourth most abundant of all the elements. In fact, the known deposits of iron ores are more than enough for all the world's expected needs.

Throughout the last century, aluminium production rose rapidly, partly because its light weight makes it the choice for aircraft construction, and its malleability and stability in air and water makes it ideal for drinks and other cans. Titanium, another metal with widespread ores, is very hard and resistant to corrosion.

In this chapter, you will learn about the methods used to produce these three metals from their ores. The chapter also explains how production costs affect the uses that each metal is put to.

Minerals and ores

Only the unreactive metals gold and platinum, and the more reactive metals silver, copper and mercury are found as pure metals in the Earth's crust. Most metals are combined with other elements in the form of minerals.

A **mineral** is a substance that has a more or less definite composition. For example, haematite is a mineral consisting mainly of iron(II) oxide (Fe_2O_3). Minerals show variation

Iron ores clockwise from the left: haematite, magnetite and iron pyrite (fool's gold). A lustrous black form of pyrite can be cut and polished to make jewellery, as shown

in appearance and chemical composition since they often contain mixtures of substances in different proportions.

An **ore** is a rock that contains a mineral. Rich ores will contain large amounts of the useful mineral and little of others. A low-grade ore may contain little useful mineral and a great deal of waste. An Iron Age smelter would have had to find the ore, separate the iron-containing mineral from the ore, and treat the mineral to extract the useful iron.

Whether it is cost-effective in the present day to use an ore depends on four factors:

- How common is good quality ore?
- How easy is it to extract the metal from the ore?
- What further processing does the metal need to make it useful?
- Is there a better alternative?

This chapter looks at iron, aluminium and titanium to see how these questions affect the use we make of these metals.

 Why are the earliest coins we have found made of gold, silver or copper?

Iron, aluminium and titanium ores

Iron
There is iron in silicates (sand and clay) and in carbonates; there are also small amounts of iron in all living things. But the ores used for iron extraction are:

Fe_2O_3, an oxide in the mineral haematite,
Fe_3O_4, an oxide in magnetite,
FeS_2, a sulphide, also called iron pyrites.

Table 1 Abundances of metals in the Earth's crust	
Element	**Mass/%**
aluminium	7.85
iron	4.12
calcium	3.18
sodium	2.33
potassium	2.33
magnesium	2.11
titanium	0.41

Aluminium
Aluminosilicates are compounds of aluminium, silicon and oxygen with other elements. They make up 82% of the rocks of the Earth's crust. Aluminosilicates occur in clays, kaolin (china clay) and many other minerals. Aluminium compounds are so common that they can be found in every handful of soil.

But the main mineral used to supply aluminium is **bauxite**, a hydrated aluminium oxide, $Al_2O_3.2H_2O$. World reserves of bauxite are estimated to be about 30 000 million tonnes. Cryolite, another mineral for aluminium extraction, is sodium aluminium fluoride, Na_3AlF_6.

Titanium
Titanium minerals are quite common. The main ores are rutile, TiO_2, and ilmenite, $FeTiO_3$.

 Oxygen is the commonest element, making up almost 50% of the Earth's crust. Where is it found?

10.2 Extracting metals from minerals

Metals are usually obtained from their minerals by reduction. The compound that provides the electrons is called the **reductant**. This is the general equation:

$$M^{n+} + ne^- \rightarrow M \quad \begin{array}{l} M = \text{metal} \\ n = \text{number of positive} \\ \quad \text{charges on the metal ion} \end{array}$$

There is usually more than one way to produce the useful metal. The choice of method will depend upon:

- the energy requirements,
- the cost of the reductant,
- any further processing required after extracting the metal.

Energy requirements
Metals typically act as reducing agents, being oxidised as they donate electrons to other atoms:

$$M \rightarrow M^{n+} + ne^-$$

The most reactive metals do this most readily.

They are never found as free metals in nature, but always in mineral compounds.

In the extraction of a metal from a mineral, we can think of the reaction as being the reverse of the reaction that forms the mineral from the metal. The energy of formation of the mineral can be worked out from known values. This gives industrial chemists an idea of the energy input needed for extraction (Table 2).

Table 2 Trend for metals of ease of losing electrons											
K	Na	Ca	Mg	Al	Zn	Fe	Pb	Cu	Hg	Ag	Ti
electrons											electrons
most				ease of losing electrons							least
easily				energy required to break bonds							easily
lost				in metal compounds							lost

The most reactive metals on the left of the table lose electrons easily and form compounds in which the metals are ions. The bond enthalpy (page 84) of these compounds is proportionately high, so that equally large amounts of energy are required to break the bonds between the metal and the rest of the compound.

Methods of reduction

For compounds of the most reactive metals, **electrolysis** is the best way to supply the amounts of energy needed to break the bonds. Thus, potassium, sodium, calcium, magnesium and aluminium are usually extracted from their minerals by electrolysis. Electrolysis reduces metal ions in the molten mineral: positive metal ions moves to the cathode where they gain electrons to form the element. Electrolysis used to produce aluminium is described in section 10.4.

For compounds containing the middle rank of metals, reduction of a mineral with **carbon** or **hydrogen** provides enough energy to reduce the oxide. So, zinc, iron, tin, lead and copper are extracted in a furnace from their oxides by reduction with carbon, carbon monoxide or hydrogen.

Metals which lose electrons more easily can also **displace** metals which lose electrons less easily from their compounds. For example, titanium, on the far right of Table 2, is reduced to the metal from its chloride using a displacement reaction with magnesium metal.

Minerals containing mercury and silver, to the right of the table, are so unstable that they **decompose on heating** in air to form the metal, which is why they are occasionally found in nature as the **native** element.

The cost of the reductant

Electrical energy is expensive, so extraction processes that depend on electrical energy are often sited near cheaper electricity sources. For example, the aluminium plant at Lochaber in Scotland takes advantage of cheap hydroelectric power available in the area.

Chemical reduction processes usually rely on carbon or carbon monoxide. Carbon monoxide is produced from coke in a furnace. Coke consists almost entirely of carbon and is made by heating coal in the absence of air. If a lot of coal is used in the extraction process, the plant is sited on a coalfield to minimise transport costs.

Further processing

From a mineral, it is relatively easy to produce iron metal that is 95% pure. This is called pig iron or cast iron. Unfortunately, cast iron is not very useful because impurities such as phosphorus and sulphur make it brittle. So, after extraction, the iron is purified to about 99% purity. This obviously costs more money, energy and time.

Most iron is processed into steel which is dealt with on pages 146 and 147.

KEY FACTS

- Haematite, Fe_2O_3, magnetite, Fe_3O_4 and iron sulphide, FeS, are the main iron-bearing minerals in commercially valuable ores.

- Aluminium ore contains the mineral bauxite, $Al_2O_3.2H_2O$

- Titanium is extracted from rutile, TiO_2, and ilmenite, $FeTiO_3$.

- Metals are obtained from their minerals by electrolysis, by reduction of the mineral heated with carbon, displacement by a more electronegative metal, or by decomposition on heating.

- The choice of the extraction method depends on the energy required by the process, the cost of the reductant, and any further processing the metal requires before use.

10.3 Iron and steel

Uses

With its many steel alloys, iron is the most common metal produced today – 19 million tonnes in the UK per year, and about 1.5 billion tonnes a year world-wide. It appears in everything from motor cars and ocean-going liners to food cans and the screws in self-assembly furniture.

Iron has been worked for thousands of years and, in the past, the nations that developed the most successful iron industries became the major industrial and imperial powers.

In the nineteenth century the Industrial Revolution began in Britain which had huge deposits of iron ore, together with the coal needed to extract iron from the ore. The iron and steel produced helped the British Empire to flourish.

Extraction

Iron extraction involves the reduction of the mineral oxide in iron ore. The reducing agents in the blast furnace are coke (C) and carbon monoxide (CO).

The blast furnace

A mixture of crushed iron ore, coke and limestone is fed into the top of the **blast furnace** (Fig. 1), named after the blasts of air, heated to 1000 °C, that are forced into the bottom of the furnace. The air contains 20% oxygen.

1　In the blast furnace, coke is oxidised to carbon dioxide, an exothermic reaction:

$$C(s) + O_2(g) \rightarrow CO_2(g) \quad \Delta H = -392 \text{ kJ mol}^{-1}$$

2　The carbon dioxide reacts endothermically with coke to form carbon monoxide:

$$CO_2(g) + C(s) \rightarrow 2CO(g) \quad \Delta H = +172 \text{kJ mol}^{-1}$$

3　Iron(III) oxide in the ore is reduced to iron by the carbon monoxide in a reaction which overall is exothermic.

$$Fe_2O_3(s) + 3CO(g) \rightarrow 2Fe(s) + 3CO_2(g)$$
$$\Delta H = -27 \text{ kJ mol}^{-1}$$

The iron falls to the bottom of the blast furnace, where it melts.

4　Alternatively, iron(III) oxide is reduced to iron(II) oxide by carbon monoxide:

$$Fe_2O_3(s) + CO(g) \rightarrow 2FeO(s) + CO_2(g)$$

5　Then, in parts of the furnace where the temperature is high enough, coke reacts with iron(II) oxide, reducing it to metallic iron:

$$FeO(s) + C(s) \rightarrow Fe(s) + CO(g)$$

All the reactions involving iron are simple reductions:

$$Fe^{3+} + 3e^- \rightarrow Fe$$
$$Fe^{3+} + e^- \rightarrow Fe^{2+}$$
$$Fe^{2+} + 2e^- \rightarrow Fe$$

The reductants are either carbon or carbon monoxide, which themselves are oxidised.

3 How much iron can be obtained from 125 tonnes of iron(III) oxide, Fe_2O_3? Hint: See page 50.

Using limestone to remove impurities

The limestone, $CaCO_3$, is added to remove impurities in the iron ore. Most iron ores are between 30% and 95% iron oxides. The rest is mainly made up of the impurities silicon(IV) oxide, SiO_2 (sand or clay) and aluminium oxide, Al_2O_3.

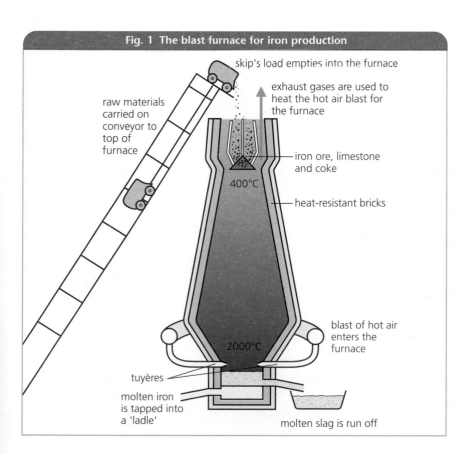

Fig. 1 The blast furnace for iron production

skip's load empties into the furnace

raw materials carried on conveyor to top of furnace

exhaust gases are used to heat the hot air blast for the furnace

iron ore, limestone and coke

400°C

heat-resistant bricks

blast of hot air enters the furnace

2000°C

tuyères

molten iron is tapped into a 'ladle'

molten slag is run off

1 At the high temperatures inside the blast furnace, limestone decomposes:

$$CaCO_3(s) \rightarrow CaO(s) + CO_2(g)$$

2 The calcium oxide reacts with the silicon(IV) oxide and aluminium oxide:

$$CaO(s) + SiO_2(s) \rightarrow CaSiO_3(s)$$
$$\text{calcium silicate}$$

$$CaO(s) + Al_2O_3(s) \rightarrow CaAl_2O_4(s)$$
$$\text{calcium aluminate}$$

The mixture of calcium silicate and calcium aluminate is liquid at blast furnace temperatures and is called **slag**. This slag does not mix with the molten iron, but forms a separate layer. Molten slag is less dense than molten iron, so it floats on top and can be tapped off.

Slag is not wasted. It can be solidified, broken up and used as hard core in the foundations of buildings and roads, and also as an ingredient of cement.

  Why are coke, limestone and iron ore mixed together before being loaded into the blast furnace?

Minimising energy costs

Iron can only be extracted from its ores at very high temperatures, using a great deal of energy. So, to minimise the expense, the production of iron is operated as a **continuous process**, 24 hours a day, 365 days a year, often for several years without a break. Round the clock, raw materials are added and products are removed.

A large furnace may produce 1000 tonnes of iron a day, and a modern plant will have several blast furnaces on site. It will use sophisticated computerised systems to monitor and control the input and output of each furnace.

The iron and steel works are integrated, operating like an assembly line. Any interruption in the production of iron from the blast furnace would stop the input of iron for steel production, and the delay and restart costs could amount to millions of pounds. Consequently, a plant is only ever shut down for maintenance work.

  Describe how continuous operation of an iron and steel works tends to keep running costs as low as possible.

Further processing of cast iron

The iron that comes from the blast furnace, called **pig iron** or **cast iron**, is not pure iron. A typical sample might contain 4–5% carbon, 1% silicon, 0.5% manganese, 0.1% phosphorus and 0.03% sulphur. The carbon content of cast iron makes it brittle and it melts sharply at 1227 °C without softening first. Because of this, cast iron cannot be worked into sheets or drawn out into wire.

Steel making

Most iron is converted to steel. There are many different types of steel which are all alloys of iron. An **alloy** is a mixture of two or more elements, at least one of which is a metal. They are mixed when molten and allowed to cool to form a uniform solid.

A steel contains mainly iron with, typically, 0.3% or so of carbon and small, carefully measured amounts of transition metals including titanium, vanadium, chromium, manganese, nickel, niobium and tungsten, chosen to give the steel particular properties to suit its use, such as rigidity, flexibility and ease of welding. But before these transition metals are added, the iron must first be treated in the converter (Fig. 2).

Table 3 gives the composition of a few alloys of iron. The balance is made up of iron.

Table 3 Common alloys of iron	
Alloy	**Composition/%**
Cast iron	C 3.5, Si 1.2, P 0.05–0.1, S 0.05–0.1, Mn 0.5–1.0
Mild steel	C 0.15, Si 0.03, P 0.05, S 0.05, Mn 0.05
Stainless steel	Cr 18, Ni 8
Chrome steel	C 1.0, Cr 2.5
Carbon steel	C 1.0

Steel used for car bodies contains moderate amounts of carbon, but high-carbon steels, which are harder, are used for making tools. Adding tungsten makes steel even harder, and tungsten steels are used for high-speed cutting tools. Titanium steel is used in spacecraft because it stands up well to very high temperatures. The stainless steel used for making cutlery contains chromium and nickel, and resists corrosion very well.

  Put in order the tensile strength of steels required for use in car bodies and bridges.

Desulphurisation

Molten iron from the blast furnace can be tapped off to remove sulphur. Magnesium powder is added which combines with sulphur to form magnesium sulphides, which are removed as slag.

The converter

Steel is made in an enormous container called a **converter**, about the size of an average three-bedroom house. The molten iron at 1400 °C is channelled from the blast furnace to the converter.

Any remaining sulphur can be removed in the converter by adding more magnesium powder to the molten iron before the next stage.

This stage is called the **basic oxygen process**. The word basic is used because the basic compound calcium oxide is one of the reactants. The carbon content is lessened and all but traces of unwanted elements are removed. Then, other elements can be added according to the type of steel required.

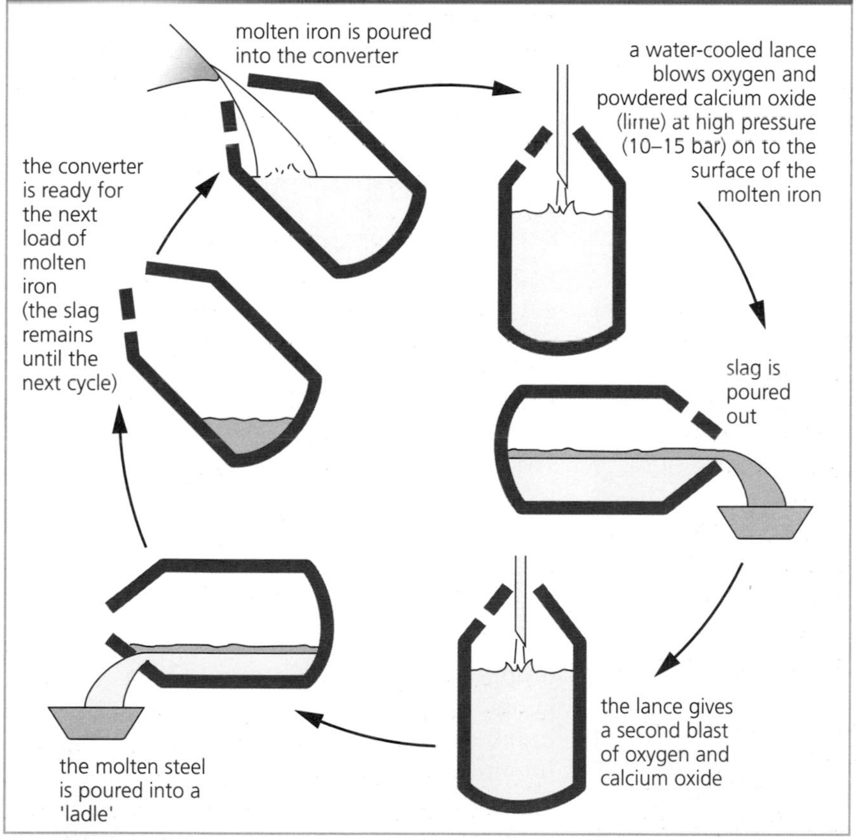

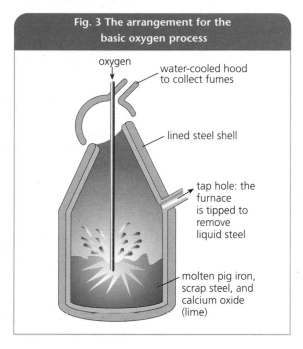

Fig. 3 The arrangement for the basic oxygen process

oxygen

water-cooled hood to collect fumes

lined steel shell

tap hole: the furnace is tipped to remove liquid steel

molten pig iron, scrap steel, and calcium oxide (lime)

Oxygen is blown at very high pressure at the surface of the molten iron. Carbon, silicon and phosphorus in the iron react with the oxygen to form oxides:

$$2C(s) + O_2(g) \rightarrow 2CO(g)$$
$$Si(s) + O_2(g) \rightarrow SiO_2(s)$$
$$4P(s) + 5O_2(g) \rightarrow P_4O_{10}(s)$$

The gas products escape. The reactions are exothermic so, if necessary, to bring down the temperature, scrap iron and steel are added.

More oxygen is blown into the molten iron, and the basic oxide, calcium oxide, is added. This reacts with the solids silicon(IV) oxide and phosphorus(V) oxide, which are acidic. They form a slag which floats to the surface and can be run off.

 7 Reactions in the converter are very exothermic. Why is this an advantage?

Fig. 2 Stages in steel making

molten iron is poured into the converter

a water-cooled lance blows oxygen and powdered calcium oxide (lime) at high pressure (10–15 bar) on to the surface of the molten iron

the converter is ready for the next load of molten iron (the slag remains until the next cycle)

slag is poured out

the molten steel is poured into a 'ladle'

the lance gives a second blast of oxygen and calcium oxide

KEY FACTS

■ Iron oxides are reduced in the blast furnace. Coke and carbon monoxide are the reducing agents.

■ The main impurities in iron ores are silicon(IV) oxide and aluminium oxide.

■ Impurities in iron ore react with limestone in the blast furnace to form slag which is run off from the top of the molten iron.

■ Production of cast iron in a blast furnace is a continuous process.

■ Most of the iron produced in blast furnaces is converted to steel in a converter using the basic oxygen process.

10.4 Aluminium

Properties and uses

The advantages of aluminium are that it is light, strong and can be made into thin sheets. The metal is half as dense as copper or steel. It is also an excellent conductor of heat and electricity, it reflects light and radiant heat and is non-magnetic.

Although the metal is reactive, it does not corrode easily because a clean aluminium surface exposed to the air quickly reacts with the oxygen in the air to form an almost invisible, thin coating of aluminium oxide. This coating is very unreactive and protects the metal below from further attack by oxygen.

Extraction by electrolysis

Aluminium is too reactive to be extracted by reducing aluminium oxide with carbon or carbon monoxide. Therefore, not surprisingly, the age of aluminium production started much later than the Iron Age.

Aluminium was not successfully extracted until the nineteenth century when Friedrich Wohler managed to reduce aluminium chloride with potassium metal (see Table 2:

Aluminium reflects heat, so it can be used to keep foundry workers cool

metals on the left displace metals on the right). The displacement reaction is:

$$AlCl_3 + 3K(s) \rightarrow Al(s) + 3KCl(s)$$

But the process was expensive and aluminium remained just a scientific curiosity.

Then, in 1855, a large pillar of aluminium was presented to the public at the Paris Exposition.

At the 1855 Paris Exposition, a pillar of aluminium was exhibited, seen here behind the display of imperial crown jewels

A French chemist, Henri Etienne Sainte-Claire Deville, had succeeded in preparing aluminium by the electrolysis of sodium aluminium chloride. The price of aluminium dropped immediately from $1225 per kilogram to $38 per kilogram, and continued to fall steadily as technology found new uses for aluminium.

Aluminium has been used so widely partly because there are plentiful supplies of high grade ores, and partly because it can be extracted from its ores economically, by electrolysis.

The mineral bauxite is used as the source of the oxide. High grade bauxite can contain up to 70% aluminium oxide, $Al_2O_3.2H_2O$, along with the impurities iron(III) oxide and silicon(IV) oxide.

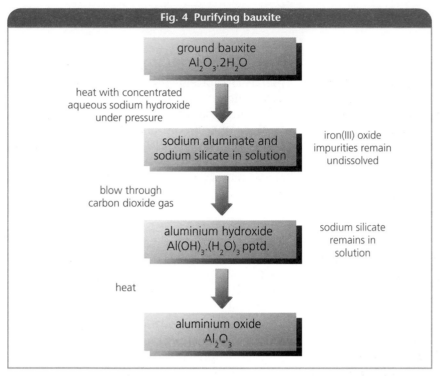

Fig. 4 Purifying bauxite

ground bauxite
$Al_2O_3.2H_2O$

heat with concentrated
aqueous sodium hydroxide
under pressure

sodium aluminate and
sodium silicate in solution

iron(III) oxide
impurities remain
undissolved

blow through
carbon dioxide gas

aluminium hydroxide
$Al(OH)_3.(H_2O)_3$ pptd.

sodium silicate
remains in
solution

heat

aluminium oxide
Al_2O_3

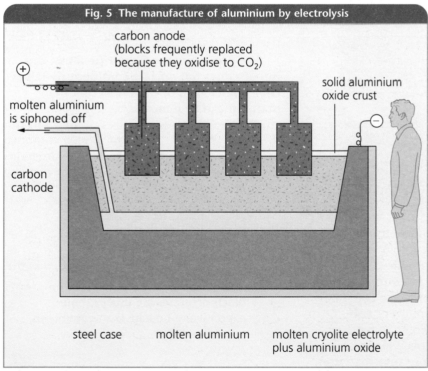

Fig. 5 The manufacture of aluminium by electrolysis

carbon anode
(blocks frequently replaced
because they oxidise to CO_2)

solid aluminium
oxide crust

molten aluminium
is siphoned off

carbon
cathode

steel case   molten aluminium   molten cryolite electrolyte
plus aluminium oxide

To purify the aluminium oxide, the mineral bauxite is ground and reacted with sodium hydroxide, giving aluminium hydroxide which is heated to give the pure oxide, as shown in Fig. 4.

Aluminium oxide has a high melting point, 2050 °C. The cost of keeping it molten is too great for industrial scale electrolysis, so it is mixed with cryolite which has a much lower melting point and allows the molten mixture to be kept at 850 °C. Cryolite is Na_3AlF_6, systematic name sodium hexafluoroaluminate(III).

Electrolysis of Al_2O_3 is carried out in an iron bath called a cell and lined with graphite which acts as the cathode (Fig. 5). The ions attracted to the cathode are Al^{3+} and Na^3. The ions attracted to the anode are O^{2+} and AlF_6^{3-}. The reactions for aluminium oxide are:

reduction at the cathode: $Al^{3+} + 3e^- \rightarrow Al$
oxidation at the anode: $2O^{2-} \rightarrow O_2 + 4e^-$

The anode is a series of carbon blocks. They have to be replaced regularly because, at the high temperature that the cell reaches, the carbon reacts with the oxygen that is given off. Since the carbon blocks are expensive, replacing them regularly is a large part of the cost of the process. Molten aluminium collects on the floor of the cell and is siphoned off at intervals. A cell can produce about 1300 kg of aluminium a day.

 Give the oxidation states of each type of atom in cryolite.

Minimising energy costs

Much of the cost of producing aluminium is for the electric power. As well as breaking down the aluminium oxide, current is used to maintain the temperature of the cell. This means that aluminium works are usually placed near to sources of cheap electrical power, often a hydroelectric power station.

 Why are aluminium works in the UK located in Scotland?

KEY FACTS

- Aluminium is extracted from bauxite by electrolysis.

- The bauxite is first purified with hot sodium hydroxide solution.

- The purified aluminium oxide is dissolved in cryolite to produce an electrolyte that is molten at a lower temperature than pure molten aluminium oxide.

- Most of the cost of aluminium production is due to the large amounts of energy required as electricity.

10.5 Titanium

Properties and uses

Titanium is a very strong, low density metal. Its density is half the density of steel. It does not corrode even under extreme conditions because, like aluminium, it forms a layer of protective oxide on its surface when exposed to air. Titanium has excellent strength at high temperature. When the titanium industry started in the 1950s, titanium was called 'the wonder metal' and was viewed as a replacement for stainless steel.

Titanium alloys meet the requirements of jet turbine blades: they have to work reliably at high temperatures for long periods under great stress

Today, titanium is used extensively in the aerospace industry which accounts for 50–80% of the titanium produced. Yet, though it is 100 times more common in the Earth's crust than copper, we use 200 times more copper than titanium every year.

The reason it did not come to replace stainless steel is that it proved far more expensive to extract from its ores than iron.

Extraction by displacement

Titanium minerals are fairly common, especially rutile or titanium(IV) oxide, TiO_2, and the iron compound ilmenite, $FeTiO_3$. Attempts to reduce titanium(IV) oxide with carbon fail, since titanium carbide is formed, as shown by the equation:

$$TiO_2(s) + 3C(s) \rightarrow TiC(s) + 2CO(g)$$

Reduction of the oxide using more reactive metals also produces impurity problems, and it is difficult and expensive to eliminate the reductant from the titanium.

Instead, titanium manufacture starts by converting titanium(IV) oxide to the chloride, $TiCl_4$, by heating it with carbon in a stream of chlorine gas:

$$TiO_2(s) + 2Cl_2(g) + 2C(s) \rightarrow TiCl_4(g) + 2CO(g)$$

Titanium chloride is liquid at standard temperature and can be purified by fractional distillation.

The titanium can then be extracted from its chloride by the **Kroll process** (Fig. 6) which takes place inside a furnace. Titanium(IV) chloride and liquid magnesium are heated in an unreactive crucible in an inert atmosphere of helium or argon gas. The reduction reaction is a displacement:

$$TiCl_4(g) + 2Mg(l) \rightarrow Ti(s) + 2MgCl_2(l)$$
$$\Delta H = -504 \text{ kJ mol}^{-1}$$

The procedure is a **batch process**: the furnace does not operate continuously but is cooled after each operation so that the titanium can be removed.

The Kroll process produces titanium in the form of a 'sponge'. Titanium sponge contains up to 30% impurities. The impurities include magnesium chloride, $MgCl_2$, which is driven off from the sponge by high temperatures that make it volatile.

10

a Why is an inert atmosphere needed in the Kroll process?

b Batch processes are usually more expensive to operate than continuous processes. Why?

As an alternative to magnesium, sodium can be used as the reductant:

$$TiCl_4(g) + 4Na(l) \rightarrow Ti(s) + 4NaCl(s)$$

The sodium chloride is removed by leaching with dilute hydrochloric acid. Although the temperature of the sodium is held initially at 550 °C, the exothermic reaction raises it to nearly 1000 °C.

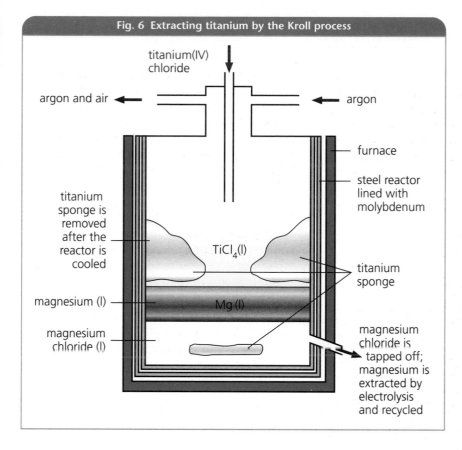

Fig. 6 Extracting titanium by the Kroll process

titanium(IV) chloride

argon and air ←

argon →

furnace

steel reactor lined with molybdenum

titanium sponge is removed after the reactor is cooled

TiCl₄(l)

titanium sponge

magnesium (l)

Mg (l)

magnesium chloride (l)

magnesium chloride is tapped off; magnesium is extracted by electrolysis and recycled

Production costs

In the Kroll process using magnesium, the energy required to convert titanium(IV) chloride to titanium sponge is about 1.3×10^5 kJ kg^{-1}, of which 97% is used to produce the magnesium. It is an expensive process to operate and because of this, titanium has not replaced stainless steel, and its use has been restricted to items for which titanium's properties are essential.

12 For years while the Mary Rose, Henry VIII's flagship, was recently being restored, it was kept in moist, dark conditions to preserve the timbers. A scaffold of titanium supported it. Suggest why this metal was used.

KEY FACTS

■ Titanium cannot be extracted by reduction with carbon as the carbide and not the metal is formed.

■ Titanium is extracted from titanium chloride by displacement with magnesium.

■ Titanium is extracted by an expensive batch process. This explains why the metal is only used in high value situations where the cost is less important than titanium's properties.

10.6 The economics of extraction

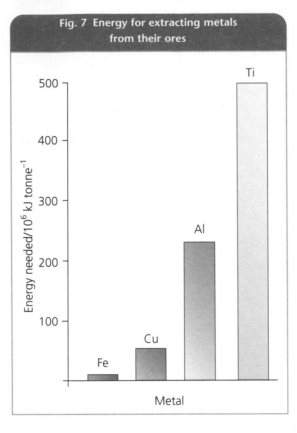

Fig. 7 Energy for extracting metals from their ores

Energy needed/10⁶ kJ tonne⁻¹ (y-axis, marked 100, 200, 300, 400, 500)

Bars labelled: Fe, Cu, Al, Ti

Metal (x-axis)

Iron ore and coal are readily available in the UK relatively cheaply, and the energy costs of the extraction process are quite low. This makes iron a cheap metal to produce. Steel works are usually sited alongside the extraction plant for easy transfer of cast iron, minimising transport costs. Today, there remain iron and steel works at Llanwern and Port Talbot in Wales, and at Scunthorpe and on Teesside in the north of England.

High-grade aluminium ore is readily available and cheap, but the energy for its extraction is several times the energy for iron extraction. But on balance, aluminium is still a relatively cheap metal to produce and is preferable for many uses.

Titanium ores are also cheap and plentiful. However, the extraction process consumes large amounts of energy. This makes titanium production expensive and hence the metal is expensive. Its use is limited to situations where titanium's unique non-corrosive, high strength, low density properties are more important than the cost.

10.7 Recycling

Aluminium

The main cost of aluminium production is for the energy to extract aluminium from the ore. This is relatively high, even when the plant is sited near cheap energy supplies.

But aluminium is easily recycled: about 40% of all the aluminium used in the UK is recycled. You are probably familiar with schemes to collect aluminium drinks cans and foil.

Economic benefits of recycling

Recycling aluminium uses just 5% of the energy for extracting aluminium from the mineral. The scrap cans are first shredded and the paint removed before the metal is melted down into ingots 8 metres long and weighing around 26 tonnes each. About one and a half million cans go to make one ingot. These ingots are rolled into thin sheet metal from which more drinks cans can be cut.

In the UK alone, we consume about 400 000 tonnes of aluminium each year. In the US this figure rises to between 4 000 000

Recyclable aluminum carries the triangular Alu symbol.

and 4 500 000 tonnes a year. So recycling aluminium is profitable big business.

13

a Describe the savings in costs involved in recycling aluminium.

b List the environmental benefits of recycling aluminium.

c If the amount of recycled aluminium increased to twice its present level, what would be the percentage saving on extraction costs, compared to producing all aluminium from its ore?

Iron

Recycling iron and steel is heavier business done by specialist metal reclaiming companies, because objects of iron and steel tend to be bulky – trains, ships and cars for example.

The first step is to break them down to a manageable size. Torch cutters produce smaller scrap, but it is the car crushers followed by shredders that reduce whole car bodies to fist-sized pieces of dense metal. A shredder can process up to one car per minute. The iron and steel, which can be magnetised, is separated from other metals in rotating magnetic drums. Then the scrap is melted and recast.

Recycled iron and steel now accounts world-wide for 45% of all iron and steel produced. The recycling industry produces nearly 100% pure metal, so there are big energy savings compared to starting with iron ores with their high non-metal content. There are some eight companies in the UK which produce steel from recycled iron and steel.

Social and economic benefits of recycling

There are environmental advantages of using recycled iron. Mining for iron ore devastates large areas of land with quarries and heaps of spoil and slag. Restoring the appearance of the landscape can be very costly.

The gases produced from the blast furnace are poisonous. Carbon monoxide is toxic to all invertebrates, and the sulphur impurities – about 1.5% in UK ores – produce sulphur dioxide which causes acid rain.

Iron ore deposits are a finite resource: the cost-effective mines will be exhausted one day. In the mean time, as deposits dwindle they become more expensive to mine, simply because we use the more readily available sources first. So as ores become scarcer, recycling becomes more economically favourable.

14

a Describe the environmental benefits of recycling iron.

b From the graphs in Fig. 8, is there a general trend over time in the recycled amount of either aluminium or iron and steel?

c Suggest reasons that might account for the fluctuations in percentage recycled.

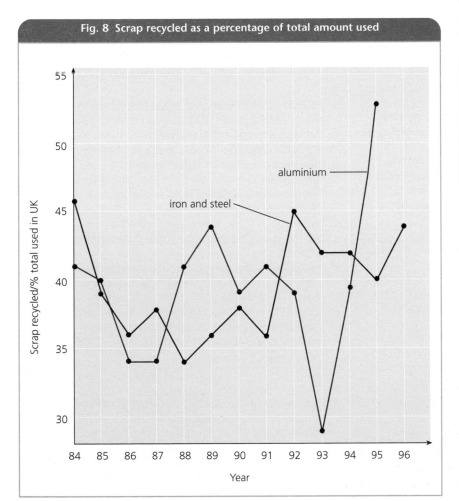
Fig. 8 Scrap recycled as a percentage of total amount used

- Recycling metals requires less energy, at less cost, than extraction of the metals from their ores.
- Aluminium is recycled from cans and foil collected by the public.
- Iron and steel are recycled by specialist metal reclaiming companies who are equipped to break up large objects.

KEY FACTS

1

a Iron can be obtained form its oxide, Fe_2O_3, by reaction with carbon, aluminium or hydrogen. Write an equation for the reaction in each case. (3)

b State, with an explanation, which of the reducing agents used above is likely to lead to
  i) the cheapest iron,
  ii) the purest iron. (4)

c State two compounds formed during the extraction of iron in the blast furnace which lead to environmental pollution. In each case identify the type of pollution caused. (4)

d Outline the essential chemistry of the process for converting crude iron into carbon steel. (2)

NEAB CH05 March 1999 Q1

2

a i) What type of chemical reaction is always involved in the extraction of a metal from its ore?

  ii) Which element is most likely to be combined with a metal in its ore? (2)

b i) Give an overall reaction to show the industrial extraction of iron from its ore.

  ii) What environmental problem may arise during this extraction even if pure iron ore is used as the starting material? (1)

  iii) Explain what further environmental problem might occur if the ore was contaminated with sulphide ores. (2)

c Aluminium is extracted from its purified ore by electrolysis.
  i) Name the ore. (1)
  ii) Give the essential condition for this electrolysis. (1)
  iii) Write the equations for the reactions occurring at each electrode. (2)
  iv) Explain why aluminium is more expensive to extract than iron. (2)
  v) Aluminium itself is used as a reagent for the extraction of other metals. Give an equation to show this use of aluminium in the extraction of an appropriate metal. (1)

NEAB CH05 February 1996 Q1

3

a Give **two** reasons in each case, other than low cost, why iron and aluminium are the most commonly used metals. (4)

b Write an equation, or two half-equations, to show the essential reactions occurring during the extraction of these metals from their oxides. (3)

c Tungsten is prepared in a pure form by high temperature reduction of tungsten(VI) oxide with hydrogen.
  i) Construct an equation for this reaction.
  ii) Suggest why carbon is not used as the reducing agent.

iii) Suggest one advantage (other than purity of product) and one disadvantage of using hydrogen as the reducing agent on an industrial scale. (4)

NEAB CH05 June 1999 Q1

4

a Select **three** different general methods for the extraction of metals. For **each** method you select, state the starting materials, the conditions used and give one example of a metal extracted by this method. (9)

b i) Indicate the essential chemistry involved in the removal of carbon from impure iron in the manufacture of steel. (2)

  ii) Give two reasons why steel is less expensive to produce than titanium. (2)

  iii) Give one reason why titanium is used for certain applications despite the extra cost of this metal as compared to steel. (1)

NEAB CH05 June 1996 Q1

5

a Titanium can be prepared in the laboratory by passing titanium(IV) chloride vapour and hydrogen through a furnace at 1000 °C.
Construct an equation for the reaction which occurs. (1)

b Industrially, a different reducing agent is used with titanium(IV) chloride. Give the reducing agent, state two essential conditions used and write an equation for the process. (4)

c Suggest two reasons why the method described in part (a) is not the preferred route on an industrial scale. (2)

d Suggest why titanium is manufactured by the method you have given in part (b) rather than by the reduction of titanium(IV) oxide with carbon. (2)

e Suggest two reasons why there has been much research into finding cheaper routes for the manufacture of titanium. (2)

NEAB CH05 March 1998 Q2

6

a Outline, by giving starting materials, conditions and equations, how iron and aluminium are extracted commercially. (9)

b State **two** possible pollution problems that may arise in the extraction of iron. (2)

c Give **two** reasons why these metals are used so extensively despite iron being prone to rusting and aluminium metal being expensive to extract. (2)

d Explain why some metals which are relatively scarce in the Earth's crust are used more commonly than plentiful metals such as titanium. (2)

NEAB CH05 February 1997 Q7

Recycling aluminium

The aluminium drinks can shows how good design and attention to chemical processes can save energy. The modern can has a mass of only 16 g and a metal wall only an eighth of a millimetre thick. It is also made in two parts today (a closed cylinder and a top.) Along with other packaging and containers, drinks cans use up 10-15% of all the aluminium produced.

The production cycle of the can-making process is shown in diagram 1, where 2.5 kg of aluminium fed in from the smelter results in 1.0 kg of cans. All the losses are shown on the diagram at each stage. By comparison, diagram 2 shows what happens if the losses from each stage are recycled in the process.

This recycling within the can production system and the recycling of aluminium cans by the public can lead to great energy savings in producing primary aluminium and hence lower costs.

As well as the information above, you will need to use the information from the whole of this chapter, and do further research, perhaps using the internet, to answer the following questions.

1 Aluminium can-making process

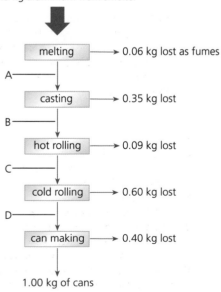

2 Aluminium can-making process plus recycling of waste

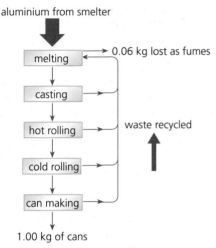

1 List other uses of aluminium. Suggest 3 main groups and give examples of each.

2

  a How many drinks cans can be made from 1.0 tonne of aluminium?

  b Insert the mass of aluminium remaining at each of the points A - D on diagram 1.

  c How much aluminium is recycled in diagram 2?

  d How much aluminium is needed from the smelter in diagram 2?

3 State, with reasons, which is the least efficient part of the can making system in terms of:

  a aluminium,

  b energy.

4 What is the percentage saving in aluminium in diagram 2?

5 If percentage efficiency is defined as being Output/Input x 100, calculate what is the materials conversion efficiency of:

  a diagram 1 with no recycling,

  b diagram 2 with recycling.

6 Summarise the environmental and economic benefits of recycling aluminium.

11 Nomenclature and isomerism

What does a chemical name tell you? It all depends on the name. Chemistry is littered with different names for the same chemicals, some of them a lot more helpful than others.

Take the label on a bottle of lager. It says 4% alcohol. Alcohol is the common name for the ingredient that makes us relax and enjoy ourselves, but it tells us nothing about the chemistry. A chemist knows the alcohols as a large family of related chemicals, and the one in the bottle as ethanol.

Stain Devils remove stains because they contain a cocktail of dry cleaning solvents. The main ingredient is trichloromethane, which used to be called chloroform. Daz is a trade name. It and other washing powders contain the surfactant alkylbenzenesulphonate.

This is just the tip of a very big iceberg of different names for the same things. We now use an agreed international naming system for chemicals based on their structure and molecular formula, because it is helpful to us as chemists. Yet it is not going to replace the trade names and old common names we are all familiar with.

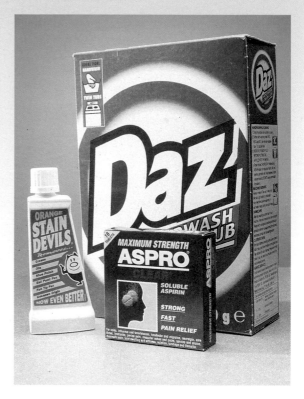

More confusingly, add a layer of brand names. Aspro is one of several brand names for the same medication, all containing the substance whose common name is aspirin. Now add another layer! The old scientific name is acetylsalicylic acid. Acetyl comes from *acetum*, the Latin for acetic acid, which is vinegar. Salicylic comes from the Latin for the willow tree, since aspirin was first extracted from its bark. But unless you knew all that, the name acetylsalicylic acid would be completely meaningless. The new systematic name of 2-ethanoyloxybenzenecarboxylic acid explains the structure to a chemist, but you wouldn't ask for it in Boots™.

11.1   What's special about carbon?

About 7 million carbon compounds are now known. The number increases all the time as chemists discover and synthesise new ones. The reason there are so many carbon compounds is that carbon, in Group IV ($1s^2\ 2s^2\ 2p^2$), has four electrons available for bonding and a unique ability to make strong covalent bonds with other carbon atoms and other non-metal atoms.

Chains of carbon atoms in polymers can reach thousands of atoms long and can include single, double and triple bonds. Carbon atoms can also join together in complicated ring and sphere structures.

Organic and inorganic compounds

Because carbon compounds are so important in nature and industry and so numerous, their study makes up a separate branch of chemistry called **organic chemistry**. There are more organic compounds than compounds of all the other elements put together.

Originally, organic compounds were those that burnt or charred when heated. They usually came from living things. Today, organic chemistry is the study of all carbon compounds, including many synthesised in laboratories and never found in nature. The two exceptions to this rule are carbon dioxide and carbon monoxide which are usually placed in inorganic chemistry.

Inorganic chemistry is the study of non-carbon compounds. Inorganic compounds were those that melted or vaporised on heating, but returned to their original state when cooled. Early chemists thought that only inorganic compounds could be synthesised in the laboratory because organic compounds from living things needed a vital force (a life force). This idea was dispelled by the discovery in 1828 that urea, NH_2CONH_2, naturally found in urine, could also be made in the laboratory.

Carbon–carbon bonding

It is carbon's ability to form strong links with itself and other non-metals that makes it unique. This single feature accounts for incredibly complex and varied carbon-based structures: at temperatures and pressures found on Earth, the stability of carbon bonds enabled carbon to become the basis for the materials of life.

Table 1 Bond energies	
Bond	**Bond dissociation energy/kJ mol^{-1}**
C—C	347
C=C	612
C≡C	838
Si—Si	226
N—N	158
P—P	198

How strong is a carbon–carbon bond? Table 1 gives the bond dissociation energy for a range of bonds. The **bond dissociation energy** is the energy needed to break the bond and separate the atoms. It is clear from

Fig. 1 Compounds with single, double and triple carbon–carbon bonds

Lauric acid, a long-chain fatty acid

Vitamin A

Ethyne

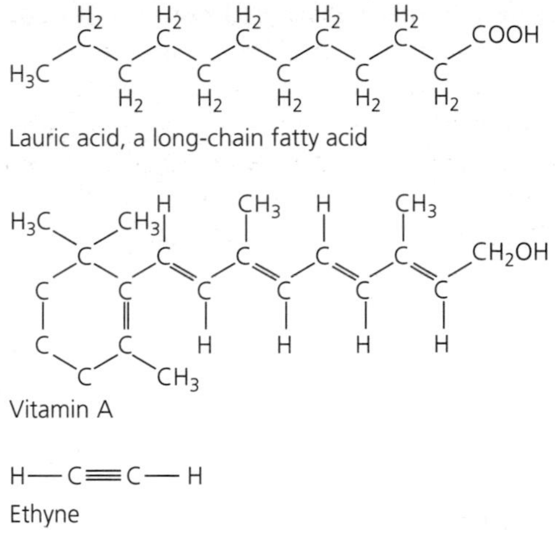

the data that the carbon–carbon bond is much stronger than other covalent bonds between atoms of the same element.

Silicon, also in Group IV, is the element most similar to carbon. With a lower dissociation energy, the Si–Si bond is weaker than C–C. Silicon can form short chains with other silicon atoms, but these compounds are unstable and decompose at room temperature and atmospheric pressure.

Most carbon–carbon bonds are single covalent bonds. Many are found in long chains, as in fatty acids (Fig. 1). Double carbon–carbon bonds are common in organic compounds, for example in Vitamin A. Triple carbon–carbon bonds are rare: there is a triple bond in ethyne, HC≡CH, and in its family of compounds.

1 Draw a dot and cross diagram to show:

a a carbon–carbon single bond,

b a carbon–carbon double bond.

2 Draw a dot and cross diagram to show the electronic configuration in:

a carbon dioxide,

b a nitrogen molecule.

3 Explain why nitrogen and phosphorus are unlikely to form compounds containing long chains of nitrogen and phosphorus atoms.

11.2 Molecular shapes

Fig. 2 The tetrahedral arrangement of bonds on the carbon atom in methane

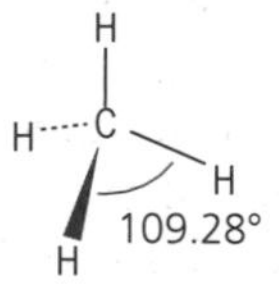

The arrangement of bonds around the central carbon.

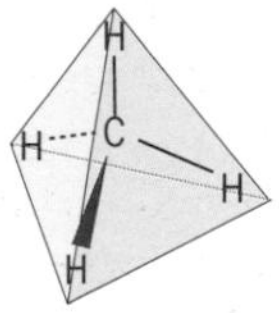

Hydrogens are at the four corners of a tetrahedron.

► The bond comes out of the plane of the paper

...... The bond goes into the plane of the paper

—— The bond lies on the plane of the paper

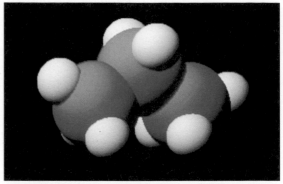

A space-filling model of propane: this shows better than a ball and stick model the volume and spatial arrangement of atoms

The four covalent bonds around a carbon atom form a tetrahedral structure. Fig. 2 shows methane. Each bond angle is 109.28°, and the way each bond is drawn indicates its 3D position.

Fig. 3 shows the three-dimensional formula of propane: the chain of atoms H–C–C–C–H is a zig-zag in the plane of the paper. The other hydrogen atoms are in front or behind the paper. The ball and stick model in Fig. 3 gives a better idea of how the atoms are spaced in a molecule, while the space-filling model in the photograph gives a more accurate representation of the spatial arrangement of the tightly packed atoms.

Fig. 3 The arrangement of atoms in a propane molecule

Molecular formula: $CH_3CH_2CH_3$

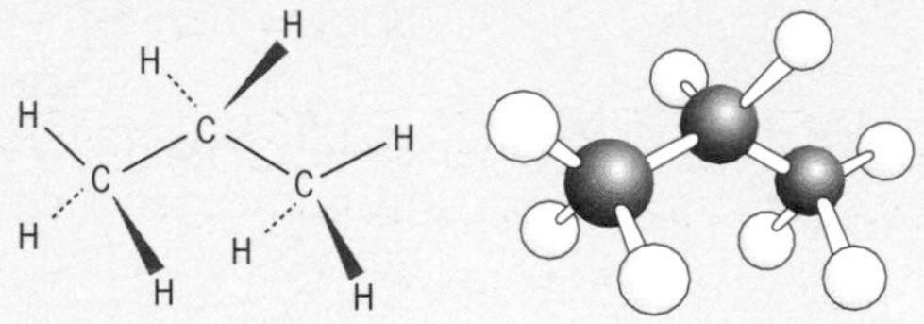

11.3 Molecular formulae in chain compounds

We can describe molecules in different ways. You have already come across empirical formulae on page 45. An empirical formula gives the ratio of different types of atoms in a molecule, such as CH_2O for glucose, and a molecular formula gives all atoms in a molecule; glucose is $C_6H_{12}O_6$.

A general formula is a formula for a family of compounds. It gives the ratio of atoms in any compound in the family, along with any special arrangements of atoms.

A general formula allows you to create a particular molecule simply by multiplying up the number of atoms. For example, the general formula for all alcohols is $C_nH_{2n+1}OH$. The –OH group is the significant group, meaning it is characteristic of the alcohols. It has no multiplication number because there is only one –OH group in any alcohol. For the numbers of the other atoms, C and H, you multiply. For example, ethanol has two carbon atoms, so $n = 2$, giving C_2H_5OH.

The structural formula gives the numbers and types of atoms in a molecule, and shows how they are bonded together.

In a structural formula, single bonds are written as a single line and double bonds as a double line. The structural formula is sometimes called the **displayed formula** or the **graphical formula**. Different ways to express formulae are summarised in Table 2.

Table 2 Types of formulae			
	Ratio of atoms present	Total number of atoms present	Structure of molecule
Empirical formula	Yes	No	No
Molecular formula	Yes	Yes	No, but identifies significant functional groups
General formula	Yes	No	No, but identifies significant groups
Structural formula	Yes	Yes	Yes

4

a A mass of hydrocarbon contains 240 g carbon and 40 g hydrogen. What is its empirical formula?

b Its relative molecular mass is 142 g. What is its molecular formula?

c Suggest a structural formula.

Functional groups and homologous series

A significant group identified by the general formula for a family of chemicals is called the **functional group**. It is the reactive portion of the molecule, and all organic molecules with the same functional group behave chemically in a similar way. For example in alcohols, the –OH group is the functional group. It determines the chemical properties of the molecule. Functional groups for other families include the C=C group in alkenes and the C=O group in ketones.

A **homologous series** is the name we give to a family of molecules that can all be represented by a general formula. All members of a homologous series therefore have the same functional group (or groups).

All the chemicals in a homologous series share the same chemical properties, while their physical properties differ but show trends. For example, the alkanes are all chemically similar because they all have the C–H functional group. The size of the molecule then affects physical characteristics such as melting point and boiling point, which increase steadily through the series.

Since the functional group identifies the homologous series of a chemical, it is used to name the molecule. Table 3 shows the main functional groups and how they name chemicals. If a molecule has a C=C functional group, it is an alkene and so the name ends in the letters -ene. Molecules with the –Cl group begin with chloro-.

We will return to the naming of organic molecules in section 11.5.

Table 3 Homologous series and functional groups				
General formula	**Homologous series**	**Name (suffix or prefix)**	**Functional group**	**Example**
C_nH_{2n+2}	alkanes	suffix -ane	C–H	ethane, C_2H_6
C_nH_{2n}	alkenes	suffix -ene	C=C	ethene, C_2H_4
	haloalkanes	prefix chloro-	–Cl	chloroethane, CH_3CH_2Cl
$C_nH_{2n+1}OH$	alcohols	suffix -ol	–OH	ethanol, C_2H_5OH
		prefix hydroxy-		
	aldehydes	suffix -al	$-C{\overset{H}{\underset{O}{}}}$	ethanal, CH_3CHO
	ketones	suffix -one	C=O	propanone, CH_3COCH_3
		prefix oxo-		3-oxobutanoic acid, CH_3COCH_2COOH
$C_nH_{2n}COOH$	carboxylic acids	suffix -oic acid	$-C{\overset{O}{\underset{OH}{}}}$	ethanoic acid, CH_3COOH
	esters	suffix -oate	$-C{\overset{O}{\underset{OCH_3}{}}}$	methyl ethanoate, CH_3COOCH_3

KEY FACTS

- The study of the compounds of carbon is called organic chemistry.

- Carbon forms strong covalent bonds with other carbon atoms.

- Families of carbon compounds with the same functional group are called homologous series.

- The empirical formula gives the ratio of different atoms in a molecule.

- The molecular formula gives the numbers and types of atoms in a molecule.

- The general formula gives the ratios and arrangement of atoms in compounds of a homologous series.

- The structural formula gives the numbers and types of atoms in a molecule, and shows how they are bonded together.

11.4 Homologous series of chain compounds

The alkanes

Alkanes make useful fuels because of their highly exothermic reactions with oxygen. Their general formula is C_nH_{2n+2}. The bonds are all single bonds. Such compounds are called **saturated hydrocarbons**.

Occurrence of methane

The smallest alkane is methane, CH_4, commonly called 'natural gas'. In the UK it is extracted from large supplies found with crude oil under the North Sea where both gas and oil were formed by plants and animals decaying over millions of years. Crude oil itself is a mixture of alkanes.

Methane is also produced wherever rotting vegetation decays anaerobically (without oxygen) under a layer of water. Enormous quantities of methane, together with carbon dioxide, come from paddy fields. Unfortunately, the gases cannot be collected, but enter the atmosphere where they act as greenhouse gases.

In a similar process, the digestion of plant material in the intestine of cows produces methane. One cow can belch 500 dm³ of methane gas every day, enough to boil the water for a cup of coffee if we could collect it!

Table 4 Chemical formulae of the first six alkanes

Name	Molecular formula	Structural formula	Empirical formula
methane	CH_4	H–C–H (with H above and H below)	CH_4
ethane	C_2H_6	H–C–C–H (with H's above and below)	CH_3
propane	C_3H_8	H–C–C–C–H	C_3H_8
butane	C_4H_{10}	H–C–C–C–C–H	C_2H_5
pentane	C_5H_{12}	H–C–C–C–C–C–H	C_5H_{12}
hexane	C_6H_{14}	H–C–C–C–C–C–C–H	C_3H_7

Table 5 The first six alkyl groups

Name	Formula
methyl	CH_3-
ethyl	C_2H_5-
propyl	C_3H_7-
butyl	C_4H_9-
pentyl	$C_5H_{11}-$
hexyl	$C_6H_{13}-$

Names of alkanes

Table 4 shows the first six alkanes, and Table 5 shows the **alkyl groups** derived from them. In a molecular formula, the alkyl group is often given the letter R.

5 Give the molecular and structural formulae for alkanes with 15 and with 30 carbon atoms in their chains.

The alkenes

The **alkenes** are a homologous series of compounds each containing one or more double bonds between carbon atoms. Because they can add more atoms or groups across the double bond, they are called **unsaturated hydrocarbons**. Table 6 shows the first five alkenes. The ending -ene means that there is a double bond in the molecule.

Although, like alkanes, the alkenes contain only carbon and hydrogen atoms, their chemistry is very different. The double bond is the functional group, and its position can vary in molecules from butene onwards.

The alcohols

The **alcohols** are the homologous series of compounds with the functional group -OH. Table 7 lists the first six alcohols.

Table 7 The first six alcohols	
Name	**Molecular Formula**
methanol	CH_3OH
ethanol	C_2H_5OH
propan-1-ol	C_3H_7OH
butan-1-ol	C_4H_9OH
pentan-1-ol	$C_5H_{11}OH$
hexan-1-ol	$C_6H_{13}OH$

Table 6 Chemical formulae of the first five alkenes			
Name	**Molecular formula**	**Structural formula**	**Empirical formula**
ethene	C_7H_4		CH_2
propene	C_3H_6		CH_2
but-1-ene	C_4H_8		CH_2
pent-1-ene	C_5H_{10}		CH_2
hex-1-ene	C_6H_{12}		CH_2

KEY FACTS

- Alkanes are hydrocarbons with single bonds between the carbon atoms.
- Alkenes are hydrocarbons with one or more double bonds between the carbon atoms.
- Halogenoalkanes are alkanes in which one or more of the hydrogen atoms have been replaced by a halogen atom.
- The alcohols have the functional group –OH.
- Carboxylic acids have the functional group –COOH.

Useful homologous groups

Alkenes: good starting materials

The alkenes are very useful to the chemical industry. Because they readily add atoms and groups across double bonds, they are used as the starting materials for making compounds that are used everywhere, such as the plastics of window frames and food bags, and additives in petrol.

The synthesis of a compound at a chemical plant usually involves a sequence of reactions. The process takes the starting chemical and changes it step by step. The chemicals made at the steps between starting material and the final product are called 'synthetic intermediates', and the sequence of reactions is called the 'chemical route'.

In the chemical route starting with an alkene, a first synthetic intermediate is often a **haloalkane**, in which one or two halogen atoms - usually chlorine or bromine - are added to the alkene. A halogen atom increases reactivity, so that in later steps other functional groups can be inserted, or a carbon chain can be extended. The naming of haloalkanes is dealt with in Application A on page 165.

Poly(chloroethene), commonly known as the plastic PVC, has ethene as its starting material. The first synthetic intermediate adds two chlorine atoms across the bond. The chemical route is:

ethene	→	1,2-dichloroethane	→	chloroethene	→	poly(chloroethene)
$CH_2=CH_2$		$CH_2Cl–CH_2Cl$		$CH_2=CHCl$		$–[–CH_2–CHCl–]–$
an alkene		a dichloroalkane		a chloroalkene		a poly(chloroalkane)

Carboxylic acids: an alternative to fingerprints

The functional group of the carboxylic acids is –COOH. The name always ends in -oic, with the stem taken from the alkyl group in the compound.

Name	Molecular formula
ethanoic acid	CH_3COOH
propanoic acid	C_2H_5COOH
butanoic acid	C_3H_7COOH
pentanoic acid	C_4H_9COOH
hexanoic acid	$C_5H_{11}COOH$

For example, ethane gives ethanoic acid.

Carboxylic acids have characteristic smells. Ethanoic acid smells vinegary, but many others have far more unpleasant smells, especially the longer chained carboxylic acids. Smelly sock odour is butanoic acid.

A trained dog can easily identify a suspect from the faintest whiff of sweat on a discarded item

Every human has his or her own unique mixture of carboxylic acids in their sweat, which enables police to identify criminals. Their sniffer dogs are far more sensitive to the odour of carboxylic acids than humans, and can match up a suspect with just a hint of their body odour on an item of clothing.

We spend a small fortune every year trying to mask our body odour

11.5 Classifying and naming organic molecules

Of all the organic compounds, the homologous families covered so far are just a few of the chain compounds. These are part of a larger category, the **aliphatic compounds**. To make sense of the enormous number of different carbon-containing compounds, they have been sorted into three categories, shown in Table 8.

Table 8 Classifying organic molecules		
Category	**Molecular structure**	**Examples**
aliphatic	straight or branched chained carbon atoms	octane, trichloromethane, soaps
alicyclic	closed rings of carbon atoms, which contain single or multiple bonds	glucose, buckminsterfull-erenes
arenes	include a benzene ring	polystyrene, TCP, some perfumes, some surfactants

IUPAC naming rules
We give compounds systematic names according to rules established by the International Union of Pure and Applied Chemistry, known as IUPAC. These rules are used throughout the world. The naming method fills several books, but we include only the relevant parts here.

Ordering functional groups
A molecule can have more than one functional group. The principal functional group, which determines its name, depends on an order of priority established by IUPAC. This is the order of priority for some of the functional groups:

    carboxylic acid
    ester
    aldehyde
    ketone
    alcohol

If present in a compound, the carboxylic acid group is the principal functional group. It is given as its suffix in the name of the compound.

Rules for an aliphatic compound

1 Identify the principal functional group present, and so the homologous series. This gives the suffix.

2 Check for the presence of double bonds in the carbon chain.

3 Select the longest continuous carbon chain that contains the principal functional group and the maximum number of unsaturated bonds. This gives the main part or stem of the name.

4 Number the carbon atoms from the end that give the lowest possible number to the principal functional group.

5 Identify additional functional groups. These provide the prefix or prefixes and are numbered according to their position. Use commas to separate numbers and hyphens to separate numbers and letters.

The following examples show how these rules apply to molecules.

Naming alkanes

1 All functional groups are C–H.
2 There are no double bonds, so it is an alkane.
3 The longest chain is 5 carbon atoms long. This gives the suffix -pentane.
4 There is a branching methyl group. Numbering from the nearest end of the carbon chain, it is attached to carbon atom 2. This gives the prefix 2-methyl.
The name is **2-methylpentane**.

```
          H
          |
       H– C –H
    H  H  |  H  H
    |  |  |  |  |
  H–C— C— C— C— C–H
    |  |  |  |  |
    H  |  H  H  H
       H– C –H
          |
          H
```

1 All functional groups are C–H.
2 There are no double bonds, so it is an alkane.
3 The longest chain is 5 carbon atoms long. This gives the suffix -pentane.
4 There are two branching methyl groups. Numbering from the end nearest to a branching methyl group, the first is on carbon 2 and the second is on carbon 3.
The name is **2,3-dimethylpentane** (di- means two).

Naming alkenes

When naming an alkene, the rule is always to count the end carbon nearest the double bond as carbon 1, so as to give the lowest number in the name.

```
      H  H  H
      |  |  |    H
  H—C—C—C=C
      |  |  |    H
      H  H       H
```

1 The functional group is C=C.
2 The carbon–carbon double bond means that the compound is an alkene. The suffix is -ene.
3 There are 4 carbon atoms in the chain, so the prefix is but-.
4 The double bond starts at carbon 1.
The name is **but-1-ene**.

```
      H  H  H  H
      |  |  |  |
  H–C—C=C—C–H
      |     |
      H     H
```

1 The functional group is C=C. The suffix is -ene.
2 There is one double bond.
3 The longest continuous carbon chain is 4 carbons long. The stem is but-.
4 The double bond begins on carbon atom 2.
The name is **but-2-ene**.

6 Draw the structural formula for the following.

a hex-2-ene

b dec-3-ene

7 Why is it not possible to have an alkane named but-3-ene?

For the naming of haloalkanes, see Application A on page 165.

Naming alcohols

1 The alcohol group -OH is on carbon 1, so the suffix is -1-ol.

```
      H  H  H
      |  |  |
  H—C—C—C—OH
      |  |  |
      H  H  H
```

2 There are no carbon–carbon double bonds.
3 There are 3 carbons, so the prefix is propan-.
The name is **propan-1-ol**.

Naming aldehydes

```
          H
          |
       H– C –H
       H  |  H
       |  |  |    O
  H–C—C—C—C
       |  |  |    H
       H  H  H
```

1 The functional group is -CHO, so the compound is an aldehyde. The suffix is -al.
2 There are no carbon–carbon double bonds, so the compound is derived from an alkane.
3 The longest chain has 4 carbons, so the suffix is butanal.
4 Carbon 3 is attached to a methyl side-group. The prefix is 3-methyl
The name is **3-methylbutanal**.

Naming ketones

```
      H  H  O  H  H  H
      |  |  ‖  |  |  |
  H–C—C—C—C—C—C–H
      |  |     |  |  |
      H  H     H  H  H
```

1 The functional group is C=O, with C attached to 2 other carbons: the compound is a ketone, the suffix is -one.
2 There are no carbon–carbon double bonds.
3 The chain is 6 carbons long, so the prefix is hexan-.
4 The carbonyl group is on carbon 3, making the suffix -3-one.
The name is **hexan-3-one**.

Naming carboxylic acids

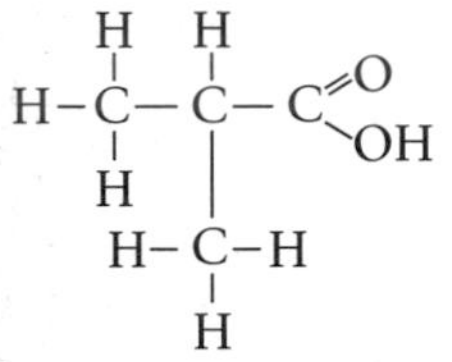

1 The principal functional group is carboxylic acid. The suffix is -oic acid
2 There are no carbon–carbon double bonds.
3 The longest continuous carbon chain is three carbons long. The stem is propan-.
4 There is an additional functional group, a methyl group, on carbon atom 2.

The name is **2-methyl propanoic acid**.

8 Give the molecular and structural formulae for the following.

a octan-2-ol

b hexanoic acid

c pent-2-ene

d 2,2-dimethylbutane

9 Give the molecular and structural formulae for the following.

a propane

b propene

c propan-1-ol

d propanoic acid

APPLICATION A

Using IUPAC rules to name haloalkanes

Haloalkanes are alkane molecules in which one or more of the hydrogen atoms are replaced by a halogen atom, such as chlorine or fluorine.

Haloalkanes rarely occur naturally; they are usually synthesised in the laboratory. They have become the goodies and baddies of organic chemistry. On the positive side, they are used to make everything from synthetic blood, anaesthetics, a range of plastics and non-stick surfaces for frying pans.

However, since the 1950s, they have also been used as aerosol propellants known as CFCs, chlorofluorocarbons. CFCs are stable, non-toxic, non flammable and have no odour. They make the ideal aerosol propellant. Unfortunately, they also collect in the stratosphere and convert ozone, O_3, into oxygen, O_2. Ozone in the upper atmosphere prevents much high-energy UV radiation from reaching the earth and damaging plant and animal cells. Chemists are now providing safe alternatives.

Naming haloalkanes

1 The stem of the name is taken from the number of carbon atoms in the alkane skeleton.
2 The presence of a halogen is shown by the prefix *fluoro-, chloro-, bromo-, iodo-*.
3 The number of each halogen atom is shown using mono-, di-, tri-, tetra-, penta-, hexa- before the prefix.

4 The position of each halogen atom is shown using numbers before the prefix.
5 If more than one type of halogen is present, they are listed in alphabetical order.

1 Name the following haloalkanes.

a

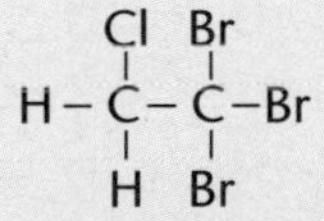

b

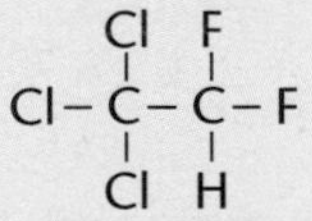

c

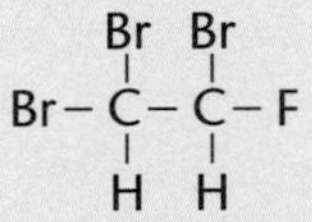

d

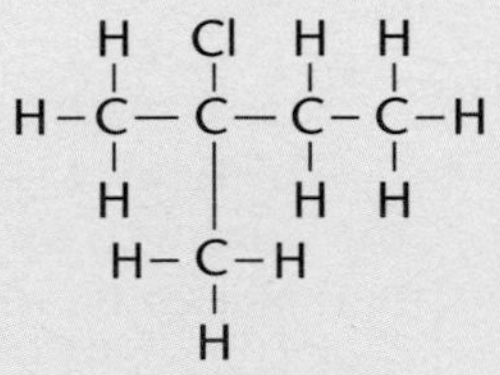

e

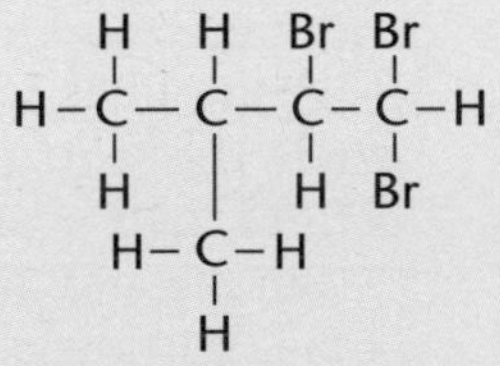

11.6 Isomers

Isomers have the same molecular formula, but different arrangements of atoms. Isomers may be structural isomers or stereoisomers.

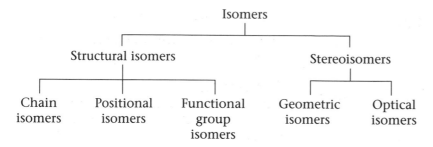

Structural isomers

Substances with the same molecular formulae but different structural formulae are called **structural isomers**. Structural isomers can be of three different types:

Chain isomers
Positional isomers
Functional group isomers

Chain isomers

Consider the molecular formula C_4H_{10}. There are two possible structural formulae for this molecular formula:

1
```
    H  H  H  H
    |  |  |  |
H−C− C− C− C−H
    |  |  |  |
    H  H  H  H
      butane
```

2
```
    H   H   H
    |   |   |
H−C−  C −  C−H
    |   |   |
    H   |   H
      H− C−H
         |
         H
   2-methylpropane
```

Butane and 2-methylpropane are structural isomers. Both belong to the same homologous series, the alkanes. This means they share similar chemical properties. However, they differ in their boiling points:

b.p. butane = −0.5 °C
b.p. 2-methylpropane = −11.7 °C.

The type of isomer present can be shown by the shortened form of the structural formula: butane can be written as:

$CH_3CH_2CH_2CH_3$

and 2-methylpropane as:

$CH_3CH(CH_3)CH_3$

where the sequence of groups in the formula defines their position in the molecule.

Butane and 2-methylpropane are examples of chain isomers. Chain isomers occur in all carbon compounds over 4 carbon atoms long, and the longer the chain, the higher the number of isomers possible. C_4H_{10} has two chain isomers, but $C_{40}H_{82}$ has an estimated 6.25×10^{13} chain isomers.

Chain isomers of C_5H_{12}

1
```
    H  H  H  H  H
    |  |  |  |  |
H−C− C− C− C− C−H
    |  |  |  |  |
    H  H  H  H  H
```
pentane $CH_3CH_2CH_2CH_2CH_3$

2
```
    H  H   H   H
    |  |   |   |
H−C− C−  C −  C−H
    |  |   |   |
    H  H   |   H
        H− C−H
           |
           H
```
2-methylbutane $CH_3CH(CH_3)CH_2CH_3$

3
```
         H
         |
      H− C−H
    H  |   H
    |  |   |
H−C−  C − C−H
    |  |   |
    H  |   H
      H− C−H        2,2-dimethylpropane
         |          CH_3(CH_3)_2CH_3
         H
```

Note that there are only three chain isomers for C_5H_{12}. The C–C bond rotates so that, although we may draw a carbon chain as a straight line, it actually twists and changes shape continually, so that:

```
    H  H   H
    |  |   |
H−C− C−  C −H
    |  |   |
    H  H   |
        H− C−H
           |
        H  C  H
           |
           H
```
is the same as 1, and

```
         H
         |
      H− C−H
    H  |   H  H
    |  |   |  |
H−C−  C − C− C−H
    |  |   |  |
    H  H   H  H
```
and
```
            H
            |
         H− C−H
       H  |   H
       |  |   |
   H−C−  C − C−H
       |  |   |
       H  H   |
           H− C−H
              |
              H
```
are the same as 2.

How many chain isomers are possible for C_6H_{14}?

Positional isomers

Positional isomers have their functional groups in different positions.

Positional isomers for C_4H_8

$$H \backslash C=C-C-C-H$$ but-1-ene
$CH_2CHCH_2CH_3$ and

$$H-C-C=C-C-H$$ but-2-ene
$CH_3CHCHCH_3$

But-1-ene and but-2-ene are positional isomers. They have essentially the same chemical reactions because they possess the same functional groups.

Positional isomers for alcohols $C_4H_{10}O$

$$H-C-C-C-C-OH$$ butan-1-ol
$CH_3CH_2CH_2CH_2OH$

$$H-C-C-C-C-H$$ butan-2-ol
$CH_3CH_2CH(OH)CH_3$

a Explain why it is sometimes confusing to use the molecular formula for an alcohol.

b Draw structural formulae for all the possible positional isomers for hexanol.

Functional group isomers

Functional group isomers have the same molecular formulae but different functional groups and so belong to different homologous series.

Functional group isomers for the molecular formula C_2H_6O

There are two functional group isomers:

1
$$H-C-C-OH$$
ethanol

2
$$H-C-O-C-H$$
methoxymethane

Ethanol belongs to the homologous series of alcohols, while methoxymethane is an ether.

Functional group isomers for the molecular formula C_3H_6O

Functional group isomers are:

1
$$H-C-C-C=O$$
propanal

2
$$H-C-C-C-H$$
propanone

Propanal is an aldehyde and propanone is a ketone.

Stereoisomers

Stereoisomers have the same molecular formula but a different arrangement of their atoms in space. There are two types of stereoisomers:

    Geometric isomers   Optical isomers

Geometric isomers

Alkenes with a double bond show geometric isomerism. The double bond C=C does not rotate and fixes the rest of the molecule in a set position. If the alkene has two different groups on each end of the double bond, then two structures are possible.

Geometric isomers of but-2-ene

$$H_3C \backslash C=C \diagup CH_3$$
$$H \diagup \quad \backslash H$$

$$H_3C \backslash C=C \diagup H$$
$$H \diagup \quad \backslash CH_3$$

cis-but-2-ene
b.p. 4 °C
m.p. −139 °C

trans-but-2-ene
b.p. 1 °C
m.p. −106 °C

We use the prefixes *cis* and *trans* to distinguish between the two isomers. *cis* means that the two like groups are on the same side of the double bond and *trans* means that they are on opposite sides.

Optical isomers

When two compounds have the same molecular and structural formulae but one cannot be superimposed on the other (Fig. 4), they are called **optical isomers** (optical because they differ in the way their crystals affect polarised light). One is the mirror image of the other.

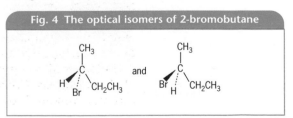

Fig. 4 The optical isomers of 2-bromobutane

EXTENSION — Fats and oils

Cis and *trans* isomers are important in fats and oils. Fat and oil molecules consist of a molecule of propane-1,2,3-triol bonded to three carboxylic acid molecules (Fig. 4).

Structure of a fat or oil

Fatty acids $R-\overset{\overset{O}{\|}}{C}-OH$

Propane-1,2,3-triol

R^1, R^2 and R^3 are long hydrocarbon chains

The carboxylic acid part of the fat molecule is often called a fatty acid chain because it consists of a long chain of carbon atoms (R in the diagram above) with a carboxylic acid group at one end. The length of the carbon chain and the presence or absence of double bonds depends on the source of the fatty acid. Fatty acids from animal fats all have single bonds and so they are saturated.

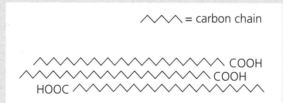

= carbon chain

shape of molecules means that they can lie side-by-side, and solidify

Animal and vegetable fats and oils

This straight chain character of the carbon chain aids allows saturated animal fats, such as butter, cheese, lard, to be solid at room temperature.

Fatty acids from vegetable sources contain one or more double bonds, so they are unsaturated. If the fatty acids have a *trans* structure, as shown below, then they will more easily solidify at room temperature. But most vegetable oils contain *cis* structures and the fatty acid chains do not pack so easily to solidify. Vegetable oils are liquid at room temperature.

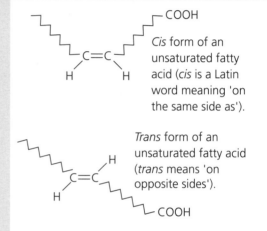

Cis form of an unsaturated fatty acid (*cis* is a Latin word meaning 'on the same side as').

Trans form of an unsaturated fatty acid (*trans* means 'on opposite sides').

Manufacturers market Flora as a polyunsaturate, meaning that there is more than one double bond in the fatty acid chains. The presence of unsaturated fatty acid chains is now thought to help prevent cholesterol building up in the blood vessels and causing heart disease.

Identifying organic compounds

Chemists no longer carry out lengthy experiments to determine molecular mass and the position of functional groups in a molecule when trying to identify an organic compound. Instead, they use infrared (IR) spectroscopy, nuclear magnetic resonance spectroscopy and mass spectrometry to piece together information about the structure of a molecule.

IR spectroscopy

The atoms in a molecule vibrate about their bonds with a set frequency. The vibration may be stretching or bending. The molecule will absorb energy in the IR region of the electromagnetic spectrum that corresponds to the natural frequency of the vibration. So if the full range of IR radiation is passed though a sample, the amounts of energy absorbed at different frequencies can be recorded on a spectrum. Each frequency is converted to its wavenumber, which is the number of wavelengths per centimetre.

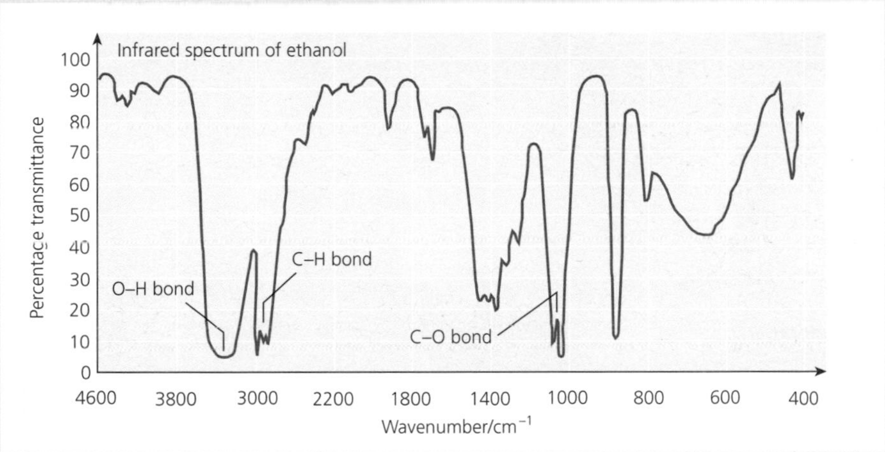

The absorptions of different bonds in a molecule follow fairly set patterns and this can be used as an identification tool.

If a person is suspected of drinking and driving and a roadside breathalyser test has proved positive, he is taken to the police station where police use the IR spectroscopy facility built into the intoximeter to accurately measure the concentration of alcohol in the blood. The intensity of the peak at 3000 cm^{-1} is used to measure the alcohol content of the blood.

Using an intoximeter

Infrared spectrum of ethanol

O–H bond
C–H bond
C–O bond

Percentage transmittance

Wavenumber/cm^{-1}

- Structural isomers have the same molecular formula but different structural formulae.

- Chain isomers have different arrangements of carbon and hydrogen atoms in their chains.

- Positional isomers have their functional groups in different positions.

- Functional group isomers have different functional groups and belong to different homologous series, but have the same molecular formula.

- Geometric isomers occur when there are two different groups on each carbon atom of a double bond between two carbon atoms.

EXAMINATION QUESTIONS

1

a Alkane **C** has a relative molecular mass of 170 and occurs in the kerosene fraction obtained by the fractional distillation of petroleum.

  i) Write the general formula for the homologous series of alkanes. (1)

  ii) Deduce the molecular formula of alkane **C**. (2)

b Three hydrocarbons, **D**, **E** and **F**, all have the molecular formula C_6H_{12}.

  D decolourises an aqueous solution of bromine and shows geometric isomerism.

  E also decolourises an aqueous solution of bromine but does not show geometric isomerism.

  F does not decolourise an aqueous solution of bromine.

Draw one possible structure each for **D**, **E** and **F**.

NEAB CH03 June 1997 Q6

2

a Explain the meaning of the terms *empirical formula* and *molecular formula*. (3)

b Give the three molecular formulae for organic compounds which have the empirical formula CH_2O and relative molecular masses below 100.

NEAB CH03 June 1998 Q7

3

a Give the structural formulae and names of the four isometric alkenes of molecular formula C_4H_8. (8)

b Identify the stereoisomerism shown by two of the above structures. Explain how this type of stereoism arises. (2)

c Deduce the structure of an isomer of molecular formula C_4H_8 which is not an alkene. (1)

NEAB CH06 June 1998 Q4(Modified)

4

a Give one structural formula in each case for the following components of crude oil:

  i) the isomer of C_5H_{12} with the lowest boiling point

  ii) a saturated compound with molecular formula C_5H_{10}

NEAB CH03 June 1999 Q2(Part)

5 The bromoalkane, $CH_3CH_2CHBrCH_3$, can be formed by reaction of $CH_3CH=CHCH_3$ with HBr.

a Name $CH_3CH_2CHBrCH_3$. (1)

b Name the type of stereoisomerism shown by $CH_3CH=CHCH_3$ and explain how this type of stereoisomerism occurs. (2)

NEAB CH03 February 1997 Q3(Part)

Carbon management

The main waste product of fuels we burn is carbon dioxide, which we now think has caused the gradual rise in global temperatures of the last hundred years. The rise is called global warming. The mechanism we use to explain the rise is called the greenhouse effect.

The greenhouse effect is concerned with the trapping of infrared radiation by atmospheric gases. Incoming sunlight passes through the atmosphere relatively easily but when it is radiated from the surface as infrared radiation the gases in the atmosphere reflect some of it back. This makes the atmosphere effectively a 'one way' filter for heat. Carbon dioxide and methane are the main greenhouse gases, although water vapour in the air has a very significant effect.

Only a small proportion of the carbon on the planet exists as carbon dioxide in the atmosphere. The vast majority of carbon is locked up in solid compounds. Environmental chemists are finding ways to reduce the greenhouse effect and slow global warming. One way is to bury carbon compounds in landfill sites.

It has been argued that, far from being a 'blot on the landscape', landfill sites were performing a useful job by taking carbon out of circulation. Estimates are that 78% of the carbon in paper and 97% of the carbon in wood never actually rots down in landfill sites. This carbon isn't available to form carbon dioxide, which is why the landfill sites are called 'carbon sinks'. Landfill sites: environmental dream or nightmare? To some extent, it all depends on what we fill the site with – carbon compounds good, almost everything else, bad.

We throw away less, by weight, than our grandparents did. Table A1 shows the changes.

Table A1 Mass, density and volume of weekly household waste			
Date	Mass/kg	Density/kg/m3	Volume /litres
1936	17	290	59
1963	14	200	70
1990	12	140	85

The waste in our bins has also changed over the years as Table A2 shows. The numbers are percentage composition of the waste.

Table A2 Household waste analysed by type/%					
Type of waste	1967	1974	1978	1980	1992
plastics	2	4	6	8	7
glass	8	9	8	9	10
textiles	2	3	3	3	4
metals	7	10	8	8	8
paper & Board	31	28	28	29	33
vegetable Matter	14	20	28	25	20
ash	32	20	12	14	10
miscellaneous	4	6	7	4	8

National Household Waste Analysis Project DoE Project Profile 009 (1992)

1 a Draw a graph to show the variation in composition of household waste from 1967 to 1992. Show all the types of waste on one graph and indicate clearly each type by using a code. You may use a computer graph drawing package.

b What observations can you make from this composite graph? How do any trends you notice fit in with, for example, changes in lifestyle or advances in chemical technology?

c Compare the mass of household waste with the volume of household waste from 1936 to 1990. What can you conclude?

d Suggest some reasons for your conclusion.

2 a Which waste materials contain carbon?

b The carbon-containing components can be burnt rather than dumped in a landfill site. But is this more environmentally friendly? Prepare a discussion document for a local council to debate whether to continue with a landfill site or to build an incinerator. The incinerator option would include a boilerhouse and generator. This would generate some electricity for the local area and supply heat for a District Heating Scheme for an old people's home, some flats and a small office block.

Think carefully about the way to present this paper to stimulate discussion, e.g. what are the advantages/disadvantages of each scheme as you see them, both locally and globally?

12 Petroleum and alkanes

Crude oil deposits are found all over the world. Although there has been great excitement about the oil fields of the North Sea, the UK has a mere 0.4% of the world's oil reserves. The majority are concentrated in the Middle East, as the bar chart below right shows. The limited nature of the oil supply and its concentration in a politically volatile part of the world can lead to severe supply problems. In the last 40 years there have been oil wars, price fixing and, most serious of all, the Gulf war (1981).

The war began when Iraq occupied Kuwait, a tiny country with a thriving economy based on its abundant oil deposits. Kuwait was a major exporter of oil and its products. The invasion caused international outcry and then a military response. Oil fields and installations were seen as legitimate targets by both sides and the NATO forces quickly drove the Iraqis out of the country again. However, as they retreated, they set the oil fields on fire in an attempt to further disrupt the ecomony and hamper the return to normality. This continued the terrible waste of such a precious natural resource and also caused environmental disruption of enormous proportions.

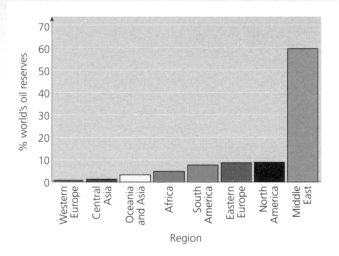

A bar chart showing the distribution of the world's oil reserves.

12.1 Petroleum

Petroleum is another name for crude oil. Its name refers to the fact that it occurs naturally in pockets within rocks; the word petroleum means 'rock oil'. Crude oil in its natural form is a thick, tarry substance that is difficult to ignite. In its raw state it isn't very useful; it needs to be processed to separate out its most valuable constituents such petrol, lubcricating oils, heating oils and power station fuel. Crude oil is also the source of the raw materials used to make detergents, plastics, paints, anti-freeze, synthetic rubber and medicines. Seventy per cent of organic chemicals are produced from crude oil and a massive 3000 million tonnes of crude oil products are used worldwide every year.

In this section we look at how crude oil formed, what it contains and then we go on to investigate the processes that make it useful to the modern industrial world.

The origin of crude oil deposits

Over 400 million years ago, much of the Earth was covered in sea. Life had evolved but it consisted of primitive cells such as bacteria, algae and single-celled animals and plants. There were no larger organisms; this was 200 million years before the appearance of the dinosaurs. Although the individual organisms were small, there were vast numbers of them and they grew and reproduced rapidly in the warm oceans. As they died, they sank to the bottom and formed thick layers of decomposing organic material. Over many years, layers of sediment built up on top of this organic layer and it eventually formed sedimentary rock. During the early stages, bacteria that were able to survive without oxygen continued to break down the organic material in the layer. Over millions of years, the high pressures created by the weight of the overlying layers and the high temperatures generated by decomposition converted this layer of biomass into crude oil and natural gas.

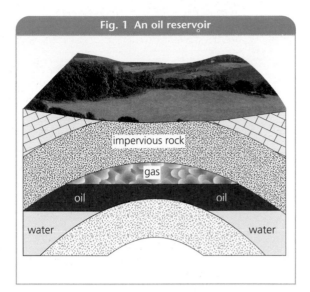

Fig. 1 An oil reservoir

impervious rock

gas

oil   oil

water   water

The liquid crude oil seeped into porous rock deposits above. If only porous rock was present, the oil could get up to the surface, forming shallow lakes. In other places, the porous rocks were overlaid by a layer of impervious rock which prevented oil travelling any further and an oil reservoir was created. Natural gas often forms a pocket at the surface of oil resevoirs (Fig. 1).

1 The oil trapped in porous rock is more difficult and more expensive to extract. It can be flushed out with steam.

a How does steam remove oil from the rock?

b How would the price of oil determine whether it is economical to extract oil trapped in porous rock?

When an oil resevoir is tapped into, the high pressure forces the oil to the surface at high speeds (left). Oil wells must be capped quickly to avoid wasting the precious resource.

Crude oil is a sticky, tarry substance (above); it is easy to see why it causes so much environmental damage when oil spills occur.

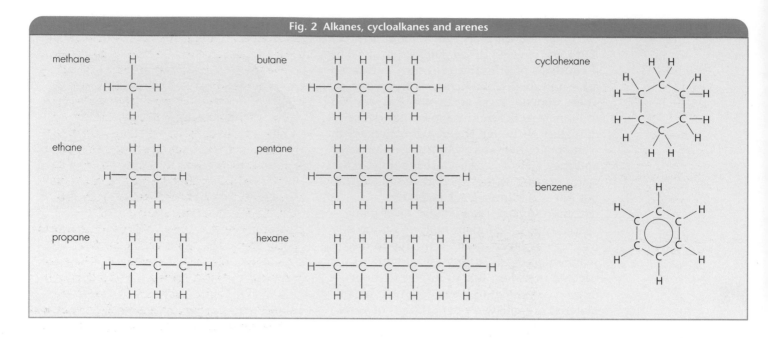

Fig. 2 Alkanes, cycloalkanes and arenes

What does crude oil contain?

Crude oil is a mixture of about 150 different hydrocarbons. Hydrocarbons are compounds that contain only carbon and hydrogen. The majority of hydrocarbons in crude oil are straight chain **alkanes**, but the mixture also contains **cycloalkanes** and **arenes**. Fig. 2 summarises the structure of these important hydrocarbons.

The exact composition of crude oil depends on the conditions in which it formed. Samples from different parts of the world have slightly different amounts of each type of hydrocarbon, called its 'fingerprint' (Table 1).

This fingerprint makes it possible to identify the source of an unknown sample by analysing the proportion of hydrocarbons it contains.

 A sample of crude oil contains 24 per cent gas oil. What is its likely origin?

Fractional distillation of crude oil

Crude oil is separated into mixtures of hydrocarbons with similar boiling points. These mixtures are called crude oil **fractions**. They are separated by **fractional distillation** at an oil refinery. Separation is possible because individual hydrocarbons in in the fractions all have different boiling points.

The crude oil is heated until it vaporises. The gases pass into a fractionating column (Fig. 3). A temperature gradient is created between the bottom of the column and the top. The bottom of the column is kept at about 340 °C and there is a gradual cooling as vapours pass up the column. The temperature at the top is about 110 °C. Any hydrocarbons that remain liquid at temperatures as high as 340 °C fall to the bottom of the column and are removed as residue. This is not wasted; it contains useful materials such as lubricating oil. At temperatures as high as 350 °C, some of the components of the residue start to break down.

Table 1 Different crude oils				
	Percentage composition			
Type of crude oil	Petrol	Kerosine	Gas oil	Fuel oil
North sea oil	23	15	24	38
Arabian light	18	11.5	18	52.5
Arabian heavy	21	15	21	43
Iranian heavy	21	13	20	46

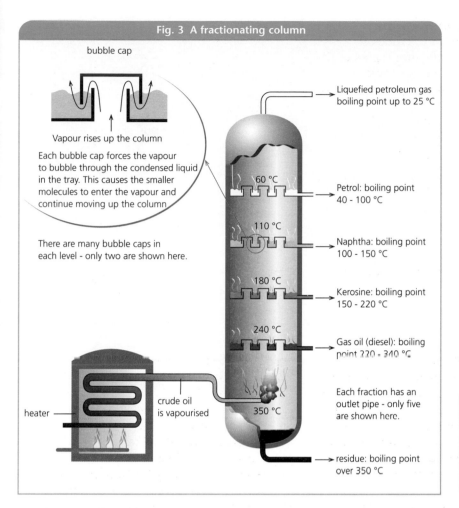

Fig. 3 A fractionating column

bubble cap

Vapour rises up the column

Each bubble cap forces the vapour to bubble through the condensed liquid in the tray. This causes the smaller molecules to enter the vapour and continue moving up the column

There are many bubble caps in each level - only two are shown here.

heater

crude oil is vapourised

60 °C

110 °C

180 °C

240 °C

350 °C

Liquefied petroleum gas boiling point up to 25 °C

Petrol: boiling point 40 - 100 °C

Naphtha: boiling point 100 - 150 °C

Kerosine: boiling point 150 - 220 °C

Gas oil (diesel): boiling point 220 - 340 °C

Each fraction has an outlet pipe - only five are shown here.

residue: boiling point over 350 °C

The smaller hydrocarbons rise up the column in their gaseous state. As a particular hydrocarbon reaches the level in the column where the temperature is equal to its boiling point, it reverts to its liquid state and is collected in trays. Only the most **volatile**, those with the lowest boiling points, reach the top of the column. The major fractions obtained by fractional distillation of crude oil and their major uses are shown in Table 2.

The **primary distillation** of crude oil does not separate individual hydrocarbons. Each fraction contains a mixture of hydrocarbons that have boiling points within a specific range. Fractions can be further separated to obtain purer products. These are **secondary distillations**. The fraction that has a boiling point above 350 °C has to be distilled under reduced pressure. This **vacuum distillation** reduces the boiling point of the remaining hydrocarbons and allows them to be distilled out at lower temperatures.

3 The smallest hydrocarbons in crude oil have the lowest boiling points and *vice versa*. Where in the fractionating column are the following collected:

a the smallest molecules?

b the largest molecules?

Table 2 Fractions from crude oil			
Name of fraction	**Boiling range/°C (approximate)**	**Number of carbon atoms in hydrocarbon**	**Uses**
LPG (Liquefied petroleum gas)	up to 25	1–4	Calor gas, camping gas
Petrol (gasoline)	40–100	4–12	Petrol
Naphtha	100–150	7–14	Petrochemicals
Kerosine (paraffin)	150–250	11–15	Jet fuel, petrochemicals
Gas oil (diesel)	220–350	15–19	Central heating fuel, petrochemicals
Mineral oil (lubricating oil)	over 350	20–30	Lubricating oil, petrochemicals
Fuel oil	over 400	30–40	Fuel for ships and power stations.
Wax, grease	over 400	40–50	Candles, grease for bearings, polish
Bitumen	over 400	above 50	Roofing, road surfacing

Why fractional distillation works

Separation of the fractions in crude oil depends on the different boiling points of the hydrocarbons present. How can these differences be explained?

As we have seen, most of the hydrocarbons in crude oil are straight chain alkanes. The petrol fraction includes alkanes that have a carbon chain with between 5 and 11 carbon atoms. The electronegativities of the carbon and hydrogen atoms in an alkane with this chain length are 2.5 and 2.1 respectively. Since these electronegativities are very similar, the intermolecular forces in a mixture of short chain alkane molecules are very weak. The **van der Waals** forces are so weak that they cannot hold the molecules close together, even at room temperature, to form a liquid or a solid. This is why short chain alkane compounds such as methane, (CH_4), ethane (C_2H_6), propane (C_3H_8) and butane (C_4H_8) exist as gases at room temperature and atmospheric pressure.

In the longer chain alkanes, van der Waals forces exert an effect, as they have a greater length of molecule to act over (Fig 4). The longer the molecules, the greater the forces between them and the less likely the molecules can separate to form a gas. More energy is needed to to change the alkane from a liquid to a gas and the boiling point of alkanes increases with chain length, as Fig. 5 shows.

Alkanes that have chain lengths between C_5 and C_{17} are liquids at room temperature and atmospheric pressure. Viscocity of the liquids increases with chain length. Alkanes with even longer carbon chains are solids.

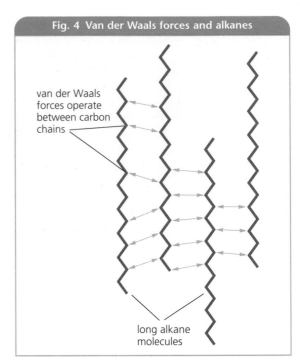

Fig. 4 Van der Waals forces and alkanes

van der Waals forces operate between carbon chains

long alkane molecules

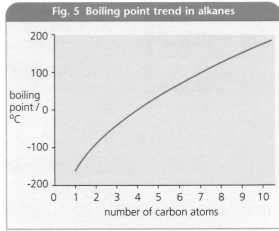

Fig. 5 Boiling point trend in alkanes

boiling point / °C

number of carbon atoms

Making efficient use of oil fractions

Typical yields of the oil fractions obtained by primary distillation are shown in Table 3. This table also shows the relative demand for each fraction and it is immediately obvious that the two do not match. Some fractions outstrip supply while others fall short.

 4 Explain why the boiling point of hexane (69 °C) is lower than the boiling point of heptane (98 °C).

Table 3 Supply and demand for oil fractions		
Fraction	Approximate supply (per cent)	Approximate demand (per cent)
Liquefied petroleum gas	2	4
Petrol and naptha	16	27
Kerosine	13	8
Gas oil	19	23
Fuel oil and bitumen	50	38

Cracking

The most useful oil fractions tend to contain the shorter chain hydrocarbons. Petrol for cars contains alkanes with carbon chain lengths from C_5 to C_{10}. Ideally, almost 30 per cent of the fractions produced from fractional distillation need to be in this range to meet the demand for petrol. Only 16 per cent of the fractions fall into this range.

The problem is solved by **cracking**. Cracking is the chemical splitting of long chain alkanes into shorter chain hydrocarbons. It involves a free radical reaction in which a carbon–carbon and carbon–hydrogen bonds are broken. Free radical reactions are covered later in this chapter.

The overall summary reaction is:

High M_r alkanes $\rightarrow$ smaller M_r alkanes + alkenes (+hydrogen)

Two main processes are used; **thermal cracking** and **catalytic cracking** but the overall result is the same. Cracking always produces alkenes but the molecules can break up in several different ways, forming a mixture of products that then need to be separated by fractional distillation. Two possible fragmentations of the $C_{14}H_{30}$ molecule are:

$$C_{14}H_{30} \rightarrow C_7H_{16} + C_3H_6 + 2C_2H_4$$
$$C_{14}H_{30} \rightarrow C_{12}H_{24} + C_2H_4 + H_2$$

A steam cracker in the Joint Venture Olefine 6 complex at Wilton. The complex was commissioned in 1979 and is jointly owned by ICI and BP. It is the largest unit in Europe, with the capacity to produce almost 800 000 tonnes of ethene per year. This is used mainly by the polymer industry; the ethene is transported away from the plant by underground pipelines.

Thermal cracking

The process of thermal cracking uses heat to provide the energy required to break the C–C and C–H bonds. When longer chained alkanes are heated in the absence of air, the bonds in the molecules vibrate more vigorously. This increased vibration breaks the bonds and splits the alkanes. At the lower end of the temperature range, carbon chains tend to break in the centre of the molecule. Some of the shorter chained alkanes produced can be used in petrol. With increasing temperature, the cracking shifts towards the end of the chain, leading to a higher proportion of low molecular weight alkenes. The double bond in an alkene makes it a reactive molecule, far more reactive than an alkane with the same chain length. Alkenes, particularly ethene (C_2H_4) can be used as a starting point for the chemical industry (see Chapter 13, page 188).

5

a What is the functional group of an alkene?

b What is the general formula of the alkenes?

The bonds that need to be broken to crack an alkane are strong. The bond enthalpies are:

ΔH(C–C) = 347 kJ mol^{-1}
ΔH(C–H) = 413 kJ mol^{-1}

This means that high temperatures (between 400 and 900 °C) and high pressures (up to 7 000 kPa) are needed. As less energy is needed to break C–C bonds, more of these bonds are broken in the reaction. To avoid decomposition of alkanes into their consituent elements, the time that they are exposed to such conditions needs to be very short. This exposure time, called the residence time, is about one second.

6

a Write an equation to show the cracking of dodecane, $C_{12}H_{26}$ to produce propene and 4-methyloctane.

b Draw the structural formula for 4-methyloctane.

c Suggest how the products could be used.

Thermal cracking – a free radical reaction

Alkane molecules split by a reaction called a free radical mechanism. Thermal cracking is initiated by homolytic fission of a C–C bond. This means that each carbon atom from the C–C bond gets one of the covalently shared electrons from the bond. Two alkyl radicals are formed. Each alkyl radical can then take a hydrogen atom from another alkane molecule to produce a different alkyl radical and a shorter chain alkane. For example octane splits into a two alkyl radicals, one containing C_5 and the other containing C_3.

$$CH_3(CH_2)_6CH_3 \rightarrow CH_3CH_2CH_2CH_2CH_2^{\bullet} + {}^{\bullet}CH_2CH_2CH_3$$

The longer alkyl radical can remove a hydrogen from another octane molecule, forming a C_8 alkyl radical and pentane.

$$CH_3(CH_2)_6CH_3 + CH_3CH_2CH_2CH_2CH_2^{\bullet} \rightarrow$$
$$CH_3(CH_2)_5CHCH_3 + CH_3(CH_2)_3CH_3$$

Alternatively, more bonds can break in the alkyl radical and an alkene, in this case ethene, and a shorter C_3 alkyl radical are formed.

$$CH_3CH_2CH_2{-}CH_2CH_2^{\bullet} \rightarrow CH_3CH_2CH_2^{\bullet} + CH_2{=}CH_2$$

7 Why does the cracking of alkanes always produce an alkene?

Most organic reactions involve the breaking and making of covalent bonds. In a covalent bond, two atoms share electrons. For example, when the bondin hydrogen chloride breaks, the electrons can be arranged in one of two ways:

Firstly, each atom receives one electron. This produces a hydrogen radical and and a chlorine radical. This is called **homolytic fission**:

$$H{-}Cl \rightarrow H^{\bullet} + Cl^{\bullet}$$

Secondly, both electrons can go to the same atom, creating two charged particles. The atom receiving two electrons has a negative charge and the other atom has a positive charge. This is called **heterolytic fission**:

$$H{-}Cl \rightarrow H^+ + Cl^-$$

Other reactions that occur during thermal cracking include:

Dehydrogenation. This involves the loss of one molecule of hydrogen to produce alkenes from alkanes and aromatic hydrocarbons from cycloalkanes.

Isomerisation. This occurs when unbranched alkanes are converted into branched isomers and when cycloalkanes are rearrangee, eg methylcyclopentane into cyclohexane.

Cyclisation. This takes place, often with loss of hydrogen, when alkanes rearrange to form cycloalkanes and aromatic hydrocarbons, eg heptane through methylcyclohexane into methylbenzene.

The conditions required for thermal cracking makes the process expensive but its advantage is that it can be used on all long chain alkane fractions, including the residue that comes out of the bottom of the oil fractionating column. Mixtures of products are refined by further fractional distillation.

Catalytic cracking

Cracking can also be carried out at much lower temperatures using a catalyst. Synthetic zeolite catalysts are crystalline alumino-silicates that have now largely replaced clay catalysts. Zeolite is a rock that contains aluminium, silicon and oxygen. Its regular atomic structure creates a network of holes (Fig. 6). Zeolites made industrially have pores of an exact size. This is important because this is where the reactions involved in catalytic cracking take place Fig. 7). Long chained alkane molecules fit into the pores and when the catalyst-alkane mixture is

Fig. 6 Structure of zeolite

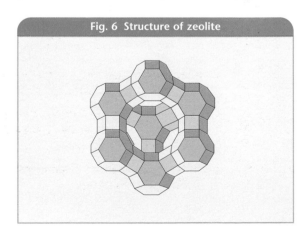

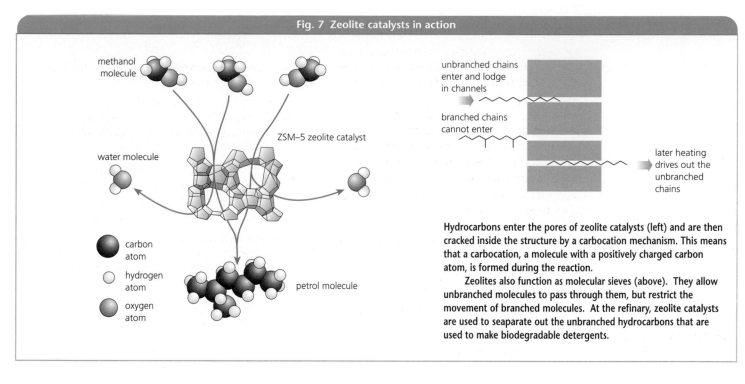

Fig. 7 Zeolite catalysts in action

methanol molecule

ZSM–5 zeolite catalyst

water molecule

● carbon atom

○ hydrogen atom

● oxygen atom

petrol molecule

unbranched chains enter and lodge in channels

branched chains cannot enter

later heating drives out the unbranched chains

Hydrocarbons enter the pores of zeolite catalysts (left) and are then cracked inside the structure by a carbocation mechanism. This means that a carbocation, a molecule with a positively charged carbon atom, is formed during the reaction.

Zeolites also function as molecular sieves (above). They allow unbranched molecules to pass through them, but restrict the movement of branched molecules. At the refinary, zeolite catalysts are used to seaparate out the unbranched hydrocarbons that are used to make biodegradable detergents.

exposed to a slight pressure and a temperature of about 450 °C, cracking occurs. This process is efficient and produces more branched chain molecules than thermal cracking. Branched hydrocarbons burn more easily and so are more useful as fuels. catalystic cracking is the major method of producing petrol.

Catalytic cracking breaks large alkanes into branched alkanes, alkenes, cycloalkanes and aromatic hydrocarbons. For example, decane splits into ethene and 2-methylheptane:

$$CH_3(CH_2)_8CH_3(g) \xrightarrow[\text{Zeolite catalyst}]{400\text{–}500\ ^\circ C} CH_2=CH_2(g) + CH_3\text{–}CH\text{–}(CH_2)_4\text{–}CH_3\ (l)$$
$$\underset{\text{CH}_3}{|}$$

decane   ethene   2-methylheptane

 Why is catalytic cracking cheaper than thermal cracking?

Petroleum as a fuel

Many fractions obtained from crude oil are used as fuels because they react exothermically when they burn in oxygen. When we use petrol in cars, kerosine in aircraft, fuel oil, heating oil, diesel and natural gas, we are using the energy available from that exothermic reaction. But burning hydrocarbons also releases carbon dioxide, a greenhouse gas that contributes to global warming.

Impurities in crude oil can also cause environmental problems. Crude oil contains sulphur and after fractional distillation, these are found in the petrol fraction. When petrol burns, sulphur also reacts with oxygen to form sulphur dioxide and this is released ino the atmosphere with the exhaust gases (see Table 4). Sulphur dioxide reacts with water and oxygen in the atmosphere to form sulphuric acid, which can cause acid rain.

KEY FACTS

- Petroleum (crude oil) is a mixture of alkanes, cycloalkanes and arenes.

- The hydrocarbons in crude oil have different boling points and can be separated by fractional distillation.

- As the alkane carbon chain increases in length, the boiling point increases.

- Cracking splits longer alkane molecules into shorter more useful molecules, such as those used in petrol and the chemical industry.

- Thermal cracking involves heating alkanes until the vibration in the bonds causes them to split.

- Catalytic cracking involves a zeolite catalyst and can be carried out at lower temperatures.

APPLICATION A

Making better petrol

Petrol burns most efficiently if the air–petrol vapour mixture in the cylinder is compressed before it is ignited. But this compression can lead to premature ignition. The result is a sudden increase in pressure, which is heard as a 'knocking' or 'pinking' sound in the engine. The problem of auto-ignition and knocking has been solved in the past by adding tetraethyl lead(IV) to petrol. Most countries are now phasing out its use since it adds lead pollution to car exhaust gases and so contributes to lead pollution. An alternative is to use petrol mixtures with a high percentage of branched chained alkanes. Branched alkanes produced by catalytic cracking cause less knocking than straight chain alkanes.

As a measure of their knocking liabilities, fuels are given an octane number. Heptane, a straight-chain alkane causes terrible knocking and so has an octane number of zero. The branched alkane 2,2,4-trimethylpentane produces hardly any knocking and so is given an octane number of 100. This and other high octane fuels are used as motor fuels.

1 What is the structural formula of 2,2,4-trimethylpentane?

2 Write equations for the combustion of:
a heptane;
b 2,2,4-trimethylpentane.

3 Explain why four-star petrol was phased out on December 31 1999 in the UK.

4 What is the molecular formula of tetraethyl lead (IV)?

APPLICATION B

Use your ideas on processing crude oil

Output of refined products from refineries in the UK in 1997	
Products	**Thousands of tonnes**
Gases, butane and propane	1 950
Other petroleum	139
Naphtha and feed stocks	2 854
Motor spirit	28 260
Industrial and white spirit	128
Kerosine:	
aviation fuel	8 342
burning oil	3 336
Gas/diesel oil	28 778
Fuel oil	11 747
Lubricating oil	1 231
Bitumen	2 258
Petroleum wax	65
Petroleum coke	598
Other	680

1 What percentage of the total output of UK refineries will be burnt to release energy?

2 When alkanes burn, carbon dioxide is released. What is the environmental consequence of this?

3 What percentage of the total output of UK refineries is used as motor fuel?

4 Suggest how catalytic cracking has contributed to the figures in the table.

Crude oil, like coal contains a proportion of sulphur, some of which remains after fractional distillation.

5 What is produced when sulphur burns?

6 What effect does the product have on the environment?

7 What measures can be taken to lessen the problem?

This child is right at exhaust fume level.

12.2

12.2 The alkanes

As we saw in Chapter 11, the general formula of an alkane is C_nH_{2n+2} and Table 6 on page 161 describes the first six alkanes in the homologous series. In this section we look at the alkanes in more detail.

Remember that alkanes are not very reactive because their C–C and C–H bonds are strong. A chemical reaction that involves breaking these bonds requires a lot of energy. Alkanes do not attract polar molecules or ions such as H^+ or OH^- and so will not react with them. The few reactions of alkanes include combustion and their reactions with the halogens.

Combustion

When alkanes are heated in a plentiful supply of oxygen, combustion occurs. Initially heat is needed to start the bond breaking process (Fig. 8). Once bond breaking has started, bond formation can begin and energy is released. Some of this released energy is used to break more bonds and the reaction proceeds without further imput of energy. In fact, like all hydrocarbons, alkanes burn in air or oxygen in very exothermic reactions. The minimum energy needed to start the reaction is called the **activation energy**, (E_A).

When enough oxygen is present, alkanes burn to produce carbon dioxide and water.

Combustion reactions of alkanes are of vital importance in fueling our way of life.

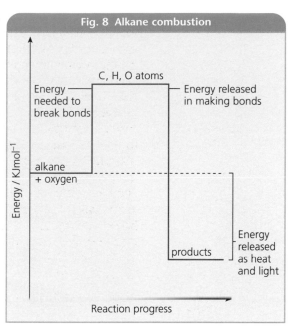

Fig. 8 Alkane combustion

This is called **complete combustion**:

$$CH_4 + 2O_2 \rightarrow CO_2 + 2H_2O$$
$$\Delta H^\ominus = -890 \text{ kJ mol}^{-1}$$
$$C_4H_{10} + 6\frac{1}{2}O_2 \rightarrow 4CO_2 + 5H_2O$$
$$\Delta H^\ominus = -2880 \text{ kJ mol}^{-1}$$

If there is insufficient oxygen present, carbon monoxide or carbon and water are produced instead of carbon dioxide and water. This is called **incomplete combustion**:

$$CH_4 + 1\frac{1}{2}O_2 \rightarrow CO + 2H_2O$$

$$C_4H_{10} + 4\frac{1}{2}O_2 \rightarrow 4CO + 5H_2O$$

You can see the difference between complete and incomplete combustion in a science lesson. When a bunsen burner is burning with the hole open, the flame is blue and complete combustion of gas is taking place. When the air hole is closed, combustion of the gas is incomplete; the flame is yellow and luminous because of the carbon particles it contains. Any apparatus heated in a luminous flame becomes coated in black soot.

9 Write an equation for:

a the complete combustion of octane.
b the incomplete combustion of nonane.

EXTENSION Carbon monoxide poisoning

The carbon monoxide that forms during incomplete combustion is extremely hazardous. Badly maintained gas central heating boilers, which produce carbon monoxide because of an inadequate supply of air are a common cause of accidental death by carbon monoxide poisoning.

Carbon monoxide is poisonous because it reacts irreversibly with the haemoglobin in red blood cells. Usually, haemoglobin transports oxygen from our lungs to all body cells. The oxygen combines with haemoglobin to make oxyhaemoglobin. The bond formed is a weak bond and oxygen is easily given up when required. If carbon monoxide is breathed in, it combines with haemoglobin and forms carboxyhaemoglobin. The bond is stronger than that between oxygen and haemoglogin and it is difficult to break.

Carbon monoxide was once a common cause of poisoning. The gas has no smell or colour and does not irritate the eyes or the lungs, so people can easily inhale it without being aware of anything wrong. Moreover, carbon monoxide poisoning is cumulative. Repeated exposure to small amounts of carbon monoxide over a long period of time can raise the proportion of carboxy-haemoglobin until it builds up in the blood to a fatal level.

Until 1967, when natural gas became available, plentiful supplies of carbon monoxide were being fed directly into people's homes in the form of coal gas. Nearly everyone used coal gas for heating and cooking. Because the coal gas contained up to 14 per cent carbon monoxide, suicides resulting from people putting their head in a gas oven were common. Other people died accidentally from faulty appliances. Between 1961 and 1965, about 800 people died in carbon monoxide poisoning incidents in the UK along. The problem today is not quite as bad but faulty gas appliances can still cause fatal accidents.

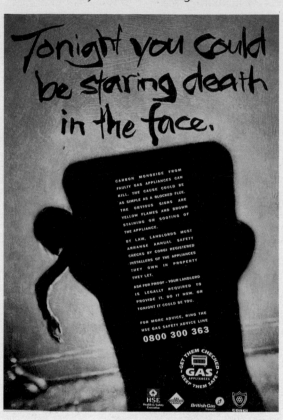

All gas appliances should be inspected regularly, since carbon monoxide can form during faulty combusion.

Pollution and alkane combustion

We use many combustion reactions of alkanes to provide us with energy. Burning gas or oil or even candles involves burning alkanes. In a car engine, the combustion of alkanes with a chain length between C_6 and C_{10} produces a large volume of hot gases to power the motor. Today's engines are the most efficient in the history of engineering but they are not capable of complete combustion; petrol engines always produce pollution. Some of the gases produced by the combusion of petrol are shown in Table 4.

Carbon monoxide is formed by the incomplete combustion of petrol vapour:

$$C_8H_{18} + 8\tfrac{1}{2}O_2 \rightarrow 8CO + 9H_2O$$

This is why running a car engine in a confined space is potentially lethal (see Extension box, above). Car engines also produced oxides of nitrogen and unburned hydrocarbons. Oxides of nitrogen form when

Table 4 Combustion products of an average car engine		
	Percentage of exhaust gases by volume	
Gas	Non-catalytic cars	Catalytic cars
Carbon dioxide	14	15
Carbon monoxide	1.0	0.2
Oxygen	0.7	0
Hydrogen	0.25	0
Hydrocarbons	0.06	0.01
Nitrogen oxides	0.2	0.02
Sulphur dioxide	0.005	0.005

the air/petrol mixture is sparked and explodes. The temperature of the burning petrol vapour can reach up to 2500 °C and this provides sufficient activation energy for nitrogen to react with oxygen to form some nitrogen monoxide (see Table 4):

$$N_2 + O_2 \rightarrow 2NO$$

Nitrogen monoxide reacts easily with more oxygen to form nitrogen dioxide. With water and more oxygen, nitric acid is formed in the atmosphere:

$$2NO + O_2 \rightarrow 2NO_2$$
$$4NO_2 + 3H_2O + O_2 \rightarrow 4HNO_3$$

Nitric acid is a major component of acid rain; rain that has a pH similar to lemon juice and that causes massive damage to trees and buildings (Fig. 9). In sunlight, nitrogen dioxide also reacts with oxygen or hydrocarbons to form an irritating photochemical smog.

10 What other polluting gas is responsible for acid rain?

These trees in the Czech Republic (below) have been killed by acid rain. Unpolluted rain has a pH of about 5.6 because of the carbon dioxide that occurs naturally in the atmosphere; rainwater in most iindustrialised countries has a pH of between 4 and 4.5. Some cities in the US (below right) are bathed in acid for that has the same acidity as lemon juice.

Catalytic converters

Catalytic converters are fitted to cars to help to reduce the emission of gases such as the nitrogen oxides, and sulphure dioxide. The definition of a catalyst is that it changes the rate of a chemical reaction, but remains chemically unchanged at the end of the reaction. The catalysts in catalytic converters are no exception; the reaction takes place within their structure, but the catalyst remains unchanged.

Most catalytic converters are 'three-way'. They are designed so that nitrogen oxides oxidise carbon monoxide to carbon dioxide and are themselves reduced to nitrogen. Unburnt hydrocarbons are also oxidised to carbon dioxide and water.

$$2CO \text{ (g)} + 2NO \text{ (g)} \rightarrow 2CO_2 \text{ (g)} + N_2 \text{ (g)}$$

The catalyst used is a mixture of platinum, rhodium and palladium – second or third row transition metals. Transition metals can have several different oxidation states and this makes them good catalysts.

The catalyst is spread in a very thin layer over the surface of a metal oxide or ceramic honeycomb that has a large surface area (see Fig. 10 on the next page). The reactions that occur in the catalytic converter remove up to 90 per cent of the harmful gases in car exhaust. Cars fitted with catalytic converters should only use unleaded fuel; lead poisons the surface of the catalyst.

11 The platinum in the catalytic converter oxidises the hydrocarbons to carbon dioxide and water. Write an equation to show the oxidation of heptane.

12 Why is a large surface area needed on the catalytic converter?

13 What are the environmental effects of:

a sulphur dioxide?

b hydrocarbons?

c carbon monoxide?

d carbon dioxide?

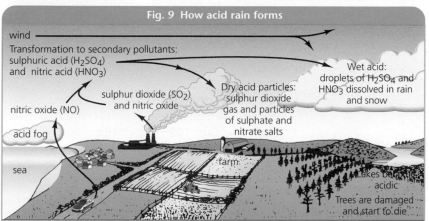

Fig. 9 How acid rain forms

wind

Transformation to secondary pollutants: sulphuric acid (H_2SO_4) and nitric acid (HNO_3)

nitric oxide (NO)

acid fog

sea

sulphur dioxide (SO_2) and nitric oxide

Dry acid particles: sulphur dioxide gas and particles of sulphate and nitrate salts

Wet acid: droplets of H_2SO_4 and HNO_3 dissolved in rain and snow

farm

Lakes become acidic

Trees are damaged and start to die

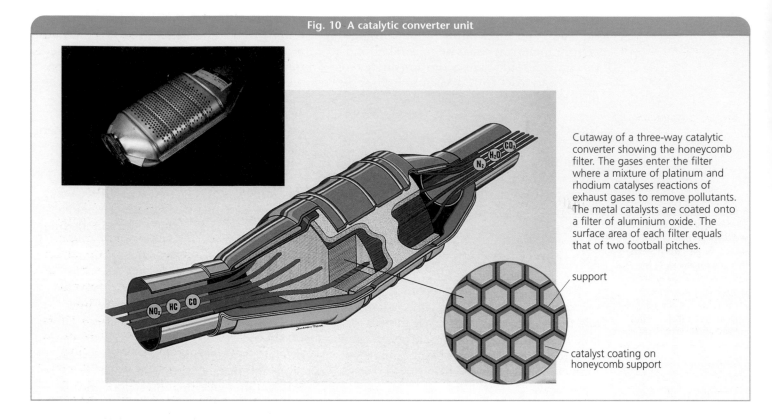

Fig. 10 A catalytic converter unit

Cutaway of a three-way catalytic converter showing the honeycomb filter. The gases enter the filter where a mixture of platinum and rhodium catalyses reactions of exhaust gases to remove pollutants. The metal catalysts are coated onto a filter of aluminium oxide. The surface area of each filter equals that of two football pitches.

support

catalyst coating on honeycomb support

Chlorination

If you mix methane gas and chlorine gas in the dark, nothing happens. But, shine ultraviolet light on the mixture and the two compounds react explosively to produce chloromethane and hydrogen chloride:

$$2CH_4(g) + Cl_2(g) \rightarrow 2CH_3Cl(g) + HCl(g)$$

During the reaction, a hydrogen atom in the methane molecule is replaced by a chlorine atom. This is called a **free-radical substitution** reaction. The step-by-step sequence of events that occur during a chemical reaction is called the **mechanism** of the reaction. Mechanisms are important for helping us to understand chemical reactions.

In this section, we look in detail at the different steps involved in the reaction between methane and chlorine. These are:

● Step 1: Initiation
● Step 2: Propagation
● Step 3: Termination

Fig. 11 shows the different parts of the reaction using dot and cross diagrams. You will need to study these as you read the text and then test your understanding with the questions that follow.

Step 1: Initiation
Methane, like all alkanes, is a non-polar and unreactive compound. A methane molecule has no areas of positive or negative charge and so does not attract charged particles. The reaction begins when ultra-violet radiation provides the energy required to split the chlorine molecule into two chlorine atoms:

$$Cl_2 \rightarrow Cl^{\cdot} + Cl^{\cdot} \quad \Delta H^{\ominus} = +243 \text{ kJ mol}^{-1}$$

The dot represents the unpaired electron.

This reaction occurs first because the Cl–Cl bond in chlorine is weaker than the C–H bond in methane. The chlorine atoms formed have an unpaired electron and are called **free radicals**. All free radicals are extremely reactive.

Step 2: Propagation
When the chlorine radical reacts with a methane molecule, the chlorine radical rips off one of the hydrogen atoms to make a molecule of hydrogen chloride. This produces another radical, a methyl radical.

$$CH_4 + Cl^{\cdot} \rightarrow CH_3^{\cdot} + HCl$$

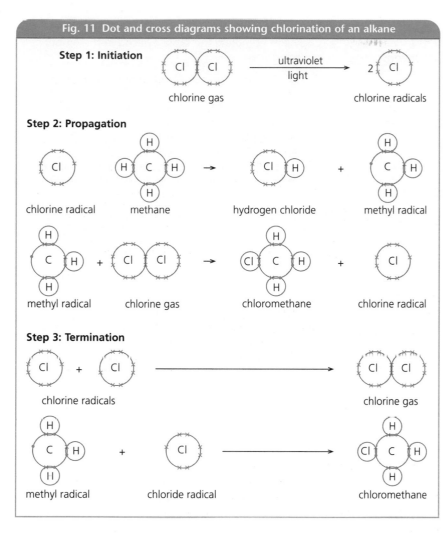

Fig. 11 Dot and cross diagrams showing chlorination of an alkane

Step 1: Initiation

chlorine gas → ultraviolet light → 2 chlorine radicals

Step 2: Propagation

chlorine radical + methane → hydrogen chloride + methyl radical

methyl radical + chlorine gas → chloromethane + chlorine radical

Step 3: Termination

chlorine radicals → chlorine gas

methyl radical + chloride radical → chloromethane

The methyl radical then reacts with another chlorine molecule to produce chloromethane and another chlorine radical.

$$CH_3^{\cdot} + Cl_2 \rightarrow CH_3Cl + Cl^{\cdot}$$

This step is called a propagation step because its two stages produce another chlorine radical. It is an explosive reaction in this case because each step in the propagation phase is exothermic.

Step 3: Termination

Propagation continues until any two radicals react together to form a stable molecule. Note that compounds with more than one carbon atom are formed.

$$Cl^{\cdot} + Cl^{\cdot} \rightarrow Cl_2$$
$$CH_3^{\cdot} + Cl^{\cdot} \rightarrow CH_3Cl$$
$$CH_3^{\cdot} + CH_3^{\cdot} \rightarrow C_2H_6$$

If there is sufficient chlorine present, substitution can continue until all the hydrogen atoms have been replaced by chlorine atoms, forming dichloromethane, trichloromethane and tetrachloromethane. The likelihood of further substitution beyond the formation of CH_3Cl is reduced if an excess of methane is used in the original mixture.

Methane reacts less readily with the halogens as you go down the periodic table. The reaction with fluorine takes place in the dark. The reaction with chlorine requires light. The reactions with bromine and iodine are slower and need an input of energy to overcome the activation energy. In all cases, the products of methane's reactions with the halogens are **haloalkanes**.

14 Explain why free radicals are very reactive.

15 Draw dot and cross diagrams to show what happens when further substitution during the termination step of the chlorination of methane produces dichloromethane.

16 Bromine reacts with methane in a similar way to chlorine. Write equations to show the stages of reaction. Name the products that form.

KEY FACTS

■ Alkanes are non-polar and not very reactive.

■ Alkanes burn in oxygen to produce carbon dioxide and water in excess oxgen. This reaction is called **complete combustion**.

■ Alkanes also burn in limited oxygen to form carbon monoxide and water. This reaction is called **incomplete combustion**.

■ Alkanes react with halogens to produce halogenoalkanes by a **free radical substitution** mechanism.

■ The stages in free radical substitution are **initiation**, **propagation** and **termination**.

1

a List, in order of boiling point, any three fractions produced by the fractional distillation of crude oil, starting with the lowest. (3)

b Explain, in terms of their structure, why the fractions reaching the top of a fractionating column have the lowest boiling point. (2)

c An alkane with 14 carbon atoms is cracked to form only octane and propene.
   i)   Give the molecular formula for the alkane.
   ii) Write an equation for the cracking reaction, name the type of reaction involved in cracking and give a use for propene. (4)

NEAB CH03 June 1996

2 Gas oil (diesel), gasoline (petrol), kerosine (paraffin) and naphtha are fractions obtained from crude oil.

a Write the fractions gas oil, gasoline and kerosine in order of increasing boiling temperature and give one specific use for each of the fuels, gas oil and keosine. (3)

b The naphtha fraction is thermally cracked to produce a mixture containing methane, ethene, butene and several other molecules.
   i)   Name the type of mechanism involved in this cracking process.
   ii) Suggest how the mixture produced by cracking is separated into individual compounds.
   iii) Write an equation for the cracking of an alkane which has nine carbon atoms per molecule into methane, ethene and butene. (4)

NEAB CH03 March 1999 Q1

3 The table below shows the fractions obtained from crude oil.

Name of fraction	Number of carbon atoms	Use
Gases	1–4	bottled fuels for camping
Petrol (gasoline)	4–12	fuel for cars
Naphtha	7–14	
	11–15	jet fuel
Gas oil (diesel)	15–19	central heating fuel
Mineral oil	20–30	lubrication
Fuel oil	30–40	
Wax	41–50	candles
Bitumen	over 50	road surfacing

a Copy and complete the table byfilling in the empty boxes on your copy. (3)

b Give a molecular formula for each of the following components of crude oil:
   i)   the alkane which, on cracking, forms, as the only products, two moles of ethene and one mole of butane per mole of alkane.
   ii) the straight chain alkane found in the petrol fraction which contains the lowest percentage by mass of hydrogen. Refer to the table at the start of the question to deduce your answer. (2)

c Write an equation for the complete combustion of the alkane which requires 11 moles of oxygen per mole of alkane for complete combustion. (2)

NEAB CH03 June 1999 Q2(Part)

4 Some organic reactions involve the formation of free radicals. Give two examples of this type of reaction. For one of your examples, write a balanced equation and outline a mechanism for the reaction. (7)

NEAB CH03 June 1997 Q7(Part)

5 When a mixture of chlorine with an excess of methane is irradiated with ultraviolet light, a reaction occurs with chrloromethane as the main organic product. (5)

a Write an equation and a mechanism for the formation of chloromethane. (5)

b The main organic product of the reaction is chloromethane. Give two other organic compounds, one containing chlorine and the one not containing chlorine, which might be present at the end of the reaction. Explain how the compounds you have suggested are formed. (4)

NEAB CH03 June 1996 Q6(Part)

6 a
   i)   Name and give the molecular formula of the following hydrocarbon, **X**, which is a constituent of the fuel used in road vehicles. (2)

$$H_3C - \underset{\underset{CH_3}{|}}{\overset{\overset{CH_3}{|}}{C}} - CH_2 - \underset{\underset{CH_3}{|}}{CH} - CH_3$$

   ii) Using the molecular formula, write an equation for the complete combusion of **X**. (2)

NEAB CH03 June 1996 Q2 (part)

KEY SKILLS ASSIGNMENT

Fuels and the environment

The effect of road vehicles on the quality of our environment is becoming more of an issue every day. There are many proposals to limit the number of vehicles in our towns and cities in order to reduce the emission of polluting exhaust gases. These gases have been implicated in everything from global warming through to health problems in people and animals, and disease and damage in plants. Even some buildings in our inner cities show the effects of acid gases given out by road vehicles, factories and power stations. Some pressure groups are calling for a total ban on motor vehicles in our inner cities.

But is a total ban really a practical option? Is this radical step not a massive over–reaction? The motor car has given some people immense personal freedom and many of the cities where we live are only possible because of transport systems, whether public or private, that rely on the internal combustion engine. Maybe a better solution is to 'design away' the pollution by using cleaner fuels, more efficient engines and lighter vehicles.

Below is a table which gives some facts about two possible fuels for motor vehicle: natural gas (methane) and petrol.

1 Use the information from the table as a starting point to prepare a presentation to show either:

a the advantages of using natural gas as a fuel in vehicles, or;

b the advantages of using petrol in vehicles.

Remember that you are not writing an essay – you are preparing for a presentation. You will still need plenty of accurate, factual information but you will also need to think about how best to present it. Think about any transparencies, slides, computer graphics or charts you may use and keep a record of them in your notes. If you use computers to produce images or search for information, make sure that you show how you did this in your account.

Natural gas	Petrol
Must be compressed to be transported; it cannot be poured into a tank easily.	Contains nitrogen compounds, sulphur, lead and hydrocarbons.
High Octane rating (about 130).	A non-renewable energy resource.
Contains nitrogen, ethane, propane & hydrogen.	The source of petrol (crude oil) is easily handled and is used to synthesise new chemicals e.g. plastics, medicines.
Infrastructure to handle distribution of fuel poorly developed.	Octane rating of up to 98.
Exhaust gases are mainly water, carbon dioxide and a little carbon monoxide.	Easily transported and added to vehicle tank.
Low carbon to hydrogen ratio so high percentage in exhaust gases.	Additives such as lead tetraethyl added to make fuel of water burn slower and reduce knocking in engine.
More difficult to use as a 'chemical feedstock'. other industries.	Sophisticated infrastructure to handle fuel in place even for in developing countries.
Fuel tank in vehicle has to be reinforced to contain compressed gas.	Large % of Greenhouse Gases in exhaust fumes.
92% methane – a renewable energy source.	Exhaust gases such as sulphur dioxide and NO_x compounds which are toxic and harmful to the environment.
Engines are less noisy as 'knocking' is reduced because of higher octane rating.	Less chance of fuel leakage from tank.

13 Alkenes and epoxyethane

What do lipstick, margarine, antifreeze, bin liners, window frames and polyester material have in common? The answer is that they are all made from alkenes, byproducts of the petroleum industry. Alkenes are produced during cracking when long chained alkane molecules are broken into shorter chained and more useful alkanes. Chemists make a wide range of materials from alkenes and are now so skilled at manipulating alkene molecules that we have entered an age of designer molecules and materials. Chemists are now synthesising materials to fit a required set of properties.

Ethene is the starting material for making Melinex, the material used to make this windsurfer sail.

13.1 Structure and bonding in alkenes

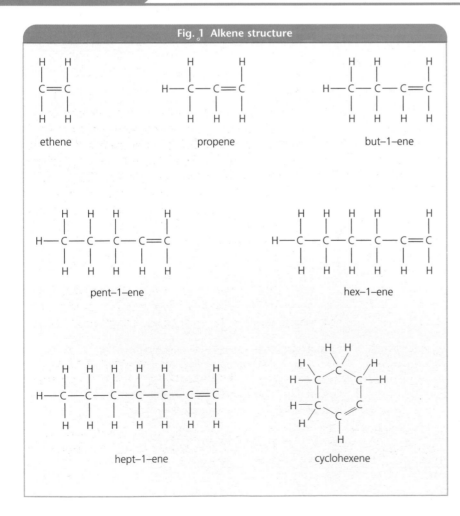

Fig. 1 Alkene structure

ethene

propene

but–1–ene

pent–1–ene

hex–1–ene

hept–1–ene

cyclohexene

Alkenes are very important to the chemical industry and are the starting point for manufacturing many other substances. Alkenes are produced during the cracking of crude oil (see Chapter 12).

Alkenes are a homologous series. Unbranched alkenes have the general formula C_nH_{2n}. Fig. 1 shows the structure of the first six alkenes in the series; ethene, propene, butene, pentene, hexene and heptene. It also shows that alkenes such as cyclohexene have a cyclic structure. In this section we look at the structure of alkenes and their reactions.

Saturated or unsaturated?

The difference between an alkene and an alkane with the same number of carbon atoms is the number of hydrogen atoms in the molecule. Ethane, for example has two carbon atoms and six hydrogen atoms. It is said to be **saturated** because it already contains the maximum possible number of hydrogens; it cannot be made to react with any more, no matter what conditions are supplied. Ethene, the corresponding alkene, has two carbon atoms and only four hydrogen atoms. Carbon must still form four single covalent bonds so to make the molecule stable, there is a double bond between the two carbon atoms. Alkenes are said to be **unsaturated** because they can accept more hydrogen atoms. The reaction converts an alkene into an alkane. We look at this reaction in more detail later in this section.

The terms saturated and unsaturated are often used to describe a range of organic chemicals, particularly large ones such as fats.

The carbon-carbon double bond

An alkene contains one double bond between one pair of its carbon atoms. This double bond is the functional group in the alkene series. It is the key to why alkenes are such reactive and useful molecules.

Fig. 2 shows the structure of ethene and the corresponding dot and cross diagram to show roughly how the electrons are shared between the different atoms.

You can see that each carbon atom is bonded to only three other atoms, two hydrogens and one carbon. Strong σ bonds form between these three atoms using three of the electrons available from the carbons. These bonds are at their most stable when the angle between them is 120°. This produces a flat molecule that is described as **planar** because all the atoms within it lie in one plane. The remaining electrons, one from the each of the two carbon atoms are also shared, forming another bond between these two atoms. This is a π bond; not just another σ bond, but a different kind of covalent bond in which the electrons are **delocalised**. The π and σ bonds in ethene are shown in Fig. 3. The 'bond areas' do not show the exact position of the electrons, they simply indicate the regions in which the electrons are most likely to be found.

The delocalised electrons that make up the π bond are held into the molecule less tightly than electrons within the σ bond. This makes the π bond a very attractive target for any positively charged groups that come near the molecule, making alkenes highly reactive – far more reactive than their parent alkanes.

The result is a molecule that has strong single covalent bonds (σ bonds) between all the atoms, with an extra, weaker covalent

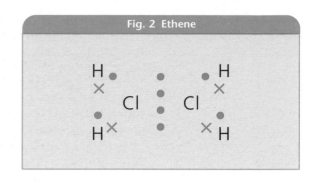

Fig. 2 Ethene

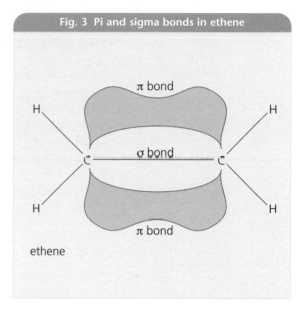

Fig. 3 Pi and sigma bonds in ethene

π bond

σ bond

π bond

ethene

bond (a π bond) between the two carbon atoms. Because the two carbon atoms are held together by two bonds, the distance between the two carbon atoms is shorter than between the two carbon atoms in ethane. However, you can also see that the combination of a strong σ bond and a weaker π bond produces a bond that is not as strong as two single bonds combined (Table 1).

1. The molecular formula of propene is C_3H_6. Draw a dot and cross diagram to show the arrangement of electrons.

2. Explain why the bond energy for the C=C bond is not twice the bond energy for the C–C bond.

3. Explain why the double covalent bond is shorter than the single covalent bond.

Table 1 Comparison of single and double carbon bonds		
Bond	Bond energy/kJ mol⁻¹	Bond length/nm
C–C	346	0.154
C=C	598	0.134

Cis and trans isomers

Many organic molecules form isomers. An isomer is a molecule made up from the same atoms but that has a different arrangement in space. Different isomers can be isolated, usually at room temperature. Sometimes, molecules have free rotation within them, allowing one form to convert to another, more or less constantly. In this case, the two forms of the molecule are **conformers**. Butane, for example, has free rotation around one of its C–C bonds and can flip from one conformer to another.

The double bond in alkenes is rigid and this prevents any rotation around the C=C bond. Rotation would require breaking the electron dense areas in the σ bond above and below the molecule and this takes too much energy. So, but-2-ene has no free internal rotation. It can still form isomers though, as Fig. 4 shows, but there is no interconversion. A molecule of but-2-ene is either one form or another. The two forms are **geometric isomers**, either **trans**- or **cis**-.

Fig. 4 Trans and cis isomers in butene

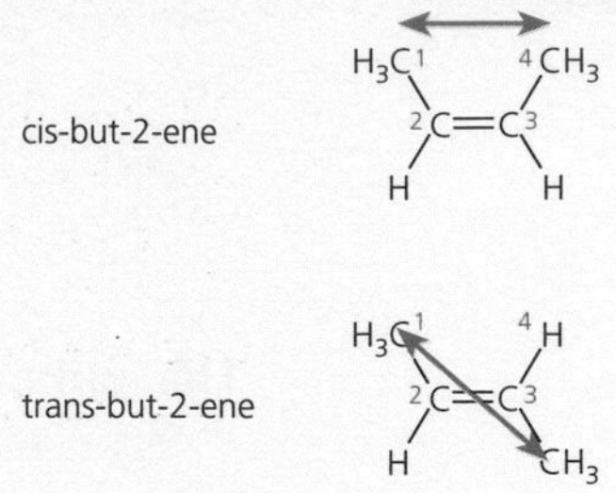

cis-but-2-ene

trans-but-2-ene

In the *cis*-isomer, the two methyl groups are on the same side of the carbon=carbon double bond. In the *trans*-isomer, the two methyl groups are on opposite sides.

4 Draw the structural formulae for:

a *trans*-pent-2-ene;
b *cis*-hex-2-ene;
c *trans*-hex-3-ene.

KEY FACTS

■ Alkenes are a homologous series with the general formula C_nH_{2n}.

■ Alkenes are unsaturated. They do not contain the maximum number of hydrogen atoms possible and have double bonds to make them stable.

■ The double bond in alkenes is called the **functional group**. It makes alkenes more reactive than alkanes.

■ A double bond consists of a strong covalent σ bond with areas of delocalised electrons above and below the σ bond, forming a weaker π bond.

■ The planar shape of the double bond allows the existence of *cis* and *trans* isomers.

APPLICATION A   **Butane isomers**

The table below gives some physical data for isomers of butane.

Name	State at room temp	Molecular mass	Density /g cm⁻³ (as liquid)	Melting point /°C	Boiling point /°C
but-1-ene	g	56.1	0.595	−185.2	6.2
trans-but-2-ene	g	56.1	0.604	105.4	1.0
cis-but-2-ene	g	56.1	0.621	−138.8	3.8

1 Why do all have the same molecular mass?

2 Why do the isomers have different densities?

3 Why is the melting point of *cis*-but-2-ene lower than the melting point of *trans*-but-2-ene?

4 How could you distinguish between the *cis* and *trans* isomers of but-2-ene?

13.2 The properties of alkenes

The first three members of the alkene series are gases at room temperature and pressure. Longer chain alkenes are liquids and solids (Table 2). An increase in the boiling point with the number of carbon atoms in the molecule is typical for all hydrocarbons.

Table 2 Melting and boiling points of alkenes			
Alkene	**Structural formula**	**Melting point/°C**	**Boiling point/°C**
Ethene	$CH_2=CH_2$	−169	−105
Propene	$CH_3CH=CH_2$	−185	−48
But-1-ene	$CH_3CH_2CH=CH_2$	−185	− 6
Pent-1-ene	$CH_3CH_2CH_2CH=CH_2$	−165	+ 30

5 Explain why the boiling points increase as the alkene carbon chain gets longer. [Hint: see page 32; Intermolecular forces.]

The reactions of alkenes

Since alkenes are unsaturated, they undergo **addition reactions** – reactions in which the double bond between the two carbon atoms becomes a single bond and other atoms are added to the molecule to form a single product:

$$CH_2=CH_2 + 2X \rightarrow XCH_2XCH_2$$

Alkenes are an important starting point for the production of margarines.

Reactions can, however, proceed only when the π bond that is part of the double carbon–carbon bond is broken. This requires energy and often can occur only when a molecule, or a part of a molecule with a strong positive charge is present. Such positively charged regions readily accept a pair of electrons from the π bond to make a more stable σ bond. Because such molecules and groups are attracted to areas of negative charge, they are called **electrophiles**. Addition reactions that are initiated by an electrophile are termed **electrophilic addition**.

We look at three main types of reactions in the alkenes in this section:

- **Hydrogenation** by the addition of hydrogen across the double bond;
- **Electrophilic addition** reactions with halogens and with sulphuric acid;
- **Hydration** to form alcohols.

Adding hydrogen to alkenes

At normal temperature and pressure, alkenes do not react with hydrogen. It takes a finely divided nickel catalyst and a temperature of 150 °C to bring about hydrogenation. The hydrogen molecule splits into two atoms on the surface of the catalyst and the two atoms then add to the same side of the double bond in the alkene. The corresponding alkane is formed:

$$CH_2=CH_2 + H_2 \xrightarrow[\text{573 K}]{\text{Nickel}} CH_3–CH_3$$

This reaction is very important in the manufacture of margarine (see the Key Skills assignment at the end of this chapter).

Addition reactions involving halogens

Alkenes undergo electrophilic addition with halogens. The reaction is rapid with chlorine, less so with bromine and is very slow with iodine. The reaction of alkenes with bromine water involves a distinctive colour change and is used as a test to distinguish an alkene from an alkane.

The reactions between ethene and bromine and between ethene and hydrogen bromide, are shown, step-by-step, on the next page.

When ethene and bromine react

When ethene is bubbled through bromine that is held under a layer of water the reaction produces 1,2-dibromoethane, a colourless oily liquid:

$$C_2H_4 + Br_2 \rightarrow CH_2BrCH_2Br$$
gas   red liquid   colourless liquid

The mechanism of the reaction involves the electrophilic addition of bromine to ethene.

Step 1: Dipole induced in bromine

Normally, the electrons in the Br–Br bond are distributed evenly between the two bromine atoms. In the presence of ethene, the high electron density of the double bond induces a dipole in the bromine molecule. One bromine atom then has a small positive charge while the other has a small negative charge:

$$Br_2 \rightarrow Br^{\delta+} - Br^{\delta-}$$

Step 2: Electrophilic attack

The positively-charged bromine atom acts as an **electrophile**, an electron seeking species. Electrons from the double bond of the ethene molecule begin to form a new carbon to bromine bond with the $\delta+$ bromine:

$$H_2C = CH_2 + Br^{\delta+} - Br^{\delta-}$$

Step 3: Bromide ion forms

The carbon–bromine bond is formed using one of the electron pairs of the carbon–carbon bond. The other carbon in the double bond becomes an electron-deficient carbocation. The electrons in the bromine–bromine bond shift towards the more distant bromine atom and the Br–Br bond breaks, releasing a bromide ion. This ion then acts as a nucleophile; it uses a lone pair of electrons to form a new bond with the carbocation:

The product of the electrophilic addition is 1,2-dibromoethane, which is used as a petrol additive. It acts as a lead 'scavenger' in leaded petrols to make them less liable to 'knocking' (see Chapter 11). Now that unleaded petrols and high octane fuels are used more commonly, the need for 1,2-dibromoethane is diminishing.

6   Explain why H_2C^+–CH_3 is a carbocation.

7   Explain why the dipole in HBr is permanent and the dipole in Br_2 is only temporary.

Ethene and hydrogen bromide

Alkenes also react with the hydrogen halides to form bromoalkanes. In contrast with its reaction with halogens, ethene reacts readily with hydrogen iodide and hydrogen bromide, but only slowly with hydrogen chloride. Ethene reacts with hydrogen bromide in the gas phase or in concentrated aqueous solution to form bromoethane.

The mechanism of this reaction is similar to that between bromine and ethene. The main difference is that, while bromine has an induced and weak dipole, hydrogen bromide has a permanent dipole:

$$H^{\delta+} - Br^{\delta-}$$

Step 1: Hydrogen acts as electrophile

The hydrogen atom in the hydrogen bromide molecule is electron deficient. When the reaction occurs in aqueous solution, the dissociated hydrogen ions $H^+(aq)$ act as electrophiles. In the gas phase, the positively charged hydrogen atom in the intact hydrogen bromide molecule acts as an electrophile and attacks the double bond of the ethene molecule. This results in the formation of a bond between the carbon and the hydrogen atom with the slight positive charge, and of a carbocation:

$$_2HC = CH_2 + H^{\delta+} - Br^{\delta-} \rightarrow H_2C^+ - CH_3 + Br^-$$

Step 2: Bromide ion reaction

The released bromide ion reacts with the carbocation to make 1-bromoethane.

$$H_2C^+ - CH_3 + Br^- \rightarrow CH_2BrCH_3$$

Fig. 5 Hydration of ethene by sulphuric acid

Sulphuric acid is an acid because it dissociates to release hydrogen ions (H+). A hydrogen ion acts as an electrophile and is attracted to the high electron density of the double bond.

The carbonium ion CH_3-CH_2^+ forms. The negative charge of -d-SO_3H is attracted to the positive charge of the carbonium ion, forming ethyl hydrogensulphate.

Adding water produces ethanol and regenerates sulphuric acid. This is hydration because, overall, a molecule of water is added to a molecule of ethene.

Ethene and sulphuric acid

This reaction is illustrated in Fig. 5. Alkenes are absorbed by cold, concentrated sulphuric acid to form alkyl hydrogensulphates. For example, ethene is absorbed by fuming sulphuric acid to form ethyl hydrogensulphate. When this is warmed in dilute sulphuric acid, hydrolysis occurs and ethanol is produced. The two reactions result in the overall addition of water to an alkene; the sulphuric acid is regenerated at the end of the reaction. Because it takes part in the reaction but is left unchanged at the end, sulphuric acid acts as a catalyst.

This is an important reaction in industry because ethyl hydrogen sulphate reacts with water to produce ethanol, C_2H_5OH. Ethanol, the alcohol in wine, beer and spirits for human consumption is always prepared by fermentation because this process also contributes a range of other chemicals that give the drink its eventual taste.

Propene can be used to produce propan-2-ol, and but-2-ene can be used to make butan-2-ol. Propan-2-ol and butan-2-ol are liquids used extensively in the chemical industry as solvents. They are also used in the manufacture of paint and cosmetics.

Today the petrochemical industry is moving away from producing ethanol using this method and is instead opting for the direct catalytic hydration of ethene, or the addition of water across a double bond. This hydration requires a pressure of 6 000 kPa and temperature of 300 °C with phosphoric (V) acid as a catalyst.

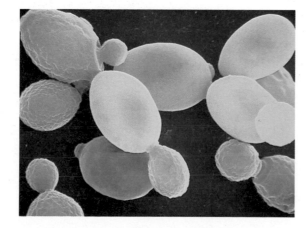

Yeast cells. Yeast is a single-celled fungus that breaks down sugar into ethanol and carbon dioxide by anaerobic respiration when grown in an environment deficient in oxygen.

8 Write an equation using structural formulae to show the mechanism for the reaction in which water is added to propene, using sulphuric acid as a catalyst, to produce propan-2-ol.

Fig. 6 Symmetry in alkenes

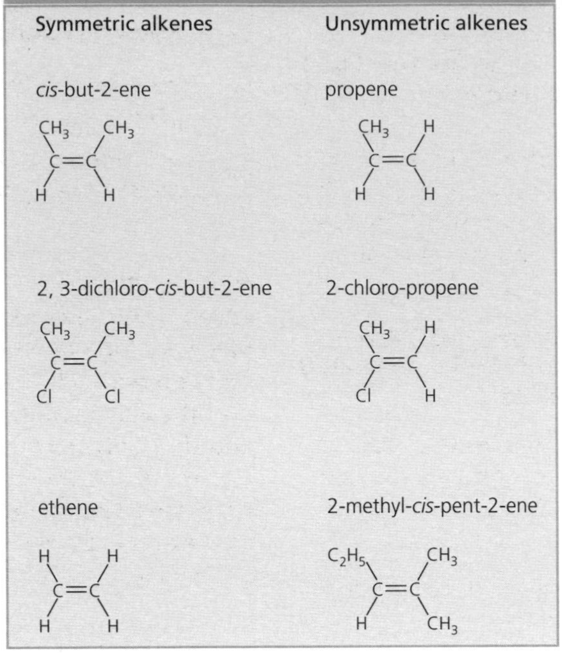

Symmetric alkenes	Unsymmetric alkenes
cis-but-2-ene	propene
2, 3-dichloro-cis-but-2-ene	2-chloro-propene
ethene	2-methyl-cis-pent-2-ene

Either;

$$CH_3(H)C=CH_2 + HBr \rightarrow CH_3CH_2CH_2Br$$
bromoethane

Or;

$$CH_3(H)C=CH_2 + HBr \rightarrow CH_3CHBrCH_3$$
2-bromoethene

Unsymmetrical alkenes

An unsymmetric alkene, such as propene, has different groups attached to the carbons of its C=C double bond. Examples of symmetric and unsymmetric alkenes are shown in Fig. 6.

The electrophilic addition of a hydrogen halide to an unsymmetric alkene can give more than one addition product, because it depends on which end of the double bond is attacked by the electrophile. For example, when propene reacts with hydrogen bromide, there are two possible products:

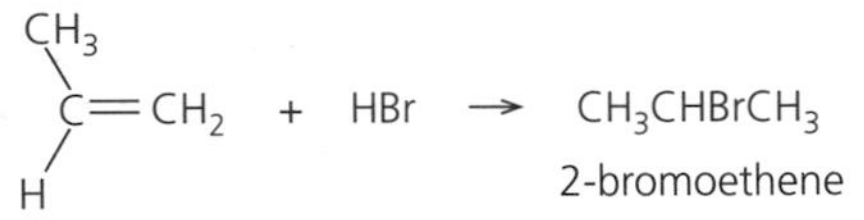

The bromine atom can be bonded to either the first or second carbon atom in the chain, depending on which end of the double bond is attacked by the proton in step 1 of the reaction (see page 192). In reality, it is mostly 2-bromoethane that forms. Why is this?

The addition product of an unsymmetrical alkene depends on the stability of the intermediate carbocation formed; in this case the carbocation. A primary carbocation, a species in which a positive carbon atom is attached to just one other carbon atom is much less stable than a secondary carbocation that is attached to two other carbon atoms. As you would expect, following this trend, a tertiary carbocation is the most stable of all. The reason for the extra stability is that the

Table 3 Primary, secondary and tertiary carbocations		
Type of carbocation	**Structure***	**Description**
Primary carbocation	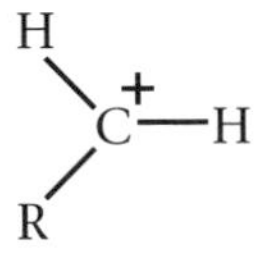	The positive carbon atom is attached to **one** other carbon atom.
Secondary carbocation	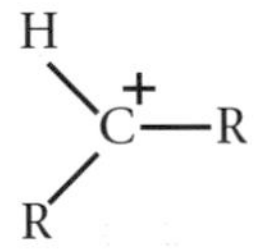	The positive carbon atom is attached to **two** other carbon atoms.
Tertiary carbocation	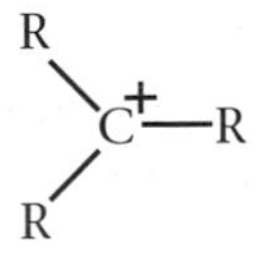	The positive carbon atom is attached to **three** other carbon atoms.
* R is used to represent an alkyl group		

alkyl groups donate electrons towards the positive carbon atom, so minimising the positive charge on the carbocation.

Table 3 summarises the stability trend and shows the structure of the different carbocations.

In an addition reaction that involves an unsymmetric alkene, the product most likely to be formed is the one that results from the most stable carbocation. An extension of **Markovnikov's rule** summarises this tendency:

An electrophile adds to an unsymmetric C=C bond so that the most stable carbocation is formed as an intermediate.

You can see how this applies to a real reaction by looking at how propene reacts with hydrogen bromide (Fig. 7).

Fig. 7 Propene and hydrogen bromide

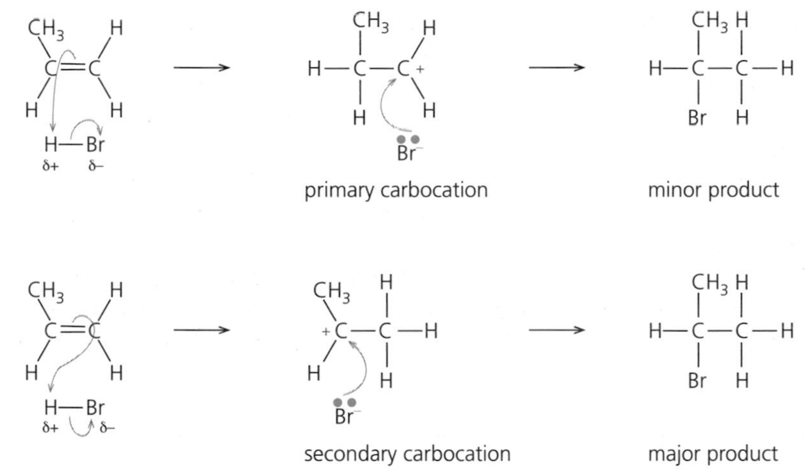

9 Predict the major product from the following reactions:

a propene and hydrogen chloride;

b pent-1-ene and hydrogen bromide;

c but-1-ene and concentrated sulphuric acid followed by hydrolysis with water.

Polymerisation

Alkene molecules can join up in chains to give very long molecules called polymers. The reaction occurs in the presence of a catalyst and the alkene monomers link to form addition polymers, which are saturated. The process is therefore known as **addition polymerisation**. Ethene molecules polymerise to make polyethene, more commonly called polythene.

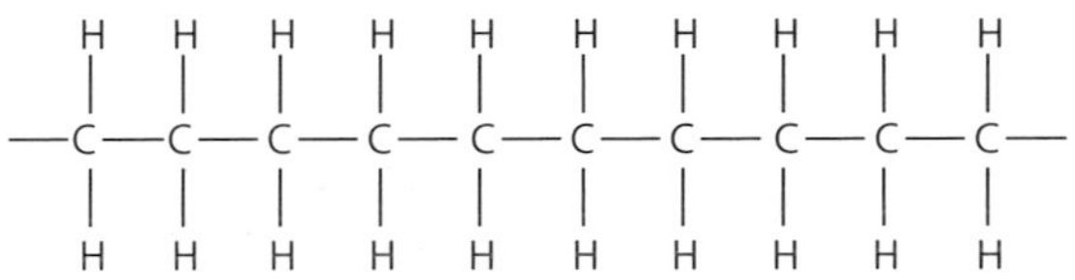

The general equation for this reaction is:

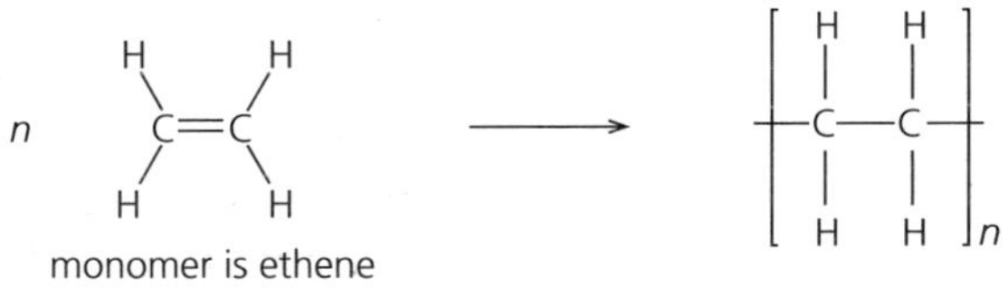

monomer is ethene

This chain may be several tens of thousands of carbon atoms long. Different alkenes produce different polymers. Ethene polymerises to poly(ethene), used for plastic bags, insulation for wires and material for squeezy bottles; propene forms poly(propene), used for clothing, carpets, ropes and twine.

Epoxyethane

Alkenes, like alkanes, burn in oxygen to produce carbon dioxide and water.

$$C_2H_4 + 3O_2 \rightarrow 2CO_2 + 2H_2O \quad \Delta H^\ominus = -1411 \text{ kJ mol}^{-1}$$

The reaction releases a lot of energy, but, unlike alkanes, alkenes are not used as fuels; they are far too useful to burn. They are used as raw materials in the chemical industry. Such raw materials are often given the industrial term **feedstock**. About 25 per cent of the ethene produced from cracking is used to make epoxyethane. Epoxyethane is a very reactive chemical and is used to make other substances such as antifreeze for engines, polyesters for textiles, detergents and solvents.

Manufacture of epoxyethane

Epoxyethane can be manufactured by the partial oxidation of ethene. If oxygen reacts with ethene in the presence of a finely divided silver catalyst at temperatures between 250 and 400 °C, epoxyethane, a **cyclic** or ring compound is produced:

$$\Delta H^\ominus = -210 \text{ kJ mol}^{-1}$$

The catalyst is a finely-divided layer, usually on a base material like alumina (aluminium oxide). During the reaction, about 20 – 30 per cent of the ethene undergoes complete combustion to carbon dioxide and water. The production of epoxyethane from ethene was first developed by Lefort in 1935. Various factors influence the efficiency of its production and the ideal reaction conditions are shown in Table 4. Chemicals such as 1,2-dichloroethene are added because they act as oxidation inhibitors. The epoxyethane produced is purified by fractional distillation.

10 About 70% of the ethene is left unreacted in the reaction mixture. Suggest what could be done with this ethene.

Table 4 Ideal reaction conditions to produce epoxyethane

Variable	Value
Amount of ethene in reaction mixture	5 to 20%
Amount of air in reaction mixture	80 to 95%
Temperature	200 to 400 °C
Pressure	1000 to 3000 kPa (10 to 30 atmospheres)
Catalyst	silver
Average conversion of ethene to epoxyethane	14%
Average conversion of ethene to all possible products	30%

Table 5 Bond angles in ethers

Bond angle	Usual value	Value for epoxyethane
	105°	70°
	109.5°	60°

Structure and properties of epoxyethane

Epoxyethane is a **cyclic ether** because it contains the C–O–C group arranged in a ring. Most ethers are chemically stable, but epoxyethane is very reactive because of the instability of this ring structure. Table 5 shows that the bond angles in the cyclic structure are very different to the usual bond angles that occur in stable ethers. This puts the cyclic structure under great strain; in order to relieve this strain, the ring is always 'ready to burst open' to react with other chemicals.

Epoxyethane is a colourless gas at room temperature. It boils at 10 °C. It is flammable and explosive. During its manufacture, the exothermic reaction must be monitored because the risk of explosion increases at the high temperatures necessary for the reactions to occur. An efficient system of heat exchangers is used to maintain the correct temperature. Problems like static electricity or creating hot spots on the catalyst surface must be avoided.

Epoxyethane also has a strong tendency to polymerise, particularly if it comes into contact with an alkali. The polymerisation reaction is very exothermic which could further increase the risk of explosion. Since it is a reactive chemical, epoxyethane also reacts with living tissue, and so is toxic. It irritates the respiratory system and damages the nervous system, and causes skin blisters and burns. Strict safety precautions have to be taken during its manufacture and the recommended limit for prolonged exposure to epoxyethane is under 25 parts per million.

Reactions of epoxyethane

The open ring structure of epoxyethane is prone to attack by nucleophilic species with a positive charge. These react with the lone pair of electrons from the ring to make a double covalent bond.

The carbon atoms in epoxyethane have a positive dipole because electron density is attracted towards the oxygen atom. Oxygen is more electronegative than carbon. Nucleophiles are attracted to the positive charges on the carbon atoms. Nucleophilic attack causes the ring to open and the subsequent reaction is exothermic. Primary products of such reactions contain 2-hydroxyethyl groups ($-CH_2CH_2OH$). Some of these products then go on to react with the epoxyethane still present.

Reaction with water

The reaction between epoxyethane and water is called **hydrolysis**. The reaction is slow at room temperature but it can be speeded up by:

- using steam at 200 °C and a pressure of 1400 kPa

- using a dilute sulphuric acid catalyst at 60 °C.

In industry, epoxyethane is treated with a ten-fold molar excess of water at 60 °C in the present of sulphuric acid. The reaction produces a **diol** – a compound containing two OH groups.

$$H_2C-CH_2(g) + H_2O \longrightarrow \quad \text{ethane-1,2-diol}$$

epoxyethane + water $\longrightarrow$ ethane-1,2-diol

The resulting aqueous solution is concentrated by 70 per cent by evaporating most of the water and is then fractionally distilled. Despite the large excess of water, the yield is only about 90%. The other product is the dihydroxyether:

$HOCH_2CH_2OCH_2CH_2OH$

Ethylene glycol, the old name for the product, is still commonly used. Ethane-1,2-diol is an important component of antifreeze. Its melting point of −12 °C and boiling point of 198 °C and the fact that it mixes completely with water makes it ideal for this application.

Most cars rely on water circulating round the engine to keep the engine cool. Antifreeze allows cars to be used when the temperature is below freezing.

Ethane-1,2-diol is 30% sweeter than sugar to taste. Unfortunately, it is very toxic because it is converted by enzymes into oxalic acid (the real poison) in the body. Death from liver and kidney failure follows quickly. However, there is an antidote – alcohol! Alcohol works as an antidote because it keeps the enzymes busy that would otherwise produce the oxalic acid and gives the body time to excrete the ethane-1,2-diol intact.

Every year, thousands of pets die from ethane-1,2-diol poisoning, usually in the autumn when radiator fluid is being changed. They are encouraged by the sweet taste and the symptoms of appearing drunk and awkward in affected animals are common to vets. Anti-freeze should always be stored in a covered container.

11 Epoxyethane is stored either by refrigerating it or by diluting it with nitrogen or carbon dioxide gas. Explain why.

12 Poly(chloroethene) makes a strong rigid plastic because permanent dipoles exist in the polymer chains and there is attraction between the opposite charge on adjacent molecules. Where do the permanent dipoles form.

Fig. 8 1,4-Benzenedicarboxylic acid

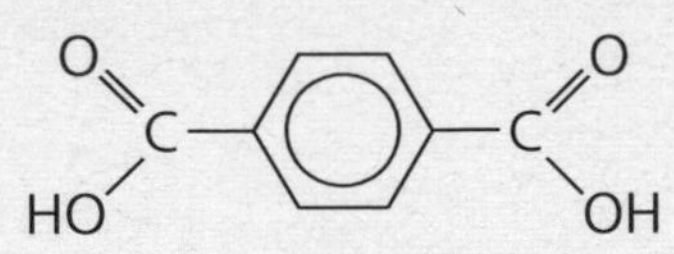

Polymerisation
Ethane-1,2-diol is an alcohol with two –OH groups. If ethane-1,2-diol reacts with an organic acid, benzene 1,4-dicarboxylic acid (Fig. 8), the polyester poly(ethyleneterephthalate) (PET), often known by its trade name of Terylene, is made (Fig. 9).

A polyester is a polymer made by linking many small molecules or monomers by

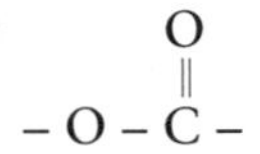

$$-O-\overset{\overset{\displaystyle O}{\|}}{C}-$$

linkages . These are called **ester linkages**. The monomers are an alcohol and an organic acid. The alcohol must have two –OH groups and the organic acid must have two –COOH groups so that reactions can happen at both ends of the molecule.

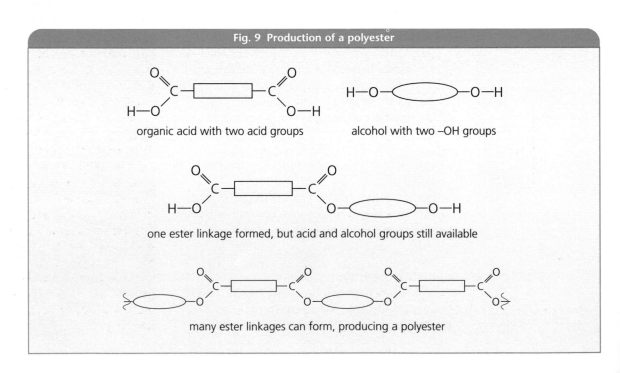

Fig. 9 Production of a polyester

organic acid with two acid groups   alcohol with two –OH groups

one ester linkage formed, but acid and alcohol groups still available

many ester linkages can form, producing a polyester

Fig. 10 The first stage in the production of PET

monomer

$+ 2H_2O$

The raw material for these polyester clothes was ethene produced during the cracking of crude oil. Ethene was converted into epoxyethane and then into polyester.

Fig. 11 The second stage in the production of PET

270–300 °C
zero pressure
antimony catalyst

PET

$+ (n-1)$ H—O—CH$_2$—CH$_2$—O—H

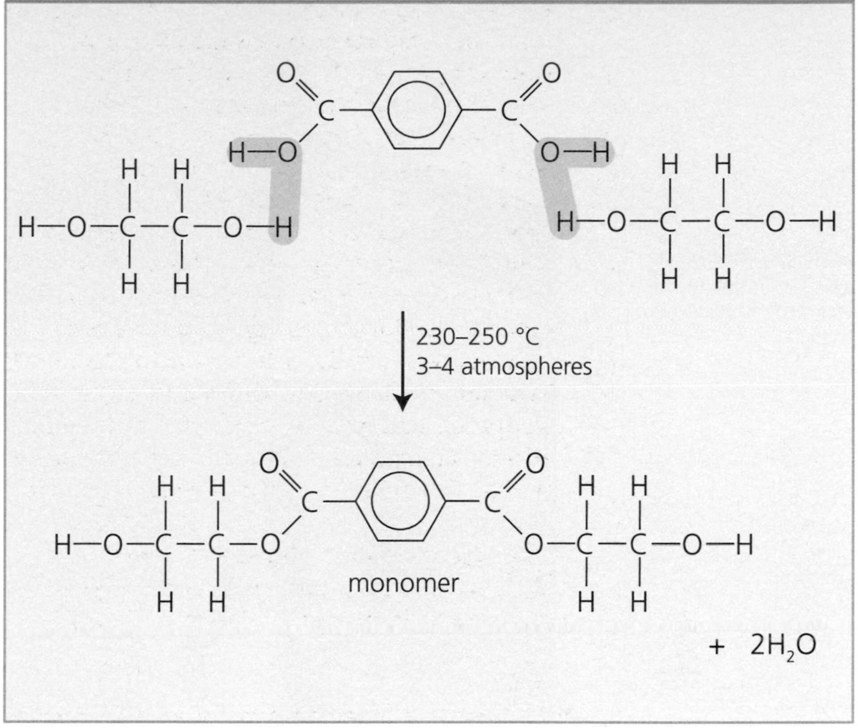

Ethane-1,2-diol reacts with benzene 1,4-dicarboxylic acid at 230–250 °C and three to four atmospheres pressure. Initially, they react in a 2:1 ratio to produce a 'monomer' for later polymerisation to PET. The reaction adds an ester group to both acid groups in the benzene 1,4-dicarboxylic acid, but leaves two –OH groups, one at each end of the monomer molecule, available for further reaction (Fig. 10).

The monomer is polymerised to PET by heating it at 270–300 °C at almost zero pressure in the presence of an antimony catalyst (Fig. 11). As the polymerisation proceeds, the viscosity of the reaction mixture increases. Viscosity is monitored to decide when the process should be stopped. The ethane-1,2-diol produced is boiled off and recycled to make more monomer. Molten polyester can be forced through a fine mesh in a process called **extrusion**. This produces long thin fibres that can be used to make a range of textiles for the clothing industry.

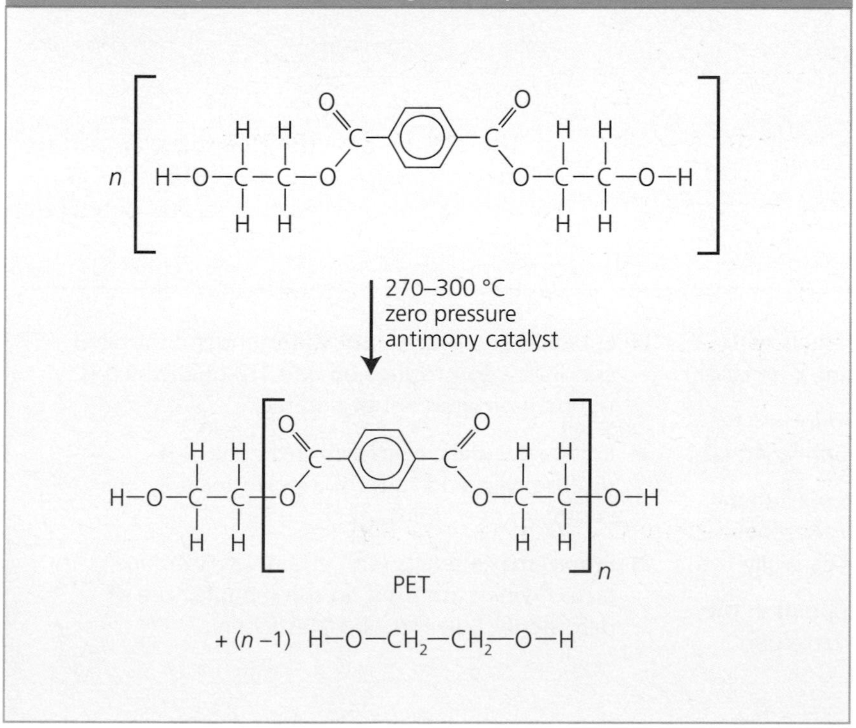

Hydration with less water

When epoxyethane is manufactured, an excess of steam is used to give the maximum yield of epoxyethane. If the amount of water used is reduced, then various poly(alkoxy) ethanols are produced.

$$H_2O \quad + \quad n\left[\begin{array}{c} H_2C \text{—} CH_2 \\ \diagdown O \diagup \end{array}\right] \longrightarrow HO(CH_2CH_2O)_nH$$

Poly(alkoxy) ethanols are an important group of chemicals used in the manufacture of plasticisers, polyurethane, solvents and detergents.

13 Draw the fully displayed formula for the poly(alkoxy) ethanol where n=3.

Poly(alkoxy) ethanols are added to lipsticks to make them feel smooth and easy to apply.

PVC is a hard rigid plastic. The addition of plasticisers to PVC during the manufacture of this fabric make the product more pliable because the long polymer chains can now slide over each other.

Reaction with alcohol

The reaction between epoxyethane and alcohols is similar to the reaction with water. The primary products are monoalkyl ethers of ethane-1,2-diol. For example, the reaction between epoxyethane and ethanol produces monoethyl ether

$$ROH \quad + \quad \begin{array}{c} H_2C \text{—} CH_2 \\ \diagdown O \diagup \end{array} \longrightarrow ROCH_2CH_2OH$$

$$\text{alcohol} \quad + \quad \text{epoxyethane} \longrightarrow \text{monoalkyl ether}$$

The monoethyl ether produced is used in the paint industry and in printing inks as a solvent and also in plasticisers and detergents.

KEY FACTS

- Under controlled conditions, ethene reacts with water to form epoxyethane. Epoxyethane is an ether.

- A permanent dipole on the C–O bond in epoxyethane makes it open to nucleophilic attack.

- The bonds in the cyclic structure of epoxyethane are strained and epoxyethane is a very reactive compound that needs to be handled carefully

- Epoxyethane is an important starting point in the manufacture of antifreeze, polyester, detergents and plasticisers.

- Epoxyethane reacts with water under controlled conditions to produce ethane-1,2-diol, which is the major ingredient of antifreeze.

- Ethane-1,2-diol reacts with benzene 1,4-dicarboxylic acid to form a polyester polymer containing ester linkages.

- Epoxyethane reacts with ethanol to produce ethers which are used in the manufacture of detergents, solvents and plasticisers.

APPLICATION B

Plasticisers

PVC is used to make cling films suitable for use in microwave ovens, as well as for making ordinary cling films. PVC is made from the monomer chloroethene by addition polymerisation:

$$n\text{CH}_2{=}\text{CHCl(g)} \longrightarrow -(\text{CH}_2{-}\text{CHCl})_n-(s)$$

chloroethene   poly(chloroethene) (PVC)

The PVC produced has long polymer chains. The carbon–chlorine bond is strongly polar and there is considerable intermolecular attraction between the polymer chains (see diagram A). PVC is therefore a strong and rigid plastic, ideal for making items such as guttering and drainpipes. It is far too rigid to be used as cling film. PVC has to be specially treated to make it more flexible.

PVC can be made more flexible by adding a chemical called a plasticiser. The plasticiser molecules penetrate the polymer and increase the distance between the polymer chains. The polar effects of the carbon–chlorine bond are weakened and the rigidity of the three-dimensional structure is reduced (see diagram B). As a result, the polymer chains can slide over each other and the plastic produced is soft and pliable.

PVC used to make cling film normally contains up to 18 per cent plasticiser by mass. The plasticisers used in cling film are compounds called esters. An ester is formed when an alcohol and a carboxylic acid react together in the presence of a concentrated acid, such as sulphuric acid. The equation for this type of reaction is:

Esters gave the general formula:

A

polychloroethene chains
plasticiser molecules

distance too great for intermolecular forces to be effective

B

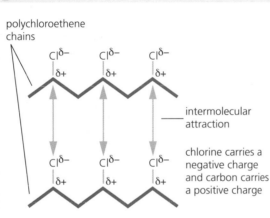

polychloroethene chains

intermolecular attraction

chlorine carries a negative charge and carbon carries a positive charge

the dipoles in the carbon–chlorine bonds attract adjacent polymer chains

Carboxylic acid   alcohol   ester   water

1 What type of intermolecular forces operate in PVC?

2 Cling film is used to wrap food and many of the plasticisers used are fat soluble. What precautions should be printed on the cling film packet and why?

3 Cling film manufacturers use low-migratory plasticisers. What do you think this means?

PVC is used to manufacture window frames and doors than need no painting and resist the elements for years.

EXAMINATION QUESTIONS

1 Propenoic acid, $CH_2=CHCOOH$, can be converted into compound A, CH_3CH_2COOH.

a Give the reagent and conditions necessary for the conversion of propenoic acid into A. (2)

b Propenoic acid can be used to make a polymer.
  i) Draw the repeating unit of the polymer. (1)
  ii) Name the type of polymer formed. (1)
  NEAB CH03 June 1995 Q1(Part)

2 Outline a mechanism for the addition of hydrogen bromide to 2-ethylbu-1-ene, $(CH_3CH_2)2C=CH_2$, and explain why only one major organic product is obtained. (7)
  NEAB CH06 June 1997 Q4(Part)

3
a The reaction between ethene and concentrated sulphuric acid is an example of the first stage of a general method used to form alcohols from alkenes. Write an equation for the reaction and name the type of mechanism involved.

b Suggest a reagent which could be used to convert the product obtained in part (a) into ethanol. Name the type of reaction taking place. (2)

c Predict the major organic product of the reaction between but-1-ene and hydrogen bromide. Explain the basis for your prediction.(4)
  NEAB CH06 June 1996 Q5(Part)

4
a Why is it necessary, in the direct synthesis of epoxyethane from ethene and air, to have the efficient removal of the heat generated? (1)

b i) Explain briefly why epoxyethane is highly reactive and write an equation for the reaction between one mole of epoxyethane and one mole of ethanol. (4)
  ii) Give the repeating unit of the polymer formed when one mole of ethanol reacts with an excess of epoxyethane. (1)

c Predict, by means of an equation, how one mole of epoxyethane reacts with one mole of ammonia. (1)
  NEAB CH06 June 1997 Q5

5 Formation of epoxyethane by the partial oxidation of ethene by air, in the presence of a catalyst, is an exothermic process ($\Delta H = -210$ kJ mol^{-1}).

a Write an equation for the reaction, name the catalyst and suggest a hazard associated with the process. (4)

b i) Name the type of reaction which takes place between epoxyethane and water. Writ an equation for the reaction between one mole of epoxyethane and one mole of water. (2)
  ii) Give the structure of the compound formed when the product in part (b) (i) undergoes a further reaction with two more of epoxyethane. (1)
  NEAB CH06 June 1998 Q6

6 Ethene can be converted into two different hydrocarbons one of which is a gas and the other a solid of high relative molecular mass.

Give the structure of each product, state the types of reaction involved and, for the gaseous product only, give the conditions necessary for its formation. (5)
  NEAB CH03 June 1997 Q8(Part)

7
a Give the structures of the two carbonium ion intermediates formed when pent-2-ene reacts with hydrogen bromide. (2)

b Name the two isomeric organic products which result from this reaction. (2)

c Indicate why these two products are obtained in approximately equal amounts. (1)
  NEAB CH06 March 1998 Q4(Part)

Margarine – still the healthy option?

In recent years, margarine has enjoyed an image as a 'healthy alternative' to butter. This has been mainly due to the perception that the unsaturated fats in margarine are healthier than the saturated fats found in butter. However, recent research suggests that *trans*-fatty acids found in margarine are linked with heart disease, though the link has yet to be proved. Just another health scare or should we really be worried?

The answer lies in the chemistry of the hydrogenation process used to manufacture margarine. In this process some of the unsaturated fatty acids are converted into saturated fatty acids. This also leads to some rearrangement of the fatty acid structure from *cis* to *trans*. It is the double bond between carbon atoms which stops the chain of carbon atoms rotating in an unsaturated chain which makes two isomers possible. These are the *cis*- and *trans*- forms. The chains can rotate in a saturated chain because there are no double bonds. Normally, fats from plant sources contain only *cis*-fatty acids and are mostly unsaturated fatty acids. Animal fats contain both isomers and are mainly saturated fatty acids.

Up to 25% conversion from *cis*- to *trans*- has been detected in analysis. Food processing doesn't seem to change the amount of *trans*-fatty acid but varying amounts of *trans*-fatty acids have been detected by chemists all over the world. See the table below.

Percentage of trans-fatty acids in some foods	
Food Product	**% *trans*-fatty acids**
Margarine	0.6 - 23.5
Cakes & Biscuits	0 - 15.5
French fries	5.8 - 32.8
Animal & dairy fats	1.5 - 10.6

So why are these *trans*-fatty acids a problem? Unlike *cis*-fatty acids, they interfere with metabolic processes in the body as enzymes do not recognise their shape. This means that they are treated as toxic. *Cis*-fatty acids (such as linoleic, linoleneic and arachidonic acids) are essential for a healthy diet as they are not found in the body and are needed for essential metabolic processes.

Trans-fatty acids, even though they are unsaturated, seem to increase blood cholesterol levels close to those associated with saturated fatty acids. Hence the link with heart disease. Research at King's College, London has established that there seems to be a threshold level above which *trans*-fatty acids can be potentially dangerous. However, the problem is that the consumer at present cannot establish the amount of *trans*-fatty acids are in a food product such as margarine. Why? Because they are often lumped together on labelling with *cis*-fatty acids as mono- or polyunsaturated fats. Sometimes food labels include a mention of saturated fats. So far the food industry has resisted efforts to relabel its products to distinguish between *cis* and *trans* forms of fatty acids.

1 Look up the prefixes *cis* and *trans* in a dictionary and write down their definitions. This will help you with question 2.

2 Using this definition, draw a structural diagram to illustrate the difference between a *cis* and *trans* version of a fatty acid. You must put in the correct types of bonds.

3 Explain why *cis* and *trans* are considered to be isomers.

4 What is the chemical difference between a fat and an oil?

5 Draw up a table showing the similarities and differences between *cis*- and *trans*- fatty acids, saturated and unsaturated fatty acids, their main natural sources, uses and effects in body metabolism.

6 Why is the statement in adverts suspect when it states that a spread is 'healthy because it is low in saturates'? What do you think the advertiser is trying to imply?

7 Carry out a survey of at least 50 food items and find out how the amounts of fats are described.

a Record the type of food, the amount of fats present and how they are described and the manufacturer. Try to cover as many types of food as possible.

b Analyse the data set for average fat content for different group of foods. Estimate the mean, median and range of fat content for each group of foods.

14 Haloalkanes

Chloroform, now called trichloromethane, was an early and effective anaesthetic. It could cause liver damage though, which was a drawback to its safety. Ethoxyethane (then simply called ether) was also used as an early anaesthetic, but ethoxyethane is very flammable and it proved dangerous in an operating theatre. Ideally, an anaesthetic needs to be a gas or a volatile liquid to enable it to be be administered easily to the patient, who inhales the anaesthetic and absorbs it through the thin lining of the lungs. Anaesthetics must also be nonflammable, non-toxic and capable of producing deep anaesthesia.

The presence of any halogen atom in an alkane chain reduces flammability but different alkanes can affect the usefulness of potential anaesthetics. We now know, for example, that the chlorine atoms in trichloromethane cause the anaesthetic effect. The more chlorine atoms present in the alkane, the more powerful the anaesthetic but also the more toxic the compound. So dichloromethane is a weak anaesthetic, but not very toxic, trichloromethane is a stronger anaesthetic and more toxic and tetrachloromethane is a very strong but extremely toxic anaesthetic.

Introducing fluorine atoms into the haloalkane reduces the toxicity. The carbon–fluorine bond is stronger than the carbon–chlorine bond and fluoroalkanes do not react as readily with

Illustration of how a leg amputation was performed in 1592. Before anaesthetics, surgery was a painful last resort.

chemicals in living cells. Just over thirty years ago, the anaesthetic 2-bromo-2-chloro-1,1,1-trifluoroethane was used for the first time in hospitals. Its trade name is Halothane. The fluorine atoms in halothane make it unreactive, non toxic and non-flammable. The chlorine atom produces anaesthesia. The bromine atom raises the boiling point so that Halothane is a liquid at room temperature and can be stored easily.

Understanding the chemistry of anaesthetics has made modern surgery safe and bearable. How can we predict the behaviour of new halo-compounds before we test them out on humans?

2-bromo-2-chloro-1,1,1-trifluoroethane

14..1 Haloalkanes

Drug companies have developed many other anaesthetics and, like trichloromethane, many are **haloalkanes**.

A haloalkane is an alkane in which one or more of the hydrogen atoms have been replaced by a halogen atom. Haloalkanes are also called **halogenoalkanes**.

The compounds shown in Fig. 1 are all haloalkanes. You may need to revise page 165 in Chapter 11 if you are uncertain about naming haloalkanes. Remember that when there is more than one halogen in the compound, the halogens are listed in alphabetical order.

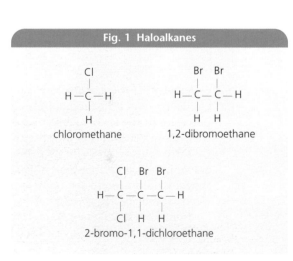

Fig. 1 Haloalkanes

chloromethane

1,2-dibromoethane

2-bromo-1,1-dichloroethane

The carbon–halogen bond

Haloalkanes are covalently bonded to make simple molecules. Within the haloalkane molecule, the halogen atoms are more electronegative than the carbon atoms. Each halogen atom attracts electrons towards itself and away from the carbon atom. We say that the halogen atom **withdraws** electrons from the covalent bond. This produces a small negative charge on the halogen atom and a small positive charge on the carbon atom. The result is that the carbon–halogen bond is **polar**; it has a **permanent dipole**.

The dipole tends to attract other charged molecules. Molecules with positive regions are attracted to the halogen atoms while molecules with negative regions are attracted to the carbon atom. This attraction is often the first step in a chemical reaction.

As Fig. 2 shows, the structure of haloalkanes is very similar to that of the corresponding alkane; even the bond angles are the same.

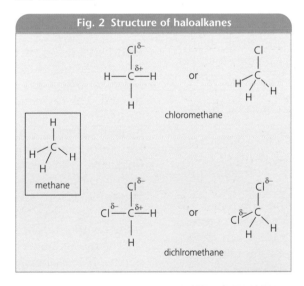

Fig. 2 Structure of haloalkanes

chloromethane

methane

dichloromethane

Chloromethane is a starting point for the manufacture of the explosive TNT.

---

1 Draw the structural formula for

a 2,2-dibromo-1,1-dichloropropane

b 1,2-dichloro-1,2-dibromopropane

c 2-chloro-2-methylbutane

2 Mark the position of the permanent dipoles in the formulae that you have drawn for question 1.

Primary, secondary and tertiary haloalkanes

Haloalkanes containing one halogen atom can be classified as primary, secondary or tertiary haloalkanes, according to the position of the halogen atom in the molecule.

- A primary haloalkane has two hydrogen atoms bonded to the carbon with the halogen atom:

$$Cl - \underset{\underset{H}{|}}{\overset{\overset{H}{|}}{C}} - R$$

- A secondary haloalkane has one hydrogen atom bonded to the carbon with the halogen atom:

$$Cl - \underset{\underset{R}{|}}{\overset{\overset{R}{|}}{C}} - H$$

- A tertiary haloalkane has no hydrogen atoms bonded to the carbon atom with the halogen atom:

$$Cl - \underset{\underset{R}{|}}{\overset{\overset{R}{|}}{C}} - R$$

3 Are the following primary, secondary or tertiary haloalkanes?

a 2-chloro-2-methylbutane?

b 1-chloropropane?

c 2-chloropropane?

Table 1 Physical properties of haloalkanes				
Haloalkane	Formula	Melting point °C	Boiling point °C	Density g cm⁻³
chloromethane	CH_3Cl	−97	24	0.92
chloroethane	C_2H_5Cl	−136	12	0.90
1-chlorobutane	$CH_2ClCH_2CH_2CH_3$	−123	79	0.89
2-chlorobutane	$CH_3CHClCH_2CH_3$	−121	68	0.87
2-chloro-2-methylpropane	$CH_3CCl(CH_3)CH_3$	−25	51	0.84

Physical properties of haloalkanes

Most haloalkanes are liquids or gases at room temperature. The physical properties of five haloalkanes are summarised in Table 1.

The boiling points of the haloalkanes depend upon the intermolecular forces that operate. Haloalkanes with longer carbon chains have more points for induced dipole attraction between the molecules. This attraction means that more energy is required to overcome the intermolecular forces, so the boiling point of longer-chained haloalkanes is higher than that of shorter haloalkanes. For example, 1-chlorobutane has a higher boiling point than chloroethane, which in turn has a higher boiling point than chloromethane.

Comparing fluoro- and chloroalkanes

If you compare the boiling point of a fluoroalkane with that of a corresponding chloroalkane you find that it is the size of the halogen that makes the difference. So, fluoromethane has a lower boiling point than chloromethane which in turn has a lower boiling point than bromomethane.

The number of halogen atoms per molecule also has an effect. A bromoalkane with two bromine atoms boils at a higher temperature than a bromoalkane with only one bromine atom (see Table 2).

4 What would be the state of each of the haloalkanes in Table 1 at 25 °C?

5 Use the information given in Table 2 to plot graphs of the boiling points of:

a chloroalkanes with 1,2,3 and 4 carbons;

b bromoalkanes with 1,2,3 and 4 carbons;

c iodoalkanes with 1,2,3 and 4 carbons.

d Explain how the graphs show the effect of adding halogens to alkane molecules.

Table 2 Boiling points of haloalkanes	
Primary haloalkane	boiling point K
Fluoromethane	195
Chloromethane	249
Chloroethane	258.4
1-chloropropane	319.7
1-chlorobutane	351.5
Bromomethane	277
bromoethane	311.5
1-bromopropane	344.1
1-bromobutane	374.7
Iodomethane	316
iodoethane	345.4
1-iodopropane	375.5
1-iodobutane	403.6

Bond strengths in haloalkanes

The strength of the carbon–halogen bond in a haloalkane depends on the type of halogen present. The carbon–fluorine bond is the strongest and a great deal of energy is need to break it (Table 3). This means that substances containing carbon and fluorine tend to be unreactive. The carbon–chlorine bond is not as strong as the carbon–fluorine bond but is still strong enough to give stability to compounds containing carbon and chlorine. As a result, these compounds are also not very reactive.

The most famous but least environmentally popular haloalkanes are the **chlorofluorocarbons** or CFCs. In these alkanes, every hydrogen atom has been replaced by either a fluorine atom or a chlorine atom. Many molecular formulae are possible. The names and formulae of some CFCs are given in Table 4.

Table 3 Bond dissociation enthalpies	
Bond	Bond dissociation enthalpy kJ mol⁻¹
C–F	467
C–Cl	346
C–Br	290
C–I	228

Molecular formula	Name	CFC designation	Uses
$CFCl_3$	trichloro-fluoromethane	CFC11	blowing foam plastics, refrigeration, air conditioning
CF_2Cl_2	dichloro-difluoromethane	CFC12	blowing foam plastics, refridgeration, air conditioning, aerosol propellant, sterilsation and food freezing
$C_2F_3Cl_3$	trichloro-trifluoroethane	CFC113	solvent
$C_2F_4Cl_2$	dichloro-tetrafluoroethane	CFC114	blowing foam plastics, refrigeration, air conditioning
C_2F_5Cl	chloro-pentafluoroethane	CFC115	refrigeration, air conditioning

Table 4 Some CFCs and their uses

Halon fire extinguishers, once used on fires near electrical equipment, are now being replaced by carbon dioxide gas extingusihers

Chlorofluorocarbons

CFCs are very stable compounds because of their strong carbon–fluorine and carbon–chlorine bonds and they persist in the atmosphere for many years. Some of the CFCs released in 1990s will still be present in the upper atmosphere in 2010. The carbon–bromine bond is less stable and bromoalkanes react more easily than fluoroalkanes and chloroalkanes. The carbon–iodine bond is the weakest of all and is easily broken in chemical reactions.

 Draw the structural formula for the CFCs in Table 4.

Halons

If the haloalkane contains bromine atoms as well as fluorine and chlorine atoms, it is called a **halon**. Halons are very unreactive and are heavier than air. They have been used in fire extinguishers because they can form a blanket over a fire, excluding oxygen and do not react themselves. Unfortunately, halons also cause the same environmental problems as CFCs and research is underway to find substitutes.

KEY FACTS

- Haloalkanes are alkanes in which one or more hydrogen atoms are replaced by a halogen atom.

- Haloalkanes are covalently bonded.

- The carbon-halogen bond is polar.

- Haloalkanes can be primary, secondary or tertiary, depending on how many hydrogen atoms are attached to the carbon atom with the halogen atom.

- Most haloalkanes are liquids or gases at room temperature.

- Longer carbon chained haloalkanes have higher boiling points than shorter carbon chained haloalkanes because more energy is need to overcome the induced dipole attractions.

- The C–F bond is the strongest carbon-halogen bond and the C–I bond is the weakest.

APPLICATION A

Infamous CFCs

When CFCs were first developed, their stability and lack of reactivity, together with the fact that they were odourless and tasteless, made them an excellent choice for use in aerosol sprays. They could act as the propellant in the aerosol, without affecting or reacting with the contents. Their lack of reactivity also led to their use in fire extinguishers and as solvents to dissolve oils and refrigerants. Their usage grew from the 1920s, reaching an all-time high in the 1960s. Only after this did we realise that our use of CFCs was storing up serious environmental problems.

CFCs have carbon-fluorine bonds and carbon to chlorine bonds. The carbon–fluorine bond is very stable, but in the upper atmosphere, the carbon to chlorine bond breaks to release an atom of chlorine, called a chlorine free radical. The equation is:

$$CF_3Cl \rightarrow CF_3{}^{\cdot} + Cl^{\cdot}$$

This is called homolytic fission because one electron from the covalent C–Cl bond ends up with the chlorine radical and the other electron with the CF_3 radical. The dot represents the unpaired electron. The chlorine free radical is very reactive.

Oxygen in the upper atmosphere forms a layer of ozone gas, O_3. Ozone absorbs UV light and prevents it from reaching the Earth. UV light has damaging effects on living organisms, causing increased rates of skin cancer in human beings.

The chlorine radical reacts with ozone, forming chlorine monoxide:

$$Cl + O_3 \rightarrow ClO^{\cdot} + O_2$$

Chlorine monoxide is also a free radical and since oxygen atoms are also present in the upper atmosphere, the two react:

$$ClO^{\cdot} + O \rightarrow Cl^{\cdot} + O_2$$

The chlorine radical is regenerated. The overall result is a reaction between ozone and oxygen atoms:

$$O_3 + O \rightarrow 2O_2$$

This is a chain reaction. It is estimated that one chlorine radical can break down 100 000 ozone moleules. Less ozone in the upper atmosphere means more UV radiation reaching the Earth and by the late 1970s scientists had detected a thinning of the ozone layer. This thinning has now developed into holes over Antarctica and more recently over the Arctic.

In 1987 an international treaty called the Montreal Protocol restricted the use of CFCs and in 1989, 93 nations agreed to phase out their production and use of CFCs.

Which brings us back to the stability of CFCs. It will be many years before their ozone depleting ability decreases. Some CFCs have a lifetime of up to 100 years in the atmosphere so it will be well into this century before depleting ozone ceases to be a problem.

Coloured satellite map showing the ozone hole over Antarctica in September 1999. The hole had reached its maximum area for 1999; a massive 9.8 million sequare miles.

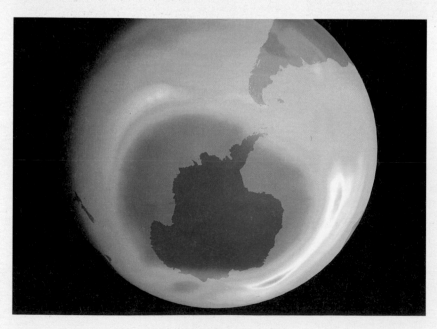

1 Oxygen exists in two molecular forms, O_2 and O_3. Draw dot and cross diagrams to show the bonding in O_2 and O_3

2 Describe how CFCs deplete the ozone layer.

3 Use dot and cross diagrams to explain why chlorine monoxide is a free radical.

4 Ozone is constantly being regenerated in the upper atmosphere by the action of cosmic particles on oxygen. When the rate of regeneration is less than the rate of depletion, what is the effect on the Earth?

5 Explain how our use of CFCs illustrates the positive and negative effects of science.

14.2 Chemical reactions of haloalkanes

Haloalkanes cannot undergo addition reactions because they have no double bonds or triple bonds. They are already saturated with hydrogen atoms. Haloalkanes can undergo two types of reactions:

- **Substitution reactions**; a halogen atom is swapped for another atom or group of atoms in the haloalkane;

- **Elimination reactions**; one hydrogen atom and one halogen atom are removed from the molecule, and a double bond forms between two carbon atoms. This produces an alkene.

Substitution reactions

The polar nature of the carbon–halogen bond means that molecules or ions with a lone pair of electrons are attracted to the electron deficient carbon atom of the carbon-halogen bond. Remember that electrons are drawn towards the halogen atom because it is more electronegative. A molecule with a lone pair of electrons is called a **nucleophile** .

The nucleophile must be able to donate a pair of electrons to form a covalent bond with the electron deficient carbon atom. When a nucleophile is attracted to a carbon atom in a haloalkane, substitution occurs. This reaction is called **nucleophilic substitution**. The carbon–halogen bond is broken and a carbon–nucleophile bond forms. Haloalkanes undergo nucleophilic substitution with:

- Hydroxyl ions;
- Ammonia;
- Cyanide ions.

7 Which haloalkane is used to make:

a ethanol?

b 1-butanol?

c 2-butanol?

Nucleophilic substitution by hydroxide ions

The electron configuration of the hydroxide is:

lone pair of electrons

The lone pairs of electrons are areas of high electron density and are attracted to the carbon atom of the carbon–halogen bond.

An example of this reaction is the reaction between 1-bromopropane and sodium hydroxide solution. The overall reaction is:

$$CH_3CH_2CH_2Br + OH^- \rightarrow CH_3CH_2CH_2OH + Br^-$$
1-bromopropane   1-propanol

We show the mechanism as:

The curly arrow shows the movement of a pair of electrons. The OH^- nucleophile is attracted to the carbon atom and donates one of its lone pairs of electrons to form a covalent bond. The carbon–bromine bond breaks, forming a bromide ion.

Water reacts slowly with haloalkanes, but if sodium hydroxide is used to provide the hydroxide ions and the reactants are boiled, the reaction proceeds much more rapidly.

Fluoroalkanes do not react with hydroxide ions because the carbon–fluorine bond is too strong and does not break. Chloro-, bromo- and iodoalkanes react with increasing vigour as the atomic number increases.

Nucleophilic substitution by ammonia

The electron configuration of ammonia is:

A lone pair of electrons forms an area of high electron density, which is attracted to the electron deficient carbon atom of the carbon-halogen bond.

When ammonia reacts with 1-bromopropane, the mechanism is:

The curly arrow shows the movement of a pair of electrons.

The lone pair of electrons in the ammonia molecule is attracted to the slightly positive carbon atom of the carbon–bromine bond. The lone pair of electrons is used to form a covalent bond with the carbon atom and the carbon–bromine bond breaks.

2-methylethylamine is the substance in chocolate thought to be responsible for making people chocoholics. It can be prepared by reacting ammonia with a haloalkane.

The overall reaction is:

$$CH_3CH_2CH_2Br + NH_3 \rightarrow CH_3CH_2CH_2NH_2 + HBr$$
1-bromopropane   propylamine

The hydrogen bromide produced by this reaction will react with ammonia to produce ammonium bromide. The propylamine produced acts as a nucleophile and reacts further with the haloalkane. The yield of propylamine is less than expected theoretically because secondary, tertiary and quaternary ammonium salts are formed. Using a large excess of concentrated ammonia ensures that the main produce is the primary amine.

8 Which haloalkane could be used to make butylamine. Write an equation for the reaction.

Nucleophilic substitution by cyanide ions

The electron configuration of the cyanide ion is:

lone pair $\longrightarrow \left[\begin{array}{ccc} \times & & \times \\ \times & C & \times \\ \times & & \times \end{array} \; N \; \begin{array}{c} \bullet \bullet \end{array} \right]^{-}$ lone pair
of electrons   of electrons

The negative charge on the carbon atom in the cyanide group is attracted to the slightly positive charge of the carbon atom in the carbon-halogen bond.

When 1-bromopropane reacts with the cyanide nucleophile, the mechanism is:

$$-\overset{|}{\underset{|}{C}}{}^{\delta+}\!\!-\!Br^{\delta-} \qquad \overset{\bullet\bullet}{CN^{-}}$$

The carbon atom of the CN^- ion donates a pair of electrons to the carbon-bromine bond and the C–Br bond breaks. Butanenitrile and a bromide ion form.

The overall reaction is:

$$CH_3CH_2CH_2Br + CN^- \rightarrow CH_3CH_2CH_2CN + Br^-$$

Nucleophilic substition by ammonia in haloalkanes is used to produce hexane-1,6-diamine to make nylon.

Drug manufacture

Many drugs are complicated organic molecules that may contain several functional groups and ring and chain structures. Manufacturing them involves a series of steps to build up the molecule from a simple starting compound. Phenobarbitone is used in sleeping pills and to control epilepsy. Its structure is:

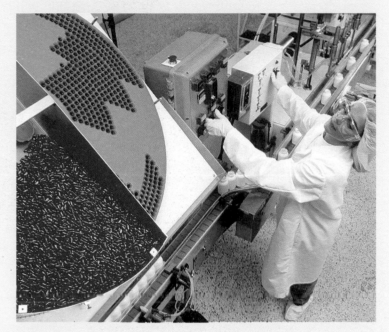

The starting compound is methyl benzene and the first four steps in its manufacture are:

STEP 1   STEP 2   STEP 3

methyl benzene

Amphetamines

Amphetamines were once used to treat obesity, mild depression and some behaviour disorders in children. Today, they are 'pep-pills', that provide a sense of well-being and alertness but that can lead to serious addiction. Their chemical structure is similar to that of adrenaline. This hormone is made naturally in the body where it acts as a stimulant on the central nervous system. Amphetamines are made using an organic halogen compound as an intermediate. The synthesis is:

1-phenylpropan-2-ol

Phenobarbitone

1 Which step increases the length of the carbon chain?

2 Which reagents and what conditions are used in this step?

3 Describe the mechanism of this reaction.

4 What mechanism is involved in the first step?

5 Which compound is the

a hydrocarbon;

b organic acid;

c nitrile?

6 Step 3 is an hydrolysis reaction. What reagents and conditions will be needed?

Amphetamines

7 What is the mechanism for the reaction shown in step 2 in diagram C?

8 Why is concentrated ammonia used instead of dilute ammonia?

9 Why is amphetamine a primary amine

Sodium or potassium cyanide dissolved in ethanol are usually used to provide the cyanide ion, so that either sodium bromide or potassium bromide forms.

This reaction is very important because it changes the length of the carbon chain. In the above example the reactant has three carbon atoms in its chain and the product has four. When chemists are manufacturing an organic chemical, they prefer to start with a chemical with a hydrocarbon with the same number of carbon atoms as the chemical they want to make. But sometimes, it is not possible to start with the correct length carbon chain; it has to be lengthened or shortened. The reaction with the cyanide ion lengthens the chain by one carbon atom and so provides a valuable manufacturing route. For example, the nitrile produced can now be hydrolysed to produce a carboxylic acid.

Refluxing ethanenitrile with dilute hydro-chloric acid produces ethanoic acid (Fig. 3):

$$CH_3CN(l) + 2H_2O(l) + HCl(aq) \rightarrow CH_3COOH(aq) + NH_4Cl(aq)$$
ethanenitrile   ethanoic acid

Elimination reactions

In an elimination reaction a haloalkane forms an alkene and a hydrogen halide. Elimination reactions are usually carried out by reacting the haloalkane with a strong base, such as potassium hydroxide or sodium hydroxide in ethanol to provide OH⁻ ions. The hydroxide ions with their lone pair of electrons can accept a proton and act as a base.

When bromoethane and potassium hydroxide in ethanol react, the elimination reaction is:

bromoethane $\xrightarrow[\text{in ethanol}]{\text{KOH}}$ ethene $+$ H₂O $+$ Br⁻

However, the yield in this reaction is less than one per cent, so a more suitable example is the reaction between 2-bromopropane and potassium hydroxide. The elimination reaction is:

2-bromopropane $\xrightarrow[\text{in ethanol}]{\text{KOH}}$ propene $+$ H₂O $+$ Br⁻

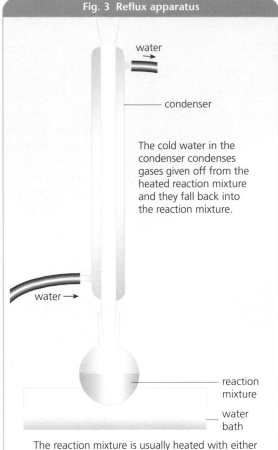

Fig. 3 Reflux apparatus

water →

condenser

The cold water in the condenser condenses gases given off from the heated reaction mixture and they fall back into the reaction mixture.

water →

reaction mixture

water bath

The reaction mixture is usually heated with either a water bath or an electric heater.

The reflux apparatus keeps the reaction mixture at its boiling point for as long as is needed for the reaction to occur.

9 Draw the structural formula for:

a pentanenitrile;

b propanenitrile.

10 Explain why nucleophilic substitution by cyanide ions is an important reaction in the chemical industry.

11 How could you make:

a butanoic acid from 1-chloropropane?

b pentanoic acid from 1-chlorobutane?

The mechanism for the reaction between 2-bromopropane and potassium hydroxide is:

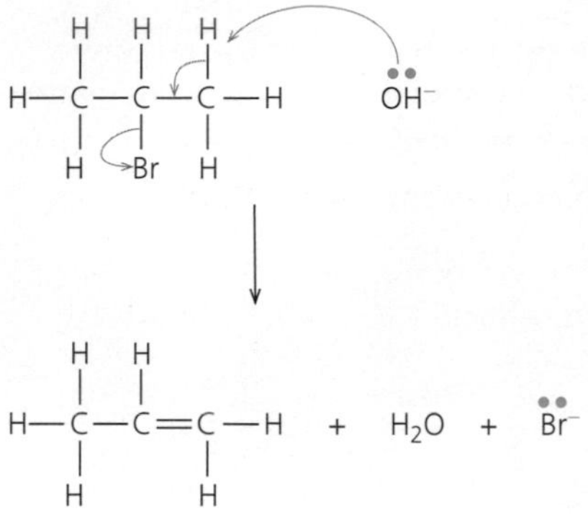

1 The curly arrows show the movement of a pair of electrons. Electron density is drawn towards the bromine atom and the C-Br bond breaks. A bromide ion forms.

2 The lone pair of electrons in the hydroxide ion is donated to a hydrogen atom. A molecule of water is made and a double bond forms between the two carbon atoms.

But you have read earlier in this chapter that the hydroxide ion also acts as a nucleophile towards haloalkanes and carries out nucleophilic substitution reactions. This means that two reactions with the hydroxide ion are possible; either a substitution reaction,to make an alcohol, or an elimination reaction. Which reaction takes place depends on the conditions of the reaction (see Table 5). In some conditions both substitution and elimination reactions take place, especially with secondary haloalkanes.

So elimination is much more likely with a strong base dissolved in ethanol at a high temperature. Whether the haloalkane is primary, secondary or tertiary also influences the type of reaction. Tertiary haloalkanes are more likely to undergo elimination reactions than secondary haloalkanes and secondary haloalkanes are more likely to undergo elimination than primary haloalkanes.

12 What are the likely products of the following reactions:

a chloromethane dissolved in ethanol with concentrated sodium hydroxide solution at high temperature?

b Chloroethane dissolved in water with a dilute solution of sodium hydroxide at room temperature?

Table 5 Predicting the products of reacting a haloalkane with an hydroxide

Conditions	elimination reaction	substitution reaction
Base	strong	weak
Solvent	ethanol	water
Temperature	high	low

KEY FACTS

- Haloalkanes undergo substitution reactions and elimination reactions.
- A halogen atom is swapped for another atom or a group of atoms in a substitution reaction.
- One hydrogen atom and one halogen atom are lost in an elimination reaction and an alkene is formed.
- Nucleophiles are attracted to the electron deficient carbon of the carbon-halogen bond.
- Haloalkanes undergo nucleophilic substitution with hydroxide ions, ammonia and cyanide ions.
- Haloakanes undergo elimination with hydroxide ions in ethanol.
- The conditions of the reaction help to determine whether a substitution or elimination reaction takes place between hydroxide ions and a haloalkane.

1 When 3-bromo-2-methylpentane, $(CH_3)_2CHCHBrCH_2CH_3$, reacts with aqueous potassium hydroxide, an alcohol is formed.

a Name the type of reaction taking place and give the role of the reagent .(2)

b Give the structure of the alcohol formed and outline a mechanism for its formation. (3)

c When 3-bromo-2-methylpentane reacts with ethanolic potassium hydroxide, two isomeric alkenes are formed.
  i) Name the type of reaction taking place and give the role of reagent. (2)
  ii) One of the reaction products is 2-methylpent-2-ene. Give the structure of this alkene and outline a mechanism for its formation. (4)
  iii) Give the structure of the second alkene which is also formed in this reaction. What type of stereoisomerism is shown by this compound? (2)

NEAB CH06 June 1999 Q4(Part)

2

a Name the type of reaction taking place when 2-bromopropane is converted into propene in the presence of a strong base. Outline a mechanism for this reaction. (5)

b Give the structural formula of 2-bromo-2-methylbutane. (1)

c Give the structural formula of the two alkenes obtained when 2-bromo-2-methylbutane reacts with ethanolic potassium hydroxide. Deduce the names of these two products. (4)

NEAB CH06 June 1996 Q4

3

a At room temperature, chloromethane reacts very slowly with aqueous sodium hydroxide to form methanol. Name and outline a mechanism for this reaction. (3)

b Explain why the above reaction is much faster when carried out at 80 °C rather than at room temperature. (2)

NEAB CH03 June 1996 Q6(Part)

4

a Give the structure of 3-bromopentane. (1)

b Name and outline the mechanism for the reaction taking place when 3-bromopentane is converted into pent-2-ene in the presence of a strong base. (5)

c What type of stereoisomerism is shown by pent-2-ene? (1)

NEAB CH06 March 1998 Q4(Part)

5

a Give the structure of 2-bromo-2,3-dimethylbutane. (1)

b Name the type of reaction which could be used to convert this compound into 2,3-dimethylbutan-2-ol and suggest a suitable reagent and appropriate conditions. (3)

NEAB CH06 February 1997 Q1(Part)

The chemistry of the ozone hole

You have probably read in the papers about the worldwide problem of releasing CFCs into the atmosphere. But why is there all this fuss?

The answer to this lies in the effect of ultra-violet (UV) radiation on the bonds between the halogens and carbon in haloalkanes. The strength of the bond between carbon and halogen decreases as you move down Group VII. So when a CFC gets into the stratosphere the chlorine is more easily removed by the UV radiation than the fluorine. Although CFCs are heavier than air, they still get into the upper atmosphere (the stratosphere) by being carried up by winds and air currents – in much the same way that dust from volcanoes can get there. There are two ways in which pollutants are removed from the air - deposition, when the rain 'washes' the pollutant out, and chemical reactions. The first option won't work because CFCs are insoluble in water. The second is a non-starter because CFCs are unreactive in the lower atmosphere.

So chlorine exists in the stratosphere as a free radical (Cl·) and this free radical is very reactive. It reacts with ozone (O_3) to produce oxygen and a chlorine-oxygen radical (ClO·).

This chlorine-oxygen radical reacts with an oxygen radical and then chlorine radical is once again set free to start the process all over again. Consequently the chlorine is not used up in the stratosphere in the destruction of the ozone. The chlorine will persist for tens of years according to current estimates. Cuts made now in CFC use could take decades to show up in the ozone layer. What makes the problem worse is that CFCs are supposed to have been reduced according to International agreements. But there seems to be a 'black market' in these chemicals as many developing countries are wanting to have the same consumer products as the 'developed countries' (e.g. refrigerators, freezers, foam rubber for insulation, furnishing, sound proofing, packaging, aerosols.).

1 Why are CFC's so stable? Explain in terms of the carbon-halogen bonding for each member of Group VII.

2 If CFC's are more dense than air - how is it that they get into the stratosphere? Why don't they just sink to the ground?

3

a Explain why a small amount of CFC can do a large amount of damage to the ozone layer.

b Write a few equations to illustrate the possible chemical mechanisms involved.

4 CFC's are useful because they are very stable. What makes them unstable in the upper atmosphere?

5 A suggestion for 'mending' the hole in the ozone layer has been made in a newspaper article. The writer suggests that we should send up balloons filled with ozone and let the ozone out at the height where the hole appears, so replacing the 'missing' ozone. Write a letter to the newspaper to explain why this may not work in practice.

6 The hole in the ozone layer is the subject of many claims and counter claims from governments, environmentalists and industry. At times there can be some dangerously over-simplified statements made. Sometimes the claims made are simply lies. Add to this the fact that our understanding of the issue is changing all the time and you can see how difficult it can be for members of the public to get hold of reliable, useful information.

a Research the subject of ozone depletion on the internet. This is probably the source of the most up to date information – but is also a source of the kind of wild claims made by people on all sides of the argument.

b Prepare a simple two page document giving the current state of understanding of ozone depletion and the likely implications of this problem. Your document should also include information about how people are responding to the challenge of ozone depletion and your considered opinion on the likely developments in the situation over the next 25 years. Remember to keep records of all of the documents, websites and other sources of information you use to produce your final report.

15 The alcohols

People have fermented fruit juices and solutions of sugar in water to produce alcoholic drinks for thousands of years. Workers who built the Eygptian pyramids were given a beer ration and since early times alcoholic drinks have been taxed by kings and governments to provide revenue. Recently, the amount of tax payable has been based on the percentage of alcohol in the drink. In the UK, spirits such as whisky, gin and vodka contain the highest percentages of alcohol and this used to be measured in degrees proof. Historically, the accepted method of determining the alcohol content of a spirit involved mixing the spirit with water and then pouring the mixture onto gunpowder of specified composition. 100 degrees proof spirit is able to just ignite the gunpowder. In the UK, 100 degrees proof spirit contains 57.155% alcohol by volume at 20 °C. In the USA 100 degrees proof spirit contains 50% alcohol by volume at 20 °C. Today the amount of alcohol in most drinks is stated on the bottle as a percentage by volume.

Pure alcohol is poisonous and is not legally available for consumption in this country. Whilst limited intakes of dilute solutions loosen inhibitions and relax muscles, larger intakes can cause unconsciousness, vomiting and even liver damage with prolonged use. This liver damage kills hundreds of alcoholics in the UK every year. It is illegal to distil wine or beer in the UK to obtain alcohol without an excise license. These are usually only granted to companies such as whisky distilleries.

Making alcoholic drinks is a complex craft. Wine, which can contain anywhere between 8 and 15% alcohol, is produced with great care. Wine tasters (top) can check if a wine is good. Whisky (right) is usually about 40% alcohol.

15.1   The homologous series of alcohols

The term alcohol is commonly used to describe ethanol, CH_3CH_2OH, usually with reference to alcoholic drinks. In chemistry books the same term refers to the complete homologous series of alcohols of which ethanol is just one member (see Chapter 11). Fig. 1 shows some examples of alcohols.

Alcohols consist of an hydroxyl group covalently bonded to an alkyl or cycloalkyl chain. The hydroxyl, or OH group, is the functional group. In this chapter we see how alcohols are classified, how they are produced industrially and look at some of their physical and chemical properties.

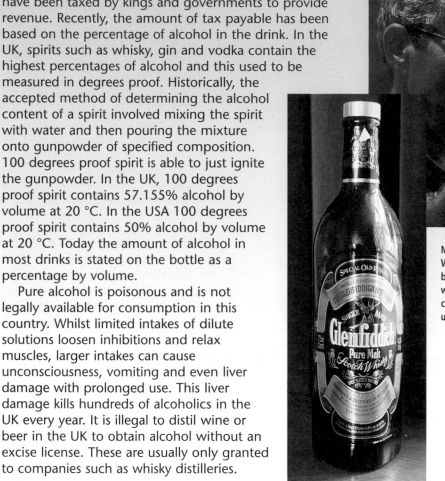

Fig. 1 Alcohols

propan-1-ol

ethanol

cyclohexanol

H H
| |
H—C—C—O—H
| |
H H
ethanol

H H H
| | |
H—C—C—C—H
| | |
H OH H
propan-2-ol

H CH₃ H
| | |
H—C—C—C—H
| | |
H OH H
2-methylpropan-2-ol

Classifying alcohols

Alcohols can be classified as **primary**, **secondary** or **tertiary**, depending on the number of carbon atoms attached to the carbon atom with the hydroxyl group. Primary alcohols such as ethanol have one carbon atom attached to the carbon with the hydroxyl group. Secondary alcohols such as propan-2-ol have two carbon atoms attached to the carbon atom with the hydroxyl group. Tertiary alcohols such as 2-methylpropan-2-ol have three carbon atoms attached to the carbon atom with the hydroxyl group. Fig. 2 summarises the general structures of primary, secondary and tertiary alcohols (note that complete structures are not shown.)

1 Draw the structural formulae and give the names of the first six alcohols that have a hydroxyl group on the first carbon atom in the chain.

2 Draw all the possible positional isomers for an alcohol with five carbon atoms.

3 Which of the following are primary, secondary or tertiary alcohols?

a 2-methylbutan-1-ol

b pentan-3-ol

c butan-1-ol

d methanol

e decan-3-ol

f Draw the structural formula for each of the alcohols above.

4 All alcohols with three or more carbon atoms have positional isomers. Draw the structural formula for a primary, a secondary and a tertiary alcohol with the molecular formula C_4H_9OH

Fig. 2 Primary, secondary and tertiary alcohols

Primary alcohol

H
|
C—C—OH
|
H

Secondary alcohol

H
|
C—C—OH
|
C

Tertiary alcohol

C
|
C—C—OH
|
C

EXTENSION ## Monohydric, dihydric, trihydric and polyhydric alcohols

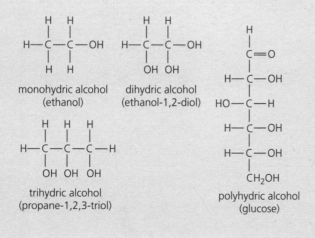

monohydric alcohol
(ethanol)

dihydric alcohol
(ethanol-1,2-diol)

trihydric alcohol
(propane-1,2,3-triol)

polyhydric alcohol
(glucose)

Alcohols can also be classified according to the number of hydroxyl groups present in a molecule. Ethanol has one hydroxyl group and is a **monohydric** alcohol.

A **dihydric** alcohol has two hydroxyl groups per molecule, a **trihydric** alcohol has three hydroxyl groups per molecule and a **polyhydric** alcohol has many hydroxyl groups per molecule.

Ethane-1,2-diol, the ingredient of antifreeze is a dihydric alcohol. Propane-1,2,3-triol, sometimes called glycerol, is a trihydric alcohol and is an essential component of all fat molecules. Glucose has 5 hydroxyl groups per molecule and so is a polyhydric alcohol.

KEY FACTS

■ Alcohols are a homologous series with hydroxyl functional groups.

■ The chemical names of all alcohols end in -ol.

■ Alcohols can be classified as primary, secondary or tertiary depending on the number of carbon atoms bonded to the carbon atom carrying the hydroxyl group.

Producing alcohol

Alcohol can be produced by fermentation of sugar or by hydration of ethene. Typically, alcohol intended for human consumption in alcoholic drinks is made by **fermentation** whereas alcohol required for industrial processes is produced by **hydration**.

Fermentation of sugars

Ethanol in alcoholic drinks is made by the fermentation of sugars in fruits, usually grapes. The skins of grapes are naturally covered in microscopic fungi called yeasts, which ferment the sugars in the grapes to alcohol. Fermentation depends on anaerobic respiration which is respiration without oxygen. Initially, the yeasts respire aerobically but the oxygen in the solution is rapidly used up and respiration switches to anaerobic. Yeast is a living organism and respiration is controlled by a series of enzymes, collectively called **zymase**.

The reaction is complex and involves a number of stages but can be summarised as:

$$C_6H_{12}O_6(aq) \xrightarrow{40\ ^\circ C} 2CH_3CH_2OH(aq) + 2CO_2(g)$$
$$\text{glucose} \qquad\qquad \text{ethanol}$$

The best wines are made from grapes with sufficient sugar to produce high levels of ethanol. Fermentation produces between 8 and 15 per cent ethanol by volume in water. At this concentration of ethanol, the environment becomes toxic to the yeast and fermentation stops. Drinks with higher percentages of ethanol have to have extra ethanol added (the fortified wines like port and sherry) or be distilled (the spirits like whisky and rum).

APPLICATION A ## Champagne bubbles

In a good champagne the bubbles continue to rise steadily for a long time after the champagne has been poured in to the glass. Cheaper sparkling wines usually have a shorter, sharp burst of bubbling. One theory claims that when carbon dioxide is produced during the production of champagne, it reacts with the ethanol to form diethylpyrocarbonate, $C_2H_5OCOOCOOC_2H_5$.

Diethylpyrocarbonate decomposes slowly to release carbon dioxide and hence champagne produces a slow release of carbon dioxide bubbles. If carbon dioxide is simply added to wine under pressure, it dissolves and does not react. The pressure is released when the bottle is uncorked and the carbon dioxide is released quickly.

1 Write an equation to show the release of carbon dioxide from diethylpyrocarbonate.

2 Draw the structural formula for diethylpyrocarbonate.

3 What effect will chilling champagne have on the release of carbon dioxide bubbles?

Hydration of ethene

The cracking of longer-chained alkanes to produce shorter alkanes suitable for motor fuel also produces large amounts of ethene gas. This gas is used as the feedstock or starting point for a range of important organic chemicals (see Chapter 12) Ethene gas is used to make about one third of the world's ethanol supply.

If a molecule of water is added to a molecule of ethene, an ethanol molecule is made. This reaction is called hydration. The details of this reaction are shown in Fig. 3.

On an industrial scale, ethene is reacted with steam at 300 °C and 6 000 kPa in the presence of a phosphoric(V) acid catalyst.

This petrol attendant in Brazil is filling a car with ethanol fuel.

Fig. 3 Hydration of ethanol

Ethene can be converted to ethanol using concentrated sulphuric acid as a catalyst. When ethene is bubbled through concentrated sulphuric acid, ethyl hydrogen sulphate is formed:

$$\underset{\text{ethene}}{\text{H}_2\text{C}=\text{CH}_2} \text{ (g)} + \underset{\substack{\text{concentrated} \\ \text{sulphuric acid}}}{\text{H}_2\text{SO}_4\text{(l)}} \longrightarrow \underset{\text{ethyl hydrogen sulphate}}{\text{H}_3\text{C}-\text{CH}_2-\text{OSO}_2\text{OH (l)}}$$

Adding water hydrolyses these to form ethyl hydrogen sulphate, ethanol and sulphuric acid:

$$\underset{\substack{\text{ethyl hydrogen} \\ \text{sulphate}}}{\text{CH}_3\text{CH}_2\text{OSO}_3\text{H(l)}} + \underset{\text{water}}{\text{H}_2\text{O(l)}} \longrightarrow \underset{\text{ethanol}}{\text{CH}_3\text{CH}_2\text{OH(l)}} + \underset{\substack{\text{sulphuric} \\ \text{acid}}}{\text{H}_2\text{SO}_4\text{(l)}}$$

The sulphuric acid catalyst takes part in the reaction, but remains unchanged at the end. The overall result is the addition of water across the double bond. The process is carried out industrially using a catalyst of phosphoric acid.

$$\underset{\text{ethene}}{\text{CH}_2\text{CH}_2\text{(g)}} + \underset{\text{water}}{\text{H}_2\text{O(l)}} \xrightarrow[\text{H}_3\text{PO}_4 \text{ catalyst}]{300\,°\text{C, 60 atmospheres}} \underset{\text{ethanol}}{\text{CH}_3\text{CH}_2\text{OH(l)}}$$

Uses of industrially produced ethanol

The ethanol produced may be used as a fuel, a solvent or as an intermediate in the production of other chemicals. It is not usually suitable for human consumption, but can be purchased in shops as methylated spirits.

Methylated spirits is a mixture of industrial alcohol with a small amount of methanol and a purple dye to distinguish it from pure ethanol. Methylated spirits is highly toxic due to the methanol and is not suitable for human consumption even when diluted. It avoids excise duty (tax) because it is not safe for human consumption.

5 Write an equation to show how ethene is produced when decane is cracked.

6 Write an equation for the combustion of ethanol.

KEY FACTS

■ Ethanol for human consumption is produced by the fermentation of sugars by yeasts.

■ Fermentation is catalysed by a series of enzymes called zymases.

■ Most ethanol for use in industry is produced by the hydration of ethene gas.

15.2 Physical properties of alcohols

As with alkanes, alkenes and haloalkanes, trends in the physical properties of the primary alcohols depend upon the number of carbon atoms per molecule. The physical properties of the secondary and tertiary alcohols are, in addition, influenced by the shape of the molecules. Table 1 gives some physical data for some alcohols.

The table shows that the boiling points of the primary alcohols increase with the length of the carbon chain. There are two types of intermolecular forces that operate between alcohol molecules. The carbon chains of the alcohols have weak induced dipoles. These set up induced dipole-dipole intermolecular attractions between alcohol molecules. In order for an alcohol to boil, enough energy has to be supplied to overcome these intermolecular forces. The longer chain primary alcohols have more sites for

Table 1 Physical properties of simple alcohols				
Alcohol	Structural formula	Melting point /°C	Boiling point /°C	State at 25 °C
methanol		−94	65	liquid
ethanol		−117	78	liquid
propan-1-ol		−127	98	liquid
propan-2-ol		−89	83	liquid
butan-1-ol		−90	117	liquid
butan-2-ol		−115	100	liquid
2-methylpropan-2-ol		26	82	liquid

intermolecular attractions and therefore have higher boiling points. Secondary and tertiary alcohols have structures that do not allow the alcohols to lie so close together and so intermolecular forces are weaker than in the primary isomer and the boiling points are lower as a consequence.

Secondly, hydrogen bonds exist between the oxygen atoms in the hydroxyl groups and the hydrogen atoms in the hydroxyl groups. The hydroxyl group is polar with the electron density drawn towards the oxygen atom. This gives the oxygen atom a small negative charge (δ^-) and the hydrogen atom a small positive charge (δ^+). This part of the molecule has a permanent dipole.

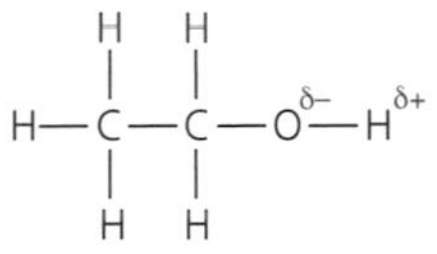

The oxygen atom of one molecule attracts the hydrogen atom of another molecule and a hydrogen bond forms. The hydrogen bonds that form between molecules of decan-1-ol are shown in Fig. 4.

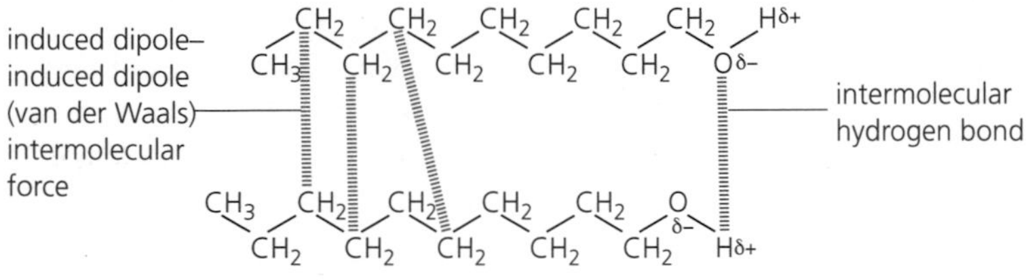

Solubility of alcohols in water

Wine and beer are mixtures of ethanol and water with dissolved flavourings and sugars. In order for the water and ethanol to mix, the ethanol molecules and the water molecules must be attracted to each other. Ethanol and water mix completely because hydrogen bonds form between the hydroxyl groups in ethanol and the hydroxyl groups in water molecules (Fig. 5).

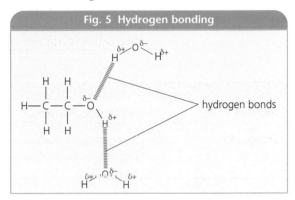

Fig. 5 Hydrogen bonding

But, as the primary alcohol chain increases in length. the solubility of the alcohols in water decreases. This is because the induced dipole-dipole attractions are greater between the longer chained alcohols and the alcohol molecules are more attracted to each other than to water molecules. So they do not dissolve.

7 Explain why alkanes with low molecular mass are gases whereas alcohols with low molecular mass are liquids.

8 How would you expect the solubility of propan-1-ol in water to compare to the solubility of decan-1-ol in water? Explain your answer.

Fig. 4 Hydrogen bonding in decan-1-ol

induced dipole–induced dipole (van der Waals) intermolecular force

intermolecular hydrogen bond

15.3 Chemical properties of alcohols

When alcohols react, the reaction either involves the hydroxyl group, the carbon skeleton or both. The most familiar reaction involving the complete molecule is combustion. Almost all alcohols burn easily, often with a pale blue flame, to produce carbon dioxide and water. Reactions involving the hydroxyl group have two possibilities:

- the C–O bond is broken (substitution and elimination reactions);

- the O–H bond is broken to release a hydrogen ion (the alcohol acts as an acid).

Alcohols are so valuable in industry as intermediate compounds simply because they can undergo so many different types of reaction.

a What are intermediate compounds?

b Explain why an alcohol acts as an acid when the O–H bond breaks.

Oxidation reactions

Combustion is one type of oxidation reaction. In organic chemistry, oxidation is regarded as the gain of an oxygen atom or the loss of two hydrogen atoms. Reduction is the opposite and can be considered as the loss of an oxygen atom or the gain of two hydrogen atoms. The chemical that supplies the oxygen or removes the hydrogen is called the oxidising agent. The chemical that removes the oxygen or supplies the hydrogen is called the reducing agent.

Oxidation of alcohols involve both the carbon skeleton and the functional hydroxyl group. Primary, secondary and tertiary alcohols give different products on oxidation:

$$\text{Primary alcohol} \xrightarrow{+[O]} \text{aldehyde} \xrightarrow{+[O]} \text{carboxylic acid}$$

$$\text{Secondary alcohol} \xrightarrow{+[O]} \text{ketone}$$

$$\text{Tertiary alcohol} \rightarrow \text{DOES NOT OXIDISE}$$

APPLICATION B

Singed eyebrows are off the menu

A new clean-burning fuel for lighting fires could end the ritual havoc of the summer barbecue with its billowing smoke, blackened sausages and accidental flash fires.

The fuel, which comes as a nondrip gel, is made from almost equal amounts of ethanol, fermented from sugar cane, and cellulose. It burns without smoke, giving off water and carbon dioxide as waste products. "It's nontoxic, won't flare and doesn't taint food," says Nick Malpeli, director of Kwick Cook of Bristol, the firm that developed the fuel.

Conventional fire-lighting fluids are based on kerosene (paraffin), a highly flammable petrochemical that can flare up if you douse the charcoal with too much fluid. Solid lighters are usually based on hexamine, a compound often used in explosives. It produces a lot of smoke, which contains potential carcinogens and blackens food with soot.

By contrast, only about 0.1 per cent of the new fuel turns to soot. The mixture of cellulose and ethanol would naturally burn with a bluish flame. But, for safety reasonson, Kwik Cook has added table salt to turn the flame a highly visible yellow. Tiny amounts of Bitrex, an extremely bitter substance, have been added to discourage people from consuming the fuel for its alcohol. Trial sales of the gel are now starting in Britain.

Source: Matt Walker. New Scientist, June 1999

1 Write an equation for the combustion of alcohol.

2 Write an equation for the combustion of the alkane kerosine ($C_{10}H_{22}$).

3 Write an equation for the combustion of hexamine ($C_6H_{13}NH_2$).

4 Suggest a reason why kerosine and hexamine both produce more smoke and soot than ethanol.

Oxidation of primary alcohols

When ethanol is oxidised, two hydrogen atoms are removed, one from the carbon skeleton and one from the hydroxyl group.

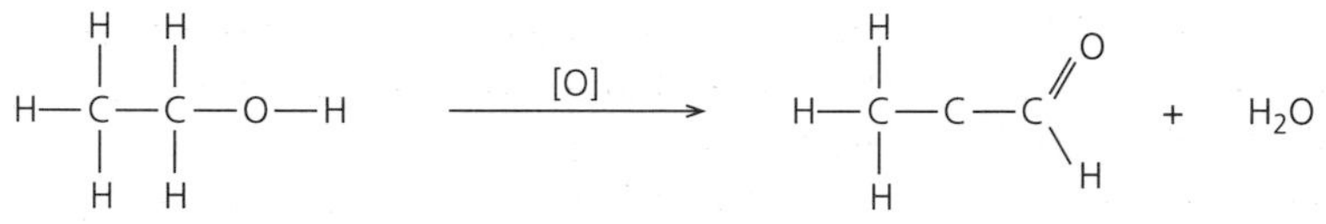

This produces a new functional group, the **-CHO group**, or **aldehyde group**. The names of aldehydes all end in 'al'. The first part of the name is taken from the alkyl group present. So the aldehyde formed by the oxidation of ethanol is ethanal. The oxidising agent used in the laboratory is acidified potassium dichromate(VI) solution. This is potassium dichromate(VI) solution with sulphuric acid added.

The complete equation is very complicated, so we use [O] to show oxygen and 2[H] to show hydrogen. The square brackets indicate that the oxygen and hydrogen are not present as atoms but are supplied or removed as part of a chemical reaction.

The equation can be summarised as:

$$CH_3CH_2OH(l) + [O] \rightarrow CH_3CHO(l) + H_2O(l)$$

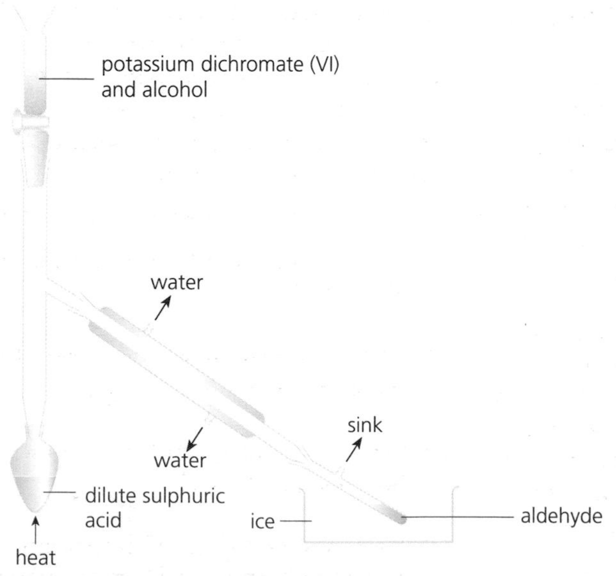

This reaction must be carried out at room temperature to prevent further oxidation of the products. If a higher temperature is used, then two atoms of hydrogen will be removed and one atom of oxygen gained to form a carboxylic acid.

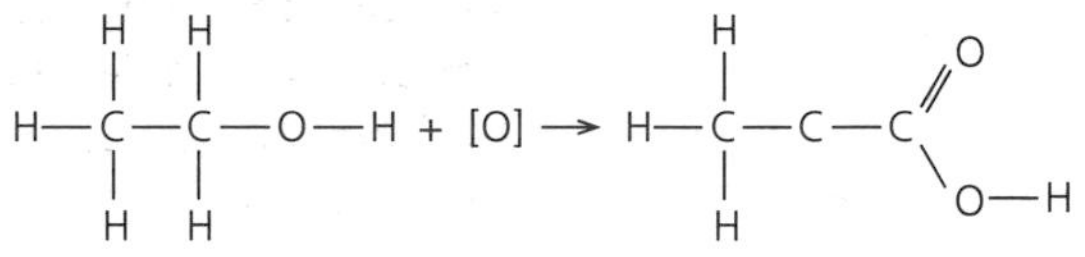

The carboxylic acid formed is ethanoic acid. (You have read about the homologous series of carboxylic acids in Chapter 11.)

The equation can be written as:

$$CH_3CH_2OH(l) + 2[O] \rightarrow CH_3COOH(l) + H_2O(l)$$

Either acidified potassium dichromate(VI) or acidified potassium manganate(VII) (dilute sulphuric acid added to acidify both) can be used as the oxidising agent and the mixture is refluxed (see Chapter 14).

Oxidation of secondary alcohols

Propan-2-ol is a secondary alcohol. When it is refluxed with acidified potassium dichromate(VI), two hydrogen atoms are removed and a ketone is produced. Ketones are a homologous series with a C=O functional group. The names of all ketones end in -one.

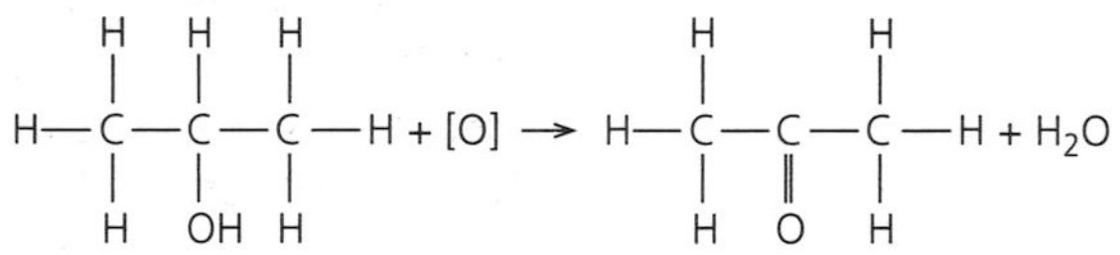

Propanone is an important industrial solvent and is manufactured from propan-2-ol. It is the solvent in cheaper nail polish removers.

11 Write equations for the reactions, and name the products formed when:

a butan-1-ol is oxidised;

b butan-2-ol is oxidised.

Fig. 6 Oxidising a primary alcohol to an aldehyde

APPLICATION C	Wine or vinegar?

Home brewers need to take care that unwanted microbes don't ruin all their hard work.

Vinegar is mostly ethanoic acid and water, plus flavourings and colourings. Industrially,vinegar is produced from cheap wine or cider by oxidising the ethanol in the wine to ethanoic acid. The oxidising agent used is the oxygen in the air and the process is caused by a bacteria named Acetobacter. The bacteria oxidise the alcohol to ethanoic acid as a source of energy.

The type of vinegar produced depends upon the alcoholic liquor used; cider makes cider vinegar and red wine makes red wine vinegar.

Unfortunately, the same reaction can cause home brewers to produce vinegar instead of wine. Acetobacter is present in the air and contamination of the fermenting brew can introduce the offending bacteria. A flavoured solution of ethanoic acid results. Even if a bottle of wine is left uncorked for a few days, it will turn vinegary because of the large numbers of these bacteria in the air.

1 Write an equation to show how vinegar is made from wine.

2 What precautions do the wine-makers need to take to prevent the formation of ethanoic acid?

Tertiary alcohols

Primary and secondary alcohols both have hydrogen atoms bonded to the carbon carrying the hydroxyl group. These hydrogen atoms are removed in the oxidation process. But tertiary alcohols have no hydrogen atoms on the hydroxyl carrying carbon. Tertiary alcohols cannot therefore be oxidised since this would involve the breaking of a carbon–carbon bond.

$$H-\overset{\overset{\displaystyle H}{|}}{\underset{\underset{\displaystyle H}{|}}{C}}-\overset{\overset{\displaystyle CH_3}{|}}{\underset{\underset{\displaystyle OH}{|}}{C}}-\overset{\overset{\displaystyle H}{|}}{\underset{\underset{\displaystyle H}{|}}{C}}-H$$

2-methylpropan-2-ol

2-methylpropan-2-ol is a tertiary alcohol. The carbon bonded to the hydroxyl group is bonded to three other carbon atoms. There are no hydrogen atoms available for oxidation.

Testing for alcohols

When primary, secondary and tertiary alcohols are oxidised using either acidified potassium dichromate(VI) or acidified potassium manganate(VII), the oxidising agents are themselves reduced and there is a colour change. Acidified potassium dichromate(VI) changes from orange to green because chromium(VI) ions are reduced to chromium(III) ions. Acidified potassium manganate(VII) changes from purple to colourless because purple manganate(VII) ions are reduced to colourless manganate(II) ions. The colour changes are shown in the photographs at the top of the opposite page.

Since primary, secondary and tertiary alcohols all give different products with oxidising agents, these reactions, or the lack of them, can be used to distinguish between the different classes of alcohol. We can also distinguish between a primary and secondary alcohol by indentifying whether an aldehyde or a ketone is formed in oxidation reactions.

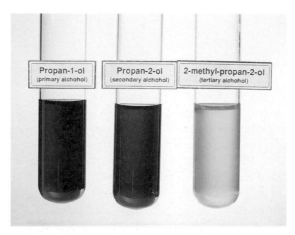

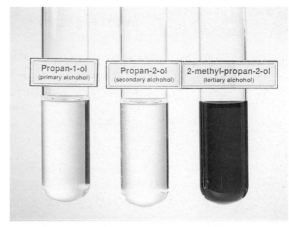

During the oxidation of primary and secondary alcohols using acidified potassium dichromate(VI), the colour changes from orange to green, but tertiary alcohols do not change.

During the oxidation of primary and secondary alcohols using acidified potassium manganate(VII), the colour changes from purple to colourless, but tertiary alchols do not change.

Tollen's reagent

Tollen's reagent is a mixture of aqueous ammonia and silver nitrate. The active substance in Tollen's reagent is a complex of silver(I) ions as $[Ag(NH_3)]^{2+}$. When Tollen's reagent is warmed with an aldehyde, silver atoms are produced. These can be made to coat the test tube and produce an effect called a silver mirror.

The silver mirror is produced because the silver(I) ions are reduced to silver atoms as the aldehyde is oxidised to a carboxylic acid in the reaction. The equation for the oxidation of ethanal is:

$$CH_3CHO(aq) + 2Ag^+ + H_2O(l) \rightarrow CH_3COOH(aq) + 2Ag(s) + 2H^+(aq)$$

The tube on the left shows ammoniacal silver nitrate before the addition of the aldehyde. The tube on the right shows that the aldehyde reduces the $[Ag(NH_3)_2]^+$ to Ag to give the silver mirror effect.

Fehling's solution

Fehling's solution contains blue copper(II) ions as a copper complex. The copper(II) ions act as a weak oxidising agent and will oxidise an aldehyde to a carboxylic acid.

When ethanal is heated with Fehling's solution, the following reaction occurs:

$$CH_3CHO + 2Cu^{2+} + 2H_2O \rightarrow CH_3COOH + Cu_2O + 4H^+$$

The copper(I) ions in copper(I) oxide are brick red and copper(I) oxide is insoluble in water. So a brick red precipitate forms as the copper(II) ions are reduced to copper(I) ions.

Ketones have no effect on Fehling's solution or on Tollen's reagent, so these reactions can be used to distinguish between an aldehyde and a ketone.

The unreacted Fehling's solution is blue because of the copper II complex ions it contains (left). After oxidation of the aldehyde, the copper (II) ion is reduced to Cu_2O, which forms a brick red precipitate (right).

225

APPLICATION D

Sweet chemistry

Glucose and fructose are simple sugars. Both sugars have two structures, a ring structure and a chain structure. In a solution of the sugar, both forms exist in equilibrium, with the ring structure most abundant. The diagram on the left shows the chain structures for glucose and fructose.

Fructose is sometimes called fruit sugar because it occurs naturally in fruit. Glucose is the end product of the digestion of starch in your digestive system. The presence of OH groups on several adjacent carbon atoms is thought to be responsible for their sweet tastes.

1 Which sugar is an aldehyde and which is a ketone?

2 How could you use Fehling's solution to distinguish between glucose and fructose?

3 Why do Biologists often call glucose a 'reducing sugar'?

4 Which sugar will reduce Tollen's reagent to give a silver mirror?

5 Glucose and fructose are both soluble in water. Explain why.

glucose

fructose

Many people restrict their intake of sugars in order to keep their weight down. Other, such as diabetics avoid sugar because it makes their blood sugar levels abnormally high and makes them very ill. Artificial sweeteners add sweetness to food without affecting blood glucose levels or adding excessive energy. Sorbitol is an artificial sweetener with the structural formula:

sorbitol

6 Would you expect sorbitol to dissolve in water and why?

7 What effect will sorbitol have on Fehling's and Tollen's reagents?

8 Suggest why sorbitol tastes sweet.

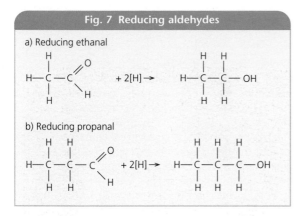

Fig. 7 Reducing aldehydes

a) Reducing ethanal

b) Reducing propanal

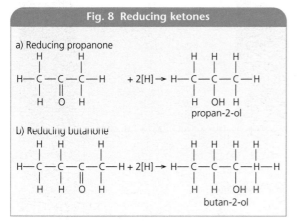

Fig. 8 Reducing ketones

a) Reducing propanone

propan-2-ol

b) Reducing butanone

butan-2-ol

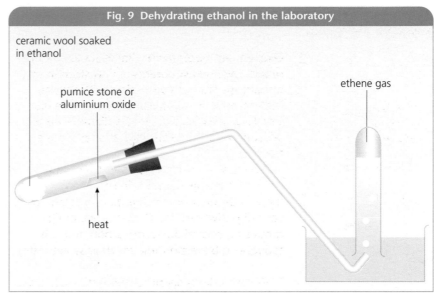

Fig. 9 Dehydrating ethanol in the laboratory

ceramic wool soaked in ethanol

pumice stone or aluminium oxide

ethene gas

heat

Reducing aldehydes and ketones

Primary alcohols can be oxidised to aldehydes and secondary alcohols can be oxidised to ketones. It therefore follows that, if an aldehyde is reduced, a primary alcohol will be obtained and if a ketone is reduced, a secondary alcohol will be produced. Aldehydes and ketones can be reduced using either sodium tetrahydridoborate(III), $NaBH_4$, dissolved in aqueous alcohol, or lithium tetrahydridoaluminate, $LiAlH_4$ dissolved in ethoxyethane.

The reduction of ethanal and propanal is shown in Fig. 7. The reduction of propanone and butanone is shown in Fig. 8

12 What is produced when

a butanal is reduced,

b pentan-2-one is reduced?

Elimination reactions of alcohols

Elimination reactions involve the loss of a molecule of water from an alcohol to form an alkene. The reaction is often called dehydration because water is lost from the molecule. During the reaction, the carbon-oxygen bond in the alcohol breaks and one hydrogen atom is lost from the carbon skeleton. The reaction for ethanol is:

The conditions for the reaction involve heating with a suitable catalyst such as sulphuric acid or phosphoric(V) acid. In the laboratory, this can be carried out by passing ethanol vapour over heated pumice stone or aluminium oxide. The ethene produced is collected over water (Fig. 9). The mechanism of the reaction is shown in Fig. 10.

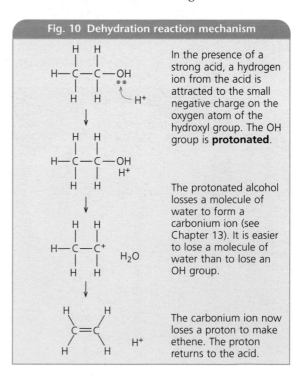

Fig. 10 Dehydration reaction mechanism

In the presence of a strong acid, a hydrogen ion from the acid is attracted to the small negative charge on the oxygen atom of the hydroxyl group. The OH group is **protonated**.

The protonated alcohol loses a molecule of water to form a carbonium ion (see Chapter 13). It is easier to lose a molecule of water than to lose an OH group.

The carbonium ion now loses a proton to make ethene. The proton returns to the acid.

EXTENSION

Starting points for plastics

Most ethene comes from the fractional distillation of crude oil and its subsequent cracking. But oil reserves are finite; one day, probably in your lifetime, we will exhaust supplies. Ethene is an important starting point for the manufacture of many plastics. An alternative route for making plastics could be:

Plant sugars $\xrightarrow{\text{fermentation}}$ Ethanol $\xrightarrow{\text{elimination}}$ Ethene $\xrightarrow{\text{polymerisation}}$ Polythene

Plastics from aldehydes

You read in Chapter 13 that ethene can polymerise to form the plastic polythene and that this is an example of an addition polymerisation.

Methanal has the formula:

Methanal molecules polymerise like this:

The plastic is called polymethanal. Polymethanal is a strong plastic because it has covalent links between the chains that make the molecular structure very rigid. It is called a thermoset plastic. Thermoset plastics do not soften on heating and can be used for electrical fittings and appliances like electrical sockets and kettles.

Methanal was also used to make Bakelite, one of the first plastics ever made. Bakelite is also thermosetting and was commonly used to make electrical fittings. They were always brown in colour and older houses may still retain some of these today. Bakelite was made from methanal and phenol, C_6H_5OH, a carbon ring with an OH group.

phenol

methanal

The three dimensional network gives Bakelite a strong structure.

1 Describe the reaction between methanal and phenol to produce Bakelite.

2 Why do you think this is called condensation polymerisation?

- Oxidation of primary alcohols produces an aldehyde. Further oxidation produces a carboxylic acid.

- Oxidation of a secondary alcohol produces a ketone.

- Tertiary alcohols do not oxidise easily.

- Aldehydes produce a silver mirror with Tollen's reagent, ketones do not.

- Aldehydes reduce blue Fehling's solution to brick red copper(I) oxide, ketones do not.

- Aldehydes are reduced to primary alcohols using a suitable reducing agent.

- Ketones are reduced to secondary alcohols, using a suitable reducing agent.

- Alcohols undergo elimination reactions to produce an alkene and a molecule of water.

EXAMINATION QUESTIONS

1 Butan-1-ol can be oxidised by acidified potassium dichromate(VI) using two different methods.

a In the first method, butan-1-ol is added dropwise to acidified potassium dichromate(VI) and the product is distilled off immediately.
  i) Using the symbol [O] for the oxidising agent, write an equation for this oxidisation of butan-1-ol, showing clearly the structure of the product. State what colour change you would observe. (3)
  ii) Butan-1-ol and butan-2-ol give different products on oxidisation by this first method. By stating a reagent and the observation with each compound, give a simple test to distinguish between these two oxidation products. (3)

b In a second method, the mixture of butan-1-ol and acidified potassium dichromate(VI) is heated under reflux. Identify the product which is obtained by this reaction. (1)

c Give the structures and names of two branched chain alcohols which are both isomers of butan-1-ol. Only isomer 1 is oxidised when warmed with acidified potassium dichromate(VI). (4)

NEAB CH03 February 1997 Q4

2

a Write an equation for the oxidation of pentan-2-ol by acidified potassium dichromate(VI) showing clearly the structure of the organic product. You may use the symbol [O] for the oxidising agent. (2)

b Pent-2-ene can be formed by the dehydration of pentan-2-ol. Give the reagent and conditions used. Outline a mechanism for this reaction. (6)

c Alcohols A, B and C are branched-chain isomers of pentanol.

A cannot be oxidised by acidified potassium dichromate(VI).

B can be oxidised by acidified potassium dichromate(VI) but cannot be dehydrated.

C can be oxidised by acidified potassium dichromate(VI) and can also be dehydrated.

Draw a possible structure for each of the three alcohols. (3)

NEAB CH03 June 1998 Q3

3 a
  i) Give the structure of 3-methylbutan-2-ol. (1)
  ii) Name and outline the mechanism for the reaction taking place when 3-methylbutan-2-ol is converted into 2-methylbut-2-ene in the presence of a strong acid. (5)
  iii) Explain why 3-methylbut-1-ene is also formed in this reaction. (2)

b Give the structure of the product obtained when 3-methylbutan-2-ol is treated with acidified potassium dichromate(VI). (1)

NEAB CH06 June 1998 Q5

4 Alcohol X has the structure

$$(CH_3)2C(OH)CH(CH_3)_2$$

a Name alcohol X. (1)

b Name and outline the mechanism for the reaction occurring when alcohol X is converted into 2,3-dimethylbut-2-ene in the presence of a strong acid. (5)

c Give the structure of, and name an isomer of 2,3-dimethylbut-2-ene which is also formed in the reaction. Explain why two products are obtained. (4)

NEAB CH06 June 1999 Q3

5

a Ethanol can be produced industrially from ethene or from sugars such as glucose, C6H12O6. For each route, name the method used, write an equation for the reaction and give one necessary condition. Suggest, with a reason, which route is likely to become the major method of production in the future. (8)

b Ethanol can also be produced in a reaction involving reduction. Give a suitable reducing agent and write an equation for the reaction. You may use [H] to indicate the reductant in your equation. (2)

NEAB CH03 June 1997 Q8

6 Two isomeric products of molecular formula C_6H_{12} are formed when 2,3-dimethylbutan-2-ol reacts with concentrated sulphuric acid.

a Name the type of reaction taking place and give the structure of the carbonium ion intermediate formed. (2)

b Explain briefly why two products are formed and give the structures of these isomers. (4)

NEAB CH06 February 1997 Q1(Part)

Breathalysers and alcohol

Drinking and driving has become socially unacceptable as statistics clearly show the correlation between road accidents and drivers who drink too much.

The chemistry behind the way in which drivers are checked for alcohol in their blood has undergone several important changes in the last 35 years. The relationship between the amount of alcohol in the blood and the amount in breath is not simple. The ratio of alcohol in the blood to alcohol in the breath is about 2300:1. This posed a problem for the early breathalysers which were based on chemical reactions. They only sampled the air from the top of the lungs, whereas the air from deep in the lungs is needed to really establish how much alcohol there is in the blood stream, and therefore whether a driver is over the limit.

One of the first chemical breathalysers was based on potassium dichromate(VI) acidified with sulphuric acid. This makes the dichromate a bright yellow-orange colour which turns green as the ethanol is oxidised to ethanoic acid. Silical gel coated with the acidified potassium dichromate(VI) is used to absorb the breath sample as the person being tested blows into the tube.

Modern breathalysers work on the same principle as the fuel cell. A 1.5 cm³ sample of deep lung air is drawn by a piston and the breath sample is passed over the surface of a platinum catalyst. This acts as the anode. The alcohol from the breath sample is then oxidised on the surface of the platinum to produce an electron flow (or electric current). It is the size of this electric current which determines the amount of alcohol in the blood stream.

If a driver's breath analysis falls between 35 and 50μg of alcohol per 100 cm³, then a blood or urine sample is taken. This is analysed using gas chromatography equipment.

1

a Calculate how much blood alcohol in 100 cm³ is the same as 1 μg of breath alcohol in 100 cm³.

b Calculate the equivalent amount (in μg per 100 cm³ of breath) of 80 mg per 100 cm³ of blood alcohol.

c What blood alcohol levels correspond to the 30-50μg of breath alcohol?

2 Write a balanced equation to show:

a the reaction of potassium dichromate (VI) with sulphuric acid.

b the oxidation of ethanol to ethanoic acid.

Table A1 Blood alcohol levels in mg/100 cm³ of blood									
	Time since drink /mins								
Dose / units	0	15	30	45	60	75	90	105	120
1	7	14	23	21	18	15	11	9	–
2	7	21	36	39	37	32	27	20	–
3	7	34	57	61	58	52	49	40	–
4	7	40	70	78	76	71	67	60	–

Table A2 Kerb bumpings by 40 drivers given different amounts of alcohol					
	Units of alcohol drunk				
Driving period (mins since drinking)	0	2	3	4	5
0–20	68	64	97	59	86
21–40	32	68	79	75	112
41–60	51	58	87	58	93
61–80	58	65	87	68	68

Table A3 Measures of drinks containing 1 unit of alcohol	
Drink	Quantity
Beer, cider, lager	half pint
Table wine	glass
Port, sherry	glass
Spirits (rum, whisky, brandy etc)	single measure

Much of the research that informs legal limits for blood alcohol was done in the late 1950's. The Medical Research Council investigated how quickly alcohol was absorbed and cleared by the body. They also looked at how these amounts affected driving. The doses given in the tables shown above correspond roughly to the units of alcohol used to give drinkers an idea of the strength of drinks. Use the data on the rate of clearing of alcohol in Table A1 to answer the following questions.

The three glasses in the top photograph show a unit of alcohol in each of the three drinks shown. Notice the difference in volume between a unit of alcohol in beer (typically 4% alcohol) and vodka (typically 40% alcohol).

3

a How long after taking a drink does it take for blood alcohol levels to reach a maximum value?

b What is the maximum blood alcohol level for a person who has drunk: i 2 units ii 4 units?

c How many units of alcohol in the following drinks:
i one pint of beer?
ii a double whisky?
iii three glasses of sherry?
iv two pints of lager?

d Predict the blood alcohol level for someone, one hour after they have drunk a pint of beer.

4

a Display the data from Table A1 in the most effective way to show how blood alcohol varies over time after drinking different amounts.

b Estimate the blood alcohol levels after two hours for someone who has drunk 3 units of alcohol.

5 The legal limit for alcohol is 80mg/100 cm³ of blood. None of the people in this test had a blood alcohol level this high. What evidence can you find that their driving skills were reduced? Prepare a letter to the local paper suggesting the current limit is too high.

The Periodic Table

Relative atomic masses given in brackets refer to the isotopic mass of the most abundant isotope of the elements concerned.

Key:

atomic no
symbol
name
relative atomic mass

metal | non–metal

Group	I	II												III	IV	V	VI	VII	O
Period 1	1 **H** hydrogen 1.0																		2 **He** helium 4.0
2	3 **Li** lithium 6.9	4 **Be** beryllium 9.0												5 **B** boron 10.8	6 **C** carbon 12.0	7 **N** nitrogen 14.0	8 **O** oxygen 16.0	9 **F** fluorine 19.0	10 **Ne** neon 20.2
3	11 **Na** sodium 23.0	12 **Mg** magnesium 24.3												13 **Al** aluminium 6.9	14 **Si** silicon 28.1	15 **P** phosphorus 31.0	16 **S** sulphur 32.1	17 **Cl** chlorine 35.5	18 **Ar** argon 39.9
4	19 **K** potassium 39.1	20 **Ca** calcium 40.1	21 **Sc** scandium 45.0	22 **Ti** titanium 47.8	23 **V** vanadium 50.9	24 **Cr** chromium 52.0	25 **Mn** manganese 54.9	26 **Fe** iron 55.9	27 **Co** cobalt 58.9	28 **Ni** nickel 58.7	29 **Cu** copper 63.5	30 **Zn** zinc 65.4		31 **Ga** gallium 69.7	32 **Ge** germanium 72.6	33 **As** arsenic 74.9	34 **Se** selenium 79.0	35 **Br** bromine 79.9	36 **Kr** krypton 83.8
5	37 **Rb** rubidium 85.5	38 **Sr** strontium 87.6	39 **Y** yttrium 88.9	40 **Zr** zirconium 91.2	41 **Nb** niobium 92.9	42 **Mo** molybdenum 95.9	43 **Tc** technetium (98)	44 **Ru** ruthenium 101.1	45 **Rh** rhodium 102.9	46 **Pd** palladium 106.4	47 **Ag** silver 107.9	48 **Cd** cadmium 112.4		49 **In** indium 114.8	50 **Sn** tin 118.7	51 **Sb** antimony 121.8	52 **Te** tellurium 127.6	53 **I** iodine 126.9	54 **Xe** xenon 131.3
6	55 **Cs** caesium 132.9	56 **Ba** barium 137.3	57 **La** lanthanum 138.9	72 **Hf** hafnium 178.5	73 **Ta** tantalum 181.0	74 **W** tungsten 183.9	75 **Re** rhenium 186.2	76 **Os** osmium 190.2	77 **Ir** iridium 192.2	78 **Pt** platinum 195.1	79 **Au** gold 197.0	80 **Hg** mercury 200.6		81 **Tl** thallium 204.4	82 **Pb** lead 207.2	83 **Bi** bismuth 209.0	84 **Po** polonium (209)	85 **At** astatine (210)	86 **Rn** radon (222)
7	87 **Fr** francium (223)	88 **Ra** radium (226)	89 **Ac** actinium (227)	104 **Unq** unnilquadium (261)	105 **Unp** unnilpentium (262)	106 **Unh** unnilhexium (263)	107 **Uns** unnilseptium (262)	108 **Uno** unniloctium (265)	109 **Une** unnilennium (266)										

Lanthanides

58 **Ce** cerium 140.1	59 **Pr** praseodymium 140.9	60 **Nd** neodymium 144.2	61 **Pm** promethium (145)	62 **Sm** samarium 150.4	63 **Eu** europium 152.0	64 **Gd** gadolinium 157.3	65 **Tb** terbium 158.9	66 **Dy** dysprosium 162.5	67 **Ho** holmium 164.9	68 **Er** erbium 167.3	69 **Tm** thulium 168.9	70 **Yb** ytterbium 173.0	71 **Lu** lutetium 175.5

Actinides

90 **Th** thorium 232.0	91 **Pa** protactinium (231)	92 **U** uranium 238.1	93 **Np** neptunium (237)	94 **Pu** plutonium (244)	95 **Am** americium (243)	96 **Cm** curium (247)	97 **Bk** berkelium (247)	98 **Cf** californium (251)	99 **Es** einsteinium (254)	100 **Fm** fermium (253)	101 **Md** mendelevium (256)	102 **No** nobelium (254)	103 **Lr** lawrencium (257)

Glossary

absolute zero The temperature $-273\ °C$ or $0\ K$, at which the volume of a gas is theoretically zero and has no energy. See also **Kelvin temperature scale**.

acid A substance which has a tendency to release protons, hydrogen ions, H^+. A strong acid, such as nitric acid, releases hydrogen ions readily. Weak acids, such as ethanoic and other organic acids, release hydrogen ions far less readily.

acid–base titration An experimental procedure to determine the amounts of acid and base in aqueous solution that react exactly together. Knowing the concentration of one of the reactants, the concentration of the other reactant can be calculated.

actinides The 14 elements, A_r 90 to 103, which follow actinium, A_r 89.

activation energy The minimum energy required by particles in collision to bring about a chemical reaction.

addition polymerisation The addition reaction of many molecules of a monomer to form one large molecule of polymer. No other substances are formed. Ethene forms poly(ethene) by addition polymerisation.

addition reaction A reaction in which two molecules react together to form one molecule.

alcohols Alcohols have the general formula R–OH, where R is an alkyl group. Their names end in -ol. Ethanol, C_2H_5OH, is an alcohol. A primary alcohol has the general formula RCH_2OH. A secondary alcohol has the general formula R^1R^2CHOH. A tertiary alcohol has the general formula $R^1R^2R^3COH$.

aldehyde A carbonyl compound with the general formula RCHO. The names of aldehydes end in -al. Ethanal, CH_3CHO, is an aldehyde.

alkane A hydrocarbon with the general formula C_nH_{2n+2}. The first three alkanes are CH_4, C_2H_6 and C_3H_8.

alkene A hydrocarbon with the general formula C_nH_{2n}. Alkene molecules contain double bonds. The first two alkenes are C_2H_4 and C_3H_6.

alkyl group A group of atoms with the general formula C_nH_{2n+1} forming part of a molecule.

allotropes Different forms of the same element, having element structures. Carbon has several allotropes: diamond, graphite and the fullerenes.

alloy A mixture of two or more elements, at least one of which is a metal. Alloys are usually designed to give a required set of properties.

alpha particle A particle consisting of 2 protons and 2 neutrons. It is the same as a helium nucleus that has lost its electrons.

amphoteric Having both acidic and basic properties. For example, aluminium oxide is an amphoteric oxide. It forms salts both with acids and with alkalis.

anion A negatively charged ion that is attracted to the anode during electrolysis.

arene An aromatic compound which is a hydrocarbon. All arenes contain one or more benzene rings. Benzene and naphthalene are arenes.

atom A single unit of an element.

atomic mass See **relative atomic mass**.

atomic number, symbol Z The number of protons (and therefore of electrons) in an atom.

atomic radius The distance from the centre of the nucleus to the outermost electrons of an atom.

Avogadro constant The number of particles in one mole of a substance: $6.022 \times 10^{23}\ mol^{-1}$.

balanced equation A chemical equation where the number and types of atoms in the products equals the number and types of atoms in the reactants.

base A substance which has a tendency to gain protons. Bases which dissolve in water are called alkalis. Strong bases gain protons readily.

basic oxygen process The process of steel making

batch process An industrial process which is started and stopped at intervals. In titanium production, the extraction apparatus is loaded, operated, cooled and emptied, before the cycle is repeated. Each cycle produces a batch of titanium.

bauxite hydrated aluminium oxide, $Al_2O_3.2H_2O$.

blast furnace Industrial furnace for the extraction of iron from its ore. Blasts of hot air are blown at a mixture of iron ore, coke and limestone to produce iron, carbon dioxide, carbon monoxide and slag.

bond dissociation energy, symbol $\Delta H^{\ominus}_{\text{diss}}$ The standard molar enthalpy change of bond dissociation. The enthalpy change when one mole of bonds of the same type are broken in gaseous molecules under standard conditions.

bond enthalpy The amount of energy released when a bond is broken. It equals the amount of energy absorbed when the same bond is made. It is measured as the energy in kilojoules per mole of bonds.

carbonium ion or **carbocation** A group in which a carbon atom bonded to three other atoms has an unpaired electron at the position of the fourth bond that gives the group a positive charge. Examples are $\cdot CH_3$, the methyl carbonium ion, and $\cdot C_2H_5$, the ethyl carbonium ion.

carbonyl compound A compound containing the functional group $>C=O$. Carbonyl compounds include aldehydes and ketones.

carboxylic acids Organic acids having the general formula RCOOH. Their names end in -oic acid. Ethanoic acid has the formula CH_3COOH.

catalyst A substance that usually speeds up the rate of a chemical reaction. It changes the nature of the intermediate compounds formed between reactants and products and so reduces the activation energy. A catalyst remains chemically unchanged at the end of the reaction.

catalytic cracking The process which uses high temperature and a catalyst to break up long-chain hydrocarbon molecules from crude oil into smaller, more useful molecules such as ethene.

cation A positively charged ion that is attracted to the cathode during electrolysis.

chemical equation A chemical reaction expressed in chemical symbols showing reactants and products. The equation shows how many molecules or atoms react together, and how many molecules or atoms are formed.

chemical formula It shows how many atoms of each element combine together to make a substance.

chemical properties The chemical reactions of a substance.

chlorofluorocarbons or **CFCs** Hydrocarbons in which some or all the hydrogen atoms have been replace by chlorine and fluorine atoms.

closed system A system from which reactants and products cannot escape, and to which substances cannot be added. A chemical equilibrium is possible only in a closed system.

collision theory A theory to explain how chemical reactions occur, which states that for a reaction to happen, particles have to collide with a minimum amount of energy.

complex ion An ion that contains a central atom to which other atoms or ions are bonded. In a transition metal complex, the transition metal is the central atom. The atoms or ions bonded to the central atom are called ligands. An example is the tetraamminecopper(II) ion $Cu(NH_3)_4^{2+}$.

compound A substance whose particles contain two or more atoms.

conducts electricity Allows an electric current to pass through.

contact process The process used to make sulphuric acid from sulphur, oxygen and water.

continuous process An industrial process in which a material is produced continuously. An example is iron, with the iron ore fed continuously into the apparatus and cast iron continuously removed.

converter Container in a steel works in which steel is made.

coordinate bond A covalent bond in which the shared electron pair originates from the same atom. It can be written as X→Y, showing that the shared electron pair originated from X.

coordination number The number of ligands to which a central metal atom is bonded in a complex ion. For example, in the tetraamminecopper(II) ion $Cu(NH_3)_4^{2+}$, the coordination number of copper is 4.

covalent bond A bond in which two atoms share one or more pairs of electrons. A hydrogen molecule, H–H, has a single covalent bond. In a double covalent bond there are two shared pairs of electrons, such as in the oxygen molecule, O=O.

cracking The process of breaking up the long-chain hydrocarbons in crude oil into shorter chain hydrocarbons that can be used in the chemical industry and for fuels.

crude oil A mixture of hydrocarbons formed naturally by the decomposition of marine animals over millions of years.

cycloalkane An alkane with a cyclic structure.

dative covalent bond Another name for a coordinate bond.

d block The elements in the Periodic Table between Groups II and III in Periods 4, 5 and 6, known as the transition elements. In each period, a d orbital within an outer s orbital is being filled.

delocalised electrons Electrons that are not located at one particular atom, but are free to move between all atoms in the structure. Examples of materials with delocalised electrons are metals, graphite and benzene.

diol An alcohol with two –OH groups.

dipole A molecule (or ion) with a positive charge in one part and a negative charge in another, separated by a short distance. The dipolar nature is due to the uneven distribution of electrons. Temporary dipoles form in non-polar molecules such as N_2 because, at any instant, electron distribution within the molecule may not be even. Molecules containing different atoms, such as hydrogen chloride, are polar. They have permanent dipoles because the electron distribution is always uneven. Bonding between atoms of different electronegativity causes this unevenness.

displacement reaction A chemical reaction in which an atom in a compound is replaced by another atom, e.g. chlorine displaces bromine in potassium bromide.

displayed formula or **graphical formula** or **full structural formula** A chemical formula that shows every atom and bond.

dissolve Particles of solute mix separately and intimately with particles of solvent.

dot-and-cross diagram A drawing representing the electrons in a molecule. Dots and crosses are used to indicate their atom of origin.

dynamic equilibrium A stage in a reaction where the forward reaction equals the backward reaction so that there is no net change in the concentration of the substances involved in the reaction.

electrical conductor A material that conducts electricity.

electrolysis Passing an electric current through a substance with charged particles that are free to move, and causing a chemical change.

electron A negatively charged particle. Electrons orbit the atomic nucleus in energy levels. Atoms of different elements have different numbers of electrons. The number of electrons is always equal to the atomic number of the element.

electron affinity A measure of the attraction of an atom for an electron or electrons. It is measured as the amount of energy in kJ mol^{-1} required to remove an electron from a gaseous negative ion.

electron configuration The arrangement of electrons in an atom, written in number and letter symbols, e.g. for Na it is $1s^2 2s^2 2p^6 3s^1$.

electron density map A diagram of a molecule in which lines connect areas of equal electron density. It shows the position of the atoms (or ions) and gives information about the bonding.

electron pairs Bonding electron pairs occur in a covalent bond between two atoms, and include one electron from each atom, except in the case of a coordinate bond where they come from one atom only. Non-bonding electron pairs, or lone pairs, take no part in bonding, e.g. HCl has one bonding electron pair, together with three non-bonding electron pairs on the chlorine atom.

electronegativity The tendency of an atom to gain or retain electrons. Elements whose atoms gain electrons easily are the most electronegative. Fluorine is the most electronegative element. Elements whose atoms lose outer electrons easily are described as being electropositive. Caesium is the most electropositive element.

electrophile An electron-seeking group. Electrophiles are positively charged, e.g. the nitryl group NO_2^+.

electrophilic addition A reaction in which an electrophile is attracted to an area of high electron density. The electrophile adds on to the atom or group in an addition reaction.

electrophilic substitution A reaction in which an electrophile is attracted to an area of high electron density. The electrophile replaces an atom or group in a substitution reaction.

electrostatic forces of attraction The attraction between positive and negative ions in e.g. a crystalline ionic compound.

element A substance which cannot be broken down into any simpler substance by chemical means. All atoms of an element have the same atomic number.

elimination reaction A reaction in which the products include a small molecule, often water. The small product molecule is said to be eliminated from the reacting molecule(s).

empirical formula The simplest formula of a compound, showing the ratio of the numbers of atoms in the molecule, e.g. CH_3 is the empirical formula of ethane, C_2H_6.

endothermic reaction A chemical reaction in which energy is absorbed.

energy The ability to do work.

energy barrier The minimum amount of energy (activation energy) that reactants must have before a reaction can occur.

energy level One of the fixed range of energies which electrons in atoms can possess; sometimes described as shells and sub-shells. An electron in an atom requires a particular amount or quantum of energy to move from one energy level to the next.

energy profile diagram A diagram showing the energy changes in a chemical reaction.

enthalpy Energy associated with a chemical reaction.

enthalpy change An amount of energy that is transferred (absorbed or released) during a chemical reaction.

equilibrium The state reached in a reversible reaction at which the rates of the two opposing reactions are equal, when the system has no further tendency to change. This is a dynamic equilibrium, as reactants and products are both still being formed, but at equal rates.

equilibrium position The dynamic stage in a chemical reaction where the forward reaction equals the backward reaction, so that there is no net change in the concentrations of the substances involved in the reaction.

equivalence point The exact neutralisation point of an acid–base titration.

ester linkage An –O– linkage connecting small molecules or monomers.

exothermic reaction A chemical reaction in which energy is released.

f block The elements of the Periodic Table based on the lanthanide and actinide series, in which electrons are filling an f orbital within outer shells.

fermentation The process by which carbohydrate reacts with water in the absence of oxygen, producing ethanol and carbon dioxide, often catalysed industrially by enzymes in microorganisms such as yeast.

fraction A product of fractional distillation, collected over a specific temperature range. A fraction contains hydrocarbons from crude oil of similar chain length.

fractional distillation Process used to separate the components of crude oil into groups of hydrocarbons of similar chain length. The crude oil is heated until it vaporises and the products within a set boiling point range are collected.

functional group A reactive atom or group of atoms in an organic molecule that largely determine the properties of the molecule.

gamma ray High energy radiation, often emitted in the decay of radioactive elements, which can penetrate most materials.

geometric isomers Isomers resulting from different spatial arrangements of functional groups relative to a double bond. They are called *cis* when groups are on the same side of the double bond, and *trans* when groups are on different sides.

giant atomic structure A structure that contains many millions of atoms all bonded together, e.g. as in diamond and graphite

graphical formula See **displayed formula**.

group The elements in a column (vertical row) of the Periodic Table, e.g. Group II elements are the elements in the second column of the Periodic Table, from beryllium to radium.

halide A compound containing a halogen atom. It can be ionically bonded, as in metal halides, e.g. NaCl, or covalently bonded, as in non-metal halides, e.g. HCl(g) or PCl_5.

haloalkane or **halogenoalkane** An alkane molecule in which one or more of the hydrogen atoms are replaced by a halogen atom.

halon A haloalkane containing combinations of bromine, chlorine and fluorine atoms.

Hess's law If a chemical change can occur by more than one route, then the overall enthalpy change for each route must be the same, provided that the starting and finishing conditions are the same.

heterogeneous catalysis A reaction for which the catalyst and the reactants are in different states, e.g. a solid iron catalyst in the Haber process reaction:
$$3H_2(g) + N_2(g) \rightarrow 2NH_3(g)$$

heterogeneous equilibrium An equilibrium in which the reactants are in different states, e.g. the equilibrium mixture obtained by heating ammonium chloride in a sealed tube:
$$NH_4Cl(s) \rightarrow NH_3(g) + HCl(g)$$

heterolytic fission The breaking of a single covalent bond (a bonding pair of electrons) so that the two electrons remain on one atom. Ions are formed: the atom taking the two electrons is negatively charged and the atom with no electrons from the bond is positively charged, e.g. the dissociation in solution of hydrogen bromide,
$$H:Br(g) \rightarrow H^+(aq) + Br^-(aq)$$

homogeneous catalysis A reaction for which the catalyst and the reactants are in the same state, e.g. the oxidation of sulphuric(IV) acid is catalysed by transition metal ions in solution.

homogeneous equilibrium An equilibrium in which all the reactants are in the same state, e.g. the equilibrium mixture obtained by heating hydrogen and iodine in a sealed tube:
$$H_2(g) + I_2(g) \rightleftharpoons 2HI(g)$$

homologous series A series of organic compounds with the same general formula, each successive member of the series having one more carbon atom in its molecule, e.g. the alkanes, C_nH_{2n+2}.

homolytic fission The breaking of a single covalent bond (a bonding pair of electrons) so that one electron remains with each atom. The species formed are called radicals and each has an unpaired electron, e.g. the gaseous state dissociation of chlorine, $Cl:Cl \rightarrow Cl\cdot + Cl\cdot$

Hund's rule of maximum multiplicity Electrons organise themselves so that, as far as possible, they remain unpaired, occupying the maximum possible number of sub-level orbitals.

hydration The addition of water. In organic chemistry examples include the conversion of alkenes to alcohols, and in inorganic chemistry the formation of aqua ions by the addition of water ligands to metal ions, e.g. hydration of $CuSO_4$ to form $CuSO_4.nH_2O$.

hydrogen bonding The intermolecular bonding between dipoles in adjacent molecules in which hydrogen is bonded to a strongly electronegative element, e.g. intermolecular hydrogen bonding in H_2O, NH_3 and HF.

hydrolysis The splitting up of a compound by reaction with water, e.g.
ester hydrolysis:
$$CH_3COOCH_3 + H_2O \rightleftharpoons CH_3COOH + CH_3OH$$
hydrolysis of aqua ions:
$$[Al(H_2O)_6]^{3+} + H_2O \rightleftharpoons [Al(H_2O)_5(OH)]^{2+} + H_3O^+$$

ideal gas A gas made up of particles of zero size, with no forces acting between them. Ideal gases exist only in theory, not in practice, but nitrogen, oxygen, hydrogen and the inert gases behave like ideal gases at high temperature and low pressure. Under these conditions they obey the ideal gas equation.

ideal gas equation A mathematical description of the relationship between volume, temperature and pressure for an ideal gas:
$$pV = nRT$$
where pressure p is measured in N m^{-2} (Pa), volume V is measured in m^3, n is the number of moles of gas, R is the molar gas constant with the value of 8.314 J K^{-1} mol^{-1}, and temperature T is measured in K.

incomplete combustion Combustion reactions in which there is insufficient oxygen for full oxidation, e.g. incomplete combustion of hydrocarbons produces carbon monoxide instead of carbon dioxide.

induced dipole An uneven charge distribution in a particle (molecule or atom). It occurs when a charge in an adjacent particle causes movement of electrons within the particle. One region of the particle becomes negative and another part positive: the particle is said to be polar.

inert gas Elements in Group 0 (or VIII).

inorganic chemistry The study of compounds that do not contain carbon. (Carbon dioxide and carbon monoxide are the usual exceptions.)

intermolecular bonding Bonding between molecules, not within molecules. There are several types of intermolecular bonding, including van der Waals forces and hydrogen bonds.

ion A particle consisting of an atom or group of atoms that carries a positive or negative electric charge. An atom forms an ion when it loses or gains one or more electrons.

ionic Description of a substance which contains ions.

ionic compounds Compounds with ionic bonding, containing ions.

ionic equations A concise method of writing down the important changes to the ions in a chemical reaction.

ionisation energy The energy required to remove one mole of electrons from one mole of atoms of an element to a distance at which the electrons are no longer influenced by the positive charge of the nuclei. The energy required to remove one mole of the outermost electrons from one mole of atoms of the element is called the first ionisation energy. The atom becomes a positively charged ion:
$$X(g) \rightarrow X^+(g) + e^-$$
Removing a further mole of electrons represents the second ionisation energy:
$$X^+(g) \rightarrow X^{2+}(g) + e^-$$

irreversible reaction A reaction where the equilibrium lies to the right, i.e. the reactants react to make the products, but the products do not react to make the reactants.

isomers Compounds that have the same molecular formula but different structural formulae.

isotopes Atoms that have the same atomic number but different mass numbers. They are atoms of the same element, with the same numbers of protons and electrons but different numbers of neutrons, e.g. isotopes of chlorine are written as chlorine-35 and chlorine-37 (or $^{35}C(el)$ and $^{37}C(el)$, where 35 and 37 are mass numbers.

Kelvin temperature scale or **absolute temperature scale** Measured in kelvin K, the temperature scale is based on the theory that at 0 K (–273 °C), the volume of a gas becomes zero. 273 K is 0 °C.

ketone A carbonyl compound with the general formula: $RR^1C=O$. Propanone, CH_3COCH_3, is a ketone.

kinetic theory Also called the kinetic molecular model, it describes the movement due to kinetic energy of particles in solids, liquids and gases.

kinetics of reaction or **rate of reaction** The study of factors that affect the way in which the concentrations of the reactants and products change with time during a chemical reaction.

Kroll process The industrial process used to extract titanium from titanium chloride.

lanthanides The 14 elements, A_r 58 to 71, which follow lanthanum, A_r 57.

lattice A geometric arrangement of positions. Crystal structures are based on lattices with the particles in a geometric pattern.

law of conservation of energy Energy cannot be created or destroyed, only changed from one form to another.

Le Chatelier's principle When an equilibrium reaction mixture undergoes a change in conditions, the composition of the mixture adjusts to counteract the change. For example, if the concentration of one of the reactants in an equilibrium mixture is suddenly increased, the equilibrium will adjust so as to reduce the increase in concentration.

lone pair A non-bonding pair of electrons in a molecule.

mass A measure of the amount of matter in a substance.

mass number, symbol A The number of protons plus the number of neutrons present in an atom.

mass spectrometer A scientific instrument used to produce a mass spectrum.

mass spectroscopy A technique used to find the relative atomic mass of an element or the relative molecular mass of a molecule. It can identify the types and amounts of any isotopes present in an element or compound.

mass spectrum A chart from a mass spectrometer showing the relative abundance of different ionised atoms and molecules.

Maxwell-Boltzmann distribution For a sample of gas at a particular temperature, it represents the number of gas molecules at each energy over the whole range of energies present, and can be represented by a curved graph.

mineral A naturally occurring compound of more or less definite composition, found in rocks.

molar gas constant, symbol R The proportionality constant in the ideal gas equation.

molar mass The mass of one mole of a substance. For example, the molar mass of magnesium is 24 g mol^{-1}.

molar volume The volume occupied by one mole of any gas. It is 22.4 dm^3 at standard temperature and pressure.

molarity The concentration of a solution expressed in mol dm^{-3}.

mole An amount of substance that contains 6.022×10^{23} particles. The particles may be atoms, ions, molecules or electrons.

molecular formula A formula showing the number and types of atoms present in a molecule, e.g. the molecular formula for calcium carbonate is $CaCO_3$.

molecular ion A molecule that has lost one or more electrons.

molecule A particle containing two or more atoms.

monomer A molecule that can react with many other similar molecules to build up a large molecule, a polymer, e.g. the monomer ethene gives rise to the polymer poly(ethene).

mononuclear ion An ion with a single charge on its nucleus.

negatively charged ion An atom or group of atoms that has gained one or more electrons to become negatively charged. See also **cation**.

neutralisation point In a titration, the point at which exactly enough of one reactant, for example an acid, has been added to a reaction mixture to react with all of another reactant, an alkali. The mixture has then changed from being alkaline to being neutral.

neutron A neutral (uncharged) particle in the atomic nucleus. Its mass is approximately 1 atomic unit.

nucleophile An atom or group of atoms that is attracted to a positive charge, e.g. NH_3, –OH and H_2O.

nucleophilic addition reaction A reaction in which a nucleophile is attracted to a positively charged molecule or group and reacts with it, e.g. the reaction between the nucleophilic bromide ion and a carbocation: $Br^- + CH_3=CH_2^+ \rightarrow CH_2BrCH_2Br$.

nucleophilic substitution reaction A chemical reaction in which one nucleophile replaces another in a molecule. For example, in the reaction of bromoethane with alkali, the nucleophilic hydroxide ion replaces the bromide ion in the bromoethane molecule: $C_2H_5Br + OH^- \rightarrow C_2H_5OH + Br$

nucleus The central part of an atom occupying a tiny fraction of its volume, with electrons orbiting round it. The nucleus consists of tightly packed positively charged protons and neutral neutrons.

optical isomers Compounds whose molecules, though alike in every other way, are mirror images of each other.

orbital The region in an atom where an electron is most likely to be found.

ore Rock that contains a mineral.

organic chemistry The chemistry of carbon compounds. Several million different carbon compounds are known.

oxidant Another term for oxidising agent.

oxidation A process in which a species loses one or more electrons; also defined as an increase in oxidation state of an element. Oxidation and reduction occur together in a redox reaction.

oxidation state or **oxidation number** The charge that an element would have if it were totally ionically bonded. For an ion, it is the charge on the ion. In a covalent compound, it is the theoretical number assigned to each atom in a molecule if it were an ionic compound. For example, in water the oxidation state of hydrogen is +1, and that of oxygen is –2, even though water is covalently bonded. Oxidation state can change in a redox reaction. The oxidation state of elements is zero.

oxidising agent An element or compound that gains electrons from a reducing agent which itself loses electrons. The oxidising agent is reduced, and the reducing agent is oxidised.

particle An atom, molecule, ion, complex or sub-atomic component.

parts per million, p.p.m. A unit used to express low concentrations. It is not always easy to visualise such low concentrations. Analogies can help: one part per million is one second in 12 days of your life, or one penny out of £10 000. 1 p.p.m. is the same as 1 mg per 1000 g (1 mg per 1 kg).

p block Elements of the Periodic Table in Groups III to O.

period The elements in a horizontal row in the Periodic Table, e.g. Period 2 elements are the elements in the second horizontal row of the Periodic Table, from lithium to neon.

Periodic Table A classification of the elements in order of their atomic numbers. Elements with similar properties appear in columns, known as groups. Metals lie on the left of the table and non-metals on the right, with a gradual change of properties across the rows, or periods.

permanent dipole A molecule in which one part always has a slightly positive charge, and another always has a slightly negative charge.

planar Description of a molecule whose shape is flat.

plasticiser A substance added to a plastic in order to increase its flexibility.

polar molecule A covalent molecule with atoms of different electronegativities. The electron density of the bonding electrons lies towards the more electronegative atom.

polymer A large molecule formed when many smaller monomer molecules react together, e.g. plastics like polythene, and synthetic fibres like nylon and terylene.

polymerisation The reaction of monomers to form polymers.

positively charged ion An atom or group of atoms that has lost one or more electrons to become positively charged.

precipitate An insoluble (solid) product formed from a reaction in solution.

primary distillation The first distillation of crude oil to obtain fractions containing a mixture of hydrocarbons.

primary steam reforming A stage in the manufacture of ammonia by the Haber process in which methane and

steam react to form hydrogen and carbon dioxide.

proton A positively charged particle in the atomic nucleus. Its mass is approximately 1 atomic unit.

protonation The addition of a proton, written as H^+, to another molecule or particle.

radical A species which has an unpaired electron available for bonding. A radical is formed by homolytic bond breaking.

radioactivity The property of the atoms of certain heavy elements which break up into smaller atoms, emitting energy. Protons, neutrons, electrons are some of the particles that may also be emitted.

rate curve The curve of a graph showing rate of reaction as the concentration of a product or reactant against time. The gradient on the curve at a particular point on the curve will give the rate of reaction at that time.

rate of reaction The change over time of the concentration of a reactant or a product of a reaction. Its units are mol dm^{-3} s^{-1}.

reaction goes to completion All the reactants react to make the product.

redox reaction A reaction in which oxidation and reduction both occur. One species is oxidised, while another is reduced. The two processes can be shown as half-equations.

redox titration A procedure in which amounts of reducing agent or oxidising agent can be determined accurately in a redox reaction. An indicator is need to show the point at which all of the limiting reactant has reacted.

reducing agent An element or compound that loses electrons to an oxidising agent, which itself gains electrons in the process. The reducing agent is oxidised, and the oxidising agent is reduced.

reductant Another term for reducing agent.

reduction A process in which a species gains one or more electrons. It can also be defined as a decrease in oxidation state for an element. Reduction and oxidation occur together in a redox reaction.

refluxing Boiling a liquid in a flask with a condenser attached, so that the vapour condenses and flows back into the flask. This keeps the liquid at its boiling point without any loss by evaporation.

relative abundance The amount of each isotope of an element as it occurs naturally, expressed as a percentage or proportion (ratio).

relative atomic mass, symbol A_r The mass of one atom of an element compared with one-twelfth of the mass of one atom of carbon-12.

relative charge The electrical charge on an atomic particle, compared to another. A proton has one positive charge and an electron has one negative charge.

relative molecular mass, symbol M_r The mass of one molecule of an element or compound compared with one-twelfth of the mass of one atom of carbon-12.

reversible reaction A chemical reaction which can take place in both directions and so does not go to completion. A mixture of reactants and products is obtained when the reaction reaches equilibrium. The composition of the equilibrium mixture is the same whether the reaction starts from the substances on the left or the right of the reaction equation.

saturated Description of an organic compound that contains the maximum number of hydrogen atoms possible. It contains only single bonds between the carbon atoms.

s block Elements of the Periodic Table in Groups I and II.

secondary distillation Distillation of the fractions obtained from primary distillation of crude oil. This stage can separate mixtures into pure substances.

shell A term used to describe electron energy levels in an atom. The numbers 1, 2, 3... denote the shells, and correspond to the numbers of the periods in the Periodic Table.

single covalent bond A bond between two atoms in which two electrons are shared, one from each atom.

slag Waste material from mining.

solute A substance that dissolves in another, usually a liquid.

solution A solute dissolved homogeneously in a solvent.

solvent The liquid component of a solution, such as water or alcohol.

sparingly soluble Only very slightly soluble.

specific heat capacity The amount of energy required to raise the temperature of 1 kg of a substance by 1 K.

spectator ions Ions present in a solution that do not take part in the reaction.

spectrometer An instrument used to measure the absorption of electromagnetic radiation by substances. There are different types of spectrometer (infrared, ultraviolet, NMR and so on) according to the type of radiation that is being studied.

spin diagram A diagram which shows the direction of spin of electrons in an atom.

standard conditions A temperature of 298 K, or 25 °C, and a pressure of 1 atmosphere (101 kPa).

standard enthalpy change of combustion, symbol $\Delta H_c^\ominus$ The energy transferred when one mole of a substance burns completely in oxygen under standard conditions.

standard enthalpy change of formation, symbol $\Delta H_f^\ominus$ The energy absorbed when one mole of a substance is formed from its elements in their standard states.

standard state The most stable physical state (solid, liquid or gas) of a substance at 1 atmosphere pressure and at a stated temperature, usually 298 K.

stereoisomers Isomers that have the same molecular formula and structural formula but different arrangements of their atoms in space. Optical and geometrical isomers are stereoisomers.

strong nuclear force The attractive force that binds the particles of the nucleus.

structural formula A formula that shows how the atoms are bonded together in a compound. It can either be written out in full, with each bond shown, or as groups of atoms in sequence.

structural isomers Isomers having the same molecular formula, but different structural formulae. Butane and 2-methylpropane are structural isomers of C_4H_{10}.

sub-shell A term used to describe the orbitals or energy levels in an atom. Each sub-shell contains pairs of electrons. Sub-shells are given letters: s contains up to one electron pair, p contains up to 3 electron pairs, d contains up to 5 electron pairs.

surroundings The environment in which a chemical reaction takes place. The immediate surroundings include the vessel and any other associated apparatus, nearby objects and the atmosphere around them. Strictly speaking, the term applies to *every* object that is not a component of the reaction mixture that is the system.

synthesis The production of one compound from two (or more) reactants.

system In chemistry, the term is used to mean the reaction mixture.

temporary dipole See **induced dipole**.

thermal cracking Using heat to break C–C and C–H bonds in the cracking of crude oil.

titration An experimental procedure to measure a precise amount of one substance of a known concentration which reacts exactly with a measured amount of another.

transition metals Elements whose atoms or ions have incomplete electron sub-shells within the outermost shell. First-row transition metals (scandium to copper) have an incomplete 3d subshell.

transition state In a chemical reaction when bonds are being broken and new bonds are being formed, the transition state is an intermediate form between reactants and products.

unsaturated hydrocarbon A compound that contains one or more double bonds between the carbon atoms.

vacuum distillation Secondary distillation of the fraction of crude oil that boils above 350 °C, carried out under reduced pressure to lower the boiling points.

van der Waals forces Weak attractive forces between temporary dipoles in adjacent molecules. These forces give rise to intermolecular bonding and are one hundredth to one-tenth as strong as typical covalent bonds.

volatility The ease with which a substance changes from liquid to gas.

X-rays Radiation emitted when high energy electrons strike a solid target.

Answers to questions

Chapter 1

1. a. Cathode rays are attracted to the positive anode and can be deflected by a magnetic field.
    b. Canal rays travel away from the anode.
    c. The heavier particles were deflected less by the magnetic field.
2. Alpha particles; do not penetrate paper.
3. a. The proportion of alpha particles fired at thin sheets of gold foil which were reflected or deflected indicated that a tiny proportion of the volume of the atom had most of its mass.
    b. Alpha particles are positively charged, the nucleus deflected some alpha particles, so the nucleus must also be positively charged.
    c. Most alpha particles passed straight through, so most of the atom must be empty space.

4.

	Protons	Neutrons	Electrons
^{35}Cl	17	18	17
^{37}Cl	17	20	17

5. a. $H_2(g) \rightarrow 2H^+(g) + 2e^-$
    b. $He(g) \rightarrow He^+(g) + e^-$
6. A^{2+}
7. (page 13) $1 = H^+$, $2 = H_2^+$, $12 = C^+$, $13 = CH^+$, $14 = CH_2^+$.
7. (page 16) 2 = energy level 2, p = sub-level, 6 = 6th electron to fill the sub-level
8. a. $[Ne]\ 3s^2\ 3p^4$
    b. $[Ne]\ 3s^2\ 3p^1$
    c. $[Ar]\ 3d^1\ 4s^2$
    d. $[Ar]\ 3d^9\ 4s^2$
9. a. Fe^{2+}: $1s^2\ 2s^2\ 2p^6\ 3s^2\ 3p^6\ 3d^6$
    b. Cl^-: $1s^2\ 2s^2\ 2p^6\ 3s^2\ 3p^6$
    c. Al^{3+}: $1s^2\ 2s^2\ 2p^6$
    d. S^{2-}: $1s^2\ 2s^2\ 2p^6\ 3s^2\ 3p^6$
11. b. Decrease down Group I: the increasing shells of electrons shield the nuclear charge.
    c. The pattern is similar.
12. The graph shows that the first electron is relatively easy to remove, then ionisation energies increase because electrons are progressively more difficult to remove. These increases show the pattern of the p and s sub-levels.

Application A
1. a. mass of H atom = $(9.109 \times 10^{-31})\ +\ (1.672 \times 10^{-27}) = 1.673^{-27}$ kg
    b. mass of H_2 molecule = $1.673^{-27} \times 2 \times 1000 = 3.346^{-24}$ g
    c. number of electrons = $(1.674 \times 10^{-27})\ /\ (9.109 \times 10^{-31}) = 1837.7$
2. a. $1.674 \times 10^{-27} \times 10^3 = 1.674 \times 10^{-24}$ g
    b. $9.109 \times 10^{-31} \times 2 \times 10^8 = 1.822^{-22} = 1.822^{-19}$ g
    c. $0.311 \times 10^3 = 311 = 3.11 \times 10^2$ g
3. a. diameter = 8 nm = 8×10^{-9} m = 8×10^{-7} cm
    b. mass = $1.6 \times 10^8 \times 1.67 \times 10^{-27} \times 10^{17}$ kg = $0.02672 = 2.672 \times 10^{-2}$ kg = 26.72 g
4. a. $7/0.07$ nm = 100 times
    b. $64\ 450 \times 1.67 \times 10^{-27} = 1.076 \times 10^{-19}$

Application B
1.

	Protons	Neutrons	Electrons
^{238}U	92	146	92
^{235}U	92	143	92
^{234}U	92	142	92

2. a. ^{234}U, ^{235}U, ^{238}U
    b. ^{234}U is deflected most because it has least mass.
    c. Total mass of 100 atoms = $(0.01 \times 234) + (0.015 \times 235) + (0.975 \times 238)$
        $M_r = 2.34 + 3.525 + 232.05 = 237.9$

Chapter 2

1. a. $K^+ = 1s^2\ 2s^2\ 2p^6\ 3s^2\ 3p^6$; $O^{2-} = 1s^2\ 2s^2\ 2p^6$
    b. $Na^+ = 1s^2\ 2s^2\ 2p^6$; $N^{3-} = 1s^2\ 2s^2\ 2p^6$
    c. $Fe^{3+} = 1s^2\ 2s^2\ 2p^6\ 3s^2\ 3p^6\ 3d^6\ 4s^2$; $O^{2-} = 1s^2\ 2s^2\ 2p^6$
2. A carbon atom forms 4 covalent bonds. But 8 electrons cannot be shared between 2 atoms. You cannot have a quadruple bond, so C_2 is not possible. A triple bond is possible in carbon compounds, but it leaves a non-bonded electron on each atom which is not possible in C_2. Therefore, carbon cannot form a simple molecule.
    Two iodine atoms can share 2 electrons in 1 covalent bond.
3. There are no free electrons or other charged particles to carry the charge.
4. Outer electrons are free to move in a metal, but are attached to an ion in an ionic compound. There are positive and negative ions in an ionic compound, but all ions in a metal are positive.
5. 'Inert' or noble gases are very unreactive and form few compounds.
6. (page 31) The nucleus of the small fluoride ion attracts electrons to itself and

---

its electron cloud is not distorted. Bromide is a larger negative ion with more electrons. Its electron cloud is easily distorted by the small, highly charged Al^{3+} ion. This makes $AlBr_3$ largely covalent.

6. (page 34) Without hydrogen bonding, b.p. H_2O could be about 210 K and b.p. HF about 180 K.
7. M_r ethanoic acid, CH_3COOH, is 60. Hydrogen bonding produces particles with the formula $2(CH_3COOH)$, M_r 120.
8. The diagram should show hydrogen bonds between: the terminal O in ethanoic acid's COOH group and an H atom in water; the H in the COOH group and an O atom in water.
9. Attraction between oppositely charged ions in ionic crystals makes a very rigid structure. In a malleable substance, the particles need to be able to slide over each other.
10. a. Ammonia has 3 bonding electron pairs and 1 non-bonding electron pair.
    b. Water has 2 bonding electron pairs and 2 non-bonding electron pairs.
11.

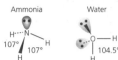

Application A
1. Covalent: sugar, candle wax, propane gas, coal. Ionic: salt. Metallic: spoon.

Chapter 3

1. Iron(II) titanate is $FeTiO_3$.
    Sum of A_r values = $55.8 + 47.9 + 3(16.00) = 151.7 = M_r$
    Iron(III) titanate is $Fe_2(TiO_3)_3$.
    Sum of A_r values = $2(55.8) + 3(47.9 + 48.0) = 399.4 = M_r$
2. Naturally occurring sulphur has four isotopes in different proportions with mass numbers 32, 33, 34, 36. The relative atomic mass is the average mass.
3. a. CH_2O b. CH_2
4. a. oxygen = 36%
    b.

	%	$\%/A_r$	Ratio
Fe	28	28/55.8	0.5
Ti	36	36/47.9	0.75
O	36	36/16	2.25

    Ratio Fe : Ti:O = 1 : 1.5 : 4.5 = 2 : 3 : 9
    So empirical formula = $Fe_2Ti_3O_9$
    M_r = 339.9. Mass of empirical formula = 339.9,
    so molecular formula = $Fe_2(TiO_3)_3$
5. a. $6/24 = 0.25$ mol Mg
    b. $60/100 = 0.6$ mol $CaCO_3$
    c. $106.5/35.5 = 3$ mol HCl
6. a. $0.72 \times 16.0 = 11.52$ g O
    b. $1.3 \times 58.5 = 76.05$ g NaCl
    c. $0.1 \times 101.8 = 10.18$ g Al_2O_3
7. a. Mass 1 hydrogen atom = $1.0079 / (6.023 \times 10^{23})$ g = 1.6734×10^{-24} g
    b. Mass 1 mercury atom = $200.59 / (6.023 \times 10^{23})$ g = 3.3304×10^{-22} g
8. a. $0.85 \times 1.5 = 1.275$ mol
    b. $(376.3/1000) \times 0.2 = 0.075$ mol
    c. $(16.4/1000) \times 2.0 = 0.0328$ mol
9. a. $10 \times 0.85 \times 165.9 = 1410.15$ g
    b. $(350/1000) \times 2 \times 40 = 28$ g
    c. $(9.4/1000) \times 0.01 \times 158 = 0.0148$ g
10. a. $C_2H_5OH + 3O_2 \rightarrow 2CO_2 + 3H_2O$
    b. $2Al + 6NaOH \rightarrow 2Na_3AlO_3 + 3H_2$
    c. $6CO_2 + 6H_2O \rightarrow C_6H_{12}O_6 + 6O_2$
    d. $C_3H_8(g) + 5O_2(g) \rightarrow 3CO_2(g) + 4H_2O(l)$
    e. $2Al(s) + 6H_2SO_4(l) \rightarrow Al_2(SO_4)_3(aq) + 3SO_2(g) + 6H_2O(l)$
11. $NO_3^- + H^+ \rightarrow HNO_3$
12. 19.5 g zinc = $19.5/65.4 = 0.3$ mol
    $Zn + 2HCl \rightarrow ZnCl_2 + H_2$ 0.3 mol zinc produces 0.3 mol hydrogen
    $T = (273 + 30)$ K = 303 K
    $V = (0.3 \times 8.31 \times 303 \times 10^3) / 100\ 000 = 7.56$ dm^3

Application A
1. It reduces the yield.
2. H_2SO_4 used annually to produce $CaSO_4 = (160 - 15) \times 1000 = 145\ 000$ tonnes
    M_r $H_2SO_4 = 2 + 32 + 64 = 98$. M_r $CaSO_4 = 40 + 32 + 64 = 136$
    No. tonnes $CaSO_4$ per year = $145\ 000 \times 136/98 = 201\ 225$
3. Waste discharged to air: new process led to reduction; discharged to water: very big reduction as H_2SO_4 is used to make $CaSO_4$. Non-hazardous waste discharged to land: big increase, likely to be waste materials from process between sulphuric acid and chalk. Hazardous waste to land: no change.

Chapter 4

1 atomic no. 43 = technetium, 61 = promethium, 75 = rhenium

2 **a** mass no. = 99 **b** 43 electrons

3 **a** $1s^2\ 2s^2\ 2p^5$; p block
   b $1s^2\ 2s^2\ 2p^6\ 3s^2\ 3p^6\ 4s^2$; s block
   c $1s^2\ 2s^2\ 2p^6\ 3s^2\ 3p^6\ 3d^{10}\ 4s^2$; d block

4 **a** Period 4 **b** p block **c** Group VI **d** 6

5 **a** strontium $1s^2\ 2s^2\ 2p^6\ 3s^2\ 3p^6\ 3d^{10}\ 4s^2\ 4p^6\ 5s^2$; s block
   b fluorine $1s^2\ 2s^2\ 2p^6$; p block
   c gold $1s^2\ 2s^2\ 2p^6\ 3s^2\ 3p^6\ 3d^{10}\ 4s^2\ 4p^6\ 4d^{10}\ 4f^{14}\ 5s^2\ 5p^6\ 5d^{10}\ 6s^1$; d block
   d aluminium $1s^2\ 2s^2\ 2p^6\ 3s^2\ 3p^1$; p block
   e iron $1s^2\ 2s^2\ 2p^6\ 3s^2\ 3p^6\ 3d^6\ 4s^2$; d block
   f germanium $1s^2\ 2s^2\ 2p^6\ 3s^2\ 3p^6\ 3d^{10}\ 4s^2\ 4p^2$; p block

6 (page 62) The d block elements of period 4, Sc to Zn, successively add one electron to the 3d subshell which has a maximum of 10 electrons, while the p block elements, Ga to Kr, add to the 4p subshell, maximum 6 electrons.

6 (page 64) The number of protons increases across Period 2, so there is an increasing positive charge. This exerts more force on the electrons in the same level, so it becomes increasingly more difficult to remove the electrons.

7 **a** Strength of metallic bonding depends on electrostatic attraction between delocalised electrons and positive ions. The ionic radii decrease in Na, Mg and Al, so, in that order: electrons are pulled closer to a smaller, denser nucleus; the number of delocalised electrons increases; it takes more energy to separate attracting particles and melt or boil the metals.
   b Al diameter = 0.26 nm
   c surface area of: Na^+ $0.131\ nm^2$, Mg^{2+} $0.0652\ nm^2$, Al^{3+} $0.0353\ nm^2$
   d Ionic radius as % of atomic radius:
   Na = 66.2 %, Mg = 49.7 %, Al = 40.8 %

8 **a** P and S are covalently bonded. S–S bonds are stronger than P–P bonds. Molecules include P_4 and S_8. Weaker van der Waals forces hold molecules in a lattice.
   b The forces within and between the puckered rings of the eight atoms in S_8 are stronger than the four tetrahedrally arranged P_4 atoms, so S has a higher melting and boiling point.

9 **a** beryllium $1s^2\ 2s^2$; magnesium $1s^2\ 2s^2\ 2p^6\ 3s^2$;
   calcium $1s^1\ 2s^2\ 2p^6\ 3s^2\ 3p^6\ 4s^2$
   b s block: electrons in the outermost shell of each element are in s orbitals.

10 **a** Melting points decrease.
   b The attraction decreases between the metal ions and the delocalised electrons.
   c about 660–690 °C

11 $2NaOH(aq) + MgCl_2(aq) \rightarrow Mg(OH)_2(s) + 2NaCl(aq)$
   Since magnesium hydroxide is only sparingly soluble, most of the magnesium hydroxide formed makes a white precipitate.

12 **a** As a weak alkali, it neutralises acids formed by bacteria in plaque feeding on sugars in the mouth, but it does not interfere with digestion.
   b A test for carbon dioxide: insoluble $CaCO_3$ is formed.

13 The size of the Group II ions increasing down the group means that the metal ions exert less force to distort the electron cloud of chlorine, and the compounds are more ionic.

14 109°

15 **a** Be has 2+ charge and each OH has 1– charge, So total charge is 2–.
   b Be has 2+ charge and each F has 1– charge, so the total charge is 2–.

Application A

1 p block **2** $5s^2\ 5p^5$
3 **a** about 7 g cm^{-3} **b** about 200 °C **c** about 900 kJ mol^{-1}
4 **a** NaAt **b** HAt

Chapter 5

1 **a** Energy is the ability to do work.
   b Enthalpy change is the change in heat energy – given out or taken in – during any change in a system, when the system is kept at constant pressure.
   c An exothermic reaction gives out heat energy to its surroundings.
   d An endothermic reaction takes in heat energy from its surroundings.

2 When 1 mole of propane gas reacts with 10 moles oxygen gas at 298 K and 100 kPa, 3 moles carbon dioxide gas and 4 moles liquid water are formed; 2219 kJ of energy are given out as heat.

3 **a** ΔH_c hydrogen gas = –286 kJ mol^{-1}
   mass 1 mol H_2 gas is 2 g
   ΔH_c hydrogen gas = 286/2 = 143 kJ mol-1
   M_r C_3H_8 = 44. ΔH_c = –2219 kJ mol^{-1}
   For 1 g C_3H_8, ΔH_c = –2219/44 = –50 kJ g^{-1}
   Since this is greater than –47.5 kJ g^{-1} for LPG, the other 5% has a lower joulerific value.

4 **a** Energy for a rise of 1 °C in 1 g water = 4.2 J
   For a 29.6 °C rise it is 4.2 × 29.6 = 124.32 J
   b Energy 400 J = mass H_2O in g × temp change in K × 4.2 J g^{-1} K^{-1}
   mass of water = 400/(25 × 4.2) = 3.8 g

5 **a** Heat is lost to the surroundings during the experiment.
   b Increase insulation of apparatus to prevent heat loss.
   Make allowance for energy lost to calorimeter.
   Stir water to distribute heat evenly.

6 **a**
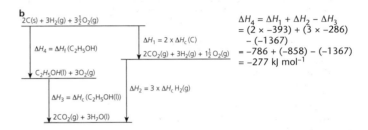

$\Delta H_4 = \Delta H_1 + \Delta H_2 - \Delta H_3$
$= (2 \times -393) + (-286) - (-1300)$
$= +228$ kJ mol^{-1}

b
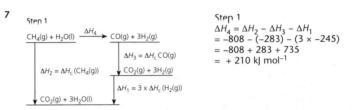

$\Delta H_4 = \Delta H_1 + \Delta H_2 - \Delta H_3$
$= (2 \times -393) + (3 \times -286)$
$- (-1367)$
$= -786 + (-858) - (-1367)$
$= -277$ kJ mol^{-1}

7
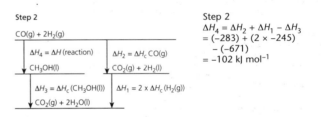

Step 1
$\Delta H_4 = \Delta H_2 - \Delta H_3 - \Delta H_1$
$= -808 - (-283) - (3 \times -245)$
$= -808 + 283 + 735$
$= +210$ kJ mol^{-1}

Step 2
$\Delta H_4 = \Delta H_2 + \Delta H_1 - \Delta H_3$
$= (-283) + (2 \times -245)$
$- (-671)$
$= -102$ kJ mol^{-1}

8
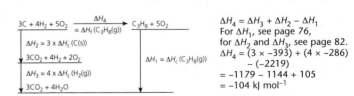

$\Delta H_4 = \Delta H_3 + \Delta H_2 - \Delta H_1$
For ΔH_1, see page 76,
for ΔH_2 and ΔH_3, see page 82.
$\Delta H_4 = (3 \times -393) + (4 \times -286)$
$- (-2219)$
$= -1179 - 1144 + 105$
$= -104$ kJ mol^{-1}

9 **a** Mean bond enthalpy = (502 + 427) / 2 = 464.5 kJ mol^{-1}
   b Values given in data books are mean values for bond energies of OH bonds in a wide range of compounds with different environments.

10

$$H\!-\!\underset{\underset{H}{|}}{\overset{\overset{H}{|}}{C}}\!-\!\underset{\underset{H}{|}}{\overset{\overset{H}{|}}{C}}\!-\!\underset{\underset{H}{|}}{\overset{\overset{H}{|}}{C}}\!-\!H + 5(O\!=\!O) \rightarrow 3(O\!=\!C\!=\!O) + 4(H\!-\!O\!-\!H)$$

Bonds broken/kJ mol^{-1}:
2(C–C) = 2 × 348 = 696
8(C–H) = 8 × 413 = 3304
5(O=O) = 5 × 498 = 2490
Total = 6490
Bonds made/kJ mol^{-1}:
6(C=O) = 6 × –743 = –4830
4(O–H) = 8 × –463 = –3704
Total = –8162
Enthalpy change of combustion = 6490 + –8162 = –1672 kJ mol^{-1}

Application A

1 Ethanol:
$C_2H_5OH(l) + 3O_2(g) \rightarrow 2CO_2(g) + 3H_2O(l)$
enthalpy change = ΔH_f(products) – ΔH_f(reactants)
= [2(–393) + 3(–286)] – (–277)
= –786 – 858 + 277
= –1367 kJ mol^{-1}
Octane:
$C_8H_{18}(l) + 12_{-}O_2(g) \rightarrow 8CO_2(g) + 9H_2O(l)$
= [8 × (–393) + 9(–286)] – [–250]
= –3144 – 2574 + 250
= –5718 + 250
= –5468 kJ mol^{-1}

2 a Octane
  b 4 times
3 a 8 moles
  b They are the same.
  c Ethanol is made from renewable sugar cane, while petrol is non-renewable.
4 You would need to know the exact composition of the mixture.

Chapter 6

1 At a particular temperature the reaction between H_2 and Cl_2 will be faster because the activation energy of the reaction is lower. More molecules will have the minimum energy needed to react when they collide.
2 At lower temperatures, fewer molecules have enough energy when they collide to react: fewer reach the activation energy.
3 $20 \times 60/2^8$ = 4.69 seconds
4 a The reaction is fastest at the beginning and gradually slows to zero.
  b The initial sharp rise in the graph means a fast rate of reaction. As the graph becomes less steep, so the reaction rate slows. When the graph is horizontal, the reaction rate is zero.
5 a $N_2(g) + 3H_2(g) \rightarrow 2NH_3(g)$
  b Raising the pressure increases the concentration of the molecules, meaning more collisions, hence the reaction rate increases.
6 NO_2 is unchanged at the end of the reaction.

Application A

1 a $N_2(g) + O_2(g) \rightarrow 2NO(g)$
  b $2NO(g) + O_2(g) \rightarrow 2NO_2(g)$
2 The activation energy is the minimum energy required by colliding molecules to react together.
3 a The E_A line should be towards the far right of the graph.
  b 0%
4 The activation energy is very much lower for nitrogen dioxide formation than for nitrogen monoxide formation.

Chapter 7

1 a At a lowered temperature, molecules have less energy and move slower, so there are fewer collisions. If the temperature is lowered enough, the reaction can appear to stop.
  b 2 moles HI
  c The reaction rate is fastest at the beginning when concentrations of reactants are highest, and gradually slows to zero, at which point the graph is horizontal - at about 80 min.
2 a The reverse reaction decreases.
  b The equilibrium shifts to the right.
3 a and c
4 a Increased temperature means increased energy. The reaction is endothermic. The equilibrium shifts to minimise the change, i.e. to absorb heat energy, so it shifts to the right.
  b The reaction is endothermic and the equilibrium shifts to the left, to absorb the energy and minimise the change.
5 a It shifts to the left.
  b No change.
  c It shifts to the right.
6 A low temperature favours the yield because the reaction is exothermic. A change in pressure has no effect according to Le Chatelier's principle.
7 a A catalyst is effective only at its surface. An increased catalyst surface area increases the rate of reaction.
  b Removing the reaction product NH_3 shifts the equilibrium to the right, giving a larger yield of NH_3.
8 a A high concentration of reactants moves the equilibrium to the right, to give a higher yield of SO_3.
  b So that the equilibrium shifts to the right: more SO_3 is produced to replace the SO_3 removed.
  c (i) Less SO_2 to be recycled means less waste. (ii) SO_2 in waste gases is a cause of acid rain.

Application A

1 The reaction is endothermic, but even the high engine temperature gives only 1% NO yield: the activation energy must be high, and the reaction rate slow. The big drop in temperature as gases reach the atmosphere effectively, brings the reaction rate to zero.
2 a (i) Reducing the pressure has no effect because there are the same number of molecules on both sides of the equation. (ii) Reducing the temperature shifts the equilibrium to the left because the reaction is endothermic and the equilibrium shifts to minimise the change.
  b Reduced pressure does not reduce NO output and it increases fuel consumption.

Application B

1 a The reaction shifts to the right.
  b It shifts to the left.
  c It shifts to the right.

Application C

1 Both reactions are exothermic. A low temperature causes the equilibria to shift to minimise the change, so they move to the right.
2 Though the reaction rate will increase, the equilibrium at 75 °C will be to the left of the equilibrium at 40 °C, so 40 °C gives a higher yield of N_2O_4 than 75 °C.
3 Lower plant and running costs.
4 The reaction is exothermic, so lower temperatures give the best yield of HNO_3.

Chapter 8

1 a $2Na(s) + Br_2(g) \rightarrow 2NaBr(s)$
    $Na \rightarrow 2Na^+ + 2e^-$
    $Br_2 + 2e^- \rightarrow 2Br^-$
    Na is oxidised; Br is reduced; Br is the oxidant; Na is the reductant
  b $4Na(s) + O_2(g) \rightarrow 2Na_2O(s)$
    $4Na \rightarrow 4Na^+ + 4e^-$
    $O_2 + 4e^- \rightarrow 2O_2^-$
    Na is oxidised; Na is the reductant.
    O is reduced; O is the oxidant.
  c $Ca(s) + I_2(s) \rightarrow CaI_2(s)$
    $Ca \rightarrow Ca^{2+} + 2e^-$; $I_2 + 2e^- \rightarrow 2I^-$
    Ca is oxidised; Ca is the reductant.
    I is reduced; I is the oxidant.
  d $3Mg(s) + N_2(g) \rightarrow Mg_3N_2(s)$
    $3Mg \rightarrow 3Mg^{2+} + 6e^-$; $N_2 + 6e^- \rightarrow 2N_3^-$
    Mg is oxidised; Mg is the reductant.
    N is reduced; N is the oxidant.
2 a Na +1, Cl –1   d K +1, S +7, O –2
  b H +1, N +5, O –2   e H +1, P +5, O –2
  c Mn +7, O –2   f Cr +6, O –2
3 a copper(I) oxide   e lead(IV) chloride
  b copper(II) oxide   f manganese(II) ion
  c manganese(IV) oxide   g manganese(III) oxide
  d lead(II) oxide   h tin(II) oxide
4 a $FeSO_4$ d $Cu(NO_3)_2$
  b TiO_2 e $FeBr_2$
  c $Mn(OH)_2$
5 a chlorine(I) oxide ion   c chlorine(V) oxide ion
  b chlorine(III) oxide ion d chlorine(VII) oxide ion
6 H_2SO_4 is sulphuric(VI) acid H_2SO_3 is sulphurous(IV) acid
7 a 2
  b $Ca(s) + 2H_2O(l) \rightarrow Ca(OH)_2(s) + H_2(g)$
  c $Ca \rightarrow Ca^{2+} + 2e^-$
    $2H_2O + 2e^- \rightarrow 2OH^- + H_2$
  d Ca is highly reactive, and so readily donates two electrons.
8 +5
9 a $N_2(g) + O_2(g) \rightarrow 2NO(g)$ c N_2O +1, NO_2 +4
  b (i) +2; (ii) nitrogen(II) oxide
10 a $NaI(s) + H_2SO_4(l) \rightarrow NaHSO_4(aq) + HI(g)$ b +2
  c Ease of oxidation of the hydrogen halides increases down Group VII: HF < HCl < HBr < HI.
    HI is readily oxidised and HF not at all.
11 a The zinc atom loses 2 electrons and is oxidised to the zinc ion in zinc sulphate. The copper ions gains 2 electrons to form a copper atom.
  b oxidation half equation: $Cu \rightarrow Cu^{2+} + 2e^-$
    reduction half equation: $2Ag^+ + 2e^- \rightarrow 2Ag$
  c The copper rod becomes coated with silver metal.
12 $MnO_4^-(aq) + 8H^+(aq) + 5Fe^{2+}(aq) \rightarrow Mn^{2+}(aq) + 5Fe^{3+}(aq) + 4H_2O(l)$

Application A

1 a p block   b 3   c +3
2 $Al(s) + Fe_2O_3(s) \rightarrow Al_2O_3(s) + Fe(s)$
   0   2(+3) 3(–2)   2(+3) 3(–2)
3 Aluminium has been oxidised to Al_2O_3 and Fe_2O_3 has been reduced to Fe.
4 Fe_2O_3

Chapter 9

1   fluorine $1s^2\ 2s^2\ 2p^5$
    chlorine $1s^2\ 2s^2\ 2p^6\ 3s^2\ 3p^5$
    bromine $1s^2\ 2s^2\ 2p^6\ 3s^2\ 3p^6\ 3d^{10}\ 4s^2\ 4p^5$

2 **a** Cl^- $1s^2\ 2s^2\ 2p^6\ 3s^2\ 3p^6$
      Br^- $1s^2\ 2s^2\ 2p^6\ 3s^2\ 3p^6\ 3d^{10}\ 4s^2\ 4p^6$
      F^- $1s^2\ 2s^2\ 2p^6$
 b   The ions are dissolved from rocks from on the sea floor.

3   Benefits: disinfecting water, in PVC, bleach and insecticides.
    Problems: environmental, e.g. pesticides, unbalancing food chains.

4   Astatine m.p. over 200 °C, real m.p. 302 °C; b.p. over 300 °C,
    real m.p. = 337 °C.

5   No because iodine is far less reactive/electronegative than fluorine.

6 **a**   molecular   **b**   ionic   **c**   ionic

7 **a**   No reaction because Au is an unreactive metal.
 b   Both Br_2 and I_2 react with Al since they are both oxidising agents and aluminium is readily oxidised. Br_2 reacts faster than I_2 to form the halide because Br_2 has the greater oxidising power.
 c   K has a low electronegativity, while the values for Br_2 and I_2 are relatively high, so K readily reacts with the halogens, faster with Br_2 since it is the stronger oxidant.

8 **a**   Brown I_2 precipitated, KCl solution formed.
      $Cl_2(aq) + 2KI(aq) \rightarrow 2KCl(aq) + I_2(s)$
 b   No reaction.   **c**   No reaction.
 d   Brown I_2 precipitated, NaBr solution formed.
      $Br_2(aq) + 2NaI(aq) \rightarrow 2NaBr(aq) + I_2(s)$

9 **a**   iodide   **b**   bromide

10 Silver halide decomposes in the light reflected from objects, to form silver particles which are dark in colour. The lighter coloured the objects, the more the silver particles produced, and the blacker the colour on a black and white photographic film.

11 (page 135) Several reactions: initially, HAt produced, then HAt oxidised to At, and H_2SO_4 reduced to SO_2 and H_2O.

11 (page 136) oxidation state = +1

12 1 atom of chlorine is oxidised (0 to +1) to NaOCl and the other atom of chlorine is reduced (0 to –1) to NaCl.

13 $Br_2(aq) + 2NaOH(aq) \rightarrow NaOBr(aq)\quad + \quad NaBr(aq) + H_2O(l)$
                     sodium bromate   sodium bromide
    $3NaOBr(aq) \rightarrow NaBrO_3(aq) + 2NaBr(aq)$

14 Chlorine dissolves in water to give an acidic solution, so litmus paper turns red. The litmus is then bleached by the chlorine.

15 The four sulphur atoms are oxidised from +2 to an averaged oxidisation number of +2.5. (Sulphur can have oxidation numbers +2, +4 and +6.)

16 no. moles sodium thiosulphate = $44/1000 \times 0.10 = 0.044$
    no. moles iodine = $44/2 \times 10^{-3} = 22 \times 10^{-3}$
    no. moles chlorine = 22×10^{-3}
    mass chlorine = $22 \times 10^{-3} \times 71$ g $= 0.156$ g = mass in 20 cm³ bleach
    mass chlorine in 1 dm³ bleach = $0.156 \times 1000/20 = 7.80$ g

Application A

1 **a**   DDT becomes more concentrated up the food chain, hence cormorants and osprey, which are secondary consumers, have the highest DDT levels in their body fat.
 b   DDT levels will be higher than in the tern or osprey.

2   Time for DDT only to reduce to 20% = 8 years
    Time if adding bacteria doubles rate = 4 years

3   Advantage: minimises adverse effects on environment.
    Disadvantage: insecticide may break down before it has time to work effectively.

Application B

1   Cl is more electronegative than C and attracts electrons towards its nucleus, to give Cl a negative charge and C a positive charge.

2   Plasticisers are not bonded to the PVC molecules and can migrate from the plastic, which is hastened by heating. This allows PVC chains to lie closer to each other and dipole–dipole attractions to operate more strongly, giving a more rigid structure.

Application C

1 **a**   bromine   **b**   bromine
 c $Br_2(l) + H_2O(l) \rightarrow HOBr(aq) + HBr(aq)$
 d   Chlorine is more readily available and so is cheaper.

Chapter 10

1   Gold, silver and copper are found native in rocks.

2   Oxygen is found as a gas in the air, in water, and combined in rocks e.g. silicates and carbonates.

3   A_r Fe = 112. M_r Fe_2O_3 = 160
    Mass of Fe in 125 tonnes Fe_2O_3 = $112/160 \times 125 = 87.5$ tonnes.

4   The reactions are faster and more complete when particles are more intimately mixed.

5   The plant does not cool down so energy wastage is kept low. If cooled, extra energy would be needed to reheat the plant.

6   Bridges require higher tensile strength steels than car bodies.

7   Exothermic reactions help to maintain the high temperature needed to keep the system liquid.

8
	Na_3	Al	F_6
Oxidation state of an atom:	+1	+3	–1

9   To be near a plentiful supply of cheaper hydroelectric power.

10 **a**   An inert atmosphere prevents oxidation of magnesium.
   b   Energy is wasted when the plant cools down and has to be reheated. This is more expensive than maintaining a constant temperature. Rate of output is lower because of interruptions.

12 Moisture does not corrode titanium. A corroding metal could contaminate the timbers and become weakened as a support.

13 **a**   Recycling uses 5% of the energy required for extraction.
   b   Recycling uses less ore, requires less mining and less energy, causes less spoiling of landscape, and less atmospheric and soil pollution.
   c   20% extracted + 80% recycled: Energy costs = 20 + (80/100 × 5) % = 24%. So saving = 76%

14 **a**   As for 13b.
   b   No clear trend for either, though the graph for recycled iron and steel scrap suggests a slight increase.
   c   Amounts of scrap collected for recycling varies, costs of ore and energy vary, so the economics of recycling vary also.

Chapter 11

1

2

3   Bond dissociation energies for N–N and P–P are substantially lower than for C–C.

4 **a**   C 240 g   240/12 = 20
       H 44 g   40/1 = 40
      ratio = 20 : 40 = 1 : 2
      empirical formula = CH_2
 b   formula mass = 12 + 2 = 14
      molecular formula = 140/14 = $C_{10}H_{20}$
 c $CH_3CH_2CH_2CH_2CH_2CH_2CH_2CHCH_2$

5   $C_{15}H_{32}$:
    $CH_3CH_2CH_2CH_2CH_2CH_2CH_2CH_2CH_2CH_2CH_2CH_2\ CH_2CH_3$,
    but there are many branched isomers, see section 11.6.
    $C_{30}H_{32}$; fully-written out form of $CH_3(CH_2)_{28}CH_3$,
    but there are very many branched isomers, see section 11.6.

6

7   Because the prefix but- means 4 carbon atoms, and functional groups are numbered to give the lowest number in the name.

8 **a** $CH_3CH(OH)CH_2CH_2CH_2CH_2CH_2CH_3$

 b $CH_3CH_2CH_2CH_2CH_2COOH$

c   CH₃CHCHCH₂CH₃

d   CH₃C(CH₃)₂CH₂CH₃

9   a $C_8H_{17}OH$; full form of $CH_3(CH_2)_7OH$
    b $C_5H_{11}COOH$; full form of $CH_3(CH_2)_4COOH$
    c C_5H_{10}; $CH_3CHCHCH_2CH_3$
    d C_6H_{14}; $CH_3CH_2C(CH_3)_2CH_3$ (two methyl groups on C2)
10 a C_3H_8; $CH_3CH_2CH_3$
    b C_3H_6; CH_2CHCH_3
    c C_3H_7OH; $CH_3CH_2CH_2OH$
    d C_2H_5COOH; CH_3CH_2COOH
11 5
12 a   It does not show where the functional group is.
    b $CH_3CH_2CH_2CH_2CH_2CH_2OH$
        $CH_3CH_2CH_2CH_2CH(OH)CH_3$
        $CH_3CH_2CH_2CH(OH)CH_2CH_3$

Application A
1   a   1,1,1-tribromo-2-chloroethane
    b   1,1,1-trichloro-2,2-difluoroethane
    c   1,1,2-tribromo-2-fluoroethane
    d   2-chloro-2-methylbutane
    e   1,1,2-tribromo-3-methylbutane

Chapter 12

1   a   Steam raises the temperature of the oil and makes it less viscous and so it is easier to flush out.
    b   Extracting oil from porous rock is expensive, so it is only profitable when the price of oil is high.
2   North Sea
3   a   at the top   b   at the bottom
4   Hexane is C_6H_{14} and heptane is C_7H_{16}. Heptane has a longer carbon chain and more sites for van der Waals forces between its molecules than hexane. Extra energy has to be supplied to overcome these forces when heptane changes from a liquid to a gas, so its boiling point is higher.
5   a   The functional group is the double bond, C=C.
    b C_nH_{2n}
6   a $C_{12}H_{26}(l) \rightarrow C_9H_{20}(l) + C_3H_6(g)$
    b

    c   As alkenes, they could be the starting materials for petrochemical synthesis. Petrochemicals include petrol additives, fuels, solvents, and polymers such as plastics.
7   When a C–C bond is broken in an alkane, and there is no hydrogen to add to the fragments to form alkanes, a double bond must re-form between two carbon atoms in each fragment, so producing alkenes.
8   Heat energy is expensive in thermal cracking. Catalytic cracking uses lower temperatures and the catalyst can be reused.
9   a $2C_8H_{18}(l) + 25O_2(g) \rightarrow 16CO_2(g) + 18H_2O(l)$
    b $2C_8H_{18}(l) + 17O_2(g) \rightarrow 16CO(g) + 18H_2O(l)$
10 sulphur dioxide
11 $C_7H_{16}(l) + 11O_2(g) \rightarrow 7CO_2(g) + 8H_2O(l)$
12 The reaction takes place on the surface of the catalyst, so a large surface area increases the rate of reaction.
13 a   causes acid rain
    b   greenhouse gases, soil pollutants
    c   toxic, fatal in higher doses
    d   greenhouse gas

14 The unpaired electron makes a free radical unstable, and by reacting with another free radical, the electrons are paired up in a stable molecule.
15

chloromethyl radical   dichloromethane

16 $CH_4 + Br_2 \rightarrow CH_3Br + HBr$
    $CH_3Br + Br_2 \rightarrow CH_2Br_2 + HBr$
    $CH_2Br_2 + Br_2 \rightarrow CHBr_3 + HBr$
    $CHBr_3 + Br_2 \rightarrow CBr_4 + HBr$

Application A
1

2   a $C_7H_{16}(l) + 11O_2(g) \rightarrow 7CO_2(g) + 8H_2O(l)$
    b $2C_8H_{18}(l) + 25O_2(g) \rightarrow 16CO_2(g) + 18H_2O(l)$
3   To reduce lead pollution from tetraethyl lead(IV) in four-star petrol.
4   $Pb(C_2H_5)_4$
Application B
1   [(1950 + 139 + 28 260 + 8342 + 3336 + 28 778 + 11 747) / total] × 100%
    = (82 552/90 366) × 100 = 91.35%
2   CO_2 is a greenhouse gas.
3   [(139 + 28 260 + 28 778)/90 366] × 100% = 57 177/90 366 × 100 = 63.27%
4   Longer chain alkanes have been cracked to produce shorter chain alkanes for petrol, etc.
5   sulphur dioxide
6   causes acid rain
7   Most of the sulphur dioxide can be removed by installing scrubbers in the chimneys of industrial plants using crude oil-derived fuels.

Chapter 13

1

2   One pair of shared electrons form a covalent bond, a σ bond, and the other pair of shared electrons make an area of delocalised electrons, a π bond, positioned above and below the σ bond. The π bond is not as strong as the σ bond, so the bond energy for C=C is not twice the bond energy for C–C.
3   In the double covalent bond, the increased region of negative charge draws the nuclei closer together.
4

5 Longer carbon chains have more van der Waals forces between adjacent molecules in the liquid state, so more energy is needed to overcome these forces and allow the chain molecules to move independently in the gas.

6 There is an unpaired electron on one of the carbon atoms. This gives the positive charge of a cation.

7 In HBr, the bromine atom has more protons than hydrogen and the bond electron density is drawn towards the bromine atom. This gives H–Br a permanent dipole. In Br–Br, the electrons are distributed evenly, so there is no permanent dipole. (A temporary dipole can be induced if Br-Br is near to a charged particle.)

8

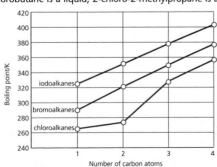

9 **a** 2-chloropropane **b** 2-bromopentane **c** butan-2-ol

10 Ethene can be separated from epoxyethane and returned to the reaction mixture.

11 Epoxyethane is very reactive. At low temperature, the rate of any reaction will be slowed down; $N_2(g)$ and $CO_2(g)$ do not react with epoxyethane.

12 Permanent dipoles exist at the $C^{\delta+}$–$Cl^{\delta-}$ bond in the polymer. The chlorine atoms are attracted to carbon atoms on adjacent molecules.

13

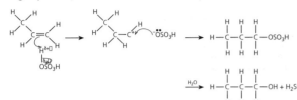

Application A

1 Isomers of the same compound always have the same molecular mass.

2 Different shaped molecules pack in different ways.

3 *trans*-but-2-ene has a straighter molecule than *cis*-but-2-ene. The straighter the molecule, the more van der Waals forces there are that can operate between molecules that align more closely. Therefore more energy is needed to overcome the intermolecular forces in the *trans* form, in order to melt the solid.

4 By comparing their boiling points.

Application B

1 Permanent dipole–permanent dipole

2 A sentence such as: Do not use to wrap fatty foods such as cheese, butter, lard, or foods containing oils.
The plasticiser esters would otherwise be transferred to food that will be eaten.

3 Plasticisers stay in the clingfilm and do not migrate into the food.

Chapter 14

1,2 **a**   **b**   **c**

3 **a** 2-chloro-2-methylbutane is a tertiary haloalkane.
   b 1-chloropropane is a primary haloalkane.
   c 2-chloropropane is a secondary haloalkane.

4 chloromethane is a gas; chloroethane is a gas; 1-chlorobutane is a liquid; 2-chlorobutane is a liquid; 2-chloro-2-methylpropane is a liquid

5

   d The graph shows that b.p. increases with the size of the halogen.

6

trichlorofluoro-   dichlorodifluoro-   trichloro-   dichlorotetra-   chloropentafluoro-
methane   methane   trifluoroethane   fluoroethane   ethane

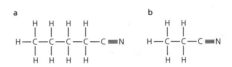

7 **a** Chloro-, bromo- or iodoethane.
   b 1-chlorobutane, 1-bromobutane or 1-iodobutane.
   c 2-chlorobutane, 2-bromobutane or 2-iodobutane.

8 Any butyl halide:
$CH_3CH_2CH_2CH_2Hal + NH_3$ $CH_3CH_2CH_2NH_2 + HHal$
butylamine

9

a   **b**

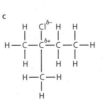

10 Because nucleophilic substitution by CN ions lengthens the carbon chain by one carbon atom.
First react the haloalkane with cyanide to obtain the nitrile, then reflux with dilute hydrochloric acid to obtain the acid, as follows.
a   dil. HCl
$CH_3CH_2CH_2Cl + NaCN \longrightarrow CH_3CH_2CH_2CN \rightarrow CH_3CH_2CH_2COOH$
b   dil. HCl
$CH_3CH_2CH_2CH_2Cl + NaCN \longrightarrow CH_3CH_2CH_2CH_2CN \rightarrow$
$CH_3CH_2CH_2CH_2COOH$

12 **a** An elimination reaction is favoured. The products are ethene and hydrogen chloride.
   b A substitution reaction is favoured. The products are ethanol and hydrochloric acid.

Application A

1

O_2 O_3

2 In the upper atmosphere, C–Cl bonds in CFCs break to release chlorine radicals. The chlorine radicals react with ozone to form chlorine monoxide radicals:
$Cl\bullet + O_3 \rightarrow ClO\bullet + O_2$

3

The unpaired electron between the atoms makes ClO very reactive and a free radical.

4 The ozone layer thins, and more UV radiation reaches the Earth's surface.

5 Positive: use in aerosol sprays, refrigerants, fire extinguishers (life saving).
Negative: the effects of a thinner ozone layer and consequent increase in UV radiation include a possible increase in the rate of melting of polar ice and snow, and an increase in damage to DNA of Earth's organisms including humans, who are more liable to get skin cancer.

Application B

1 Step 2

2 chloromethylbenzene and sodium cyanide.

3 The nucleophile is the CN^- ion. This is attracted to the positive carbon of the C–Cl bond, to which it donates a pair of electrons, and the C–Cl bond breaks.

4 free radical substitution

5 **a** methylbenzene
   b CH_2COOH **c** CH_2CN

6 water, sulphuric acid, raised temperature (reflux condenser)

7 nucleophilic substitution

8 So that the primary amine only is formed.

9 Because two hydrogen atoms are attached to the nitrogen atom.

Chapter 15

1 methanol

ethanol

propan-1-ol

butan-1-ol

pentan-1-ol

hexan-1-ol

2

3
a primary
b secondary
c primary
d primary
e secondary
f

a

b

c

d

e

4

primary

secondary

tertiary

5 $C_{10}H_{22}(l) \rightarrow C_2H_4(g) + C_8H_{18}(l)$
6 $C_2H_5OH(l) + 3O_2(g) \rightarrow 2CO_2(g) + 3H_2O(l)$
7 Hydrogen bonds occur between alcohol molecules, more energy is required to change the alcohol from a liquid to a gas, so boiling points of alcohols are higher and they are liquids at room temperature.
8 Propan-1-ol is more soluble in water than decan-1-ol because propan-1-ol's shorter carbon chain gives fewer sites for van der Waals forces, so there is less attraction between propan-1-ol molecules. Decan-1-ol has a longer carbon chain and more sites for van der Waals forces between the alcohol's molecules, reducing its affinity for water and hence its solubility in water.
10 a They are compounds formed in a chemical route between the raw materials and the product.
 b Breaking an O–H bond releases a hydrogen ion, H^+. Acids give rise to hydrogen ions.
11 a 2[O]
$C_4H_9OH \rightarrow C_3H_7COOH + H_2O$
butanoic acid
 b [O]
$CH_3CH_2CHOHCH_3 \rightarrow CH_3CH_2COCH_3 + H_2O$
butanone
12 a butan-1-ol
 b pentan-2-ol

Application A
1 $C_2H_5OCOOCOOC_2H_5 + H_2O \rightarrow 2C_2H_5OH + 2CO_2$
2

3 Lowering the temperature lowers the reaction rate so that diethylpyrocarbonate decomposes more slowly, so CO_2 bubbles are given off more slowly.

Application B
1 $C_2H_5OH(l) + 3O_2(l) \rightarrow 2CO_2(g) + 3H_2O(l)$
2 $2C_{10}H_{22}(l) + 31O_2(g) \rightarrow 20CO_2(g) + 22H_2O(l)$
3 $2C_6H_{13}NH_2(l) + 20O_2(g) \rightarrow 12CO_2(g) + 16H_2O(l) + N_2(g)$
4 Combustion is incomplete for these larger molecules, and particles of carbon (soot) remain unreacted.

Application C
1 2[O]
$C_2H_5OH \rightarrow CH_3COOH + H_2O$
2 Sterilise all containers and seal containers to prevent contamination.

Application D
1 Glucose is an aldehyde, fructose a ketone.
2 As an aldehyde glucose will reduce Fehling's solution (blue) to give a brick red precipitate of Cu^+ ions.
3 Glucose reduces Fehling's solution.
4 Glucose.
5 Hydrogen bonds form between the OH groups in the sugar and water molecules.
6 Sorbitol has OH groups so it can form hydrogen bonds, with water molecules and therefore dissolves in water.
7 No effect, so it has no aldehyde groups.
8 The presence of the OH groups is thought to account for the sweetness.

Extension
1 A polymer is formed with alternating groups from methanal and phenol.
2 Because the only other product is water.

Index